D0601582

The Secret Eye

Husband up thine ideas,
and give them stability and substance;
Write often for thy secret eye.
So shalt thou grow in wisdom.

—Martin Farquhar Tupper

Gender & American Culture

Coeditors
Linda K. Kerber
Nell Irvin Painter

Editorial Advisory Board
Nancy Cott
Cathy Davidson
Thadious Davis
Jane DeHart
Sara Evans
Mary Kelley
Annette Kolodny
Wendy Martin
Janice Radway
Barbara Sicherman

The Secret Eye

*The Journal of
Ella Gertrude Clanton Thomas,
1848–1889*

Edited by Virginia Ingraham Burr

Introduction by Nell Irvin Painter

The University of North Carolina Press

Chapel Hill and London

The paper in this book meets the guidelines for permanence
and durability of the Committee on Production Guidelines
for Book Longevity of the Council on Library Resources.

Printed in the United States of America

Library of Congress Cataloging-in-Publication Data

The secret eye: the journal of Ella Gertrude Clanton Thomas,
    1848–1889 / edited by Virginia Ingraham Burr; introduction by
    Nell Irvin Painter.
        p.   cm.—(Gender & American culture)
    ISBN 0-8078-1897-6.—ISBN 0-8078-4273-7 (pbk.)
    1. Southern States—Social life and customs—1775–1865.
2. Southern States—Social life and customs—1865– 3. Women—
Southern States—History—19th century. 4. Georgia—Social life
and customs. 5. Women—Georgia—History—19th century. 6. United
States—History—Civil War, 1861–1865—Personal narratives,
Confederate. 7. Reconstruction. 8. Thomas, Ella Gertrude Clanton—
Diaries. 9. Women—Georgia—Diaries. 10. Georgia—Biography.
I. Burr, Virginia Ingraham. II. Series.
F213.S43   1990
975—dc20   89-37188
                                                                  CIP

In remembrance of E.G.C.T.,
my parents, and A.W. L.

Contents

Gertrude Thomas

One day she said, "I wonder what will happen—
This diary that I wrote, about myself,
This story told of Georgia and her people—
Will it stay idle on some dusty shelf?
Beneath the basement stair or in the attic,
Will anybody hesitate to look
Across a hundred years or so, yet open it
And start in sweet surprise at this my book?
This is my life and I am Southern Woman—
These are my times and these events are real,
And all I'll ever ask of this accounting
Is that in reading it you'll come to feel
What a southern woman knew, I do beseech
You, stay with me, and read—if words can teach.
—Gertrude Despeaux, 1988

Preface

Few diaries of the nineteenth century compare to the journal kept by Ella Gertrude Clanton Thomas from 1848 to 1889.[1] Spanning four decades, Thomas's revealing account furnishes significant insights into the life and times of a remarkable southern woman coping with misfortune and changing attitudes during a chaotic era in our history.

Gertrude Thomas lived the myth of the antebellum South during the years before the Civil War. The daughter of a wealthy planter, an indulgent father, she was precocious, attractive, well educated, and socially prominent. Her debut as a belle in Augusta, Georgia, quickly followed by her engagement and marriage to handsome Princeton graduate Jefferson Thomas, is a familiar tale of magnolia-scented romance that ended abruptly in 1861. On the surface, the story of the Thomases is the story of many lives of that era, but Gertrude Thomas's forty-year chronicle—written with candor, uncommon lucidity, humor, and poignancy—is unique among the surviving records. Among the diverse themes addressed by Thomas are marriage, morality, childbirth, death, religion, politics, slavery, the burdens of slavery, war, education, the rights of women, poverty, and survival. Although generally fair in her assessments, brought up as she was with the "peculiar institution," she is sometimes blinded by her own experience.

Thomas wrote in fluent prose—not in the brief jottings common to many diaries. Her journal is personal, and through it we come to know Gertrude Clanton Thomas intimately as she recounts the emotions and events that touched her life. The narrative evolves like a provocative novel, and it is through Thomas's perceptive writing that the intrinsic texture of her life and times emerges. It is a fascinating text that should interest general readers as well as scholars. Thomas did not write her journal for publication, but she did recognize that it could be useful and often ex-

---

1. Journal of Ella Gertrude Clanton Thomas, 13 vols., Manuscript Department, Duke University Library, Durham, N.C.

pressed, somewhat ambiguously, the hope that others would read it. The journal ends unsatisfactorily in 1889, but in the epilogue readers will discover the redeeming climax of a resilient life.

Although a few scholars were acquainted with Gertrude Thomas prior to 1970, her journal became more widely accessible through the work of the late Mary Elizabeth Massey, professor of history at Winthrop College, who commissioned a typescript of the manuscript journal in the early 1970s. Massey did not live to complete the work she planned and, unfortunately, the several typists were inconsistent in spelling and punctuation. Where Thomas's handwriting was particularly difficult to read, the result was guesswork and blank spaces. Nevertheless, the typescript represents a herculean accomplishment and is an indispensable reference.

Reading the worn manuscript and deciphering the scribbled handwriting is no small task, as attested by Thomas's own admission: ". . . for my handwriting will daunt most persons I am well aware."[2] Her husband and one of her sisters also remarked on her illegible script. Additional hardships for the transcriber result from Thomas's use of poor pens, pale ink, and paper of inferior quality, especially during and after the Civil War. A number of pages are blotched and dog-eared. A few pages from the troubled years 1878 to 1889 have short portions cut off from the top or bottom of the page. Several entire pages have been removed. This leads to speculation as to whether Thomas or a family member was responsible for a possible act of censorship in removing words thought to be best left unsaid.

The tedious work of correcting the typescript to conform faithfully to the original manuscript, of translating and inserting missing words and sentences, and of correcting the names of persons and places has been my task during the last eight years. It has been a rewarding labor of love, one in which I willingly acknowledge the advantage of family connections and familiarity with so much of the subject matter.

V. I. B.
Salem, South Carolina
January 1989

---

2. Journal, Sept. 25, 1869.

Editor's Note

There are approximately 450,000 words in the original manuscript diary. Editing for this abridged version was an agonizing task. Thomas wrote often—sometimes two or three times in a single day—and in great detail. It was her habit to copy poetry and excerpts from her insatiable reading into the journal and to write commentary on books, sermons, and scripture passages. Although these anecdotes are intriguing and provide valuable insight into her psyche, I have reluctantly omitted most of them here. I have also deleted, entirely or in part, many entries dealing with clothes, parties, shopping, college, and the constant visiting among friends and relatives. Though interesting in themselves, such passages do not contribute measurably to Thomas's story. The result is that I have sacrificed much that is worthwhile in favor of the essential plot and themes of historical significance.

Ellipses between entries denote the deletion of one or more entire journal entries. Also deleted are some opening and closing remarks dealing primarily with weather, time, and place. These are generally repetitious. Often, when she was worried or depressed, Thomas wrote at length of everyday occurrences until she had calmed her emotions enough to write about what was on her mind. Such introductions have been deleted or shortened in some cases. Then there are her habitual, albeit natural, digressions. Unavoidably, I have used ellipses frequently, but in all cases I have tried not to disrupt the story at hand. In a few instances, I have silently deleted totally irrelevant sentences, such as, "Mrs Phinizy just called," "Cousin Amanda spent last night here," or "The bell just tolled."

The syntax, faulty as it often is, remains exactly as written by Gertrude Thomas, and I have left her erratic spelling, capitalization, and punctuation undisturbed for the most part. To avoid confusion, I have regularized quotation marks but have not corrected her use of them. I have added apostrophes—almost totally disregarded by Thomas—and I have inserted an occasional comma or period when absolutely necessary. Thomas's most common form of punctuation was the dash. I have capitalized book titles and italicized the titles of books, newspapers, and magazines. All emphasized words are Thomas's, but I have deleted some of her excessive underlining.

Spelling presented special problems; idiosyncrasies abound. As did many people of her time, Thomas spelled some words phonetically. She also used many English spellings—as in *parlour*, *sceptic*, *colour*, or *recognise*—and even poetic and Middle English words like *wifes* or *sinonym*. Much of the spelling was normal for the period and was not peculiar to Thomas. I have let such spelling stand. Only Gertrude Thomas, however, could explain why she spelled *piazza* as *piazzi* and *Baptist* as *Babtist* for forty years. She showed an annoying disregard for consistency in such letter combinations as *ie*, *ei*, *ai*, *ia*, *ll*, and *ff*. She consistently misspelled *Teusday* and differentiated little between *two* and *too*; yet she used them correctly often enough to show that she probably knew what was right. It seems reasonable to assume that hundreds of inconsistencies were the result of carelessness, haste, and fatigue. To preserve all such errors would be unfair to Thomas and disconcerting to the reader. Where poor penmanship makes the spelling all but impossible to interpret, I have given the author the benefit of the doubt. I have corrected the spelling of proper names as well as obvious slips of the pen.

Thomas often made two words out of one, as in the case of *bed room* or *up stairs*. These I have let stand. With other words, such as *today*, *tonight*, *everything*, and *anyone*, she made a mere hesitation between syllables, and I have interpreted them as one word. It would have been easier to correct all orthography and punctuation, but that would have robbed the text of its colloquial charm and Gertrude Thomas of her individuality.

Most of her numerous extracts from literature are loosely quoted. I have not identified them all, and none of the biblical quotes are identified since the source is readily available.

To identify every person walking across the pages of the thirteen volumes would have been virtually impossible and of doubtful value. Relatives are identified to the extent possible. The Clanton, Luke, Reid, and Thomas families were quite large, and a vast network of kin inhabited Columbia, Richmond, and Burke counties. I have not tried to expand the author's own identification of school friends, neighbors, and social acquaintances. The doctors of Augusta were a problem. There were several families who had more than one member practicing medicine there at the same time, among them the Eves, Fords, Joneses, Dugases, Doughtys, and Steiners. Unless these people were named by Thomas or were recognized through circumstantial evidence, I have not attempted identification. Slaves and servants are usually identified by context or by the author. I have not, in every case, identified prominent persons who are well known in our own day, such as Abraham Lincoln and Jefferson Davis, nor have I identified every officer and battle of the Civil War mentioned by Thomas.

I have put the dates of the entries into a more consistent form, and I admit to taking some literary license in paragraphing. All parentheses and extra line spacings are the author's. All ellipses and square brackets are mine.

Notwithstanding the minimal editorial intervention detailed above, this edited version of the journal of Ella Gertrude Clanton Thomas is *what she wrote*, carefully and faithfully preserved in her own words. Already recognized and quoted by historians for the past thirty years, her diary will now be available to a wider audience.

Acknowledgments

My first expression of gratitude must be to the many friends who, over the past seven years, encouraged me to undertake and persevere in editing my great-grandmother's journal. Their enthusiastic interest and support kept the fires of resolve burning.

I would like to thank Robert L. Byrd, curator of manuscripts at the Perkins Library of Duke University, for his support and kind assistance to me from the inception of my idea to edit the Thomas journal. His help has been invaluable. I should like, also, to express appreciation to the former curator, Mattie B. Russell, for her interest and helpful cooperation.

Gertrude T. Despeaux, a great-granddaughter of Gertrude Clanton Thomas, has been of invaluable help in making the Thomas scrapbooks available and in providing family memorabilia and access to certain portraits and photographs. I am deeply appreciative of her cooperation, knowing the deep affection she feels for the journal, and I'm grateful for the special relationship we share.

I am indebted to Nell Irvin Painter, author of the introduction, for proposing the publication of the Thomas journal to the University of North Carolina Press and for suggesting our collaboration. Nell's advice and guidance led to an improved and historically sound manuscript. I wish, also, to thank Iris Tillman Hill, editor-in-chief at the University of North Carolina Press, for considering this project a worthy one. I am most grateful to Pamela Upton, my editor, for her interest and expert help.

I want to express my gratitude to centenarian Madge Byne Rood and her son, the late Robert Rood, Jr., both of Augusta, Georgia, for family reminiscences not otherwise available and for the privilege of browsing among their antiques and records of the Clanton family, which date back 125 years. My numerous visits with Mrs. Rood, from 1983 until a few weeks before her death on August 20, 1988, yielded bountiful information. Her friendship was but one of the unexpected rewards I received. In the course of this work I became acquainted affectionately with my ancestors and with family members still living, several of whom I had not known heretofore. For that experience I am forever grateful.

Additional thanks go to Patricia D. Hulslander, Michael F. Despeaux, Mrs. James A. Miller, Jr., Mrs. Robert Rood, Lottie Thomas Nye (Mrs. George E.), Mrs. W. LaBorde Mathias, and Mrs. Token Thomas Norman for permitting their family portraits to be photographed. I also used one from my own collection. Other photographs come from a collection in the Reese Library of Augusta College, from the Hargrett Rare Book and Manuscript Library at the University of Georgia, from the collection of Mrs. Gertrude T. Despeaux, and from Ernest P. Ferguson of Photo Arts in Winnsboro, South Carolina. Sandy Canupp assisted me with the photography, and Thomas Freeman prepared the maps. The maps are based on an 1886 map of Georgia furnished by the Surveyor General Department in Atlanta and a historic guide to Augusta prepared by Dennis O'Shields for the Augusta Heritage Trust.

I owe a special debt to Myra Armistead, reference librarian at the Cooper Library of Clemson University, who was immensely helpful in researching literature mentioned in the journal—often with faint and confusing clues.

I gratefully acknowledge the help and services of the following: the Oconee County (S.C.) Library, the Augusta-Richmond County Library, the Reese Library of Augusta College, Historic Augusta, Inc., the Augusta Chamber of Commerce, and the archives of the Richmond County Courthouse and Magnolia Cemetery in Augusta.

Several books were enormously helpful in verifying names and dates mentioned in the journal, and I would like to acknowledge them here: Edward J. Cashin, The Story of Augusta (Augusta, Ga., 1980); Charles C. Jones, Jr., and Salem Dutcher, Memorial History of Augusta (1890; rpt., Spartanburg, S.C., 1966); Florence Fleming Corley, Confederate City: Augusta, 1860–1865 (Columbia, S.C., 1960); H. R. Casey, "Reminiscences," Columbia Sentinel, [late 1880s]; and C. Vann Woodward, ed., Mary Chesnut's Civil War (New Haven, Conn., 1981).

Charles Bisceglia deserves credit for convincing me that I could sit down to my word processor and, with no prior experience, produce the manuscript for this book. He willingly came to my aid when I had problems.

I want to express especial appreciation to Carol Bleser and Alan Schaffer of Clemson University for their friendship and genuine interest in my work. They were always available with help and encouragement when I needed it most.

My greatest debt is to Donald H. Burr for his affectionate support, his candid interest, his dedicated help in countless ways, and, most of all, his endurance through all the days, weeks, and months of my neglecting all else. To him and to my family, with special notice of Susan and Geoffrey Burr, I give sincere thanks for their understanding and for sharing my frustrations and joys while the work was in progress.

The Thomas Family

Joseph J. Thomas was a descendant of John Thomas, who settled in Jamestown, Virginia, in 1622. Joseph married Elizabeth Eskridge of Virginia, a descendant of Col. George Eskridge, patriot and guardian of George Washington's mother, Mary Ball. Their children of record were Pierce Butler, Nathaniel, Joseph Darius, and Nancy. Some members of this family emigrated to Edgefield County, South Carolina, and Burke County, Georgia. Joseph Darius Thomas of Burke County married Louisa (Loula) Kettles (Kittles) of Screvin County, Georgia.

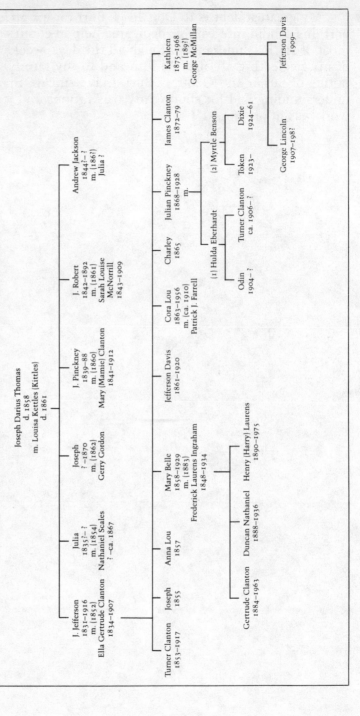

Joseph Darius Thomas
d. 1858
m. Louisa Kettles (Kittles)
d. 1861

J. Jefferson
1831–1916
m. (1852)
Ella Gertrude Clanton
1834–1907

Julia
1835?–?
m. (1854)
Nathaniel Scales
?–ca. 1867

Joseph
?–1870
m. (1862)
Gerry Gordon

J. Pinckney
1839–88
m. (1860)
Mary (Mamie) Clanton
1841–1912

J. Robert
1842–1892
m. (1861)
Sarah Louise McNorrill
1843–1909

Andrew Jackson
1844?–?
m. (1862?)
Julia ?

Turner Clanton
1853–1917

Joseph
1855

Anna Lou
1857

Mary Belle
1858–1929
m. (1881)
Frederick Laurens Ingraham
1848–1934

Jefferson Davis
1861–1920

Cora Lou
1863–1956
m. (ca. 1910)
Patrick J. Farrell

Charley
1865

Julian Pinckney
1868–1928
m.

James Clanton
1872–79

Kathleen
1875–1968
m. (1897)
George McMillan

Gertrude Clanton
1884–1963

Duncan Nathaniel
1888–1936

Henry (Harry) Laurens
1890–1975

(1) Hulda Eberhardt

(2) Myrtle Benson

Odin
1904–?

Turner Clanton
ca. 1906–?

Token
1923–

Dixie
1924–61

George Lincoln
1907–198?

Jefferson Davis
1909–

The Clanton Family

Nathaniel Holt Clanton and Catherine Newsome Clanton, with their large family, emigrated from Mecklinburg County, Virginia, in 1798, the same year Turner Clanton was born. They settled in Columbia County, Georgia, north of Augusta. Their children of record were Littlebury, James, Polly (Mary), Catherine, Nathaniel Holt, Tabitha, and Turner.

John Reid (Ried) emigrated from Virginia to Columbia County before the American Revolution. One of his daughters, Elizabeth (Betsy), married Judge James Luke of Columbia County. Their three children of record were: William, Elizabeth, and Mary Margaret.

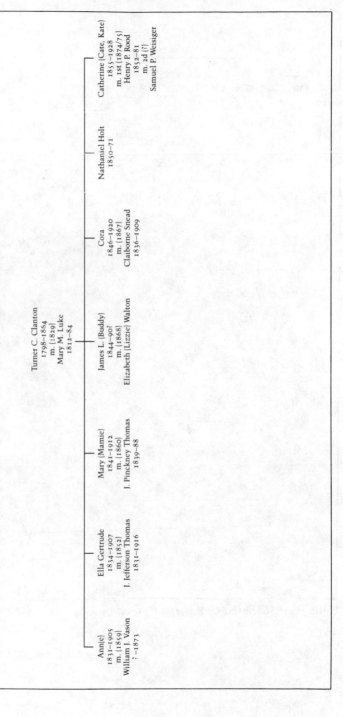

Turner C. Clanton
1798–1854
m. (1829)
Mary M. Luke
1812–84

Ann(e)
1831–1905
m. (1859)
William J. Vason
?–1873

Ella Gertrude
1834–1907
m. (1852)
J. Jefferson Thomas
1831–1916

Mary (Mamie)
1841–1912
m. (1860)
J. Pinckney Thomas
1839–88

James L. (Buddy)
1844–90?
m. (1868)
Elizabeth (Lizzie) Walton

Cora
1846–1920
m. (1867)
Claiborne Snead
1836–1909

Nathaniel Holt
1850–71

Catherine (Cate, Kate)
1855–1928
m. 1st (1874/75)
Henry P. Rood
1852–81
m. 2d (?)
Samuel P. Weisiger

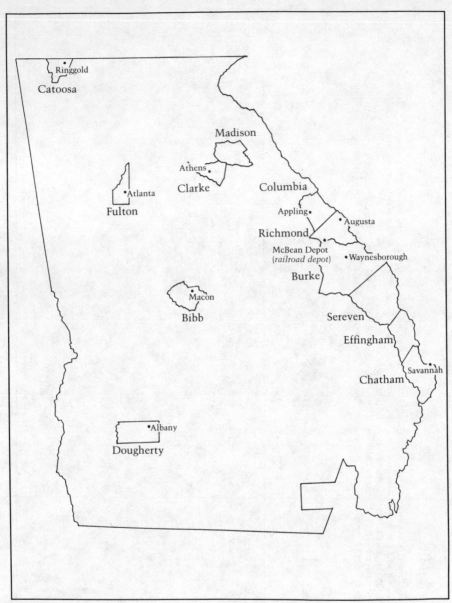

Georgia, 1886 (*based on a map prepared by Thomas Freeman*)

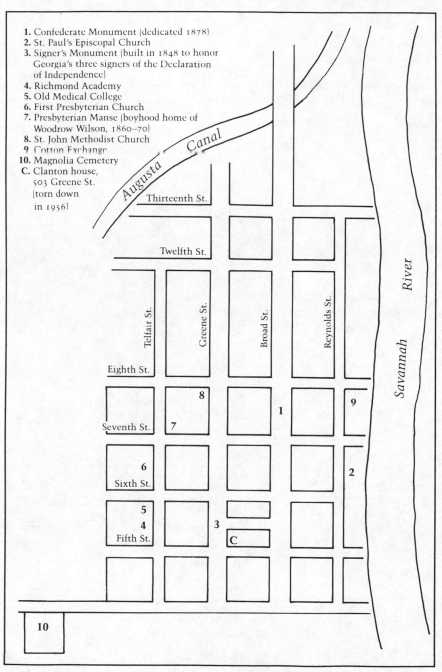

1. Confederate Monument (dedicated 1878)
2. St. Paul's Episcopal Church
3. Signer's Monument (built in 1848 to honor Georgia's three signers of the Declaration of Independence)
4. Richmond Academy
5. Old Medical College
6. First Presbyterian Church
7. Presbyterian Manse (boyhood home of Woodrow Wilson, 1860–70)
8. St. John Methodist Church
9. Cotton Exchange
10. Magnolia Cemetery
C. Clanton house, 503 Greene St. (torn down in 1956)

Augusta Canal

Thirteenth St.

Twelfth St.

Telfair St.

Greene St.

Broad St.

Reynolds St.

Savannah River

Eighth St.

Seventh St.

Sixth St.

Fifth St.

Augusta, Ga., in Gertrude Thomas's time (*based on a map prepared by Dennis O'Shields for the Augusta Heritage Trust*)

The Secret Eye

Introduction
The Journal of Ella Gertrude Clanton Thomas: An Educated White Woman in the Eras of Slavery, War, and Reconstruction

by Nell Irvin Painter[1]

Journal-keeping among the elites of the Old South was a fairly common pastime, a convention that lent weight to individual experience but that required more discipline than most could summon over the long haul. Even the best-known nineteenth-century southern journal, that of the indomitable Mary Boykin Chesnut, encompasses only the Civil War years. Other extended journals lack the detail and candor that Gertrude Thomas sustained for over two decades.[2] The journal of Gertrude Thomas is, therefore, unique. Spanning forty-one years, it presents one intelligent woman's responses to the upheavals of her times. Because Thomas was unusually articulate, her journal illuminates experiences that she shared with thousands of women but that only she documented in a persistent fashion.

In true autobiographer's style, Ella Gertrude Clanton Thomas

1. This essay was completed while I was a fellow at the Center for Advanced Study in the Behavioral Sciences at Stanford, California, with the generous support of the National Endowment for the Humanities (grant #FC-20060–85) and the Andrew W. Mellon Foundation. I am grateful to colleagues at the Center and to other scholars in southern history for their help in sorting out Gertrude Thomas's society.

At several points in this analysis I have reached conclusions with which the editor, Virginia Burr, does not agree. I have indicated these places in the footnotes to make sure that readers do not conflate her ideas with mine.

Readers should also note that I have used the entire journal rather than this abridged edition in preparing this essay; therefore occasional citations refer to entries not included in this book.

2. For example, the journal of Samuel Agnew of Mississippi, housed in the Southern Historical Collection of the University of North Carolina at Chapel Hill, is longer but less detailed.

1

exists twice: once in her own lifetime, from 1834 to 1907; and once as a rich personal text, the journal that she generated between 1848 and 1889. To an extent unusual in autobiographical literature, Gertrude Thomas the life and Gertrude Thomas the text are incongruent. The text ends in the late 1880s in Augusta, but Thomas herself lived a decade and a half longer and died in Atlanta. Having begun her woman's life as a belle, she ended it as a suffragist.[3]

Unlike the published memoirs of Myrta Lockett Avary or the revised diaries of Mary Boykin Chesnut, the Thomas journal presents unretouched, day-to-day tussles with the contingencies of life and a decades-long effort toward self-definition in the midst of privilege, Civil War, social revolution, downward mobility, and paid work.[4] The journal, its last entry dated Friday, 30 August 1889, is (unaccountably) silent on Thomas's temperance activities in the 1880s and ends before her embrace of woman suffrage in the 1890s. In contrast to the journal, which ends on a somber note, Thomas's life began anew when she moved to Atlanta in 1893 and gained prominence as a public figure.

Respecting the distinction between life and text, I will discuss them sequentially. The first, biographical section of this essay narrates Thomas's life.[5] The second section discusses the journal's main themes: identity, gender and sexuality, religion, race, labor, and the journal's great and painful secret. Readers may wish to read

---

3. Thomas's history recalls those of southern suffragists like Rebecca Latimer Felton and Caroline Merrick. See Rebecca Latimer Felton, *Country Life in Georgia in the Days of My Youth* (Atlanta, Ga., 1919), and Caroline E. Merrick, *Old Times in Dixie Land: A Southern Matron's Memories* (New York, 1901). See also Shari Benstock, "Authorizing the Autobiographical," in Shari Benstock, ed., *The Private Self: Theory and Practice of Women's Autobiographical Writings* (Chapel Hill, N.C., 1988), p. 20.

4. Myrta Lockett Avary, *Dixie after the War: An Exposition of Social Conditions Existing in the South, during the Twelve Years Succeeding the Fall of Richmond* (New York, 1906); Isabella D. Martin and Myrta Lockett Avary, eds., *A Diary from Dixie, as Written by Mary Boykin Chesnut, Wife of James Chesnut, Jr., United States Senator from South Carolina* (New York, 1905); Ben Ames Williams, ed., *A Diary from Dixie by Mary Boykin Chesnut* (Boston, 1949); C. Vann Woodward, ed., *Mary Chesnut's Civil War* (New Haven, Conn., 1981).

5. I am prevented from offering a more critical discussion of Thomas's life here by two factors: First, no letters to or from Thomas survive, making the diary virtually the only source for information on her life; second, Carolyn

the biographical section, then turn directly to the journal, before confronting my analysis.

Gertrude Thomas the Life

Gertrude Clanton was born in Columbia County, near Augusta, Georgia, in 1834. Her family belonged to the approximately 6 percent of southern whites who made up the Deep South planter elite.[6] Clanton's mother, the former Mary Luke (born in 1812), was from a wealthy rural family living near Augusta.

Mary Luke married Turner Clanton in 1829. Although he had been born in 1798 in southside Virginia, where the ambitious, rather than the "first families," scrambled for wealth, Turner Clanton had already improved his sizable inheritance and reinforced his own claim to gentility by serving two terms in the Georgia legislature.[7] The Clantons had eleven children, seven of whom lived past the age of five: Anne (whom Thomas calls "Sis Anne" in the journal), born in 1831; Ella Gertrude, born in 1834; Mary (Mamie), born in 1841; James (Buddy), born in 1843; Cora, born in 1846; Nathaniel Holt (Holt), born in 1849; Catherine (Cate/Kate), born in 1855. In 1864 Clanton's estate was valued at some $2,500,000 in Confederate dollars, and he was reckoned as one of the wealthiest planters in the state.[8]

Curry's unpublished 1987 Georgia State University dissertation, the sole full-length biography of Thomas, has not been made available for purchase by anyone but the author from University Microfilms as of May 1989.

6. In 1860 some 400,000 southern white families owned slaves, usually only one or two. Planter families, by definition, owned twenty or more slaves. The proportion of white families owning slaves decreased during the antebellum era, from 36 percent in 1830 to 31 percent in 1850 and 26 percent in 1860. Further, the proportion of slaveowners in the white population varied throughout the South, there being relatively few in the upcountry and more in the lowcountry Black Belts such as the Georgia and South Carolina hinterlands of Augusta. See James Oakes, *The Ruling Race: A History of American Slaveholders* (New York, 1982), pp. 225, 229.

7. Allan Kulikoff, *Tobacco and Slaves: The Development of Southern Cultures in the Chesapeake, 1680–1800* (Chapel Hill, N.C., 1986) pp. 148–57.

8. Information on the Luke, Clanton, and Thomas families comes from Virginia Burr, who is the great-granddaughter of Gertrude Thomas and the granddaughter of Mary Belle Thomas Ingraham (1858–1929). I have also drawn on Mary Elizabeth Massey, "The Making of a Feminist," *Journal of Southern History* 39, no. 1 (Feb. 1973): 3–22.

As a girl, Gertrude Clanton slept late, read voraciously, visited friends, dressed prettily, and wrote letters.[9] But her time became more regimented in January 1849, when she went away to Wesleyan Female College in Macon, Georgia. Gertrude was the first Clanton daughter to go away to school or college and one of a tiny minority of southern women of her generation with access to higher education. Schools for women were few, and those that existed—for example, Clanton's Wesleyan, Moravian College in Salem, North Carolina, and Mme Talvanne's in Charleston—cost anywhere from $200 to $700 per year. Wesleyan, which formed part of the antebellum movement in the South toward more rigorous education for women, was a Methodist institution that had been chartered in 1836, during a fertile period in southern evangelical education.[10]

After three years, Clanton graduated from Wesleyan in 1851 at the age of seventeen. An active and enthusiastic alumna, she twice held office in the Wesleyan Alumnaen Association and returned to Macon several times for reunions. Over the years she remained in regular touch with many of her school friends. One, Martha (Mat) Oliver, was particularly close. Gertrude Clanton grieved when Mat Oliver married for the first time, but then, as the years passed, she gradually lost interest in Mat's fate. Another school friend, Julia (Jule) Thomas, became family.[11] When Jule's charming and handsome brother, James Jefferson Thomas, began courting Gertrude in the spring of 1851, he was completing his undergraduate work at Princeton, and in the fall he pursued medical studies in Augusta.

---

9. In this abridged edition of the journal, much discussion of Thomas's visiting and reading and many descriptions of clothing have been deleted.

10. Anne Firor Scott, *The Southern Lady: From Pedestal to Politics, 1830–1930* (Chicago, 1970), pp. 68–74; Catherine Clinton, *The Plantation Mistress: Woman's World in the Old South* (New York, 1982) pp. 124–28; Jane Turner Censer, *North Carolina Planters and Their Children, 1800–1860* (Baton Rouge, La., 1984), p. 44; and Donald G. Mathews, *Religion in the Old South* (Chicago, 1977), pp. 89–91, 96–97.

11. Concerning Mat Oliver, the most interesting entries from Thomas's journal are: 2 Feb. 1849, 5 Jan., 19 Apr., 9 June, 9 July 1852, 11 Apr. 1855, 9 Feb. 1858. Thomas and Jule Thomas remained friends, even when Jule moved to North Carolina after having married Nathaniel Scales. In 1860 sibling exchange reinforced the close bonds between the Thomas and Clanton families when Jule and Jeff's younger brother Pinckney married Gertrude's younger sister Mary.

In a milieu that venerated romantic love, courtship was the great and public moment in the life of the belle, a smooth and glamorous ritual. Clanton strove to fill her role, though Jeff Thomas proved perplexing. While she did her best to appear unassailable and unmoved, he kept her off balance and insecure.[12] She pretended, even to her journal, not to be upset by his absences, silences, and suspicious maladies, but Jeff Thomas caused her distress as well as delight. Turner Clanton's lukewarm approval of the match also proved wrenching. To aggravate matters further, Jeff fell ill in 1852 and delayed the wedding for nearly a month. Ella Gertrude Clanton and Jefferson Thomas married in December 1852, then honeymooned with her family in New York City. At some point during their betrothal, Jeff had decided to abandon his medical studies, an unexplained decision that both later came to regret.

Jefferson Thomas came from a plantation family residing in Burke County, Georgia, in the Augusta environs. With both of them bringing wealth to the marriage, Gertrude and Jeff were quite well off. When they married, Turner Clanton gave Gertrude and Jeff a house, plantation, and slaves worth nearly $30,000. In the years that followed, Clanton remained in the financial picture. Even during the prosperous years of the mid-1850s, he furnished luxuries— such as the addition of a piazza on the Thomases' house—that his daughter had earlier taken for granted. Turner Clanton also gave gifts of money and supplies, such as animal fodder, that eased the Thomases' economic situation. That such gifts were so welcome indicates a degree of financial stringency. As early as 1855 Gertrude Thomas began to write about, if not to attempt seriously to reduce, her level of spending.[13]

During the 1850s, however, money did not unduly worry the young matron, and she and Jeff began their family. Beginning when she was nineteen until she was forty-one, Gertrude Thomas bore ten children, seven of whom lived past the age of five: Turner Clan-

---

12. John D'Emilio and Estelle B. Freedman, *Intimate Matters: A History of Sexuality in America* (New York, 1988), p. 94, Steven M. Stowe, "Courtship: Sexuality and Feeling," in *Intimacy and Power in the Old South: Ritual in the Lives of the Planters* (Baltimore, Md., 1987), pp. 50–121; and Thomas Journal, 26 Feb., 16 Mar., 15, 18, 30, 31 May, 5 Nov. 1852. Entries from Thomas's journal will hereafter be cited by date only.

13. 27 Apr., 9 July, 20 Aug., 29 Sept. 1855, 10 Mar. 1856, 1 Jan. 1857, 7 Feb. 1858.

ton (1853–1917); Mary Belle (1858–1929); Jefferson Davis (1861–1920); Cora Lou (1863–1956); Julian Pinckney (1868–1928); James Clanton (1872–79); and Kathleen (1875–1968).

Thomas was in her late twenties when the Civil War broke out. Like other Confederates—indeed like her northern counterparts—she rejoiced (momentarily) at the prospect of warfare, which she thought would rejuvenate a southern manhood that she feared had "degenerated" as a consequence of luxurious living. Throughout the war years, she pondered the meaning of southern national identity and worried that "the South" continued to be too indolent and too dependent upon the North intellectually. Thomas followed the progress of the war closely, was a director of the Augusta Ladies' Aid Society, sewed uniforms, made cartridges, and visited military hospitals repeatedly. During the war and after, she spoke of the Confederacy as "we."[14]

In 1861, during her period of flag-waving Confederate nationalism, Gertrude gloried in Jefferson Thomas's military service and played out their partings as if they were scenes in an opera. But by October 1861, Jeff was back home to purchase uniforms, sell Confederate bonds, and visit his plantations. His mother's and his own illnesses delayed his return to the front until November 1861. In early 1862 Gertrude began to hope that he would leave the army, and by late February 1862 he was back at home, this time to recruit volunteers and purchase supplies in Augusta and Atlanta. Jeff was in Virginia again from April to June 1862. In mid-1862 he became one of scores of Confederate officers who resigned their commis-

---

14. 15, 16 July 1861, 1 Jan. 1862. In the use of the first-person plural Thomas had a good deal of company, as illustrated in the journal of Susan Cornwall of Burke County, Georgia, quoted in LeeAnn Whites, *The Process of Feminization in the New South: Augusta, Georgia, 1860–1900* (Chapel Hill, N.C., forthcoming), p. 12. Jean Bethke Elshtain mentions Jean-Jacques Rousseau's and Machiavelli's celebration of military values (*Women and War* [New York, 1987], p. 55). See also journal entries for 15, 16 July 1861, 7 Oct. 1862. The present edition of the journal deletes much news about the progress of the Civil War. For a discussion of Confederate nationalism that accords well with Thomas's experience, see Drew Gilpin Faust, *The Creation of Confederate Nationalism: Ideology and Identity in the Civil War South* (Baton Rouge, La., 1988).

sions, complaining of favoritism and low morale.[15] Jeff purchased a substitute and joined a local militia unit that did not threaten to take him far from Augusta. Until the war faded into unfocused memory, Jefferson's record proved more a source of ambivalence to Gertrude than of pride. All told, Jefferson Thomas had spent about nine months at the front.[16]

Three years into the war, the glamor of the Confederate cause wore thin for Gertrude. Weary of the war with its shortages, inflation, and social upheaval, by 1864 she preferred to keep her husband safe at home, even if it meant losing Atlanta to the Yankees. Wearing cotton instead of linen, complaining of the discomfort of the town house they were renting, she wondered, "Oh God will this war never cease?"[17] The war came close to home in 1864, when Gen. William T. Sherman's army burned buildings on one of the Thomas plantations in Burke County and looted the storehouses and cotton-gin houses. Contemplating the possibility of Confederate defeat, Thomas began to question the deeper significance of the war.

The enduring personal meaning of the Confederate defeat for Thomas was financial, and in the loss of wealth her experience was characteristic of the planter class.[18] Like every other slaveowning family in the South, the Thomases lost every cent they had invested in slaves. And like many others, they had also invested in Confederate bonds (C$15,000) that became worthless.

To compound the tragedy of Confederate defeat, Thomas had

---

15. 27 June, 17 Sept. 1862. Both Thomas W. Thomas (of Elbert County, Georgia, in the Augusta hinterland) and Robert Toombs, who had been a U.S. senator from Georgia, resigned their commissions in early 1862. In April 1862 the Confederacy resorted to conscription in order to supply the necessary manpower. See J. William Harris, *Plain Folk and Gentry in a Slave Society: White Liberty and Black Slavery in Augusta's Hinterlands* (Middletown, Conn., 1985), pp. 144–47.

16. 18 Aug. 1861, 17 Jan. 1862. Jeff Thomas later embraced the role of Confederate veteran. As an old man he would ride about at reunions of Confederates and Princeton alumni on his favorite horse, "Dixie Will Go." He died in Atlanta in 1916.

17. 22 Oct., 21 Nov. 1864.

18. James L. Roark, *Masters without Slaves: Southern Planters in the Civil War and Reconstruction* (New York, 1977), pp. 61, 77, 196, 208.

sustained another crippling loss before the end of the war, this one personal as well as financial. Turner Clanton, who had been a source of moral and financial support over the years, died in 1864. Gertrude, therefore, stood to receive a handsome inheritance, or so she had assumed. But this was not to be the case. Sixteen years after Clanton's death, his will was finally settled, but Gertrude received relatively little from it. Without her knowledge, her husband had over the course of ten years resorted to the (not uncommon) expedient of borrowing from his father-in-law, substituting liabilities for Gertrude's inheritance. In the postwar years, Jeff went deeper into debt to Gertrude's family and his own siblings. During the hard financial times of the late 1860s and the 1870s, Gertrude missed her father keenly. The death of her father figures larger than any other event in her journal, spreading over twelve pages in the typescript for 1864 and reappearing in the years that followed.

At his best, Jefferson Thomas was an attractive and generous gentleman whom Gertrude loved deeply. But after the war, he fell apart physically and emotionally, a far-from-unique failing of the time. At the moment of defeat, Gertrude also experienced a serious crisis. She fainted, miscarried, and tormented herself with doubts. Although she would not have phrased it quite so starkly, her standing in her own eyes and that of her kin and neighbors had depended, before the war, on their owning many slaves—together with the wealth that slaveowning symbolized—and on the refinement that came with higher education.[19] Without slaveownership as a social marker, her world tottered. Emancipation shook her to the point of threatening her physical health, her religious beliefs, and her certainty about her position as a woman.

But she recovered quickly; once she had decided that slavery was wrong, she accepted the fact of emancipation. Despite the despondency and doubt that plagued her from time to time, she was able to look ahead and plan confidently to bring money into the family. By the summer of 1866 her health was good, but Jefferson's was still terrible. He brooded over the Confederate defeat and denied the justice of emancipation. His psychosomatic illnesses, his

---

19. See Elizabeth Fox-Genovese, *Within the Plantation Household: Black and White Women of the Old South* (Chapel Hill, N.C., 1988), pp. 15, 22–27.

chronic mismanagement of his plantations and his business, his bitterness at the Confederate defeat and emancipation, and his habit (acquired during the war) of swearing before his pious Methodist wife severely strained the marriage.[20]

The end of the war, which she described as "the turning point, the crisis with me," changed Gertrude Thomas's life profoundly.[21] In broader terms, the war fundamentally altered relations between men and women in the South, as both natives and visitors observed. Southern women seemed generally to have more energy and intelligence than the men, and they were suing for divorce, going out to work, and speaking up in public for the first time.[22] The thought that she might earn money had never crossed Gertrude Thomas's mind before the end of the Civil War. But after the Confederate defeat, as financial losses began to afflict the Thomases, she appreciated her education anew.[23] For the first time she contemplated salaried work as a teacher. Without discerning the relationship between her own access to paid work and the wider upheaval in women's employment opportunities, Thomas entered the universe of paid labor, both as employee and employer.

To a certain degree, Thomas gloried in the new order. "I think and think boldly," she wrote, "I act—and act boldly." Unaccompan-

---

20. Jeff Thomas had actually suffered bouts of nervous stomach and shortness of breath since 1859. But the immobilizing depressions he suffered after the war marked a deterioration in his mental as well as physical health. In her journal entry of 29 November 1868, Gertrude speaks of Jeff's depression and the terrible "strain upon his nerves & physical system." On 7 December 1870, she writes that her husband "talks about being a fit subject for the Lunatic Asylum." See also entries for 1 Jan. 1859, 17 Sept. 1862, 31 Dec. 1863, 12 Feb. 1865, 3 Dec. 1868.

21. 5 May 1865.

22. Scott, *Southern Lady*, pp. 98–99; Mary Elizabeth Massey, *Bonnet Brigades* (New York, 1966), pp. 153, 174–75, 242, 260. Other scholarship on women in war—for instance, on women in World War I—indicates that wars liberate women even as they debilitate men. See Sandra M. Gilbert, "Soldier's Heart: Literary Men, Literary Women, and the Great War," in Margaret R. Higonnet, Jane Jenson, Sonya Michel, Margaret Collins Weitz, eds., *Behind the Lines: Gender and the Two World Wars* (New Haven, Conn., 1987), pp. 199, 201, 214, 223.

23. 22 Sept., 22 Nov. 1864, 29 Mar., 5 May 1865, 9 July, 12 Oct. 1866.

ied by a man, she walked in the streets of Augusta and journeyed by train to a postwar Wesleyan reunion. In Macon she read aloud a piece of her own writing with sufficient aplomb to substitute spontaneously more appropriate wording. In 1869 she began to think about publishing her writing for money, and the temptation of writing professionally never disappeared.[24] Without remuneration, she proudly published her account of the improvements in her church, not as Mrs. Jefferson Thomas, but as Mrs. Gertrude Thomas. Even as she regretted the motives for her moving out into the world as a woman of affairs rather than as a lady, she relished her increased individuality.[25]

Reconstruction—in the strictly political sense of the term—was a brief affair in the state of Georgia (1867–70), but it did bring political upheaval in the late 1860s and very early 1870s that was accompanied by a perceptible increase in black self-confidence among women as well as men. Jefferson Thomas, the head of the local Democrats, was alarmed by black political independence. Gertrude Thomas, to the contrary, was not threatened by blacks in politics. She praised the abilities of Aaron Bradley, a black politician, and realized that were she black, she, too, would support the Radicals.[26]

Because women could neither vote nor hold office, politics was not the stuff of Thomas's day-to-day life. Nonetheless, she resented the economic ramifications of Reconstruction: unintimidated free labor that pursued better wages and working conditions. This meant that while her husband's adjustment to emancipation and Reconstruction took place largely in the more public worlds of politics and farm employment, hers was a far more intimate accommodation, pursued in the private world of house and yard and unmediated by the power of the state. No laws regulated household employment, in which there were no contracts, liens, or prosecutions for debt.

---

24. 25 Oct. 1864, 9, 22 July 1866, 20 Sept. 1869, 29 Sept., 30 Nov. 1870, 9 Feb. 1879, 21 Feb. 1880. Thomas shared this aspiration with many other southern women who had kept journals during the Civil War.

25. This use of her own (as opposed to her husband's) first name merits two mentions in the journal, on 25 March and 15 May 1880. See also 14 Dec. 1870, 2 Jan. 1871.

26. 1, 2 Nov. 1868.

For Gertrude Thomas as for her female peers, Reconstruction represented not so much a political revolution as an upheaval in labor relations. For the first time, she was not assured the help of reliable and experienced workers. Like many other formerly prosperous former slaveowners, she gritted her teeth at the thought of the "low class of people," the nouveau-riche whites (some migrants from the North) now benefiting from the service of workers whom she and her class had trained but could no longer afford to employ.[27] She further had to adjust to her husband's difficulties in business.

Jefferson Thomas's retail business, established during the war, failed after faltering for two years. In 1868 his New York creditor forced Jefferson and his partners to declare bankruptcy and sell off what was left of their inventory at a publicly advertised sale that embarrassed both of the Thomases. Just as Gertrude faced the fact of the bankruptcy of Jefferson's business, he announced to her that Belmont, their home, might well be sold for debt.[28] Between 1868 and the early 1890s, the Thomases gradually lost much of their property. City lots, plantations in Burke County, and, finally, their residence in Augusta were auctioned off for debt in the early 1870s. Their remaining properties—Belmont (which was not sold), Dixie Farm, and the Road Place—were heavily mortgaged. In 1875 or 1876 Belmont burned, and Gertrude lost the home in which she had lived during most of her married life. Faced with unanticipated frustrations, Gertrude Thomas faltered, and she wrote the word "humiliation" in her journal many a time.[29]

The worst chagrins that financial ruin entailed were the shabbiness that came from not being able to replace worn-out carpets, carriages, and clothing, the sight of her property advertised by the sheriff in the newspapers for sale at auction, and the realization that her children lacked the status that accompanied wealth. Her husband's business failures and crushing debts became public knowledge in the late 1860s, exposing their financial difficulties to everyone who read the local newspapers. Rather than let her neigh-

---

27. The quote is from 29 May 1865. See also 1 Feb., 10 Apr. 1871, 5 Jan. 1881.

28. 29 Nov. 1868.

29. See particularly 10 Jan., 6 Mar., 5 Dec. 1870, 23 June 1880.

bors see her in reduced circumstances, Thomas refused to go to town. She would not let her neighborhood literary club meet at her house until she could buy new carpets, noting sadly that she could no longer afford to replace the worn-out velvet tapestry.[30] At first the advertisements of the auctions and sheriff's sales were painful. But with the passage of time, Thomas discovered that she no longer felt the sting so acutely. By mid-1880 the public disclosure of bankruptcy no longer mortified her.[31]

She never learned to swallow what she saw as her children's lack of social advantages. Early in 1880 she cried at the thought that she could not give her children the wealth and prestige that she had enjoyed.[32] None of her children attained planter status, and the Thomas family descendants lost the social standing that had gone hand in hand with rural wealth.[33]

Downward mobility sums up Gertrude Thomas's postwar experience, and she felt it keenly. Resenting poverty and everything it implied in her life, she tortured herself by listing her expenses down to the penny, yet took pride in her ability to pay off creditors, bit by bit, week by week.[34] Through this scrimping and close figuring, she recalled the luxury in which she had been raised and which she had for so long taken for granted. At times she was amazed that she, "the child of wealth and pride," should suffer "such degradation" and saddened that hardship had prevented her oldest child, Turner, from drinking from the "golden cup" that had been held to his lips at birth.[35]

Hard times impaired Gertrude's relationship with her husband. She was aware that his inability to support the family meant that the task of providing for her children devolved upon her. To preserve her family's integrity, she used her earnings to pay taxes and wages

---

30. 12 Dec. 1870, 2 Jan. 1871, 9 Feb. 1879, 22 Jan. 1880.
31. 14 May 1869, 10 Jan. 1870, 18 Dec. 1879, 19 May 1880.
32. 10 Aug. 1879; 2 Jan., 13 June 1880.
33. Toward the end of the journal, Thomas writes of her three adult children: Turner is selling insurance; Jeff works for an express company; and Mary Belle is happily married and living in Atlanta (3 Apr. 1888).
34. E.g., 8 Feb. 1879, 3 Apr. 1888.
35. 10 Jan., 5 Dec. 1870.

on the farms—an obligation that before the war she would have assumed to have been her husband's responsibility. Yet for all her unquestioned commitment to her nuclear family, she distinguished rhetorically between her husband, on one side, and herself and her children, on the other, as though hard times had stripped the family down to its matrifocal core.[36] In a revision of the traditional roles that she had once accepted for herself and her husband, she was now a breadwinner. Gertrude became the pillar of the nuclear family, as her husband, with his debts and bad management and ill-temper, became peripheral.

Money problems also created difficulties between Gertrude Thomas and her mother, her siblings, and her in-laws, all of whom were her husband's creditors. Homestead legislation passed in 1868 allowed Jefferson Thomas to shelter $2,000 worth of real estate and $1,000 worth of personal property from seizure for debt. In the late 1860s and early 1870s, he often considered declaring one or another of their plantations a homestead. But Gertrude found this plan distasteful, as so many of their creditors were their relatives. As she saw it, to shelter their property would be to cheat their families. Over the years the Thomases argued about the homestead law, with Gertrude opposing its use on the ground that her brother James (Buddy) and her sister Mamie and her husband Pinck (who was Jeff's brother) would be badly hurt after having incurred financial risks on Jefferson Thomas's account.[37]

Even as she reproached her husband for endangering their siblings financially, she complained to her mother that it hurt to be sued by one's own sisters and accused her family of avoiding her entirely.[38] As in so many human affairs, poverty strained the bonds of family, but not, in this case, to the point of breaking. Thomas

---

36. 29 Nov. 1868; 9 Mar. 1871.

37. 29 Nov., 4, 20 Dec. 1868, 3, 4 May 1869, 9 Jan., 5, 12 Dec. 1870. The Thomases' other creditors exerted more pressure than did their families for the repayment of debt.

The Georgia homestead law of 1868 had been tailored to meet the needs of planters as well as yeoman farmers, hence the generous limits on real and personal property (Jonathan M. Bryant, " 'The Work of Negroes and Thieves': Georgia's Homestead and Exemption Laws, 1868–1877," unpublished paper, University of Georgia, 1986).

38. 29 Mar. 1865, 4 Dec. 1868, 19 June 1869, 22 Jan., 5 Dec. 1870, 9 Mar. 1871, 31 Dec. 1878.

remained close to her husband, children, mother, and siblings, and her mother contributed generously to the support of the Thomases' children for a decade and a half.[39]

Gertrude Thomas experienced pain and anguish, but she also coped with catastrophe. Her progress was uneven, but she grew strong and independent as she wavered between growing assurance in her abilities and doubts about her proper role as a wife. With the instinctive knowledge that as a mother she must provide for her children and a growing confidence in her business sense, her self-esteem increased. At the same time, she was subject to conflicting pressures. Jeff detested her giving him advice—however sound—and asked her, as his wife, to defer to his judgment. Had she been permitted, she would doubtless have managed their affairs more efficiently, certainly more vigorously.[40] But she was not willing to subject her marriage to the added tension that a such a role reversal would have imposed.

The trauma of publicly advertised bankruptcy and her husband's emotional decline of themselves made for tough times, but Thomas had to endure one last tragedy. In 1879, in the midst of economic ruin and declining status, her six-year-old son Clanton died, a loss that symbolized the death of her grand old self and the apparent bleakness of the future. Thomas grieved over Clanton as intensely as she had mourned her father.

Even though the Civil War had made teaching acceptable for respectable women and Gertrude had decided in 1865 that she wanted to teach, Jeff long opposed her plan to work for wages.[41] Finally their desperate need converted him, and she began teaching elementary school in 1878. Through all the six years that she kept school, Thomas fought off competition from other hard-up, edu-

---

39. E.g., 2 Nov. 1868, 28 Jan., 7 Mar. 1869, 3 Oct. 1882.
40. E.g., 10 Jan. 1870.
41. Gertrude was enthusiastically planning to open a school for the winter of 1865–66 on 8 May 1865, and in her journal she speaks of wanting to teach from time to time over the next several years. On 30 Nov. 1870 she records Jeff's opposition to her working.

cated women. Her teaching salary of $30 per month enabled her to pay wages and property taxes on their farm, but she still had to borrow money from her aunt and her mother to meet other expenses.[42]

Jeff Thomas often failed to meet his financial obligations, and in 1880 he was able to continue planting only after Gertrude arranged for credit.[43] He could no longer provide his wife the moral support that he had offered, for instance, when a premature baby had died in late 1855. Rather, she now complained that he never appreciated her sacrifices and that his grouchiness got on her nerves. For a while in the early 1870s they ceased sleeping together, because he—not she—was afraid of having more children, whom they could not afford to support.[44]

Gertrude Thomas found teaching elementary school tiring and frustrating, even though she took a sincere interest in the welfare of her pupils. Tempted by the hope that she could write for money, she felt she was wasting her education on the very young. She wanted to quit teaching in 1880, but her husband persuaded her to persevere, for the family depended on her salary.[45] The year 1879 represented Gertrude Thomas's lowest point, financially and emotionally. She felt old and poor and alone. "I only felt that Mr Thomas could not help me, the children could not," she wrote. "I had not one friend upon whom I could rely and before me seemed a dense high wall."[46] During the 1870s and 1880s she noticed the physical decline that accompanied her middle age.

She stayed in the classroom until her mother's death in 1884. The Thomases then moved to the Clanton mansion in Augusta, where they took in boarders. In these further reduced circumstances, Gertrude suffered a long, debilitating illness, which she suspected was related to the lack of privacy and to the emotional

---

42. E.g., 12 Apr. 1871, 4 Jan., 8 Feb. 1879. In February 1879 her salary was increased to $35 per month.

43. 23 June 1880.

44. 10 Jan., 30 Nov., 12 Dec. 1870. Intimacy between the two resumed in the early 1870s, for Clanton was born in 1872 and Kathleen in 1875. By 1880 they were again occupying separate bedrooms.

45. 8 Jan. 1880, 3 Oct. 1883.

46. 18 Dec. 1879. When Clanton died in 1879 he was a few days from turning seven. Turner was twenty-six; Mary Belle, twenty-one; Jeff, eighteen; Cora Lou, sixteen; Julian, eleven; and Kathleen, four.

strain that the presence of boarders entailed. While she was physically and emotionally vulnerable, a series of earthquakes in 1886–87 proved terrifying. In the spring of 1888, when she was about to turn fifty-four, she lamented that she was not even good for $50 worth of credit.[47] With the earthquakes and the meetings of her literary society the journal ends.

Were Thomas's life to have closed with the journal, it would have been a drama of failure, the embodiment of the ruin of the antebellum planter class. Thomas would have represented a female counterpart to Thomas Chaplin of the South Carolina lowcountry, who went from planting to teaching school.[48] But this was not Gertrude Thomas's end. Even before she stopped writing in her journal, she had begun to rally. As an officer in the Richmond County Grange, she occasionally published essays on matters of especial concern to women, one of which won a prize. She also joined women's groups, following a pattern that typified white southern women of her class and generation.[49]

In the mid-1880s Thomas became active in four organizations of the kind that were then easing into public life the southern white women who had formerly been cloistered belles: the Ladies' Missionary Society of St. John's Methodist Church in Augusta; the Hayne Circle, a literary club in Augusta (that included men and women); the Ladies' [Confederate] Memorial Association of Augusta; and the Woman's Christian Temperance Union (WCTU). She also remained active in the Wesleyan Alumnaen Society.

In the South, women's missionary societies were an innovation of the 1870s and 1880s, beginning with those sponsored by the Southern Methodist church in 1878. Such societies were an outlet that allowed women who were active in churches—a perfectly acceptable activity for middle- and upper-class southern women—to

---

47. By this point she had lost hope of receiving anything from her mother's estate (3 Apr. 1888).

48. Theodore Rosengarten, *Tombee: Portrait of a Cotton Planter* (New York, 1987), p. 299. Unlike Thomas, who grappled with hardship and wrote about it almost unblinkingly, Thomas Chaplin avoided the fundamental truths and tragedies of his postwar existence.

49. Scott, *Southern Lady*, pp. 139–52.

organize to work for goals outside their homes, families, and neighborhoods. Thomas had been an enthusiastic Methodist ever since her conversion at Wesleyan College, and missionary work represented a natural outgrowth of that lifelong allegiance.[50]

Respectable women across the South were forming women's clubs, often as a means of furthering their educations.[51] Similarly, Thomas figured among hundreds of white southern women who had been ardent Confederates and who, in the 1880s, organized memorial associations to commemorate the Civil War dead. Like many others, Thomas went from holding office in the Augusta Ladies' Memorial Society into the United Daughters of the Confederacy (UDC), formed in 1894. In the middle and late 1890s she served as recording secretary and national treasurer of the UDC.

Thousands of southern women, many of whom, like Thomas, had become accustomed to working together in missionary societies and women's clubs, took their giant step beyond familiar bounds when they joined the Woman's Christian Temperance Union in the 1880s. When her socially prominent kinswoman in Augusta, Jane Thomas Sibley (Mrs. William Sibley), founded the local WCTU, Thomas also became active. Legions of southern women flocked to the WCTU either as followers of Frances Willard or out of an abstract belief in the cause, but Thomas had additional, personal reasons for advocating temperance.

There is little question that Jefferson Thomas had a drinking problem, which may well have been of long standing. Years earlier, Jeff's father had asked Gertrude what she would do were Jeff to get drunk, and her own father harbored reservations toward her fiancé that may have been rooted in finances, personal morality, or both. During their courtship, Gertrude extracted an unspecified promise from Jeff that she hoped he would keep.[52]

---

50. Marjorie Stratford Mendenhall, "Southern Women of a 'Lost Generation,'" *South Atlantic Quarterly* 33, no. 4 (Oct. 1934): 341; and John Patrick McDowell, *The Social Gospel in the South: The Woman's Home Mission Movement in the Methodist Episcopal Church, South, 1886–1939* (Baton Rouge, La., 1982), pp. 1–11.

51. Anne Scott cites 1884–87 as the period of explosive growth of women's clubs in the South. Thomas's Hayne Circle, named for Paul Hamilton Hayne, a local poet, does not quite fit this pattern, however, as it was formed during the 1870s and included men as well as women.

52. 18 Mar. 1852, 17 Aug. 1879.

Thomas never addresses Jefferson Thomas's drinking habits directly, but the journal abounds in oblique references that indicate that she is keeping secrets. Twice, for instance, she relates the same anecdote about closeted family skeletons.[53] Unfortunately, the journal(s) from the difficult years 1871–78 no longer exist(s). The editor of this volume, Virginia Burr, who is most familiar with the journal, suspects that corroboration of family lore on Jeff's drinking might well lie there.

Thomas's attraction to the WCTU was a result of national policy as well as individual initiative.[54] Frances Willard, the second president of the WCTU, made a special effort to conciliate educated white southern women who had been Confederate supporters, and in her southern tours in the 1880s she brought into the WCTU respectable southern women (most white, some black) who were worried by social changes and appalled by widespread male drunkenness. Adopting a version of Henry Grady's New South rhetoric, Willard toured the South with a broad-gauged and ladylike brand of feminism that attracted white southerners like Caroline Merrick, a New Orleans clubwoman; Belle Kearney, a teacher from Jackson, Mississippi; and Rebecca Latimer Felton, a controversial lecturer from Atlanta who would become Thomas's colleague.[55]

Thomas served as secretary and vice president of the Augusta chapter of the WCTU. In accordance with Willard's motto, "Do Everything," southern women in the WCTU did not confine their activities to temperance. The WCTU led Thomas into concerns that she shared with Rebecca Felton and Felton's sister, Mary Latimer McLendon: penal reform, industrial education for girls, and woman suffrage.

By the time Gertrude and Jefferson Thomas had mortgaged everything they owned in and around Augusta, their fifth child, Julian (born 1863), had grown up and graduated from the Augusta Medical College in 1887. After completing a residency in New Jersey, Julian moved to Atlanta as a specialist in dermatology and preventive

---

53. 4 July 1864, 7 Feb. 1869.

54. Jean E. Friedman, *The Enclosed Garden: Women and Community in the Evangelical South, 1830–1900* (Chapel Hill, N.C., 1985), pp. 111–21.

55. Willard made nine southern tours between 1881 and 1896 (Rebecca Ragsdale Lallier, "The Woman's Christian Temperance Union, Frances Willard, and the South," unpublished paper, 1988, p. 13).

medicine. He asked his parents to live with him, an invitation they accepted. In 1893, at age fifty-nine, Thomas left Augusta and Richmond County, where she had spent her entire life. In Atlanta she continued to develop as a feminist.

Thomas worked with Mary Latimer McLendon for the creation of the Industrial School for Girls in Milledgeville, Georgia, and she followed McLendon and Felton into local and state woman suffrage organizations. In 1895 Thomas attended the meeting of the National American Woman Suffrage Association (NAWSA) in Atlanta as a delegate from the Atlanta WCTU.[56] In 1899, at the age of sixty-five, she was elected president of the Georgia Woman Suffrage Association (GWSA). During the 1890s she spoke frequently in public, traveled to WCTU, UDC, and suffrage conventions throughout the nation, and wrote for publication. In 1903 she became a life member of the NAWSA (and received a letter of acknowledgment from Susan B. Anthony). Such honors would not have seemed possible in her dismal decades after the war.

Thomas died in 1907 after suffering a stroke, and her obituaries bore witness to her prominence in public life. She had not realized her old ambition to make money as a writer, but she had established herself as a leading Georgian. By the end of her life, Thomas had become a full-fledged feminist whose stature was recognized throughout her state and region.

During her maturity, Thomas's life fortunes rose from the ashes. With the return of more sunny times, however, she never reestablished her habit of writing in her journal. Over the years her reasons for writing had changed from performing a ritual of the elite to recording family history for her children to seeking a confidante in times of trouble. After her emergence as a public figure in the 1890s and 1900s, no new motive appeared. Perhaps her published writings, which she saved in scrapbooks, exhibited those aspects of her self that she wished to preserve. Although this edition of the journal does not reproduce material from the scrapbooks in full,

---

56. The NAWSA had been formed in 1890 with the merger of the National Woman Suffrage Association, led by Elizabeth Cady Stanton and Susan B. Anthony and based in New York, and the American Woman Suffrage Association, led by Lucy Stone and her husband, Henry Blackwell, and based in New England.

Virginia Burr has drawn upon them to round out Thomas's life in her epilogue. An entirely different sort of source from the journal, the scrapbooks do not permit the kind of analysis that follows on Thomas's own writing. Nor is other private material available. The journal stands alone as the record of an elite white southern woman's experiences, responses, and growth during times of slavery, war, and Reconstruction.

The Journal of Gertrude Thomas

Considering Thomas's keen sense of gender, it is fitting that her journal owes its survival to her female descendants. Cora Lou Thomas Farrell, Thomas's daughter, became the guardian of the thirteen extant manuscript journals until her death in 1956. After Farrell's death, the journals remained in her home in Atlanta, where her niece, Gertrude Ingraham Threlkeld (who was Gertrude Thomas's granddaughter), and Gertrude Threlkeld Despeaux (Threlkeld's daughter and Gertrude Thomas's great-granddaughter) lived. The process by which the journals were transferred from private possession to the Duke University Library Manuscript Department in 1957 is not entirely clear but seems to have occurred at the instigation of the historian Katherine M. Jones. In preparing *The Plantation South* (Englewood Cliffs, N.J., 1957), Jones became the first historian to use the Thomas journals. Jones knew both the curator of manuscripts at Duke, Mattie Russell, and Thomas descendant Gertrude Threlkeld Despeaux.

Despeaux deposited the journals in the Manuscript Department at the Duke University Library, where a pioneer in southern women's history, Mary Elizabeth Massey of Winthrop College in South Carolina, discovered them. Massey commissioned the transcription of the journals. Until the present published edition, historians have generally worked from Massey's typescript. Unfortunately, the typescript is not accurate, for Thomas's handwriting is difficult to decipher, and the typists were not historians. For this edition, Virginia Burr has checked every page against the manuscript and corrected omissions and inaccuracies.[57]

Mary Elizabeth Massey was elected president of the Southern

---

57. At least three volumes of the journal, covering the years 1849–51, 1859–61, and 1871–78, have disappeared. All other missing portions reflect years in which Thomas did not write. According to Virginia Burr, the vol-

Historical Association in 1972, and her presidential address, "The Making of a Feminist," presents a brief biography of Thomas based upon the journals and scrapbooks.[58] Until now, Massey's essay represented the most sustained published scholarship on Thomas and her journal. In the pages that follow, I will examine several (but by no means all) of the themes that Thomas addressed in her journal over the years. This discussion will begin to indicate the wealth of insight that the journal offers to both historians and general readers.

Gertrude Thomas was an amazingly intelligent and independent thinker whose strength of character and perseverance against enormous obstacles set her apart from ordinary folk. More important for southern history, she was extremely articulate. The utility of her journal is not simply personal, for in many ways Thomas represents broader phenomena in southern history. As an unusually wealthy and well-educated young woman, she belonged to a small but extremely influential cohort of antebellum southerners, many of whom also lost their wealth after the Civil War. Other contemporary journals, diaries, and letters indicate that her reactions to loss were neither more rigid nor more racist than her peers'—on the contrary. In view of the racial and economic ideologies prevailing among her fellow citizens, North and South, she showed herself in many instances to be more open-minded than they. Her journal is exceptional thanks to her ability to record (most of) her thoughts in clear and honest phrasing. She peeled back the layers of conventional utterance to put into words what others left unspoken. This is not to say that the journal represents an artless record of Thomas's thoughts and experiences. It is, rather, a performance through which Thomas composes what she reveals and hides what she cannot face. Although the Thomas journal's great historical contribution lies in its revelations, its secrets are also of enormous interest.[59]

---

ume(s) from 1859 to 1861 were obviously lost. However, the volume(s) from 1871 to 1878, in which Thomas was writing candidly about hard times, may have been destroyed by Thomas or by one of her daughters in an act of censorship. The typescript of the extant volumes runs to approximately 1,350 pages.

58. Massey doubtless intended to publish more on Thomas, but her untimely death in 1974 cut short her career.

59. Shari Benstock aptly terms " 'writing the self' . . . a process of simulta-

Thomas's journal serves as autobiography as well as historical source. As with most people, Thomas's elaboration of individuality was the product of adversity, of which she experienced more than her share. But her awareness had begun to increase before the Civil War, when as an adolescent she questioned her feelings and first began to define herself and her journal.

Identity

Throughout Thomas's journal runs the overarching theme of personal identity that binds together her self, family, religion, gender, class, and race. In the dialectic of thought and language, her definition of self begins with the existential question: Why write?

Fourteen-year-old Gertrude began her journal in 1848 without posing that question. Her journal represented literate self-consciousness: an accoutrement of her style of life. Other classmates also kept journals, and when her own daughter Mary Belle reached twelve years of age, she, in turn, began a journal of her own. Thomas's journal started as an emblem of her standing as an educated person; a record of her days, her reading, and her associates, it lent her life a larger reality. She wanted the journal to reflect only the sunny side of life, and even long after she began to write in almost complete honesty, she still sought to hide unflattering truths about her family.[60]

Between 1848 and early 1852, the journal is a chronology of activities, listing visits, reading, and wearing apparel. Assuming that the journal requires a more formal language than ordinary speech ("How I wish I could wander o'er these old woods again"), Clanton often finds writing a chore, and she notes her dereliction of duty many times over.[61]

---

neous sealing and splitting" (Benstock, "Authorizing the Autobiographical," in *The Private Self*, p. 29). The clearest statement of the dramaturgy of self-presentation is found in Erving Goffman, *The Presentation of Self in Everyday Life* (Garden City, N.Y., 1959), esp. pp. 17–76, 209, 252–55.

60. Stowe, *Intimacy and Power*, pp. 1–2. See also Journal, 1 Aug. 1870, 17 Aug. 1879.

61. The quote is from 14 Nov. 1848. On 1 Aug. 1852 she apologizes for writing informally because others are in the room and distracting her. In the early years of her journal, Gertrude Clanton speaks of not having written regularly: 17, 29 Nov. 1848, 27 May 1851, 24 Jan., 6 Feb., 20 June [n.d.], 22 Aug., 2 Sept. 1852.

She first questions her motives in the entry for 7 March 1852, acknowledging the neglect of one aspect of her journal: recording her thoughts. She wonders what journals are for and how other people use them. In the midst of her courtship with Jefferson Thomas, she begins to doubt the use to which she had been putting her journal for nearly four years.[62]

She wants to record her feelings more openly but fears they will be read by others. In the spring of 1852 this concern was plausible, for she was living in her parents' house with several other literate people. But the fear of discovery persisted, even in the house where she lived with her husband, whom she knew was not interested enough in her journal to pry, with her children, who were very young, and with her slaves, who were illiterate.[63]

Her fear, I suspect, was not so much of discovery but of self-revelation, of an admission of the existence of an uncontrolled and disordered self that violated the ideals of her class and race. Children and servants expressed emotions they could not master. Educated adults did not. Thomas's reluctance to write down her turmoil reflected an attempt to avoid painful knowledge and an unwillingness to admit that she was not always serenely in control.[64]

Like her peers, Thomas placed enormous importance on appearances, particularly on the appearance of self-mastery. Mary Boykin Chesnut's mother-in-law, Mary Cox Chesnut, represented this kind of elite ideal, for with perfect good manners and seeming effortlessness she ran a household of twenty-five servants and an extended Chesnut family of six adults.[65] Just as Mary Boykin Chesnut tried but was unable to match that paragon of self-discipline, Thomas also struggled to maintain the proper facade.

As a young woman, Thomas knew that she must present a cool front and seems to have done so with remarkable success. Later, when the disappointments and tragedies accumulated, presenting

---

62. Thomas's struggle for open self-expression extended over many years. See particularly the entries for 26 May 1852, 26 June 1856, 5 May 1865. See also 2 June 1855, 20 Feb. 1857, 4 July 1864, 18 Sept. 1864.

63. E.g., 12 Apr., 12 May 1856.

64. Censer, *North Carolina Planters and Their Children*, p. 52. Journal, 19 Apr., 5 Feb. 1852, 1 Jan. 1859, 31 Dec. 1863, 16 Oct. 1865, 2 Sept. 1880. See also Sander L. Gilman, *Difference and Pathology: Stereotypes of Sexuality, Race, and Madness* (Ithaca, N.Y., 1985), pp. 20–24.

65. Elisabeth Muhlenfeld, *Mary Boykin Chesnut: A Biography* (Baton Rouge, La., 1981), pp. 41–49; Stowe, *Intimacy and Power*, p. 162.

an immobile countenance (in company or in the journal) became more difficult, yet she persevered. During the extremely disordered wartime—which made normal domestic management virtually impossible—she felt shame for not keeping her household running smoothly. Self-mastery came more easily when, infuriated, she presented an impassive front to offensive Yankees and departing servants alike. The need to appear controlled persisted, for even as her property was being sold at auction and her husband was proving exasperating, she strove to mask her distress.[66] For whom was this performance necessary? In part it was for her children, the journal's ostensible readers. Her other audiences were not spelled out, but the journal offers clues.

In her reluctance to express herself openly, even in her journal, Thomas indicates that her ultimate judges are herself and God. Hence the necessity for self-control is absolute and independent of external witness. But the journal also shows that self-control was an act to be performed before inferiors, whether children, servants, or Yankees (whose claims to gentlemanliness Thomas doubts). In this sense, self-control becomes an aspect of self-definition, a means of marking oneself off from the audience of undisciplined and therefore inferior others.[67] Thomas addressed two sorts of audiences, journal/self/God and children/servants/Yankees, and before the latter she preserved appearances to the end. But for the former audience, she freed herself nearly completely to voice and therefore to feel loss of control, relating particularly to lack of money, labor problems, and downward mobility in the years following the war, when her world fell apart.

Religion

God is present throughout Thomas's journal, in prayers and appeals to his mercy and examinations of the state of her faith. Her religion was woven into her life and her ideology, so that any cause

---

66. 29 May–3 June 1855, 1 Jan. 1859, 17 May, 22 July, 16 Oct., 31 Dec. 1865, 20 Sept. 1866, 30 July 1870, 2 Jan., 2 Sept. 1880.

67. 22 July 1865, 17 Aug. 1879, 5 Dec. 1870. See also Arno Gruen, *The Betrayal of the Self: The Fear of Autonomy in Men and Women* (New York, 1988), pp. xv, 30, 34, 59, 61–64.

or ideal in which she believed, any value she cherished, became God's as well. She measured her virtue as an individual by her worth as a Christian.

Without designating the journal a spiritual record, as did so many devout nineteenth-century Protestants, Thomas uses her journal to measure her progress as a Christian. After the death of her infant Anna Lou in 1855, she prays that God will enable her "to live during this year more in the performance of duty, with a more devout and earnest heart than heretofore." On the last day of each year she reflects on the year gone by, including a spiritual evaluation such as that in 1865, when she terms her journal the "quiet monitor which urges me by the memory of recorded vows to fulfill my promises to live nearer to God."[68] Many entries mention her falling on her knees beside her bed to pray, particularly as she confronts ever-more-unsettling realities. This is her religion of times of trial. The early pages of the journal record her conversion.

Thomas's years at Wesleyan coincided with a wave of Methodist and Baptist revivals that extended from 1846 to 1849, led to another round of revivals among Methodists and Presbyterians in the mid-1850s, and culminated in the Great Revival of the late 1850s.[69] Southern evangelicals—especially Baptists and Methodists—rededicated themselves to the values of dissenting Protestantism, employing the highly emotional camp-meeting style of the Second Great Awakening of the early nineteenth century. Although Thomas came along somewhat after the vogue of a Quaker-like Methodist simplicity of style, she did retain one aspect of the evangelical ideal of a "peculiar people": She did not dance.

Thomas's Methodism grew out of the early nineteenth-century revivals, and even in the middle of the century she participated in an evangelical Protestantism characteristic of the decades before her birth. In her journal entries of the late 1840s and early 1850s, Thomas describes a religion shared by young people, women, and

---

68. See Mathews, *Religion in the Old South*, pp. 113–14; and Journal, 1 Jan. 1858, 31 Dec. 1865. See also 27 July 1856, 25 Dec. 1864, 1 Aug. 1870, 8 Jan., 2 Apr. 1871.

69. Anne C. Loveland, *Southern Evangelicals and the Social Order, 1800–1860* (Baton Rouge, La., 1980), p. 68.

African Americans in terminology that evangelical Christianity still employs.[70]

Two emblematic phrases of the twentieth-century evangelical vocabulary are missing from Thomas's lexicon: *Jesus* and *the Lord*. Although she uses imagery associated with Jesus Christ (twice she mentions not wanting to roll the stone away from the sepulcher of her hopes), "Jesus" and "Christ" do not appear in her journal except when she is quoting others. Her concern is with God, whom she calls "God" (not "the Lord") and with the world of spirits. Three times she notes her attraction (fleeting) to Catholicism, embodied mainly in the figure of the Virgin Mary—Mary, a mother, rather than Mary, the mother of Jesus. Jesus simply does not figure very centrally in her Methodism.[71]

Revealing the older connections between black and white evangelical religion in the South, Thomas, before the Civil War, several times mentions attending black services and appreciating one especially gifted preacher.[72] (After the war, however, she became disenchanted with the political themes that Reconstruction brought into black religion.)[73]

The Methodism to which she converted in 1851 was highly emotional, favoring prayer meetings in which preachers "exhorted" "seekers after religion." "Mourners" who "struggled" might "get" religion. When they succeeded, they "shouted" the "praises of God" and were "happy." Only women shouted in church. By 1855, however, Thomas terms a woman's shouting in her church in Augusta "unusual."[74] By mid-century the practice had generally grown more restricted, associated with black rather than respectable white southern religion, as the white evangelical churches became more reserved during the late antebellum era.[75]

---

70. Albert J. Raboteau, *Slave Religion: The Invisible Institution in the Antebellum South* (New York, 1978), pp. 57–60, 67, 127.

71. 4 July 1864, 3 Sept. 1870, 22 Sept. 1882.

72. 8 Oct. 1848, 9 May 1851, 2 May, 24 June, 12, 22, 25, 27 July 1855.

73. 30 July 1870.

74. 17 May 1855. Whereas women's shouting was acceptable, although unusual, women's speaking in church was questionable. In the former case, religion presumably overwhelmed the worshiper; in the latter, the woman addressed men as well as women with authority in a public space.

75. In one unusual instance, Thomas records that one of the instructors at Wesleyan, the Reverend Myers, "was very happy and shouted" at a prayer

The opposite of getting religion was failing to make the connection with God and remaining "cold and indifferent," a phrase that echoes evangelical usage and that Thomas uses repeatedly to indicate a turning away from God.[76] She employs evangelical terminology most intensely during her years at Wesleyan, when she and her fellow students were preoccupied with the state of their souls. The central feature of this style of religion is an emotional commitment to a personal God.

At one point in 1864, Thomas deplores the lack of refinement and culture of her Methodist church in Augusta. She is attracted to the ritual and solemnity of the Episcopalian church, but finds the preaching boring. At bottom an evangelical Christian, Thomas says she prefers sermons that move her in her heart: "Oh gospel preaching is the most effective after all," she writes. "Give to me the preaching that touches the heart."[77]

This religion of the heart appealed to Thomas throughout her life, and she wanted to share it with her husband, who was a lukewarm Christian, at best. For most of their married life she longed for his conversion. When he went to the altar to accept God in 1870, she described the scene in loving detail, though his falling away from her religion she reported only briefly.[78]

Confirmed Methodist though Thomas was, her Christianity was broadly conceived. Like many respectable southerners, she saw nature (which she identified as female) as closely allied with God. Her Christianity being highly literal, she took natural phenomena, such as the clearing of the sky ("a smile direct from Heaven") or the sound of thunder ("God's voice"), as indications of God's im-

---

meeting. During that same period, she also mentions children making "a great deal of noise shouting and screaming" in church (9, 13 May 1851).

See Mathews, *Religion in the Old South*, p. xvii; and David Edwin Harrell, Jr., "The Evolution of Plain-Folk Religion in the South, 1835–1920," in Samuel S. Hill, ed., *Varieties of Southern Religious Experience* (Baton Rouge, La., 1988), pp. 24–33.

76. 10, 15 Apr. 1851, 27 Aug. 1864.

77. 17 May 1855, 25 Oct., 26 Dec. 1864. The quote is from 13 Dec. 1861.

78. 1 Feb. 1849, 8, 11, 15, 17 Apr. 1851, 25 Apr., 2, 15 May, 12 July 1855, 17 Sept. 1864, 1 Aug., 3 Sept. 1870, 31 Dec. 1879, 15 May 1880, 22 Sept. 1882. Jeff goes to the altar: 29 Aug. 1870. He has left the church: 17 Aug. 1879.

mediate presence.[79] She was also one of thousands of educated men and women in the nineteenth-century United States (including many feminists) who believed that it was possible to establish contact with a spirit world.[80]

Although northern intellectuals and reformers had known about the writing of Emanuel Swedenborg in the 1840s, Thomas did not discover his thought until 1857, when she began investigating spiritualism.[81] Like many others, her interest in establishing contact with the spirit world increased after she experienced personal loss, in this case the deaths of her father and her children. She worried whether they were happy and repeatedly (and mostly in vain) attempted to contact them, by herself or with the assistance of human mediums. Her belief in the possibility of communicating with the world of spirits shows that for Thomas, Methodism and spiritualism did not conflict. Hers, however, was a highly evangelical brand of spiritualism. Her visits to spiritualists in New York City demonstrate the limits of her willingness to stray from Methodist orthodoxy.

In the fall of 1870, Thomas accompanied her mother and older sister to New York, where they visited a medium who put them in touch with the spirit of Turner Clanton. The medium did not offend Thomas, for he presented himself as a man with a useful skill rather than as a religious practitioner. But the religion she discovered at a self-proclaimed spiritualist church did put her off. She

---

79. 6 Sept. 1857, 28 Aug. 1861, 12 July 1864, 22 July 1866, 12 Feb. 1871, 6 Sept. 1882. See also Censer, *North Carolina Planters and Their Children*, p. 18.

80. R. Laurence Moore, *In Search of White Crows: Spiritualism, Parapsychology, and American Culture* (New York, 1977), p. 3. Other mid-century Americans who were fascinated by spiritualism were William Lloyd Garrison, Harriet Beecher Stowe, Sarah Grimké, Horace Greeley, and Frances Willard.

81. The writings of the Swedish philosopher Emanuel Swedenborg, who died in 1772, circulated in the United States in the 1840s and paved the way for the spiritualist movement of the 1850s. Swedenborg described a series of spiritual spheres, through which the dead moved steadily farther away from earth. His views on the ability of the living to communicate with God, the dead, and other spirits were institutionalized in the American denomination known as the Church of the New Jerusalem and became fundamental tenets of American spiritualism. Thomas discovered spiritualism early in the movement's period of greatest influence, roughly 1850–75 (Moore, *In Search of White Crows*, pp. xv, 7, 9–10).

found the pastor of the Strangers Church at Apollo Hall at once attractive and repellent. He reinforced her hope that spirits did visit the world, but he also advanced doctrines that she found antithetical to what she called "our religion." Although the section of his sermon on spirits was persuasive, as a whole Thomas found this no proper church: "It was good so far as it went, but there was no religion there. No acknowledgement of a personal God." In the final analysis, the spiritualist minister's hands and feet were too big, his boots were coarse, and his clothes were common, short comings that weighed heavily in Thomas's system of values. Apollo Hall did not extinguish Thomas's attraction to spiritualism, though, and she continued to write of wanting to talk with the dead over a period of nearly twenty-five years.[82]

Given the depth of her commitment to her religion and its constant presence in her life, Thomas's spiritual record is most poignant in moments when she loses faith. For any Christian, particularly one so devout as she, doubting God is highly disturbing, as Thomas makes clear. Her religion briefly failed to sustain her when she feared that her son Julian was about to die, but her worst religious crises—and therefore, her strongest psychological and ideological perturbations—were three in number. The first occurred in 1864, when her father died. The second followed emancipation in 1865, and the third accompanied the first awful round of financial failures in 1869–70. She wondered why God would send the earthquakes that frightened her so in the 1880s, but this was a query rather than a loss of faith.[83]

The doubts associated with her father's death were many. How could God take away her strongest support, her admired and generous father? Turner Clanton had been ill in the past, and in 1858, when Jefferson Thomas's father died, Gertrude had faced the possibility of her own father's dying. Yet the actual event frightened her. Thomas believed that Turner Clanton, when he died, not only belonged to no church but also had contravened the sixth commandment. Desperately striving to prevent his going to hell, Gertrude

---

82. 28 Feb. 1857, 15 Apr., 27 Aug., 25 Dec. 1864, 20 Sept. 1869, 27 Jan., 29 Sept., 2 Oct. 1870, 2, 12 Apr. 1871, 16 Nov., 18 Dec. 1879, 1 Jan., 21 Feb. 1880.
83. 27 Aug., 25 Dec. 1864, 8, 14 Oct. 1865, 3 Aug. 1870, 5 Jan. 1887.

sent for the Episcopal prayer for the dying and prayed with him on his deathbed.

After his death, however, doubts as to his whereabouts tortured her "as with the whip of scorpions" in relation to what she feared was his greatest sin: sexual relations outside of his marriage. Not only had Clanton broken the commandment against adultery, but he had owned, and therefore willed to his heirs as property, his own children. This moral monstrosity made Thomas "cold and indifferent to spiritual things." In her anguish, she wrote (and later tried to erase) the pain of recognizing the provenance of part of her inheritance:

> Pa's will [illegible] giving of spirit [illegible] making a most liberal provision for all of us children but as God is my witness I would rather never of had that additional increase of property if [illegible] I would have been afraid the knowledge which was communicated at the same time, how hath the mighty fallen![84]

The crisis passed within a few months, but only after attenuating her faith and establishing doubt and a metaphor in the journal for ineffectual prayer: It did not ascend "higher than my head." She employed this image again after her second great moment of crisis: emancipation.[85]

Thomas's remarks on the meaning of emancipation reveal what thousands of former slaveowners must have felt when their way of life collapsed in the spring of 1865. But unlike most, Thomas finds words for the effect of emancipation on her religion. As if the social and ideological crises were not disaster enough, she admits that "my faith in revelation and faith in the institution of slavery had been woven together." Thomas and other Confederate supporters had sincerely attached God to the Confederacy. They had prayed earnestly, confident that God would respond to their

---

84. 15 Apr., 27 Aug. 1864. Virginia Burr's analysis is as follows: "Thomas's concern for her father's whereabouts in the spirit world was directly related to her Methodist belief in 'conversion,' i.e., confession of sins and acceptance of 'Lord and Savior [to] obtain pardon and redeeming love.' Her father was not a church member. The fact that he willed his slaves, including mulattoes, could hardly have surprised Thomas. Unlike many slaveowners, Turner Clanton specified that slave families not be separated if possible. (Quote is from 8 Apr. 1855.)" (Virginia Burr to Nell Irvin Painter, 2 Apr. 1989).

85. 27 Aug. 1864, 8 Oct. 1865.

entreaties. When the Confederate cause was lost, all that faith seemed to have been wasted.[86]

This disappointment she shared with every partisan who has ever championed war in the certainty that God is on her side. But for Confederates, whose cause finally came down to a defense of slavery, failure had an additional religious dimension. The Bible sanctioned slavery, and proslavery rhetoric had made much of that. In 1864, when Thomas tried to convince herself that slavery was right, she consulted the Bible. Once slavery actually was abolished, she admitted her quandary: "If the *Bible* was right then slavery *must be*—Slavery was done away with and my faith in God's Holy Book was terribly shaken." Employing language that she would use again when faced with unsurmountable financial problems that also taxed her religious faith, Thomas wrote that she was "bewildered."[87]

Her loss of faith after she had realized the seriousness of her family's financial difficulties was not as dramatic as the lapses that had accompanied her father's death and emancipation. In 1870 she did not lash out at God. She was no longer defiant, but her faith simply eroded under a flood of frustration. She tried to regain her old, fervent religion but admitted that "I cannot, I cannot."[88]

Thomas remained a woman of the Methodist church even after her children and grandchildren moved into more formalist denominations in the late nineteenth and early twentieth centuries. But hers was no longer the unquestioning faith of an innocent. It may be that Thomas's loss of religious conviction was implicated in the way she lived during the last twenty or so years of her life. Without sufficient religion to sustain her, she may have found it impossible

---

86. 8 Oct. 1865.

87. Ibid. The northern and southern Methodist Episcopal churches had split over the issue of slavery in 1845.

Looking back on the antebellum era from a later date, a leading southern Baptist minister, Jeremiah Jeter, wrote that slavery was divinely sanctioned, that Moses had allowed the Israelites to own slaves, and that Jesus and his apostles had preached on the responsibilities of masters and slaves (Jeter, *Recollections of a Long Life* [Richmond, Va., 1891], cited in Loveland, *Southern Evangelicals and the Social Order*, p. 188).

88. 3 Aug. 1870.

to continue her journal. Or the social activism of her mature years may have taken the place of her earlier religious faith. In either case, she left no clues.

Thomas embedded her identity as a Christian within her identity as a woman. In 1855, she was shocked when a woman spoke up in church, for St. Paul had said that women should not speak in public. When she questioned the Methodist church's provision for confession and counseling, she spoke of the inability of male class leaders to fathom a woman's nature. And in her respect for the power of nature, she spoke repeatedly of a gendered, female Nature.[89] Beyond religion, her female identity was of a piece with her identity as an individual.

Gender and Sexuality

From the moment she finished Wesleyan, Thomas wrote of herself as a woman and, over the years, exhibited an acute consciousness of gender. In particular, as a young wife and mother she defined womanhood through these roles, as they were shaped by their attendant gratification and suffering—especially suffering.[90]

With the fulfillment of her woman's role came certain pains, most of which she did not seek to conceal. She grieved for each of her children who died, whether it was a tiny infant whose life ended within a few weeks, or Clanton, who lived to be nearly seven years old. She cherished her children but hated the early weeks of pregnancy, when she felt depressed and tired. Three times she admits not looking forward to childbearing.

Despite loving her children and giving birth with comparative ease, she wrote often that she did not want to bear children too frequently. An interval of less than two years between pregnancies seemed insufficient, and she expressed pity for an acquaintance who had given birth to children only thirteen months apart. Motherhood was a joy, the mission of woman's life, but the lucky woman was not blessed at very frequent intervals.[91] For Thomas conception was a matter of chance. Unlike many northern women, and

---

89. 20 May 1855, 25 Oct. 1864, 3 Sept. 1870. "Dame Nature": 12 July 1864; "the dear and gracious Mother": 22 July 1866.

90. 1 Jan. 1859.

91. Not happy to be pregnant: 26 June 1855, 11 June 1856, 29 Dec. 1862. The need to space children: 13 June 1855, 11 June, 26 July 1856, 29 Dec. 1862.

along with her fellow southerners of both races, she did not attempt to limit the size of her family, through either abstinence or contraception.[92]

To be a woman also meant overcoming the frustrations inherent in marriage, which Thomas terms the "matrimonial quicksands against which my wayward barque has sometimes drifted."[93] She also recognized aspects of womanliness that she did not experience personally. She expresses solidarity with other women, even when they belonged to classes and races other than her own. Before the Civil War she writes that, as "a woman myself," she can sympathize with slave women who are pregnant.[94] During the war she gave money and food to a poor white woman refugee who was living in a railroad car.[95] Throughout the journal she writes sympathetically of poor women (seamstresses) who had to support their children and husbands when the latter were drunkards or otherwise unable to provide for their families. Women, she believed, were entitled to support from their husbands.[96]

Even for cases in which the men did not maintain their families or in which the marriages were miserable, she deplores separation and divorce; at the same time, she repeatedly recorded such occurrences, particularly during the 1850s. She calls divorce a disaster and, posing a hypothetical choice (that may also have been part of an argument with herself), prefers widowhood to divorce.[97] Without a doubt, most of Thomas's peers shared her views and only

---

92. See D'Emilio and Freedman, *Intimate Matters*, pp. 57–58.

93. 9 Mar. 1865.

94. 18 Aug. 1856. Thomas's sentiments toward her female employees hardened after emancipation, when she was paying them wages that represented scarce cash in the Thomas household. In a wage economy, the old gender solidarity vanished. Thomas resented the drag that young children imposed on household workers and dismissed a young mother who was about to give birth (20 June 1869).

95. On women's role: 16 Sept. 1857, 9 Feb. 1858, 1 Jan. 1859, 4 July 1864, 9 July 1866. On solidarity with other women: 18 Aug. 1856, 4, 12 July, 27 Dec. 1864.

96. 5 Dec. 1870.

97. On separations: 13 June 1855, 8 Feb. 1858. On divorces: 27 Apr. 1856, 4, 22 Nov. 1858, 14 Mar. 1859, 7 May 1869.

reluctantly conceded that separation and divorce actually occurred, an attitude particularly strong in the years before the Civil War, when the ideology of romance enjoyed great potency among wealthy southerners.

In the 1850s Thomas saw gender hierarchy as natural and right. She wrote approvingly of her husband as her "master," to whom she looked up, and of her "woman's weakness protected by man's superior strength."[98] Nevertheless, such remarks do not indicate a blind acceptance of the conventions of mid-century gender relations. Although she distanced herself from the northern movement for women's rights, Thomas held clear ideas about injustices done to women in the areas of education and sexuality. Having received far more formal education than most southern women, she knew that women were capable of absorbing more learning than most were allowed. She believed that women should have the opportunity to stay longer in school, for purely intellectual reasons. Such higher education need not be aimed toward moral ends, for southern women (i.e., white women from respectable families) received within the home sufficient moral instruction to reinforce their values. But men were another matter entirely. Men required as much education as possible to instill in them the correct notions of right and wrong, particularly in regard to sex.[99]

Before the war, Thomas writes heatedly about the sexual double standard in a manner that recalls the moral reform movement in the North. She insists that women should maintain the highest standards of sexual purity, yet recognizes that they might be raped or seduced or led astray by men. She deplores the acquittal of a local rapist because she was outraged by his having taken advantage of his wife's friend, a woman of his own class.[100] Thomas believed passionately that women who failed to remain pure should not be judged more harshly than men who were sexually impure. And she reckoned that nearly all men, particularly southern white

98. Quotes are from 11 Apr. 1855. Other comments on women's inferiority and men's superiority are found in the entries for 9 July 1852 and 1 Jan. 1856.

99. 13 Dec. 1861, 26 June 1869.

100. 23 July 1852, 30 Mar. 1856.

men (with the exception of her own husband, she says) were morally depraved.[101] Like most social purity advocates, Thomas wanted to confine sex to marriage. Her reasoning, which she could not admit to herself in her journal, was highly personal.

The journal does not make clear whether Thomas's female purity phrasing came from her evangelical Methodism or drew on the female purity movement in the antebellum North. She does not mention the northern movement, perhaps because its adherents tended toward abolitionism. Nonetheless, Thomas's wide-ranging reading of current literature would have brought her into touch with moral reform thought. Without a doubt, her mid-century convictions made the Woman's Christian Temperance Union doubly attractive to her in the 1880s, for one of the organization's basic goals was elevating men to women's standards of sexual purity. Working for temperance in the 1880s in the WCTU extended Thomas's long-standing concern for social purity and a single sexual standard.[102]

Before the war, Thomas has but little comment on the morals of blacks.[103] The slaves (termed "servants") who appear in the antebellum section of the journal are virtually all women. They are as likely to appear in the roles of women in black families as they are to appear as workers. As workers, too, they often serve in familial roles. One job that Thomas mentions several times during her antebellum childbearing years is that of wet nurse. She does not note that although these mother surrogates filled the most maternal of roles, they were bought, sold, and lent as chattel.[104]

Thomas and the other women in her family took a maternal interest in the weddings of their servants, providing the cloth and supplies from which servants made bridal costumes and party food. Even after emancipation, the custom of giving household workers

---

101. On the need for women's purity: 18 Aug. 1856, 16 Sept. 1857, 9 Feb. 1858. On men's depravity: 12 Apr. 1856, 2 Jan. 1859, 7 May 1869. See also Linda Gordon, *Woman's Body, Woman's Right: A Social History of Birth Control in America* (New York, 1976), pp. 116–17.

102. See D'Emilio and Freedman, *Intimate Matters*, pp. 152–54. Even though southern Methodists had sponsored temperance organizations as early as the 1820s and 1830s, Thomas did not abstain from consuming or serving wine (itself a source of some controversy) until well after the Civil War.

103. 2 Jan. 1859.

104. 26 Dec. 1858, 16 July 1861, 31 July 1863.

wedding provisions endured, although in attenuated fashion. The weddings of female slaves appear as special events, which Thomas describes in more detail than she does the weddings of her family, friends, and neighbors.[105]

The salient identity of female slaves in the journal is as mothers—mothers of many children, devoted mothers, mothers of the children of white men. One striking journal entry fondly describes a slave woman whose "maternal affection is the most strongly developed feeling she has."[106] Thomas describes households in which black and white women share far more than a work site. Her servants are, like her, mothers and daughters of whom she sometimes grows fond. Thomas describes slave women with varying amounts of affect; sometimes slaves appear as part of the setting of physical scenes, occasionally they come to life as individuals with whom Thomas is engaged. Thomas's experience with one of her female slaves illustrates both the boundaries and the attractions of a relationship that could become ambiguous.

Isabella, whom Thomas ultimately comes to regard as a thief and a runaway, appears as Turner's baby nurse in many entries between the spring of 1855 and the winter of 1859. Most citations are brief, but three are longer, including the confession, which Thomas finds "strange," of "a feeling amounting nearer to attachment than to any servant I ever met with in my life." After Isabella has been banished from the household, her memory haunts Thomas, who gets the blues in the kitchen where Isabella had worked.[107]

When the time came to name her baby girl, Thomas invoked the name Isabella, but sought more acceptable antecedents. The

---

105. E.g., 10 June 1852, 11 Apr. 1855. See also Marli Frances Weiner, "Plantation Mistresses and Female Slaves: Gender, Race, and South Carolina Women, 1830–1880" (Ph.D. diss., University of Rochester, 1986), p. 34. Janet Cornelius notes that slaveholders monitored slave marriages closely for discipline as well as to show support ("Slave Marriages in a Georgia Congregation," in Orville Vernon Burton and Robert C. McMath, Jr., eds., *Class, Conflict, and Consensus: Antebellum Southern Community Studies* [Westport, Conn., 1982], p. 129).

106. The quote is from 12 July 1855. For other examples of slaves as mothers, see 11 Jan. 1855, 11 May, 18 Aug. 1856.

107. Quote is from [n.d., late] Nov. 1857; other, longer entries are 19 Aug. 1855, 13 Jan. 1859. Brief mentions: 8, 11 Apr., 30 May, 24 June, [n.d., early] Nov. 1855.

baby became Mary Belle, "Mary" after Thomas's mother and sister. To explain "Belle," Thomas recalled a girlhood friend from her own race and class, Isabel Morrison Harrington. However, the chronology of entries mentioning Isabel Morrison Harrington and Isabella the slave, and the relative emotional intensity of the writing in those entries, throw Thomas's stated reason into doubt.

At the time of Mary Belle's birth, Thomas's journal shows her to have been far more involved emotionally with Isabella than with Isabel Morrison Harrington. The entries on Isabella the slave, before and after Mary Belle's birth, are full of affect.[108] Despite enormous affection for a black woman, with whom she shared her children and her house for several years, hierarchies of race and class prevented Thomas from evoking that tie directly. On the conscious level, she could only express her attraction to Isabella the slave by reaching for someone else. The child could not have been named Belle had Isabel Morrison Harrington not existed. Nor, I suspect, would Thomas have wanted to use the name Belle in the absence of Isabella the slave.

The turmoil of the war years revealed disparities between the commonly accepted stereotypes of women and their actual roles. Thomas found herself willing not only to travel without her husband, but also to mention that she and other women held property in their own rights, even though polite usage denied women—but not men—the satisfaction of calling their possessions their own.[109] The postwar section of the journal, in which Thomas faces unpleasant realities and becomes a salaried worker, favors independence of thought and action over submission to the gender hierarchy. After the war, Thomas grew less willing to rationalize her

---

108. [N.d.] Nov. 1857; 13 Jan. 1859. Virginia Burr adds that she "disagrees with the speculation that black Isabella influenced the naming of the baby despite Thomas's feeling of affection for her son's (Turner's) nurse" (Virginia Burr to Nell Irvin Painter, 2 Apr. 1989).

109. 25 Oct. 1864, 7 May 1869. In the latter entry, Thomas mentions the Reconstruction-era married women's property bill passed by the Georgia legislature in 1868 and strengthened by the state supreme court in 1869. See Suzanne Lebsock, "Radical Reconstruction and the Property Rights of Southern Women," *Journal of Southern History* 43, no. 2 (May 1977): 201–2, 209–10.

husband's shortcomings. Whereas early in her marriage, she ascribed the need to economize to Jefferson's having made a short crop and the difficulties of starting out, by 1870 she is no longer casting about for excuses. Squarely facing the facts, she cites her husband's "bad management." She writes no more of man's superior strength and woman's weakness when she is paying the bills.[110]

Much of Thomas's writing about the condition of women is unambiguous. As in many of her comments about race, she is remarkably clear, articulating concepts that most Americans failed to frame coherently. This clarity, though, does not entirely characterize her thinking about gender when her subjects are particular men and women. She did not perceive the boundaries that she built into her notions about the kind of womanliness of which she approved, nor did she fathom the extent to which a major trauma in her life—impending emancipation—threatened her status as a woman.

Entries that deal with black or poor white women show that Thomas extended her definition of women across the lines of race and class. She knew that femaleness, particularly in its sexual dimension, united all women, and her most basic feelings and fears about gender were not bounded. When she makes judgments about given women, however, she narrows her definition. Addressing her daughter Mary Belle, she writes proudly of being "a *woman* in the *proper sense*," meaning a woman who had "suffered and grown strong," a phrase she employs twice to define true womanhood. "Woman," therefore, meant married women, not merely because young, unmarried women had not faced the ultimate tests of husband and children, but also because they were of necessity ignorant of an important aspect of womanly experience, sexual intimacy. Thomas's belief in sexual purity dictated her insistence that unmarried women should not understand (or write about) "*certain subjects.*" Hence Thomas excoriates women writers such as Lissie Petite and George Sand, who broached the topic of sexuality.[111]

At one point, discussing a Civil War incident that concerns her

---

110. 29 Sept. 1855, 1 Aug. 1870, 21 Dec. 1868, 3, 14 May 1869, 5, 12, 19 Dec. 1870, 8 Jan. 1871.

111. 1 Jan. 1859, 4 July 1864, 16 Sept. 1857.

father, Thomas confuses class and gender. After Turner Clanton had offered to sell corn at his plantation to soldiers' wives at less than the inflated market price, these poor women complained that the offer was useless to them because they lacked transportation. Thomas interprets the exchange from her class's point of view: Her father had been generous to make the offer; the poor women were ingrates for complaining that Clanton had not brought the corn within their reach. The poor women's ingratitude, she says, outrages her "womanly honor," as though the poor women lacked proper female sensibilities.[112]

Beyond these relatively straightforward observations about womanliness, Thomas records a series of intensely emotional entries that betray her own fears of being superseded by another woman should she die in childbirth, of mulatto women's usurping the places of white wives, and of competition between Negro and white women for white men. Thomas's anxiety about being replaced was deeply seated and of long standing—her observations on the interchangeability of women begin before the Civil War and continue after it. But a cluster of entries written on the theme in 1865, as emancipation first threatened her world and then turned it upside down, illuminates her apprehension.[113] By undermining the foundations of her identity, emancipation exacerbates her old fears about her worth as an individual and as a woman, and she imagines scenes in which wives are displaced by other, younger women.

Considering the state of medical knowledge and the real peril that confinement represented, it is not surprising that several times in her journal Thomas confronts the possibility of dying in childbirth. Every nineteenth-century mother would have entertained similar fears. Ordinarily Thomas takes the rhetorical high road and pretends not to be disturbed by the idea of the "future Mrs Thomas." But she returns to the theme so often that her lofty protestations ("My dear madam who ever you may prove [to be,] you have my best wishes.") ring false. In the year of upheaval, she ad-

---

112. 14, 17 Apr. 1862.

113. 1 Jan. 1859; 3 Jan., 9 Mar., 27 May, 14 Oct. 1865, 7 May 1869, 13 Jan. 1870.

mits to being "tormented" by "jealous thoughts" as she envisions the "step mother who may be selected to take my place."[114]

In Thomas's case, her imagined successor represented the competitor about whom she could bring herself to write openly. But the entire issue of rivalry between women worried her. She knew that women were dependent on men financially but that men held the power to choose women and to discard them, to betray women and to break their hearts. Recognizing men's power over women's happiness, she did not trust men to exercise that power fairly. In fact, she was certain that men's moral fiber was so weak that they would not forgo sex out of respect for a wife who might be deceased or absent temporarily.

Given a situation in which men were so willing to substitute one woman for another and relatively powerless women were unable to control men's sexuality, women could do no more than compete with one another. Thomas saw such competition as taking place within and across racial lines, but she wrote with most passion when she envisioned rivals of different ages and races and when the war had undermined the racial hierarchy.

Rumors of the sexual habits of Union generals in the South reinforced Thomas's long-standing conviction that slavery had a deleterious effect on the morals of white men. As she faced the unhappy prospect of Confederate defeat, slavery's great evil became a means of exacting revenge on the North, or, more precisely, on the women of the North, the only northerners whom she considered within her reach. In bitter detail, she records the scene of a Union general's cohabitation with a young and beautiful mulatto woman who travels with him. Whether Thomas is writing from rumors or from her own imagination, the import of the anecdote is unmistakable. The black woman "usurps" the position of the general's wife in a parody of the elevation of the Negro race that Thomas imagines the abolitionists demand.[115]

---

114. 1 Jan. 1859; the quotes are from 9 Mar., 14 Oct. 1865.

In the 1830s, another southern diarist and young mother, Sarah Haynsworth Gayle, also rejected the idea of her successor. She asked her husband not to marry again in the event of her death, but she did die young, and he took a second wife (Fox-Genovese, *Within the Plantation Household*, pp. 25–26).

115. 3 Jan. 1865.

The fantasy extends to a letter that Thomas wrote (but did not send) to the wife of Gen. William T. Sherman, again playing out the drama of Negro elevation, sexual rivalry, and the revenge of Confederate women on northern women. According to the letter, General Sherman, too, reputedly travels with a young mulatto woman, whom Thomas says has been "elevated to fill your [Mrs. Sherman's] place."[116] In her fantasies, Thomas inflicts upon her female enemies in the North the most fearsome punishment she can imagine being displaced from the conjugal bed.

As the topsy-turvy times exposed her personal vulnerabilities, Thomas sensed that neither education, wealth, class, nor race provided sufficient insurance that her husband would not replace her with another woman. Several oblique comments indicate that Thomas feared that a light-skinned woman of African descent had already "usurped" her place as her husband's sexual partner and had borne a boy who was about Turner Thomas's age. Turner was born in 1853. Taking Gertrude's 1869 comments about racial competition into account, the agitation reported in the journal entries of 29 May–3 June 1855 may well concern her discovery of Jefferson Thomas's intimate relationship with another woman who is not white. There is no doubt that Thomas thought that "the serpent" had entered her home and that she had a "cross" to bear.[117]

In Thomas's particular formulation of gender relations, all women sought to bind their men to them, particularly in the crisis year of 1865. Black as well as white men were likely to wander when they could, so that black women were also vulnerable to abandonment. In May 1865, Thomas reworks the scenes in which she had imagined Union generals' infidelities, only this time she reports that the driver from the plantation in Burke County left "an ugly faithful black wife" to go off with "a good looking mulatto."[118]

In 1865 the journal is filled with evidences of extreme social trauma that is not replicated in other years. Thomas never again writes so long and intensely of women's vulnerability to displace-

---

116. Ibid. Thomas decided not to send the letter after learning that the Shermans' baby had died.

117. 26 June 1869, 17 Feb. 1871, 24 Nov. 1880. Virginia Burr does not find this analysis convincing.

118. 27 May 1865.

ment. But she returns to the theme of rivalry between women. Twice she mentions black men who are resisting the attempts of their common-law wives to marry legally and thus stabilize the relationships.[119] Just as beautiful young mulattoes might usurp the place of white wives, so African-American women also faced rivals among themselves.

As Thomas saw it, mulattoes represented the main competition to both white and dark-skinned Negro women. A few years after emancipation, having witnessed the spread of interracial liaisons among the poor, she worries about the rivalry between white and educated mulatto women. Thomas writes that in the competition for elite white men, black women have one innate advantage that education will only intensify: a "tropical, passionate nature."[120] Years earlier, she had written proudly of Confederate women as "our warm hearted children of the sun."[121] A confirmed white supremacist, Thomas keeps the racial hierarchy uppermost, yet as a woman she sees the similarity of all southern women's attractive qualities and their vulnerabilities to the whims of all men.

Race

As a plantation mistress living in a Black Belt county, Thomas was surrounded by African Americans of both sexes and all ages. Among blacks, women figure most prominently in the journal, identified by name rather than by race. Thomas often discusses race in tandem with sexuality and, after emancipation, labor. I doubt that she separated labor relations from race relations—most Americans did not—but because she wrote so extensively of the frustrations she encountered as an economically straitened employer of household workers, I will discuss labor relations separately below. Let me turn first to race.

During the antebellum period, Thomas mentions blacks only occasionally, not always as workers. They appear as social beings—at

---

119. 16 Sept. 1866, 7 May 1869.

120. 26 June 1869, 13 Jan. 1870.

121. Quote is from 3 Jan. 1865, emphasis in original. See also 12 Oct. 1866.

weddings, funerals, church services—often under Thomas's benign regard. A black preacher has a "decidedly fine command of language," and the beau of one of her servants is "one of the finest looking men I ever saw."[122] Her ability to see blacks as individuals, together with her keen sense of social and economic hierarchy, might seem to make Thomas more a class snob than a racist.[123] A closer look reveals that, even before the Civil War, she categorizes people according to race and uses pronouns to mark her boundaries.

Well before she establishes the use of the first-person plural for Confederates, Thomas is using the third-person plural to designate blacks, a usage that persists after the end of the war. Just as "we" and "our" refer to educated white southerners and Confederates, "they" and "their" indicate blacks, without normative connotations. Describing a church service that she finds intensely moving, Thomas writes: "How irrepressible a people they are! How easily their feelings are wrought upon!"[124] She is capable of drawing other generalizations about supposed racial traits. Retelling the story of her driver, who insists that he is a free man who had been cheated out of his freedom, Thomas uncharacteristically leaves incomplete a sentence fragment on the separation of the man's family. Without deploring an act that must have distressed her, she concludes that the "Negro is a cheerful being."[125] Several entries exemplify an unconscious train of thought that leads from blacks directly to horses. Black people remind her of horses, whether as objects of affection or as inferior beings, and the association would seem to increase her social distance from her servants.[126]

For all her ease in delineating racial characteristics among

---

122. 11 Apr., 24 June 1855.

123. Pierre L. van den Berghe notes that racism of what he calls the "paternalistic" type often seems superficially to resemble economic or social rather than racial discrimination, because the members of the reputedly inferior race are also poor and unschooled (*Race and Racism: A Comparative Perspective* [New York, 1967], p. 27).

124. 12 July 1855. Thomas often ascribes emotion to blacks in settings in which she, herself, has been touched emotionally (see also 2 May 1855, 29 July 1861).

125. 31 July 1863. This entry also speaks of African Americans as "naturally religious."

126. Particularly 18 Sept. 1861, but also 17 Sept. 1866, 30 Dec. 1870.

blacks, Thomas's thinking about race was less contradictory and less harsh than that of many other Americans. She believed that physiognomy indicated intelligence and ability or their reverse, as in the case of a white amateur musician whose forehead showed talent but whose jaw was "animal." But she disagrees with the belief, common among whites of her time, that blacks are intelligent according to the proportion of their white ancestry. Even during the period in which she is desperately trying to convince herself of the justice of slavery, she rejects the view that blacks are a lower form of human life or incapable of learning. Like any other people, she says, blacks would profit from instruction. Environment, therefore, makes a difference, but in a Lamarckian way, for Thomas believes that education and refinement are inheritable. Along with such beliefs, she accepts many racist platitudes that underscore racial differences and black inferiority, yet she tends to apply the same moral and intellectual standards to both races.[127] In sum, Gertrude Thomas believed that racial traits existed, that environment changed people's native abilities, and that blacks possessed a full measure of humanity but were actually, but not necessarily forever, inferior to whites.

Racial designations rarely appear in the antebellum section of the journal, which covers a period in which most people stayed in their distinct and separate social spheres and race did not need be pointed out. However, departures from the established order did occur, and the early section of the journal includes the stories of a rumored slave revolt and a case of racial confusion in Thomas's own house. Early in 1857 and again at the end of 1858, Thomas mentions the fear of slave insurrection that spread through Tennessee and Georgia at the end of 1856. Both times her response is remarkably cool, establishing a pattern that persists throughout the journal and that she uses to mark herself off from both blacks and other whites. She says that she is not afraid of blacks, not even black men, not even violent black men. While other whites are running from shadows, Thomas is proud of her physical courage, upon which others also comment. But her composure does not

127. 30 Nov. 1858. Rejects "Ariel" doctrine: 7 May 1869, 30 July 1870.

blind her to the potential for danger. Twice she evokes the image of Neapolitans who go about their lives under an active volcano—the volcano here standing for the possibility of a slave uprising.[128]

Insurrection presented a frightening but straightforward departure from the racial hierarchy. On an entirely different scale of social magnitude, an incident that took place at their home illustrates the Thomases' response to an uncertain racial situation with great potential for dishonor. When a man of undetermined race comes to see Jefferson Thomas, Gertrude is unsure how to deal with him. She decides to take the chance of treating a nonwhite as an equal rather than risk insulting a white man. Accepting Jefferson's invitation to eat with them, the man sits down at the table and takes off his hat. He looks, in Gertrude's words, "more suspicious than ever." When it turns out that the man is not white, Gertrude is outraged. The stranger had insulted her by sitting "at a white lady's table," something prohibited by racial etiquette.[129]

For Gertrude Thomas, people of mixed blood represented one of slavery's negative aspects. Ordinarily, however, her misgivings concerned mulatto women rather than mulatto men. In a very long 1859 entry on miscegenation, Thomas begins with observations on the child of one of her mother's house slaves, the child appearing "as white as any white child." Deploring the use of enslaved mulatto women as concubines, Thomas quotes Fredrika Bremer on the "white children of slavery" and regrets that their very existence—testament to the prevalence of race mixing—lowers the "tone of the South" morally. Like Mary Chesnut, Thomas thought that white southern women were "all at heart abolitionists" because of miscegenation, and like Mary Chesnut, Thomas restricted that thought to her journal. Thomas went even further than Chesnut; she not only execrated interracial sex but saw those opponents of mixed marriages who nevertheless tolerated interracial concubinage as hypocrites. To Thomas the moral reform advocate, the disaster was interracial, *unmarried* sex; men who lived with black women without marrying them were debased twice over. Slavery,

---

128. On her own lack of fear: 1 Jan. 1857, 1, 2 Nov. 1868, 10 Apr. 1871. On frightened whites: 1 Jan. 1857, 23 July 1865, 1, 2 Nov. 1868, 10 Apr. 1871. Mt. Vesuvius image: 25 Dec. 1858, 1 Nov. 1868.

129. 12 Feb. 1858.

she concluded, "degrades the white man more than the Negro and oh exerts a most deleterious effect upon our children."[130]

Thomas disapproved of the influence of slaves and of slavery upon white children. Describing the cultural interchange (in both directions) that takes place when black or white children come in close contact with adults and children of the other race, she approves of whites' influence on black children but not of blacks' influence on white children. She reserves a special anguish for the moral dimension of the peculiar institution. White male miscegenators, she felt, set a terrible example for their children and presented her with the awkward duty of explaining to her children the presence of obviously mixed-blood offspring.[131]

The war introduced an entirely new racial rhetoric. For the first time, perhaps inspired by the newspapers, Thomas writes in shrill and bigoted tones of the "vindictive passions of an inferior race." This kind of remark quickly disappears, as Thomas's initial burst of Confederate chauvinism subsides. But henceforth the journal takes far more note of blacks, as a race and as individual workers. Along with money matters, they are the journal's main concern after 1864. Having heretofore seen herself at the center of a system of black and white families in which she assumed that blacks gave their labor willingly, Thomas now became an employer in a wage system in which (at least) two sets of interests competed. The pivotal element in this transformation was the upheaval of emancipation.

If the intensity of her defense mechanisms is any indication,

---

130. 2 Jan. 1859, 17, 23 Sept. 1864, 26 June 1869. Fredrika Bremer, *The Homes of the New World: Impressions of America* (London, 1853), 1:382; C. Vann Woodward and Elisabeth Muhlenfeld, *The Private Mary Chesnut: The Unpublished Civil War Diaries* (New York, 1984), pp. 21 (4 Mar. 1861), 42–43 (18 Mar. 1861).

Catherine Clinton notes that southern aristocrats who objected to slavery because of miscegenation deplored the immorality of the slaves rather than that of the owners ("Caught in the Web of the Big House," in Walter J. Fraser, Jr., R. Frank Saunders, Jr., and Jon L. Wakelyn, eds., *The Web of Southern Social Relations: Women, Family, and Education* [Athens, Ga., 1985], p. 22).

131. 31 July 1863, 17, 27 May 1865, 1 Nov. 1868, 7 May 1869, 30 July 1870.

emancipation confronted Thomas with the most traumatic situation of her life. Unlike her father's death, which had been acutely painful, emancipation lacked precedent and established expectations. Funerals represented healing rituals, but emancipation was revolutionary, and it deeply disturbed Thomas despite her attempts to prepare for it.

In the fall of 1864, she apprehends the possibility of Confederate defeat and the abolition of slavery. For the first time, she thinks about slavery as a labor system (not merely as a source of moral endangerment). The process is not easy. She begins by deciding that "the Negro *as a race* is better off with us as he has been than if he were free, but I am by no means so sure that we would not gain by his having his freedom given him," for slavery imposes a heavy burden of responsibility on slaveholders. A few days later she slips into denial and describes what, had there been no war, would have been a perfectly normal scene. She paints a reassuring picture of her slaves at work around her, yet concludes that "to hold men and women in *perpetual* bondage is wrong." Shortly afterward, she repudiates this doubt.[132] Before she has reached firm conclusions, emancipation overwhelms her.

Thomas's response to Confederate defeat is denial. She says she feels "no particular emotion." But the next day, after Jefferson Thomas has called their slaves together to tell them they are free, her body manifests her alarm. Gertrude attends a piano lesson, at which she nearly blacks out. Without realizing consciously what has made her faint, she describes the swoon and, a sentence later, brings in freedom. At the end of a very long entry, she describes her husband's lecture that very morning to the now-emancipated servants and their delighted response. Over the succeeding days she records the departure of servants who had been with her for years and renounces any further interest in their welfare.[133]

The entries of May and June 1865 are extraordinarily valuable for understanding what emancipation meant to the white elite, because Thomas, with her characteristic intelligence, honesty, and

---

132. 17, 23 Sept. 1864; this is the first time that Thomas makes so systematic an attempt to depict what had been the normal antebellum routine. Further purposeful thinking about slavery: 17 Nov., 26 Dec. 1864, 31 Dec. 1865, 4 May 1871.

133. 7, 8, 17 May 1865.

sensitivity, articulates the betrayal that former owners were feeling. Years later she supplies the key to her confusion: Having accepted at face value the appearance of contentment that slaveholders demanded of slaves, she had taken for granted that her slaves served her voluntarily, that their labor was not, as she phrases it, "extorted." She had supposed that they were happy with her in slavery, but she sees that freedom makes them joyful.[134]

At the moment of emancipation, Thomas tries to distance herself from a situation in which she has a great emotional investment. She now feels the opposite of the old affection and, exasperated and angry, declares that "I do most heartily despise Yankees, Negroes and everything connected with them. The theme has been sung in my hearing until it is a perfect abomination. I positively instinctively shut my ears when I hear the hated subject mentioned and right gladly would I be willing never to place my eyes upon another as long as I live. . . . I feel no interest in them whatever and hope I never will."[135] Over the next few years, Thomas copes with the loss of household workers through rationalization: Those departing were not very good, and the new ones are much better.[136]

By the late 1860s Thomas had settled down psychologically, but black people continue to play a major role in her journal. Appearing primarily as employees, they also figure as political actors and competitors in a new social order.

During Reconstruction, Thomas's thinking about blacks ran along two distinct tracks, one leading toward a calm tolerance, the other into agitated fears of racial and sexual competition. Although she could not by any stretch of the imagination be termed a supporter of Reconstruction, her response was far more tempered than that of leading Democrats like her husband.

She wrote (again) of living at the mouth of a volcano and felt

---

134. 4 May 1871.

135. 12 June 1865. This is an example of what psychologists term reaction formation, in which Thomas cannot admit to any positive feelings and responds by going completely over into hatred, so as to keep her psyche intact in a time of upheaval.

136. 17, 29 May, 12 June 1865, 3 Dec. 1868.

desperate, yet she was able to discuss the crucial Reconstruction election in November 1868 with her servants and to see commonalities between their situation and her own. She confesses to her journal that "I do not in my heart wonder that the Negroes vote the radical ticket. . . . If the women of the North once secured to me the right to vote . . . I should think twice before I voted to have it taken from me." Meanwhile, her husband fills the house with guns, leads a local military company poised to attack the Republicans, and eavesdrops from under the house on the servants' political deliberations. Thomas finds this all somewhat excessive, for the two sides (well-armed white Democrats, poorly organized black Republicans) are so ill matched. She keeps her composure but denounces her white neighbors' "exhibition of fear" out of worry that panicky whites will "encourage evil passions in the Negroes."[137]

Reconstruction does alter the tenor of her remarks about blacks, however, and for the first time physical revulsion and small-minded surliness creep into her comments about educated black men. Such observations, unique in Thomas's journal, are more characteristic of twentieth-century than nineteenth-century southern racism.[138] The threat of blacks as competitors as well as servants may have lent her words an edge.

The late 1860s confronted Thomas with two disturbing realities. First, her oldest child, Turner, instead of attending college, left school at sixteen to work for his father in the fields. The interruption of Turner's education disturbed Thomas, who viewed education as a main attribute of elite standing. Turner had been born into wealth, but he now plowed beside a poor and uneducated black boy. Thomas asks herself: "Can this white boy with the aid of hereditary antecedents accomplish more than the one beside him? What are his [the white boy's] talents for?" As in her anxieties about competition between women, Thomas sees mulattoes (not blacks) as the likely rivals.[139] She contrasts her husband's action in depriving her son of his education because farm hands are scarce with the Negro mother who sacrifices to give her mulatto son an education. In a political system in which both boys will be able to vote and hold office, white supremacy is in peril. The remedy she advocates

---

137. 1, 2 Nov. 1868, 14 May 1869.
138. 28 Jan. 1869.
139. 26 June 1869, 30 July 1870.

is education for white boys in order to maintain that white supremacy, which she also sees as threatened by the other postwar innovation of social equality.

Thomas's diction discloses the second distressing reality confronting her and reveals that her anxieties about mulatto-white rivalry between women and between boys are connected and far from hypothetical. She does not mention either her husband or her son by name, although she has already written a good deal previously of her heartbreak over Jefferson's putting Turner to work in the fields. Also unnamed is the African-American plowboy, whom she describes, precisely, as "the mulatto boy, perhaps his father's son by a woman a shade darker than *his* mother."[140] Thomas cannot name Jefferson or Turner here, because to do so would shred the pretense that veils a painful fact: the existence of her husband's outside child. She generalizes the situation into a danger for all white boys of good family who are not being educated. Without adequate education, a new, post-emancipation sort of miscegenation would spread. Gertrude Thomas reports that educated white women almost never marry black men, but that poor white women have been doing so since emancipation.[141] Her great fear, at least ostensibly, was for the men. But other, unarticulated concerns may well have perturbed her.

If young men of the better classes do not receive the education they deserve, Thomas writes, they will sink into "degradation," the word she employs in the antebellum era when writing about miscegenation. Earlier journal comments reveal her awareness of the widespread practice among elite white men of cohabiting with black and mulatto women, presumably without withdrawing from the marriage market or creating a shortage of partners among the elite. Reconstruction, however, is a different time. The present danger is not so much miscegenation, which has been "so common as to create no surprise whatever," but "social equality," that is, marriage as among equals, which Thomas predicts will come about in her children's generation.[142]

---

140. 26 June 1869; emphasis in original.

141. An observer in northern Louisiana also noticed the increased occurrence of mixed unions after the war (see Nell Irvin Painter, *Exodusters: Black Migration to Kansas after Reconstruction* [New York, 1976], p. 73).

142. 2 Jan. 1859, 17, 23 Sept. 1864. The quoted phrase is from 26 June 1869, but Thomas uses virtually the same wording on 13 January 1870.

The possibility now exists that newly impoverished, uneducated men from formerly elite families will not know any better than to marry mulatto women. Brought together, then, the separate threads of Thomas's comments about race and interracial sex lead back to women, as well as men, of her own class and race in the fear that few suitable marriage partners will remain for her daughters. That her oldest daughter, Mary Belle, reached the advanced age of twenty-five before marrying must have over the years reinforced her mother's fears of spinsterhood on her behalf. Mary Belle's mother and grandmother had both married as teenagers.[143]

A less threatening (to Thomas) and more familiar racial system began to be restored with the end of Reconstruction in Georgia in 1872, and her fears of racial competition subsided. These years brought her no greater satisfaction as an employer, and Thomas did more and more of her own housework, a hard reality for which her antebellum training had not prepared her.[144] Although her husband must have taken some comfort from the Democratic party's return to political power in Georgia, Thomas saw no such dramatic improvements in her house and yard. Post-Reconstruction race relations may have been less threatening emotionally to Thomas, but labor relations continued to vex her. The entries that deal with her adjustment to the employment of paid household workers are of great value for understanding the former master class and the meanings of freedom for female workers.

Labor

In the prewar journal entries, work is often accomplished by invisible hands, so that Gertrude *has* a fire made or Jefferson *has* piles of brush burned. Often, Thomas names the workers whose actions constitute much of the fabric of everyday life, as in two entries concerning the same versatile domestic worker: "Tamah has just got out supper," and "I have been quite busy today having the front garden spaded by Tamah."[145] Thomas was the focal point in her household, and as a slaveholder, she never had to give much

---

143. 26 June 1869. Mary Belle was eleven when Thomas wrote this entry, seven years younger than the latter had been when she married. Mary Belle married the socially prominent Frederick Laurens Ingraham in 1883.

144. See also Weiner, "Plantation Mistresses and Female Slaves," pp. 281–84, 301–3.

145. 11 Apr. 1855, 20 Feb. 1857.

thought to her slaves' needs, which were automatically subordinated. Only one set of interests counted in her household: her own.[146] Emancipation abolished what had seemed to her to have been frictionless labor relations. For the first time, Thomas had to contend with employees who pursued interests of their own.

The spring of 1865 introduced Thomas to new, bilateral labor relations that were doubly complex. Of itself, emancipation would have plunged black families into turmoil, throwing issues of power and residence into question. But emancipation also occurred in the wake of a war that had further complicated gender relations among black men and women, as it had among whites. Just as southern white women had begun to seize the opportunity to write, speak, and work for wages, so black women in and around Augusta were also moving into openings that had never existed before. They could withdraw from the paid work force to stay home to care for their husbands and children, or they could sell food in the streets and railroad stations or keep other women's houses and babies for money.[147] At the same time, black men and women were not only adjusting to individual and familial autonomy but also were establishing and reestablishing relationships within their families that affected domicile and authority. The resulting upheaval tested Thomas's limits as an employer and housekeeper.

Freedwomen's increased opportunities inside and outside the work force caused a shortage in household labor that Thomas found disadvantageous. White workers seemed a natural resort to fill this gap, and in 1865 Thomas predicted that black labor would soon be displaced by white. Experience proved otherwise, and after experimenting with white workers, at least some of whom were Irish Catholics, she concluded that whites were no improvement. In the house and in the fields, workers pursued their own interests, and whites were no more selfless or reliable than blacks.[148] To make matters worse, from the point of view of an employer used to

---

146. As Orlando Patterson points out in *Slavery and Social Death: A Comparative Study* (Cambridge, Mass., 1982), the whole point of slavery is to create a class of people who lack self-interest. Slaves are by definition extensions of their owners' wills.

147. For instance, Mary Boykin Chesnut's housemaid, Mollie, kept herself and her former mistress in cash with a butter-and-egg business in which Chesnut had invested (Muhlenfeld, *Mary Boykin Chesnut*, p. 128).

148. 27, 29 May 1865, 26 June 1869, 14 Dec. 1870, 3, 8 Jan., 4 May 1871.

a permanent work force, household workers now engaged to work only one month at a time.

Free labor presented Thomas with a number of frustrations, the greatest of which was workers' new mobility, both into and out of the work force and between employers. Considering that emancipation coincided with financial losses for her family, Thomas found the second kind of mobility most trying. Chronically short of cash, she complained for years that she could afford to employ only young, inexperienced, or careless workers, who were particularly annoying within the household. Jefferson Thomas, who was acutely aware of the difficulty of keeping efficient workers, worked less intimately with his employees and disagreed with his wife on the extent to which employers should make concessions. Whereas he saw the necessity for conciliating first-rate workers, she insisted that workers meet her standards of employee-employer etiquette.[149]

Gertrude Thomas describes the degree to which deference was a touchy question on both sides. Former slaves sought to reinforce the distinction between slavery and freedom by dropping extreme forms of submission, as between an older servant and a younger member of the employer's household. On the other side, Thomas tried, as much as possible, to preserve older forms of etiquette and to widen the social distance between employers/whites and employees/blacks. In her scheme of labor relations, deference counted for more than efficiency: "[H]ands are scarce but respect is a quality I demand from servants even more than obedience. I can overlook neglected work but cannot tolerate disrespect."[150]

In the long run, Thomas seems to have won the battle for deference. During the five years following emancipation, however, the only period in which she reports the wages she is paying, a labor shortage (of farm as well as household workers) drove wages steadily upward. In 1865 Thomas paid a mere twenty-five cents per week to a full-time worker in her house; this person seems, not surprisingly, to have departed quickly, for Thomas not only offered

---

149. On inexperienced help: 29 May 1865, 21 Dec. 1868, 12 May, 1, 20 June, 20 Sept. 1869, 10 Jan., 7 Feb., 12 Dec. 1870, 2 Jan., 10 Apr., 4 May 1871. On respect: 17 May 1865, 23 Feb., 7 May, 20 June 1869, 30 Dec. 1870, 1 Feb. 1871, 16 Aug. 1880, 5 Jan. 1881.

150. 19 Dec. 1870.

minuscule wages, she put little importance on prompt payment. Wages quickly increased from thirty cents per day to wash to fifty cents per day to iron and five dollars per month for a cook. By late 1868 wages had increased to seven dollars per month plus board. In 1870 Thomas paid two young girls nine dollars per month to do the work for which, in 1865, she offered one dollar per month.[151]

Thomas may gradually have paid better wages, but her management style never became very steady. She jawboned her employees and hinted that they should leave, then was surprised when they actually quit. Others she told to leave without actually meaning for them to do so. She expected that workers would discern her wishes through intimation or overhearing.[152] Lacking the wherewithal to pay wages that first-rate workers could demand and insisting on an etiquette that workers found demeaning, Thomas shouldered more and more of the burden of household work. Keeping the house in perfect order wore her out, and eventually her standards declined. She began to wonder whether she was making the best use of her own energy, for she found housework "utterly uncongenial." Her decision to take up teaching was related not only to a need for money but also to a realization that she was already performing a great deal of unpaid labor. Considering her level of education, she concluded that she could make more efficient use of her time in another line of work.[153]

The conjunction of emancipation and impoverishment made Thomas a working woman; Reconstruction, in her experience, meant a hitherto unimaginable burden of work, whether paid or unpaid, whether she supervised it or carried it out herself. She knew that she was working and straightforwardly recorded her responses. But she also wrote a great deal more, with a significance that was not clear to her at the time. As though spellbound, she

---

151. 27, 29 May 1865, 3 Dec. 1868, 1 Aug. 1870.

152. 29 May 1865, 7, 17 May, 1 June 1869.

153. 29 Mar., 26, 29 May 1865, 1 Jan. 1866, 21 Dec. 1868, 20 Sept. 1869, 1 Aug., 30 Nov., 12 Dec. 1870. Thomas's responses to the employment of paid workers were characteristic of women of her background throughout the South. See also Weiner, "Plantation Mistresses and Female Slaves," pp. 281–84, 301–3.

described a set of labor relations of which she was no longer in charge.

Thomas writes an exceedingly long and detailed description of a physical fight between two farm workers that breaks out repeatedly right outside the Thomases' door. Verbal commands do not hinder the combatants; only threatened recourse to armed force stops the fights. The conflict enthralls Thomas because it reveals a side of life that had been hidden during slavery: violence unmediated by white control. The two men are consumed by their own fury, which bears no relation whatever to Thomas. Before the war, however, her mere presence would have subdued their conduct, for as slaves, blacks did not exhibit such independence and self-absorption. Thomas finds this new self-centeredness fascinating.[154]

Her impotence in this situation emphasizes the changes that occurred after the war. Having been securely at the top of the social and economic ladder, where she never had to be conscious of workers' concerns, much less adjust to them, Thomas fell into a less privileged rank in which her needs competed with those of others. In her new, diminished status she encountered many new sources of worry. Emancipation cost her the serenity of not having to think about getting work done.

Gertrude Thomas's Secrets

Valuable as Thomas's observations are as social history, what she withholds from her journal offers even further insights into long-standing tensions over gender and sexuality in the South and, ultimately, into the nature of nineteenth-century southern society. While it was the intensity of some of her writing that first raised my curiosity and drew me into her secrets, I realize that this part of my analysis violates the spirit of her journal. The journal represents a composed text, which, had Thomas succeeded completely, would have stressed the positive and omitted the negative. That the journal tells more than she wanted her readers to know is testimony to her continuing struggle between unburdening herself about matters about which she felt strongly and the maintenance of a self-consciously crafted persona.

Beyond the representation of a southerner of a certain class at

---

154. 10 Apr. 1871.

given historical junctures, there exists in the journal another, veiled text that is far less timely. The hidden layer of the journal, the layer of secrets, is murky, personal, and highly gendered. There are actually two great secrets in the journal, one of which, Jeff's drinking, Gertrude did succeed in hiding. The other proved too painful to suppress entirely. It is about being a woman—being a wife—and its great secret, too, is timeless.

Even when she is strongest and most outspoken, Thomas draws a veil across certain realities of her life that she shared with large numbers of other plantation mistresses. Like them, she tries not to see. But unlike the great majority of her peers, Thomas left a huge, magnificent journal. Her writing hints—through what psychologists call "deception clues" (cues that something is being withheld) and "leakage" (inadvertent disclosure) of highly charged material—that some important truths remain obscured.[155]

Both leakage and deception clues are associated with the phenomenon of self-deception, the concealment of painful knowledge from the self. The line between Thomas's deception of her readers (her children) and self-deception is not entirely clear in the journal, for Thomas's concept of her audience varied over the many years that she wrote. At times she addresses her children, at other times her God. In the later years she speaks with remarkable candor to her journal as a confidante (herself). Drawing the line between deception and self-deception may not be an indispensable task here, for, as observers as disparate as the sociologist Erving Goffman and the poet Adrienne Rich point out, the intention to mislead others quickly becomes the misleading of the self.[156]

---

155. Paul Ekman, "Self-Deception and Detection of Misinformation," in Joan S. Lockard and Delroy L. Paulhus, *Self-Deception: An Adaptive Mechanism?* (Englewood Cliffs, N.J., 1988), pp. 231–32.

Building on Sigmund Freud's observations that individuals provide nonverbal clues that undermine what they are saying, psychologists have usually looked for deception clues and leakage in the realm of nonverbal communication, which, of course, is not available in the present case. Thomas, however, provides verbal clues and verbal leakage that undermine the conventions that she expresses in her writing.

156. Goffman, *Presentation of Self*, p. 81; Adrienne Rich, *On Lies, Secrets, and Silence: Selected Prose, 1966–1978* (New York, 1979), p. 188.

The most obvious deception clue is one of Thomas's favorite refrains. Four times between 1852 (the year in which she married) and 1870, she cites this poem (or alludes to it by quoting the first line) by the Georgia poet Richard Henry Wilde:

> There are some thoughts we utter not.
>> Deep treasured in our inmost heart
>> Ne'er revealed and ne'er forgot.[157]

In addition, the intensity of portions of the writing manifests Thomas's uneasiness over certain subjects (e.g., competition between women, the dual sexual standard) without going to the heart of her distress. The most important deception clues begin with the entry of 2 June 1855, in which Thomas says: "[T]here are some thoughts we utter not and not even to you my journal . . . yet there are some moments when I must write—must speak or else the pent up emotions of an overcharged heart will *burst* or *break*. . . . With a heart throbbing and an agitated form. How can I write?" Thomas cites "one of the most exciting conversations I have ever held. A conversation which in a moment, in a flash of the eye will change the gay, thoughtless girl into a woman with all a woman's feelings" and the "chilling influence (it may be of disappointment) to wonder at the wild tumultuous throbbings of early womanhood." She says that she is troubled by something.

I have never succeeded in deciphering this confusing entry entirely, for the language is more than ambiguous; these phrases lead in two separate directions at once. Thomas's language echoes other women's private descriptions of infatuations at the same time that it represents Thomas's own language of disappointment. When she writes of "all a woman's feelings" elsewhere in the journal, she speaks of chagrin rather than fulfillment. Neither this entry nor those around it provide clues as to the cause(s) of her agitation. But she clearly manifests great anxiety over the contents of a conversation that takes place when her first child is eighteen months old.

---

157. 4 Nov. 1852, 2 June 1855, 26 June 1856 (in this citation, Thomas underlines the last two words of the poem), 10 Jan. 1870 (she cites only the first line). After writing the entry for 4 November 1852, in which she explained that Jeff's illness had postponed their wedding, quoted the first line of the poem twice in three sentences, and added that "there are some emotions too powerful for words," Thomas did not write again until 8 April 1855.

Moreover, in two other entries in the same season, she speaks of the "bitter agony" and the bitterness of "taunts and expressions" that are the lot of married women.[158]

Several years later, Thomas begins to explicate her concerns in what I call her leakage entries, in which she inadvertently reveals that certain matters are significant to her. The lengthy, intense entry of 2 January 1859 deplores miscegenation, which she acknowledges as matter "thought best for [white] women to ignore." Thomas castigates white men of uncontrolled, animal passions who buy mulatto slave women for sex. In general, Thomas had a very low opinion of all southern white men's morals, but bachelors's actions are not uppermost in her mind.[159] Rather, she laments the effect of miscegenation in "our Southern homes." While she believes that white men are more degraded by slavery (i.e., the miscegenation that accompanies the institution) than blacks, her main preoccupation is with white families.

A young mother worrying over slavery's pernicious effect on children, Thomas points away from her own nuclear family and toward the setting in which she was herself a child: her father's household.[160] She also mentions "others," whom she does not name, who are equally guilty. Thomas deplores interracial sex as a violation of the racial hierarchy but is aware that the significance

---

158. 11 Apr., 13 June 1855. See also 4 July 1864.

159. See also 12 May 1856, 7 May 1869. In the 12 May 1856 entry, Thomas includes the following cryptic comment on men's morality: "[W]ere that faith [in her husband] dissipated by *actual experience* then would be dissolved a dream in which is constituted my hope of happiness upon earth. Of course between a husband and wife, this is (or should be) a forbidden subject but to *you* my journal I would willingly disclose many thoughts did I not think that the prying eye of curiosity might scan these lines."

160. Thomas writes of her father's "estate," which would indicate a larger place than the Clanton household. Virginia Burr says: "Thomas, in referring to 'so many' mulatto children 'growing up on Pa's estate, as well as others,' includes Turner Clanton's entire estate of five plantations and the Clanton household. In that context, it is highly probable that resident overseers contributed to the mulatto population. Turner Clanton was, without doubt, guilty of miscegenation to some degree" (Virginia Burr to Nell Irvin Painter, 2 Apr. 1989). I believe, however, that Thomas would not have been so concerned about men who did not belong to her immediate family. Hence the emotional meaning of "Pa's estate" points to Clanton's own household, not to those of overseers or nonrelatives.

of the miscegenation she has in mind exceeds simple race mixing. It is also sex outside of marriage, so that some individuals worth worrying about in her father's household and in the household of "others" had violated one of the Ten Commandments. As a devout Christian who knew that there was a heaven and a hell and that the sins of the fathers were liable to be visited upon the children, she worried "upon whom shall the accountability of their [the mulatto children's] future state depend."[161]

By 3 January 1865 the combined strains of the war, her father's death, and the impending Confederate defeat have brought Thomas's anxieties closer to the surface. She writes at length about competition between women. Finally, in the 26 June 1869 entry, she writes of her son, Turner, the mulatto plowboy, and his mother who is only slightly darker than Turner's mother.

With the 26 June 1869 entry, much of Thomas's passionate writing falls into place. Gertrude Thomas worried about competition between women because it was a bothersome part of her own life as a daughter and a wife. Thus her long, impassioned comments on the effect of slavery on white families and on black women's usurpation of the places of white wives now appear as commentary on her own family's tragedy. She believed that her father had had children and that her husband had had a child outside their marriages. It is possible, though far from certain, that whatever unspeakable thing distressed her when her first child was a baby was the discovery that her husband was sleeping with someone else.

Pulling all these leakage entries together, I conclude that the great secret of Gertrude Thomas's journal is something that she experienced as adultery. As a devout, nineteenth-century Methodist, she was deeply concerned with matters of moral rectitude and divine retribution. At the same time, however, she reacted to her husband's sexual relations with a slave as people have traditionally responded to adultery—with jealousy, anger, and humiliation, not with the cool assurance of superiority.

This should come as no surprise, as some of the best-known observations about antebellum southern society make more or less the same point. Abolitionists—who are currently out of favor with historians as analysts of southern society—routinely pilloried slave-

---

161. 2 Jan. 1859.

owners for the sexual abuse of mulatto women.[162] Female visitors to the South criticized slavery for its deleterious effect on white men's morals. In the 1830s Harriet Martineau spoke of the plantation mistress as "'the chief slave of the harem.'" Fredrika Bremer, in the 1850s, coined the famous phrase about slaves of mixed ancestry that Thomas quotes in her journal. And Mary Chesnut wrote of the mulatto children present in every slaveholding household. Gertrude Thomas was far, very far, from alone.[163]

As of yet there is no way of knowing what number of married slaveowners slept with their slaves, only of recognizing that the phenomenon was exceedingly common and the testimony one-sided. White men passed over their extralegal involvements in si-

---

162. E.g., Harriet Beecher Stowe, *A Key to Uncle Tom's Cabin; Presenting the Original Facts and Documents upon Which the Story Was Founded. Together with Corroborative Statement Verifying the Truth of the Work* (Leipzig, 1853), pp. 63, 142–43; L. Maria Child, *An Appeal in Favor of Americans Called Africans* (1836; reprint, New York, 1968), pp. 23–24. Historian Ronald G. Walters quotes abolitionists who wrote of the antebellum South as "ONE GREAT SODOM" and of the male slaveowner as one who "totally annihilates the marriage institution" (Walters, "The Erotic South: Civilization and Sexuality in American Abolitionism," *American Quarterly* 25, no. 2 [May 1973]: 183, 192). See also James L. Leloudis II, "Subversion of the Feminine Ideal: The *Southern Lady's Companion* and White Male Morality in the Antebellum South, 1847–1854," in Rosemary Skinner Keller, Louise L. Queen, and Hilah F. Thomas, eds., *Women in New Worlds*, vol. 2 (Nashville, 1982), esp. pp. 67–68.

163. Harriet Martineau, *Society in America* (New York, 1837), 2:112, 118; Bremer, *Homes of the New World*, 1:382; Woodward and Muhlenfeld, *Private Mary Chesnut*, p. 42 (18 Mar. 1861).

See also Deborah Gray White, *Ar'n't I a Woman?: Female Slaves in the Plantation South* (New York, 1985), pp. 27–47; Clinton, *Plantation Mistress*, pp. 203–4, 210–22; James Hugo Johnston, *Race Relations in Virginia and Miscegenation in the South, 1776–1860* (Amherst, Mass., 1970), pp. 165–90, 243; Kenneth M. Stampp, *The Peculiar Institution: Slavery in the Ante-Bellum South* (New York, 1956), pp. 350–61; Eugene D. Genovese, *Roll, Jordan, Roll: The World the Slaves Made* (New York, 1974), pp. 413–29; Bertram Wyatt-Brown, *Southern Honor: Ethics and Behavior in the Old South* (New York, 1982), pp. 307–24; Weiner, "Plantation Mistresses and Female Slaves," pp. 131–39, 177–90; bell hooks, *Ain't I a Woman?: Black Women and Feminism* (Boston, 1981), pp. 26–41; Angela Y. Davis, *Women, Race, and Class* (New York, 1981), pp. 25–29, 173–77; Fox-Genovese, *Within the Plantation Household*, pp. 325–26.

lence, so that it fell to wives and blacks to point a finger.[164] White women, black women, and black men all deeply resented white men's access to black women and said so, although comments from the two sides of the color line are contradictory. Where black men and women saw gross racial and sexual exploitation, white women saw sexual competition, which carries connotations of equality—of some sort—between participants in the contest.

The intense hurt and anger in Thomas's entries on competition between women and sexual relations between slaveowners and slaves indicate that she experienced her husband's action as a breach in her marriage. Yet there may be an alternative and more appropriate definition of the phenomenon that Thomas deplored.

The pattern of slaveowning married men's sexual relations with women to whom they were not legally married was widespread, and these nonlegal relationships sometimes endured—like marriages. Seen another way, Thomas may have been party to a social pattern that she did not recognize and for which anthropologists use the term "polygyny." It may well have been that men like Jefferson Thomas, more than regularly committing adultery, were establishing something like polygynous marriages. Gertrude does not say how long Jeff's relationship with his slave-partner lasted, whether it was a fling or might qualify as a marriage. Evidence from the journal supports at least a suspicion that the relationship may have endured from 1855 to 1870, perhaps even until 1880, but it is far from conclusive.[165] The stresses that Gertrude reports as affecting her marriage—Jeff's irritability, his refusal to give her moral support, his withdrawal from intimacy—could as easily represent the human cost of financial ruin as an expression of the distance between partners that accompanies extramarital relationships.

There can be no well-founded representation of the circum-

---

164. E.g., Harriet A. Jacobs, *Incidents in the Life of a Slave Girl, Written by Herself*, edited by Jean F. Yellin (Cambridge, Mass., 1987). See also James M. McPherson, "The War of Southern Aggression," *New York Review of Books* 35, nos. 21–22 (19 Jan. 1989), p. 19; Carol Bleser, ed., *Secret and Sacred: The Diaries of James Henry Hammond, a Southern Slaveholder* (New York, 1988), p. xvi.

165. As late as 5 December 1870, Thomas draws a parallel between herself, Hester Prynne of *The Scarlet Letter*, and African-American women who bear mixed-race children. On 24 November 1880, Thomas writes of having her cross to bear.

stances that led to the conception of Jefferson Thomas's outside child, but other cases are clearer. James Henry Hammond, a prominent antebellum South Carolina statesman, for instance, had two slaves who were, in effect, multiple wives. Southern court records are full of litigation over which set of families might inherit from men who had had children by more than one woman.[166]

Thomas's unwillingness to spell out what was taking place in her marriage hints by indirection at her husband's adultery. Thomas was keeping secrets from herself and from her readers. Her South more or less concealed slave wives, who represented an open secret that polite people pretended not to see. Secrecy, the very heart and soul of adultery, is much of what makes adultery toxic to marriages, families, and, ultimately, society. Of itself, secrecy destroys trust, stifles intimacy, and rigidifies relationships, even when partners are not so deeply religious as Gertrude Thomas.[167]

In the early nineteenth century, Harriet Martineau understood

166. Clinton, *Plantation Mistress*, pp. 213–21.

167. Herbert Fingarette, in his classic *Self-Deception* (London, 1969), explains the tactic of not spelling out, or hiding, uncomfortable truths (see esp. pp. 43–50). Fingarette's not-spelling-out is analogous to Jean-Paul Sartre's *mauvaise foi*, which is translated as "bad faith," in the context of self-deception (Sartre, *Being and Nothingness: An Essay on Phenomenological Ontology*, translated by Hazel E. Barnes [New York, 1967], pp. 47–56).

On the antebellum South's great secret, see also Ann Taves, "Spiritual Purity and Sexual Shame: Religious Themes in the Writings of Harriet Jacobs," *Church History* 56 (1987): 65–66.

The term "toxic" is Annette Lawson's (*Adultery: An Analysis of Love and Betrayal* [New York, 1988], pp. 12, 30–31, 53). Robert S. Weiss stresses the symbolic meaning of sexual relationships in defining the damage that adultery inflicts (*Marital Separation* [New York, 1975], pp. 31–33). Frank Pittman prefers "infidelity" to "adultery" but retains the connotations that I have used in connection with adultery (*Private Lies: Infidelity and the Betrayal of Intimacy* [New York, 1989], pp. 20, 53). Mark A. Karpel stresses the shame, guilt, and loss of relational resources, i.e., violation of trust and reciprocity, that secrets cause within families ("Family Secrets: I. Conceptual and Ethical Issues in the Relational Context," *Family Process* 19, no. 3 [Sept. 1980]: 300). See also Judith A. Libow, "Gender and Sex Role Issues as Family Secrets," *Journal of Strategic and Systemic Therapies* 4, no. 2 (1985): 32–33; and Sissela Bok, *Secrets* (New York, 1982), pp. 25, 59–72. A recent southern autobiography by Sallie Bingham exemplifies the pernicious effects of not telling the truth within a family (*Passion and Prejudice: A Family Memoir* [New York, 1989]).

that adultery places enormous strains on families, and modern scholarship makes the same point. Adultery breaks the pact of sexual exclusivity in marriage and undermines the betrayed spouse's trust in the other. The consequences of such ruptures could not always be confined to the private sphere. James Henry Hammond believed, with good foundation, that his wife's angry reaction to his taking his second slave wife ruined his political career.[168]

Adultery also subverts the social order by weakening the most fundamental social relationship, upon which procreation and socialization depend. Adultery breeds moral and sexual ambivalence in children, who vacillate between the outraged virtue of the betrayed parent and the adulterous parent's indulgence in sin. Ultimately, adultery creates chaotic inheritance patterns, which in the antebellum South meant that fathers were liable to own or sell their offspring. Lillian Smith, a perceptive twentieth-century southern observer of her region, grasped the way that secrets, miscegenation, sin, and guilt combined to endow white southerners with a terrible fear of impending disaster. Smith would have agreed that southern society, with so many instances of bad faith, was pathological.[169] Women like Gertrude Thomas knew this all too well and abhorred slavery for its effect on personal and social morality. Why did they not act to keep their men at home or to protect slave women?

Given the power relations of antebellum slave society, it would have been extraordinarily difficult for plantation mistresses to have kept their husbands at home. To protect themselves from what they saw as sexual competition, women of the planter class—who

---

168. Bleser, *Secret and Sacred*, pp. 170, 134–244, 254–69.

169. See Lawson, *Adultery*, pp. 10, 35, 56–59, 221, 260; Pittman, *Private Lies*, pp. 261, 281; Philip E. Lampe, ed., *Adultery in the United States: Close Encounters of the Sixth (or Seventh) Kind* (Buffalo, N.Y., 1987), pp. 3–9, 13. Sue M. Hall and Philip A. Hall point out that adultery is often cited as a reason for denying child custody to one parent or the other. An adulterer appears to be unfit to care for children and unable to serve the child's best interests ("Law and Adultery," in Lampe, ed., *Adultery in the United States*, pp. 73–75). Thomas discusses parents who own or sell their own children (2 Jan. 1859). See Lillian Smith, *Killers of the Dream*, rev. ed. (New York, 1961), pp. 83–89, 121–24.

could not own property, vote, or hold office—would have had somehow to make slave women less vulnerable to sexual attack, to have somehow provided female slaves with some measure of power vis-à-vis wealthy white men. Perhaps the recognition that the power dynamics were so heavily weighted against them stopped white mistresses from making common cause with their female slaves. Lacking political and economic power, white women could hardly begin to shield slave women from white men. But white women rarely entertained such thoughts.

Even in the privacy of their journals, plantation mistresses found it difficult to forge rhetorical solidarity with their slaves. Instead, slaveowning women usually adopted one of the commonplaces of southern race relations: that slave women were so degraded morally that they tempted white men to sleep with them. Interracial sex, by this line of reasoning, was the fault of the slave women.

Gertrude Thomas, however, stops short of this conclusion. Although she deplores the morals of blacks, she nonetheless comes close to recognizing that slave women are powerless to resist slaveowners. Several times she writes of the moral depravity of (white) men and how slavery was "demoralizing" to them. Yet she resists the temptation (as Mary Chesnut did not) to cast clear blame on slave women. Thomas is unable to exculpate slave women directly; she cannot say that miscegenation is not their fault. But she can say of the children that "They are not to blame. Oh No!"[170]

In a long discussion of Elizabeth Gaskell's novel, *Ruth*, which is about unmarried but not interracial sexuality, Thomas explores the sexual double standard. She asks rhetorically, "Oh how many of those women are more sinned against than sinning[?]"[171] Thomas is not able to take the next step, to bring slave women into her commentary, but obviously the theme of impure women troubled

---

170. Thomas on morality, sex, and slavery: 12 Apr. 1856, 2 Jan. 1859, 17, 23 Sept. 1864, 26 June, 7 May 1869. For Mary Chesnut's comments on the low morals of black women, see Woodward and Muhlenfeld, *Private Mary Chesnut*, pp. 42–43 (18 Mar. 1861).

171. 18 Aug. 1856. See also 9 Feb. 1858, 2 Jan. 1859. It is possible that Thomas's opinions about sexually vulnerable slave women and white men's unreliability and lack of morals contributed to her later advocacy of woman suffrage.

her deeply.[172] I suspect that she avoided spelling out her ideas about sexual purity as they applied to her own household so as not to undermine the foundation of her place in her world. She could not clarify her thinking about slavery and sex and retain her social and religious identity. To absolve black women entirely and blame white men completely would have meant reaching unflattering and uncomfortable conclusions about herself, her family, and her society. She could not close the circle of meaning that connected gender and race and class.

According to the ostensible mores of her society, Gertrude Thomas was the superior of nearly everyone in it. She was a plantation mistress in a society dominated by the 6 percent of white families that qualified as planters by owning twenty or more slaves. She was an educated woman at a time when only elite men could take higher education for granted. And she was white in a profoundly racist culture.

These same hierarchies also permitted her husband certain liberties that she was denied. As in any slave society, male slaveowners in the South counted sexual access to enslaved women as one of the perquisites of masterliness. Slave women had no rights or means of resisting, nor could their families protect them (ordinarily) from the sexual advances of white men. That is, enslaved people had no legal ability to prevent or redress rape.

From the other side, neither Gertrude Thomas's economic and educational attributes nor her social status protected her from what she saw as sexual competition from inferior women. From Thomas's point of view, white men saw women—whether slave or free, wealthy or impoverished, cultured or untutored, black or white—as interchangeable sex partners.[173] She and other plantation mistresses failed to elevate themselves sufficiently as women to avoid the pain of sharing their spouses with slaves. From the masters' point of view, slave women were perfect women, for slaves

---

172. Thomas often censors herself by ceasing to write about distressing lines of thought, which she calls digressions, investigations of forbidden subjects, or potential harangues (12 May 1856, 9 Feb. 1858, 4 July 1864, 7 Feb., 7 May 1869, 17 Aug. 1879).

173. 1 Jan. 1859, 28 Jan. 1864, 9 Mar., 14 Oct. 1865, 13 Jan. 1870.

existed to fulfill their masters' wishes. The sexual availability of enslaved women was a function of their powerlessness in society, which defined their enslavement and made them such formidable competition to elite women. Thus the institution that assured plantation mistresses of their social prestige also gave them sexual nightmares. The effects of the victimization of slave women could not be contained, for (otherwise) privileged women like Gertrude Thomas felt that their husbands' adultery intruded into their own as well as their slaves' families.

Beyond the calculus of sexuality, however, the powerlessness that made slave women attractive as women to male slaveowners simultaneously made slaves attractive to mistresses as workers. For as workers, in theory at least, slaves had no interests of their own. They were on the job whenever they were needed and could be made to do whatever their owners ordered. Slaves could not leave work for reasons of their own. Powerless workers may have made ideal workers and ideal women, but those same characteristics conflicted with the gender interests of female slaveowners.

In the final analysis, slaveowning women were not willing even to imagine relinquishing the labor of their slaves, even though slavery made mistresses vulnerable as women. Stripped down and phrased most starkly, documents such as Gertrude Thomas's journal indicate that slave mistresses preferred the enjoyment of unlimited class privilege to the limitation of their husbands' opportunities for adultery. Reluctant to pit their class position against their gender interests, they avoided the facts and kept their secrets.

Conclusion

Gertrude Thomas belonged to a Deep South generation of educated white southerners that was virtually unique, sandwiched between the settling of the frontier, when planters lived in cabins and did not bother to educate their daughters, and the postwar generation of hard-scrabble elites who could no longer appeal to the Bible as an authority on the rightness of their world.

As a young woman, Gertrude Thomas was not intended to suffer losses. Even deaths—of her babies, of her father—came as a shock. She was destined, or so it seemed, to be a golden child and a golden woman, the product of wealth in a life of privilege in which superiority was taken for granted. But almost as soon as her part of the South had been settled long enough to produce a gentry with pretensions, the Civil War, Confederate defeat, and emancipation turned things upside down. Debt, not wealth, became her constant companion.

Not surprisingly, the most passionate and most memorable writing in this long and thoughtful journal concerns loss: familial, moral, social, and financial. Considering that Gertrude Thomas had been socialized into an automatic self-control that censored emotions of the intensity that makes her journal so rich, the contradiction between her self-censorious upbringing and the relative openness of her writing seems paradoxical. Although she very nearly succeeded in keeping the most intimate, painful, and common of southern family secrets, less private adversity freed her pen.

The losses that drove her to honesty, even to perplexed self-revelation, were precisely those that departed from her life's script as it had been laid out in 1852. Gertrude Thomas did not live the life that she had expected, but she survived, her good sense intact, to delineate the unexpected.

Part I   *1848–1859*

1. The Young Journalist

I sent for this paper to form a journal.
—September 29, 1848

Rochester,[1] September 29, 1848   Well I have written an account of yesterday's proceedings and as I sent for this paper to form a journal I will write what happened on Monday Tuesday & Wednesday.

At Home, September 25, 1848   I expected to write at the plantation today but the pen proved so bad that I could scarcely make a mark with it, and then I had very little ink. I had quite an unpleasant ride today. . . . I got out at the plantation wishing to come home with Pa[2] in the buggy. He was at the Tubman[3] place and I waited there three or four hours for him I never was as tired of a place in my life. I had no dinner but had two sweet potatoes roasted and an egg boiled besides a cup of butter milk. Billy Anthony[4] and a Mr Garnett were there. The latter wished to be employed as an overseer.

Well Amanda has just come upp in my room and has began a description of the people and the times so I will stop as it is an interresting subject—

Tuesday, September 26, 1848   I can scarcely tell how today has been passed. I have done little or nothing but arrange my room and

---

1. Rochester, so named by the fourteen-year-old Gertrude Clanton and sometimes called Piney Woods, was the country home of the Clantons in Columbia County, Ga., northwest of Augusta.
2. Gertrude's father, Col. Turner C. Clanton.
3. A Clanton plantation. Plantations often kept the name of an early owner, in this case Richard Tubman.
4. Billy Anthony was Gertrude's cousin, the son of Turner Clanton's sister, Tabitha Clanton Anthony.

71

the contents of my port folio. I had so many things in the latter and they were in such hurly burly and disorder that it took me some time to arrange them. The different packages of envelopes and the note paper &c.

I have just finished a hearty supper. I ate a good many preserves and nothing else. This morning I indulged in my old habit of lying in bed late so I did not take breakfast untill all the rest had partaken of theirs. Pa went to the Cummings[5] plantation and did not get home to dinner. I carried my coloured silk apron down stairs this morning after breakfast where I turned it and Ma[6] made it over again. I took a short nap before dinner which refreshed me a good deal. . . .

Wednesday, September 27, 1848 . . . I have been writing letters all the forenoon. I wrote two letters one to Mary Frazier and one to Isabella [Morrison] and a note to Martha Phinizy. The envelope in which Mary's letter was enclosed was the rather singular one Dr Neeson gave to me. The motto *Nothing else to do.* Isabella's was in a plain envelope and the motto *Rather die than change.* I sealed Martha Phinizy's note with a blue transparent wafer. Just then Sis Anne[7] came upp and wanted the candle in her room so I will stop writing. She also wishes my pen and ink to write to Mrs Luthringer for some steel beads and fringe besides tassells for a purse she is knitting. [Undated note at bottom of page: "Our Piney Woods place was named Rochester by me just after having read *Jane Eyre.* It was changed very often afterwards."]

Rochester, September 28, 1848 Last night Edmund returned from Augusta with a good many papers and Sis Anne received several Ladies papers. I was so busy reading that I forgot to write in my journal. I slept in this room last night as Pa did not return. Ma slept upp here in Sis Anne's room.

The latter went down to the Sand Hills[8] to Aunt Meiggs[9] to-

---

5. Another Clanton plantation, probably land formerly owned by the Thomas Cumming family.

6. Gertrude's mother, Mary Luke Clanton.

7. Ann (variously Anne, Annie) Clanton was Gertrude's older sister.

8. The Sand Hills, incorporated as Summerville in 1861, was a village located about three miles northwest of Augusta. Aside from the permanent residents, many prominent Augustans had summer homes there to escape the

day. She wrote to Cousin Emily and Eliza[10] yesterday and I expect they will come upp home with her this evening. Yesterday after breakfast Mary[11] and I went over to Mrs Berry's to spend the day. We took Amanda with us as a protectress. I gathered some Horse and whortle berrys on the road (sparkleberrys I meant). I wore my eternal tissue silk and black silk cape. We had a lunch of cordial and cake ham and biscuit—and apples besides cheese. Mrs Berry and I were weighing cotton (By the by I never done it before). While I was adding upp the weights Mrs Griffin rode upp and took dinner. I expected to meet Ma there and did so. . . .

Friday, September 29, 1848 I have just left them in the parlour talking and laughing while I have stolen away to write the occurrences of today— Late this evening Sis Anne came back accompanied by Cousin Eliza and George Mitchell [Emily's son]. Cousin Emily has not altered much. Still I do not think I would have known her its having been so long since she was out here last— I have been busy writing and indulging in my usual day dreams. As I have no books to read I expect my time now will be spent rather lonely and dull but I hope Cousin Emily's and Eliza's presence and company will enliven us a little— This evening after dinner I dressed again and fixed my hair. I then walked in the garden a while and gathered some flowers to dress the pots. I see I have passed this day occupied in writing this journal over. When I came home last Monday night I wrote on the leaf that I had used at Grandma's. The next night I wrote in an old copy book which I use for scribbling. The next night the same and so on. As I wished it all connected I coppied the writing off. Cousin Emily brought out Cousin Berry's dagaureotype.[12] He is taken in regimentals and looks quite handsome. I wish I could see him. . . .

---

heat and humidity of the city, which was located on the banks of the Savannah River.

9. The Meigses (alternately spelled Meiggs) were related to the Clantons through the Anthony family.

10. Emily Anthony Mitchell and Eliza Anthony were the daughters of Tabitha Clanton Anthony.

11. Mary (Mamie) Clanton, Gertrude's sister, was seven years younger.

12. Berry Clanton was the son of Nathaniel Holt Clanton of Alabama, Turner Clanton's brother. The daguerreotype was a new photographic process and a new word. Gertrude spelled it phonetically and never the same way twice.

October 1, 1848   I am writing later than usual tonight for Ma had my pen and ink down stairs and Cousin Eliza Anthony has just gone out. I was very late for breakfast this morning. After that was over we all began to get ready for church. Ma did not go this morning. Cousin Emily and Eliza besides Sis Anne went in the carriage. . . . When I got home I heard that Miss Purtenice Ramsey (or Mrs Mohorn I should say) had twins. I pity *her*. After dinner I had a suspicion that Mudge Merriweather and Josh Griffin would come over so I did not undress. Sis Anne and Cousin Eliza did. Sure enough they came and then they had to dress again. I went down stairs and done my best at entertaining Mr Merriweather. Pa assisted me untill the girls came in. The gentleman staid untill dark. I was very pleasantly entertained myself. . . .

October 2, 1848   This morning I was again late for breakfast and Ma was sick with bad cold and headache. She arose after breakfast and one of Mrs Griffin's servants brought us some chenkepins.[13] Uncle Ben came down with a note from Aunt Lamkin[14] informing us that Grand Ma[15] was quite sick. Pa went to Augusta this morning and Edmund had started also. Uncle Ben went after and overtook him. Ma promised to send for us tonight if she was any worse. She has not done so, so I trust Grand Ma is better. I wrote a note to Mrs Berry requesting her to loan me the nos. of *Graham's* magazine for September and October and to write me all the news. . . .

October 3, 1848   This morning Cousin Emily and George her little son rose and were dressed some time before I got upp so of course I was late for breakfast again. After that was over I came upp and was busy fixing my hair. I first fixed it in the way I saw Virginia Warren wear hers. I did not like it. Took it down and plaited down

---

13. Chinquapins or chinkapins—chestnuts.
14. Aunt Lamkin was Elizabeth Luke Lamkin, widowed sister of Mary Luke (Ma) Clanton. She lived in Columbia County and was a wealthy landowner. Apparently Colonel Clanton advised her in the management of her wealth and property.
15. Elizabeth Reid Luke, the widow of Judge James Luke, was still living at her homeplace in Columbia County, surrounded by a large number of nearby relatives.

my back in two plaits and have worn it so all day but find it very unpleasant. Don't think I will wear it so again soon. . . . Pa brought home a letter for Sis Anne from Fanny Morrison and I received one from Mary Frazier. A very welcome one by the by. He brought home one of the Ladies newspapers and some candy but not the book I wrote for. Well I did not expect it much. He says he did not have time to get it. I have finished the magazines Mrs Berry loaned me. She says she has several novels at home, one *The Traducer*[16] which I have read before and two others the names she did not know. I intend writing to her tomorrow and sending for them. She has no pen to answer it she says. I will have to send her one which I will do wright willingly to get a note from her. I like to hear from Mrs Berry. She generally writes notes with news in them. [Undated note: "I was only fourteen when I was corresponding with Mrs Berry"]

. . . .

Monday, October 9, 1848 I have just finished reading a letter Pa received from Jimmy Anthony.[17] It was written before his mother left Alabama for Georgia. This morning I came upp stairs after breakfast and arranged my room in some kind of order. Then I went in the garden and gathered some roses and put the leaves upp to dry. I also gathered some wild flowers and found one beautiful little flower, a perfect little gem. I have read seven of those *Graham's* magazines and have been reading some of the pieces in the January No. of 1846. One of the pieces I have just finished. It is "Grace Fleming." I was indulging in the habit I have formed of building castles in the air. Oh how delightful it is and the persons that I dream of. Oh it is *very* delightful. But *then* when awakened by the cold realities of life. . . .

. . . .

October 13, 1848 The time draws near for us to leave this dear dear place. Oh with how much regret will I leave it. This place has

---

16. *The Traducer—An Historical Romance* (1842), by Nicholas Mitchell.

17. Jimmy Anthony was the brother of William (Billy), Emily, Eliza, and Mary Anthony, Gertrude's cousins.

been the scene for the [illegible] of some of my happiest hours. And this summer will be a remarkable epoch in my life— . . .

.   .   .

November 13, 1848   More than two weeks have elapsed since I last wrote in this book. I expected to go to Augusta the next morning and with that intention went to writing a note to Rebecca Gardner. I slept in the room above the parlour that night and in the night a note was brought from Aunt Lamkin telling us that Grand Ma was quite sick so we went up there the next morning. We found Aunt Lamkin and her children. Aunt Gracey Harden and Mrs Wheat and her little girl Nell together with cousin Jane Chapler and Susan Anne Toole. They all went away in the afternoon. . . . On Saturday Jimmy Lamkin[18] came home. I think he has improved very much both in manners and appearance. On that evening Lizzie Lamkin was taken sick and in the morning it turned out to be the sore throat. . . . Pa and Ma, Sis Anne and I received invitations to Miss Mary Robinson's wedding yesterday. The invitation was written beautifully and it was very neat. Pa was so much afraid that we would take the sore throat that we came home. We found Cousin Emily and George, Mr Chitt and cousin Matilda [Reid] besides Cousin Eliza had been here ever since Saturday night. . . .

Our ride today was rendered rather unpleasant by its raining yesterday and making it sloppy. Cousin Emma [Lamkin] and I pounded upp some charcoal Saturday morning. Well I feel as though I had accomplished a task and now I will rest a little. I was not able to bring all my hickrinuts and walnuts and gave some to cousin Emma, Josey and Savanah—

.   .   .

Thursday, November 16, 1848   I was interrupted on Tuesday night while writing by Amanda's telling me that Grand Mother was *dead*. Cousin Matilda's Bram brought the news from Mrs Darby. Pa

---

18. James (Jimmy) Lamkin, his brother, Robert, and his sisters, Emma and Lizzie, were the children of Elizabeth Lamkin. Emma was two or three years younger than Gertrude.

instantly sent Edmund there for a letter. I was sick before and crying gave me such a headache that I was forced to go to bed. I found that I had caught the sore throat. Sis Anne heated some camphor and rubbed it on a flannel and put it around my neck. When Edmund came back he brought a note Mrs Oakman had left at Mrs Darby's. She said that Grand Ma was a little better. . . . I was studying some miscelaneous questions on Robins' outlines of English History. I studied several pages and read a good deal in Olney's history.[19] I have no novels to read. I wish that it were possible for me to refrain from reading one for six months or a year. I am confident I could study much better. If I could form the habit I would get along very well. It comes just as natural for me [to] write in this journal as it does for me to eat a meal.

How I wish I could wander o'er these old woods again. How much pleasure it would afford me. But I must not indulge in such sad reflections. If I go to Macon to school this winter I do not suppose I will be here the ensuing summer as the vacation is in May and December and neither months are spent here. I cannot stir out of this room but I must stop and pack upp my little articles. [Pencilled note: "I was mistaken with regard to the vacation at Macon. It always commences about the 12 of July and lasts till the 1st Monday in October."]

.   .   .

Augusta,[20] *November 18, 1848*   We got in town yesterday about two oclock before any of the waggons. Mary and Buddy[21] came in the buggy with Pa. Sis Anne Amanda and I came in the carriage. I was lying down on the front seat all the time. I went to sleep just this side of Mr Skinner's shop and did not wake upp again untill we got very near Mr Coleman's. I bore the fatigues of the ride pretty well. Our dinner was quite a simple one yesterday. I sent Amanda soon after with 10 cents for some apples. She brought me nine very fine ones. I have two of them now. . . . I would have written last

---

19. *History of the United States—on a New Plan Adapted to the Capacity of Youth* (1836), by Jesse Olney.
20. The Clanton mansion in Augusta, located at 503 Greene Street.
21. James L. (Buddy) Clanton, Gertrude's brother, nine years younger.

night but this journal was in the carriage under the front seat and I could not get it very well. I will stop writing and make me some hair greese.

．　．　．

Saturday, November 25, 1848   Here I am again in the country at Grand Mother's. Yesterday morning I arose quite late and dressed. After breakfast I felt quite badly. Sick at my stomach. I however went to school although twas after nine oclock. Susan Knight said the Philosophy lesson and in Rhetoric Mr Hard[22] first asked Mary Jane McEntee and then Isabel who was not prepared to answer his questions and then he asked Virginia Whatley. I was afraid he would question me for I had not looked at the lesson. I had studied the parsing in Thomson's *Seasons*.[23] When Mr Hard told me someone wished to see me I went down and found Amanda and Mary at the door. They told me to come home as Grand Mother was very ill and not expected to live. I made haste and when I got home I found that Sis Anne was getting ready to come upp here. . . . On this side of Mr Dickson's we met Uncle Frank who told us that Grand Mother was dead. Died about twelve oclock that day. We met Father this side of the plantation. He took Sister and Buddy in the buggy with him. I layed down on the back seat. It was quite dark when we were at Cousin Polly's.[24] . . .

．　．　．

Tuesday, December 12, 1848   Some days have elapsed since I wrote last. On Sunday Pa Ma and Buddy and the babe[25] left for the country. They requested Aunt Paull[26] to leave her boarding house

---

22. Rev. W. J. Hard, Baptist minister and private school teacher, later a professor at Mercer University.

23. *The Seasons* (1730), by James Thomson.

24. Polly Walton was most likely the daughter of Turner Clanton's sister, Mary (Polly) Lyons of Alabama and Texas. She was married to William Walton, an Augusta attorney. They lived in the Sand Hills.

25. The babe was Cora (Co) Clanton, Gertrude's sister, twelve years younger.

26. Aunt Paull was Catherine Clanton Paul (or Paull), another sister of

and stay here till they returned. She very kindly consented to do so. None of us went to church in the morning but Alathea [Paull], Cousin Eliza and Mary Anthony took dinner with us as did Jimmy Anthony. . . . Cousin Omar Paull called after Tea and sett till ten oclock. He said he would be round tonight. He promised to write me a composition and handed it to me the next morning as I was going to school. It was on the advantage of Education. Yesterday evening Mildred Eve Isabel and I went to walk after we came out of school. This morning twas raining so that I did not go to school but staid at home. I was reading over my arithmetic as far as fractions. This evening however it cleared upp sufficiently for me to go to school so I did so. Isabel has knit me a beautiful scarf— . . .

Thursday, December 14, 1848 Yesterday I attended school as usual. After I finished writing on Tuesday night Cousin Omar called and brought some Ether. Cousin Eliza took it and it had afect. Sis Anne took it afterwards and so did I but it had no effect and then Sis Anne took it again and it made her cry. We received invitations to Mrs Walton's party which was given to Mary. Yesterday I said the Rhetoric lesson and did not know the Philosophy. Mr Hard gave me a great deal of good advice which I trust may do some good. . . . This morning twas holiday as twas Thanksgiving day. After breakfast I learned my Rhetoric lesson and my Philosophy and reviewed my arithmetic from the first to addition of fractions. This evening I looked over my Grammar and Geography and read a little. As tis late I will close. Near ten oclock.

.   .   .

Monday, December 18, 1848 Nothing of importance occurred on Saturday. It continued raining all day. Ma came home late in the evening. Pa came after supper. On yesterday I did not go to church. Today I went to school. We saw the animals procession come by. All of us went to the windows. The first waggon was drawn by a Elephant. . . . I am very tired fatigued and sleepy.

Turner Clanton. She maintained a boarding house in the Sand Hills. Alathea (Althea) and Omar were her children.

Friday, December 22, 1848 On Tuesday evening we went to the show at least Pa carried Sis Anne Mary and Buddy and I. There was quite a large company assembled there. On Wednesday Mr Hard taught school till two. Yesterday evening He let us out at half past four. . . . This morning was my last morning at Mr Hard's. He got Mr McGraw to make me two pens. One I am writing with. The other I gave to Sis Anne. There was no school this evening and I employed myself reading *Henry De Cerons*.[27] Tis quite pretty I think. Cousin Amanda wrote my name on some visiting cards tonight. I expect to go out visiting tomorrow as I owe a great many visits. I want to go and see Lizzy Wilson, Mary Ann D'Antignac, Mary Dugas and several others.

Sunday, December 24, 1848 Yesterday I dressed and went out visiting in the carriage. I first called to see Susan Knight and found her at home. I then called to see Lizzy Crump and Indiana Clark. The latter was at her sister's. I then called at Mrs Robison's to see [illegible] Ramsay but she was in the country. I left my card and then called on Jane McKeen. She was at home and then called on Emma Cumming. Found Ellen Davies there and of course did not make a very long visit. I then went to see Mary Dawson. She was not at home either. I then made a mistake and called at Mrs Bryson's instead of going to see Mary McKensie as I had intended. I then went to Mrs D'Antignac's to see Mary Ann but I did not go [in] as I rung the bell and no one came to the door. After dinner yesterday I went upp to Mrs Morrison's to get Isabel to go to walk. While I was there Laura Chew came in. After she left we went to Dr Eve's but both Mildred and Lizzy were out. I called at Mr Brahe's to get my gold pencil and ear rings which I had left there to get mended. There was a great many out in the street. We stopped at Mrs Hickman's to see Virginia Whatley sometime in the evening. Cousin Robert and Amanda[28] went away this morning. Cousin Amanda gave me a very pretty purse. This morning Sis Anne bought a book called *Changes and Counter Changes*—[29] I was just interrupted by

---

27. *The Man at Arms, or Henri de Cerons* (1840), by G. P. R. James.
28. Robert Lamkin and his wife, Amanda.
29. Gertrude probably meant *Charms and Counter Charms*, written by Maria Jane McIntosh, which was a new book in 1848.

going to see Mr Knight who was drunk— But as I was going to say Sis Anne bought that book for me but will not give it to me as she has got mad with me. . . .

. . .

Saturday, December 30, 1848 . . . This evening I went out shopping with Ma and Sis Anne. Ma bought me a very pretty work box and Sis Anne one too. Hers is much the prettiest. She also bought me a thimble and some needles and thread and coloured silk and a pair of scissors besides two dresses. One a calico for a dressing gown and the other a muslin delaine. I wonder if I will be in Macon this time next Saturday night.

The last day of 1848 I went to church this morning in the carriage. Mr Evans[30] preached for us. The text was Paul's Epistle to the Hebrews tenth chapter, 19, 20, 21, 22 verses. I did not attend service this afternoon as there was no preaching in the Methodist church. Tonight I have read ten chapters in the Bible. I want Ma to give me a pocket Bible for a New Year's present. Pa gave me a dollar last night to buy me a pen knife. I have now 1 dollar and 75 cents. Tonight has been a very eventful night for me. I feel happier than I have in some time. The idea that this year will go out tonight is solemn. May we all live to see another year. . . .

. . .

January, 6, 1849 This morning I did not go out in the street but remained at home mending a pair of kid gloves. This evening I went to Mr Hard's and spent the evening there. After school Mildred Eve Isabella Morrison and Ginny Whatley went with me upp to Mr Dodge's dagareotype rooms. There was some beautiful specimens. . . . We have just had a serenade. Some gentleman playing on the guitar. I expect to leave on the cars for Macon tomorrow night.

. . .

---

30. Rev. J. E. Evans of St. James Methodist Church in Augusta.

Macon, January 8, 1849   At last I am here in Macon. We started from home Saturday night. Several of the girls called in to see me. In the morning Su Hall and Isabella Morrison called to see me. Martha Phinizy called to see me in the evening. While she was there Laura Chew called to see me. I was crying a good deal but the excitement of the ride on the cars soon engaged my attention. I *never was on the cars before at least* never since I was an *infant—* when I went to Charleston. I was awake when we passed Union Point and Greensborough and Decatur. We took breakfast at Atlanta and left there in the other train of cars for this place about eleven oclock. It was snowing when we left. We took dinner at Griffin (quite a pretty place by the by). We stopped at Mr Huson's Hotel. We next passed through Barnesville and then Forsythe. In the morning there were no ladies in the cars but Sis Anne and I and two others that did not ride far. We got here quite late yesterday evening. This Hotel is Mr Floyd's. We (at least) Sis Anne and I did not go down stairs to supper but did to breakfast. Pa has been to the college[31] and we will go there this evening. I believe I will commence a letter to Ma.

Thursday, February 1, 1849   Here I have been three weeks and have not written in this journal in which I expected to receive so much pleasure. When I first came here [to Wesleyan College] I disliked the place, found the girls unsociable. But now Thank Heaven I am glad I did come as it has been the means perhaps of my conversion. Oh how happy I am now. On Monday evening down stairs in the Chapel I was co[n]verted and made to feel how good God is. We have had prayer meeting every night since. Many of the girls have been converted. Sallie Roberts, Lou Chapman and a great many others. There has been a great outpouring of the spirit of God. . . . We have had Prayer meeting tonight. Many of the girls were happy. I hear Lou Chapman shouting now. This morning I arose quite early. Dressed for prayers and then went into the music

---

31. Wesleyan Female College in Macon, Ga. The first female college in the nation, Wesleyan was chartered in 1836 as Georgia Female College, a Methodist school. In 1843 the name was changed to Wesleyan Female College and in 1917 to its present name of Wesleyan College. Gertrude entered Wesleyan in January 1849 as a sophomore.

room afterwar[d]s where by myself I read in my Bible and prayed and then practised untill breakfast. . . .

I wrote a letter to Ma last Sunday night and I received a long one from her the day before of four pages. I have received a good many letters from home and from the girls since I have been here. Isabel Morrison Jane McKeen Bea Gardner & one or two others. I have written to Mildred Eve. . . . Several of the girls I am very much attached to. Susie Snider, Guss Hill all my roommates. Octavia Jones, Mary Jones, Stark Mays, Emily Harris, Mary Harris, Amanda Moore, Mary Evans, Evy Roby, Ginny Warren, Mary Ann Lamar and oh a great many others. I believe I love all the girls. Oh my heart is so much changed. . . .

Friday, February 2, 1849 Tonight we have had a glorious revival. Sallie Tucker, Victoria Holt, Amy Sparks, Joe Freeman, Lou Warrington besides Lou Warner have been converted. Mr [Edward H.] Myers exhorted us. . . . Martha Oliver brought me some very pretty envelopes today. They were for letters— [Added in pencil at bottom of page: "dear Mat Oliver afterwards is intimately connected with all my college life."]

.   .   .   .   .

Tuesday, Feburary 6, 1849 We had prayer meeting on Sunday night. Carrie Tompkins and Puss Pitts became converted. I set upp with Puss Tinsley on Sunday night and consequently was confined to my bed all day yesterday. Tonight all the girls or at least a good many of them joined the church. I did not as I did not receive a letter from home. I expect one tomorrow.

[At the end of this volume of the journal is a list of thirty-nine titles and "Any quantity of Magazines Godey's Graham's and &C," and this note: "All these Books I read when I was fourteen years old from the 25 of September to Christmas. I borrowed most of them, eagerly read anything and only regret that my reading had not been directed by someone." Also listed were books and several Shakespeare plays that Thomas read while she was at Wesleyan. There are no entries between February 6, 1849, and April 4, 1851. The journal mentioned in the following entry is missing.]

.   .   .

A Journal commenced on my seventeenth birthday—Friday, April 4, 1851   How rapidly time flies! I can look back and it appears but a little while since I was sixteen. How sad the thought makes me. To think I am borne so rapidly, so very rapidly upon the wings of time. And the thought will arise. How will all this end. To what end am I destined. Surely for something else than to waste the precious moments of existence as I have for the last two years—last year I shall say. My fifteenth year was an eventful and a happy era in my life. I shall ever look back with fond regret to it. In looking over a journal I commenced the last day of my fifteenth year which I continued for some time, I find that I was then rooming with Bec Lasnette, Lou Harris and Amanda Jones. Both Lou and Amanda are now married, Lou to Lavoisier Lamar, Amanda to Mr Foote a Methodist minister who is stationed this year in Vineville.

While I write I have my writing desk on my lap. I am sitting on the "trundle bed" by my table which is in the middle of the room. Saturday Joe Lou cousin Emma and I cleaned up our room and took up the carpet and scoured the floor. The "trundle bed" we placed by the fire place but yesterday and this morning it was cold enough for a fire. . . . This morning I rose quite early even before the day bell rung and attended prayers. I afterwards dressed for the day wearing my black silk dress with Swiss apron trimmed with yellow with white neck ribbon. I read over a lesson in Mental Philosophy last night. This morning Lissie Myrick was in here until 8 when I attended Mr Smith's recitation. The lesson did not come to me. I was talking with Anna Jeffers and did not prepare the Astronomy so I stayed away from recitation and from 11 to 12 I was in Fannie Floyd's room talking to her. She had been down town this morning. Mrs Desson sent me word she had my bonnet for me which she had brought on from New York.

Saturday, April 5, 1851   . . . I will now write what occurred yesterday evening. After dinner I carried Mat Oliver a sweet potatoe. As I could not see her I gave a piece of it to Soph Bond. I was conversing with her on the step when Bettie Williams (Bless her soul) called me and we were promenading the passage together until two oclock. Our conversation was in reference to a secret society got up among the girls principally the seniors which I had not been invited to join. Bett came to give me an explanation which was perfectly satisfactory. When I returned from Mr [George W.] Stone's recitation Eugenia Tucker came in with a note for me. I found it was from the *Adelphian Society* as they style themselves unanimously soliciting I should join them. I returned a note *respectfully declining*. To have joined them I should have been thrown into too close communion with the girl I most dislike in college Leab Goodall. . . . After prayers I was on the step with the girls. When I returned Jule Thomas[32] gave a white rose to me as a birthday present. I was in her room after tea.

. . .

Tuesday, April 8, 1851 Mr Smith has excused the class from reciting since there are so few girls here. It rained very hard last night. Some of the girls say we had quite a storm but I was asleep and did not hear it. The streets are so very muddy this morning but few of the day scholars are here. . . . [Saturday evening] I went with [Anna Jeffers] down to get some candles, but did not get them. Coming back I found a number of the girls on the front steps, listening to Bell Fernandez who was playing on her guitar. And here I cannot refrain from expressing myself with reference to her wonderful beauty. At the same time I consider her style almost too cold and unimpassioned. She is indeed a beautiful girl. I have taken quite a fancy to her. I remained on the steps until tea. Afterwards I went in to class meeting. A number of girls were out—more than I have seen this term. *Leab Goodall* came in. I felt all those feelings of *hatred dislike* and *contempt* which I have been in the habit of feeling when I see her come over me. They obtained complete mastery over me and I left the class room. Came up and retired in a short time to bed. Rose Sunday morning and attended prayers I believe. . . . When I returned from church I assisted Cousin Emma in writing her composition and attempted to write mine. I could not fix my attention so I went down stairs on the front collonade. I was with Camilla most of the evening. . . . We had an exhortation from Mr Evans. Oh how I love that man! And a very good meeting. I knelt as a mourner but could get no rest. At last with an effort and oh it was such an effort, I rose, walked to Leab Goodall and called her by her name. She returned no answer. What a struggle it was to

---

32. Julia (Jule) Thomas, of Burke County, was the sister of J. Jefferson Thomas.

speak to her the second time. I did so however and said, "Leab will you consider me your friend and give me your hand?" She did so pressing mine tight as she gave me hers. Oh how completely relieved I felt. It appeared as though a burden had rolled from off my soul.[33]

After prayer meeting I conversed with Leab for a short time. We promised a mutual explanation. I went to her room for the first time since she has been rooming there and she gave me a rose for myself and one for Joe. . . . I studied my Astronomy a little and then I finished my composition and wrote it off. The subject was "The Pulpit the Press and Schoolroom, Efficient Agents for the Morals of the People." It is the last composition I had to write this term until my graduating composition. I have not selected a subject for it yet. . . .

.   .   .   .

Thursday, April 10, 1851   On Tuesday night, I attended Prayer Meeting in the Parlour. Bishop Capers[34] exhorted us. Mr Evans was prevented by an engagement down town from being up here. I was very sorry indeed. Nevertheless we had a blessed and glorious conversion of souls to God. The first of the meeting everything appeared cold. Mr Myers rising made this proposition. That those who from that night intended living for God to kneel. Many knelt. Mollie Capers grew happy and shouted the praises of her maker. Laura Chew, Georgia Pope, Lissie Henderson, Lissie Jones, Rosa Lauton Ria Easterling, Bettie Williams and Leab Goodall were happy. Some of them had found a Saviour for the first time. Others were reclaimed sheep which had strayed from the fold of the "Good Shepperd." Again I felt cold and indifferent. Yesterday morning I rose early and attended Prayers. Went to Breakfast wearing my chamelion silk and red green baraishe[35] saque with pink neck rib-

---

33. When Gertrude's cousin Emma Lamkin enrolled at Wesleyan, she first roomed with Gertrude and her roommates, including Leab Goodall. Because Emma was several years younger, the other girls resented her and difficulties developed.

34. Methodist bishop William Capers of Charleston, S.C. His daughter, Mollie, was in Gertrude's class.

35. Gertrude refers to barege, a popular fabric for dresses. She spelled it as it sounded—bareshe, baraish, and, finally, barege.

bon, belt and cuffs. Joe was sick in bed all day yesterday. I stayed with her during the nine oclock recitation. . . .

Friday, April 12 [11], 1851   What a change a very great change has taken place in my every feeling. Yesterday I felt that although I had repented of my sins I was still unpardoned. In fact, I did not feel certain with reference to the state of my feelings. I doubted. Now thank Heaven I feel certain of my acceptance with God. How delightful is the thought! How transporting! How rapturous. How divine. What a change. Can I ever doubt the goodness of my God, of my Saviour? Last night we had another prayer meeting. Mr Evans was here and oh! we had a glorious meeting—

It is now after eleven. I will write on— We had a glorious manifestation of the goodness of God last night. Eugenia Tucker, Georgia Bryan, Bell Fernandez, Matt Clements, George Tucker, Mary Parish, Lissie Buford, Virginia Brown, Sallie Pierce, Mag Murphy all obtained religion. Cousin Emma too thinks she has obtained the "Pearl of great price." . . . Joe Freeman and Ella Pierce prayed very hard last night, still they do not feel their sins forgiven. I am so anxious for their conversion. I dearly very dearly love Joe and take a very great interest in her. . . .

After dinner the same day.   . . . While I was in [Fannie Floyd's room] someone came in telling me Ria Easterling was *happy*. I went in to see and remained hearing the girls sing until eleven. I had not read over my lesson. Still I went down to recitation. As it happened he did not come to our bench. After we had recited I asked to be excused and came up and commenced writing again. . . . Then I went into Bettie William's room—where I remained until dinner. A great many of the girls were in there. Joe and Ella were both seeking religion. Daughter and Rosa Solomon knelt. Sue Evans was up here also. She knelt too. Mrs Smith came in and then Mr Smith came in and prayed with us. I went to dinner. Talked with Mary Tucker on the subject of religion. How interested I feel for her. How anxious I am with reference to her spiritual welfare. . . . Before going over to Mr Stone's recitation to ask him to excuse me I went down to Daughter Solomon's room to see Bell Fernandez. She was perfectly happy lying on the bed shouting the praises of God. . . .

April the 16 [15], 1851   This is Tuesday evening. I have not written since Friday evening from various reasons one of which is that I have not been very well. I am absent from Mr Stone's recitation now because I do not feel well and will employ myself during the evening in writing my adventures since then. On Friday evening just as I finished writing I heard someone shouting. I closed my desk and went on down the passage to find out who it was. I was met on the way by one of the girls telling me Sue Evans had obtained religion in the recitation room. Going down to Daughter Solomon's room I found Anna Jeffers and Laura Chew and some other girls shouting together. Ella Pierce and Joe Freeman came in and remained for a short time. Joe soon after went out. Ella appeared to [be] some what affected. I came up for Joe but there appeared to be but little feeling on her side. I never in all my life saw such a sight as that. Joe standing apparently unheeding Ella's prayers to kneel. Finding Joe invincible, Ella rose, and then they both stood Ella declaring she would give up her search for religion if Joe would not go on with her. I whispered to Joe to kneel for Ella's sake if not for her own. The appeal was successful. She slowly sank upon her knees with her arms round Ella's waist imploring her to kneel with her. But Joe did all this with *such* a countenance so cold, so indifferent, no wonder it had no effect. She only knelt impelled by the wish to oblige Ella and be of benefit to her. The girls all appeared very much excited. All were shouting and praying and making a good deal of noise when someone said Mr Myers was coming up. Laura Chew commenced blessing him when he very *politely* requested us all to come to our rooms. I never saw a sett of girls scatter so in all my life. They all stopped shouting immediately and left the room. . . .

Thursday, April 17, 1851   While I was writing Tuesday evening Pa came. Of course no more writing was done that evening. . . . Tuesday morning I did not attend Prayers. I went to Mr Smith's recitation in Mental Philosophy but the lesson did not come to me. I did not attend Dr Ellison's[36] recitation in Astronomy or Mr Stone's recitation in Natural Philosophy. I was writing after four oclock. Joe and Ella were lying on the bed when someone knocked and Dr Ellison came in and told me *Pa* was down stairs. How perfectly delighted I was. Down stairs I ran and was welcomed by My Darling father. I went for Cousin Emma and then for Laura Chew and

---

36. William H. Ellison was at that time president of Wesleyan Female College. Edward H. Myers succeeded him the following year.

Mary Parish and Jule Thomas.[37] Soon after I dressed to go down to the Lanier House with Pa. I wore my black silk dress and lace cape. We walked down there, that is, cousin Emma Pa and I, sat in the Parlour a few minutes until we were carried to our rooms. Pa came in and sat with us until late. . . . I sat in the parlour for some time after tea. Pa came in. We then went to our rooms where I found some fruit. He had bought me a *box* of raisins, almonds, Brazilnuts, oranges and a pine apple cheese. Yesterday morning I awoke quite early and dressed. I took breakfast with the passengers and rode up to college in the omnibus with Pa. He gave me ten dollars which came just in the right time. . . .

. . . .

Wednesday, April 23, 1851   Some time has gone by since I wrote in this journal. The nine oclock bell is ringing while I write. I attended Dr Ellison's recitation on Friday at eleven oclock. As I expected he did not call on me. I do not recollect what engaged my attention from then until two oclock when I attended Mr Stone's recitation. Oh yes I do remember now. Ella Pierce was still sick in here. She was expecting her father[38] so we cleaned up the room as nice as we could and arranged everything for him, however he did not come. After Mr Stone's recitation I came up and was talking until four as I had prepared the History lesson before— I recited in Mr Myers' recitation— The Senior class were requested to remain in the Chapel after school for the Valedictory and Saludatory to be given out. The former was given to Bessie Hines. We all voted and Lou Banks received 16 votes and Sue Evans eleven votes. So of course Lou had the saludatory— To our very great surprise Lou declined the honour, saying she had particular reasons for doing so. Of course we were under the necessity of voting again when Sue Evans received every vote except two, one for Mary Evans and the other for Sophia Bond. . . .

I saw a good many people pass by at Mrs Blake's.[39] Among them were Mr and Mrs Logan, Bill Roberts, Rolland Chapman, the

---

37. All four girls were from the Augusta area.

38. Ella Pierce was the daughter of Methodist bishop George F. Pierce, the first president of Georgia Female College.

39. Gertrude was having tea with Mrs. Blake, the grandmother of a school friend, in the Vineville neighborhood of Macon.

editor, and Mike Nisbet[40] whom I have not seen in some time and by the by I heard some news this evening—heard Mike Nisbet was to fight a duel on my account with someone. All an idle report of course still such is the version of the tale in Burke County. . . .

Thursday, April 24, 1851 . . . After reading Sunday evening I went to sleep. When I awoke I found Lou and cousin Emma had made up a fire and were cooking cheese. We all played and talked enjoying ourselves until late in the evening when I dressed wearing plain white swiss and my black silk mantillette, expecting to go down town to church. . . . [Monday] I came up and wrote off some subjects to hand in to Mr Myers. They were— "What subject should a young lady write on when she graduates?" "Adversity favourable to the development of Genius." "The source of all great thoughts is sadness." "The keystone of thy mind, to give thy thoughts solidity—To bind them as in rock, to fix them as a world in its sphere is to learn from the word of the Lord, to drink from the fountain of his wisdom." The latter I think I shall take.[41] . . .

Tuesday morning when Charlotte came in to empty the water Lou asked her how Mrs Ellison's baby was? The reply was that it was *dead*. Lou and cousin went down to prayers. The roll was not called. They came back and told us that we were to have holiday. . . . [After dinner] I asked Dick Holmes to go with me to see the corpse of Mrs Ellison's baby. It was lying in the parlour with two white rose buds on each side of its little head. While in there I took up a volume of Dr [Henry] Bascomb's sermons and became very much interested in a sermon on "The Judgment." . . .

Wednesday, May 7, 1851 Nearly two weeks have passed since I have written. I had no idea how swiftly time flies! I remember last Thursday evening Dr Ellison gave out the announcement we would have holiday on Friday as that had been the day appointed by the Methodist conference for fast. There has been and is now quite a

---

40. Mike Nisbet, a young doctor in Macon, Ga., was mentioned frequently in the journal during Gertrude's senior year. He visited her in Augusta and, as later revealed, was a serious suitor.

41. The following appears in the program of the Wesleyan Female College commencement day exercises, July 11, 1851: "Learn from the Book of the Lord; drink from the well of his wisdom. Miss Ella G. Clanton."

revival of religion in our church down town. Sunday before last I attended church. I wore my white embroidered Swiss dress in the morning and my new white dress in the afternoon— I walked with Camilla Boston both times. . . .

Thursday, May 8, 1851 . . . Monday I decided upon the subject of my composition it is from Tupper,[42] a great favorite of mine. Thursday night I know we all attended Church. I think Mr Stone preached. His text was "My spirit shall not always strive with you." I again walked with Camilla Boston and slept with her that night. Neither of us attended prayers and did not rise until after breakfast. There was church down town so I came up and prepared for Church. I wore my corded Swiss dress. I tried to fast but could not. I eat a little biscuit and some molasses before starting and when I came back eat dinner as usual. I was reading in the Bible until late and then Mr Evans came up and gave us a talk in the afternoon. Ginnie Parish and Laura Chew joined the Church. We attended "Love Feast" that night. A great many persons gave their experience. More gentleman however than ladys. Mr Rogers said that "he had been upon the mountain top" exhorted the Church to "come from out the valley and let their lights shine before them." I was particularly struck with one expression he made use of, He said "Brethern some of you may die and reach Heaven before I do but when you get there just tell them I am coming." . . .

Friday, May 9, 1851 Monday morning I went over to Mr Myers' lecture in Bible. As I was returning Moll Evans told me they had an excellent meeting at church Sunday night and that Dr M Nisbet appeared to be very much excited—or rather affected. . . . Several of us received invitations to attend the Ball given in July in Princeton New Jersey. *Jeff Thomas*[43] sent them I think. That night we had an excellent meeting. I wore my black silk dress and Lissie Myrick's white Crape shawl. Mr Myers was very happy and shouted. L was there again. . . . Joe had been sick but she got up and went to

---

42. Martin Farquhar Tupper, author and philosopher. His *Proverbial Philosophy*, from which Gertrude quotes frequently, was published between 1838 and 1842 and was popular reading in that day.

43. J. Jefferson Thomas, of Burke County, graduated from Princeton University in 1851. He and Gertrude Clanton were married in 1852.

Church. Joe and Camilla walked with me. I begged Joe to go up to be prayed for but she would not be persuaded. In the course of the evening we heard Hettie Solomon had religion. Then Joe said she would go. We heard them shouting and singing. I went with Joe. Just as I got up both singing and shouting ceased. I never did feel just so awkward. I could not find Hettie and upon turning round found *Joe* had gone back to her seat. . . . Tuesday evening between three and four I listened to a funeral preached over an old woman who died in the night before—Aunt Margaret. It was preached by a negro man and was excellent. Wednesday evening I received the harshest reproof I ever did receive, from *Mr Stone* at that. It is not necessary to mention the particulars as they will never be forgotten. . . .

Tuesday, May 13, 1851 . . . [Friday] After school I received a box with cousin Emma's and my dresses. Ma sent me a beautiful scarf and my blue tissue dress to have made here. She also sent one ready made—a very handsome blue dress and a pink calico dressing gown—besides other things. Ma wrote me a letter and sent it in the box. . . . Sunday morning I attended Church. I wore my new blue dress—yellow sash— white neck ribbon and my new bonnet. The church was completely crowded. L was there. Mr Evans preached. . . . Some of us went down in the afternoon to hear Mr Myers preach. It was excessively warm. He preached from a portion of the Parable of The Prodigal Son. L was not there. In the afternoon when I returned from church I changed my dress wearing a white. Sallie Simms and I walked together. We sat in the gallery. Mike Nisbet sat just below. The children made a great deal of noise shouting and screaming. . . .

. . .

2. The Belle: Courtship and Engagement

My thoughts! Write those!
—March 7, 1852

[The first page of the following volume is blotched, dog-eared, and torn. The first eight or ten pages were written on January 5 and 6, but with frequent flashbacks dating from mid-December. Gertrude wrote, "I have been writing off and on this week." I have placed the entries in chronological order here for the benefit of the reader and to avoid confusion.]

Christmas eve of the year 1851 What a charm there has always been in Christmas associated as it has been from earliest childhood with the pleasant idea of Holiday poppers and Santa Claus. The charms derived from these sources are wanting now. My school days are over. The dignity appertaining to a young lady just released from the thraldom of a boarding school would prevent the taking pleasure in the shooting of Poppers and &c—even were I rid of my unpleasant headache from which I am now suffering and have been for some time. The idea of Santa Claus coming down the chimney which I once so firmly believed has been done away with by the addition of years and acquisition of superior (Can I call it so?) knowledge— So this Christmas eve I lift[ed] off the habit of expecting him and confined myself to giving presents to Mamie Brother [Buddy] Cora and Holt.[1] Every succeeding age shows some wonder. Every succeeding generation grows wiser and the children even have no confidence in our dear time honoured Santa Claus. I have been prevented by severe indisposition leaving the house today. . . .

---

1. Nathaniel Holt Clanton, Gertrude's baby brother (fifteen years younger), was born while she was at Wesleyan.

Christmas night, 1851 Here I am writing in the nursery— Ma is in bed sick— I am in rather a bad humour. I had promised Jule Thomas to visit her tomorrow. Received a note from her today saying she would be up for me and would expect me. Pa thinks I am too unwell. I however don't happen to agree with him— I suppose I must "yield to the powers that be" though unwillingly— This morning I was aroused by hearing the voice of Amanda calling upon Sister Anna for a "Christmas Gift." The children soon came up stairs rejoicing over their presents which we had arranged for them the night previous on their table. This morning Dr Dugas[2] called again. He found me in the sitting room lying on the sofa with a warm brick to my face. I have not dressed all day, wearing a dressing gown and saque. There was no company here today. My dinner consisted of turnip soup with a dessert of Sylabub and Charlotte Roose— Arranged Co's play house for her before dinner and then went up stairs in the attic and arranged Mamie's play house— Then arranged my things for visiting Jule— All to no purpose. . . .

Friday, December 26, 1851 I rose and dressed not expecting to have the pleasure of visiting the country.[3] A visit from which I had expected to derive much pleasure. Jule and her father[4] dined with us. After dinner Anna Jeffers called by when I learned she intended going down with Jule. I during that time was in a state of suspense. After some reflection Pa concluded I could go. I immediately hastened up stairs, hastily packed a trunk and soon was down stairs.

Jule Anna and I rode in one carriage while Gen Thomas preceded us in his buggy. Our ride was very pleasant to me. The road being entirely new and the scenery sometimes quite romantic. We arrived late. The moon was not shining so instead of indulging in a moonlight ride and conversation, as a "Dernier Resort" we took the stars as a topic. Each of us naming "a bright particular star." It was quite late when the carriage turned up the broad and lengthy avenue leading to the house. The lights were gleaming through the trees. And above all when we arrived there was Gen Thomas to bid us a hearty welcome. Jeff soon came out to shake hands. After

---

2. Louis A. Dugas was an Augusta physician.
3. Gertrude refers to the Thomas home in Waynesboro, located in Burke County, Ga. Burke was the next county south of Richmond County.
4. Gen. Joseph Darius Thomas.

going to a room and brushing our hair we descended to the parlour where we were introduced to Mr West, a young gentleman and acquaintance and roommate of Mr Thomas who was spending vacation with him. Also to Pinckney[5] a younger brother of Jules— Joe[6] and her [Jule's] mother[7] soon came in when we went in to tea. The evening passed off quite pleasantly. We retired at a late hour— When we woke the next morning we found that it was raining which continued to be the case all day. Although we did not leave the house the day passed off quickly. We were conversing, playing cards or backgammon all day.

The next morning (Sabbath) we took a long ride. I rode in a two horse buggy with Mr Jeff Thomas while Jule rode in a one horse buggy with Mr West. Anna and Joe took a ride on horseback. We all smoked a cigar after dinner in the parlour. Late in the evening we took a long walk. I with Joe. Anna with Jeff. Jule with West. The next morning (Monday) Jeff and Mr West left for Augusta. The former carrying a note to Sister Anna telling her that I had concluded to remain until next day. After breakfast Gen T would have us take a ride so Joe and I started off on horseback taking a very long and delightful tour through the woods. Jule and Anna rode with Pinck in the buggy. Late that evening we started for a walk. As we opened the gate we saw Mr Thomas returning from Augusta with a young gentleman whom upon joining us in our walk he introduced as Mr Law "a cousin of the Misses Barrett." After tea I told the fortunes (by card) of one or two members of the party. We then played "Magic Music" and afterwards Old Maid and Smoot. I had the signal good or ill fortune of bestowing whiskers on Mr Law— Nature having plentifully supplied him with mustache and goatee. The next morning (Tuesday) after breakfast we started to Augusta. I rode up with Jeff in the buggy. Jule rode in the carriage with Mr Law. Anna rode with Joe until we were nearly to Augusta when he turned off in an opposite direction.

---

5. J. Pinckney Thomas, a younger brother of Jefferson and Julia, later married Gertrude's sister, Mary (Mamie) Clanton.

6. Joseph Thomas, another younger brother. There were six Thomas children: J. Jefferson (Jeff), Julia, J. Pinckney (Pinck), Joseph (Joe), Robert (Bob) and A. Jackson (Jack).

7. Louisa (Lulah) Kettles (sometimes spelled Kittles) Thomas, wife of Gen. Joseph D. Thomas.

We arrived here before dinner. Jule remained with me until Friday. Wednesday was an unpleasant day. In the afternoon Sister Anna and I went to ride with Jule going down to Bessman's and Tobin's garden and &c. After returning we sent up a note to Jeff inviting him down to tea. He came and remained until after nine. A Buffalo came by that night. Something quite new. We went out in the Piazzi to see it and ascertain the cause of such an uproar. New Year's morning we found it was raining again. I was busy for some time after breakfast writing invitations to some young gentleman and ladies whom I wished to meet Jule here that night. After dinner I had a large fire made up in my room. I then dressed for the evening. Ellen Bryson had company the same evening. Several sent in the excuse to me of a previous engagement to her. Upon the whole we enjoyed ourselves very much. They all left about 12 oclock that night. The party consisted of about 20 or 25 persons. The next morning Friday the 2 of January Jule and I went up town riding for the purpose of buying a dress. She bought one in at Grey's. Her father met us there. The carriage had been brought up for her. . . .

Saturday, January 10, 1852 . . . Last night the bell rung and Johny Coleman came for Mamie. Sister A was lighting the camphine lamp and I brushing up the hearth when upon looking round to my great surprise Dr Nisbet entered the room. The night previous he had mentioned that he would call but I did not expect him so early and his name was not announced. He remained until a short time after ten— Together with other things I learned how much confidence can be placed in vows of unchanging friendship and love— oh—but I have promised— I will say no more but that she—the friend of my early days—[8] . . .

. . .

Monday, January 26, 1852 . . . Wednesday night Jan 14 Jimmie Lamkin called. A few minutes after Mr Dawson came. Then Dr Nisbet and soon after Mr Bones. I had the two latter to entertain. The Horse racing was going on that week consequently there was a great many strangers in our city. Thursday night Jan 15 I attended a

---

8. Gertrude refers to a breach of confidence by her college friend, Mat Oliver Wood, concerning Gertrude's feelings toward Mike Nisbet.

party at Mrs John Moore's. A very pleasant one. I went at the same time with Tom & Martha Phinizy.[9] Pa and sister Anna. The next day Saturday afternoon Jan 17 I was out for a short time with Cousin M[ary] A[nn] Danforth[10] and sister Anna— I saw Dr Nisbet for a short time. I suppose he left Augusta that afternoon. . . .

Monday 19th all day I was busy writing invitations to our party.[11] On Tuesday 20th we sent them out. In the afternoon of that day I went in the carriage taking Jane Phinizy and Mamie with me and sent in the invitations by Edmund. . . . The firemen had a new engine christened *Augusta* the night of our party. Also an alarm of fire at the City Hall late in the afternoon. I wore my white satin. There were near three hundred invitations issued. That morning I received a letter from Jule Thomas. I enjoyed myself very much that night. It is scarcely worth while writing anything concerning the party as the occurences (some of them at least) are too indelibly impressed upon memory ever to be effaced— I went in to the supper table with Mr Thomas. How *very* pleasant and agreeable he is! I did not retire until after four oclock Friday morning Jan 23. . . .

.   .   .

Thursday, February 19, 1852   Near two weeks have elapsed since writing in my journal and in those two weeks how much has happened. I find that I cannot distinctly recollect everything which has happened. That day (Monday the 9) after writing I wrote a letter to Fannie Floyd. At night I commenced one to Isabel [Morrison] Harrington when the bell rung and Mr Thomas was announced. I had been feeling quite unwell all day but dressed that afternoon so I was prepared to see him. Sister A would not come in. I passed *quite* a *pleasant evening*. He made an engagement to call the next

---

9. The John Phinizy home was next door to the Clanton's residence in Augusta, and the two families were close friends through the years. The Phinizy house is still standing on Greene Street.

10. Most southern families recognized broad networks of kin—cousins, aunts, and uncles spreading across several generations. Precise identification of someone who is labeled "cousin" is sometimes difficult, often impossible. Mary Ann Danforth was related through the Luke or Reid family and was probably the first cousin of Mary Luke Clanton. Her mother was Lissie Bridges.

11. Gertrude's debut in Augusta society.

Wednesday evening. Tuesday all day I was feeling very badly. Wednesday all of us went up to hear the Swiss Bell Ringers. Pa went with us. I don't think the Ringers exerted themselves very much as there were few there that night. After tea Mr Thomas called. He remained until near eleven oclock and requested permission to bring Mr Wynn round. I told him yes and he left. . . .

Monday, February 23, 1852 Thursday afternoon Mrs Phinizy called. While she was here Miss Singleton Mildred and Ginne Coombs called for me to walk. We went down to Bessman's garden. Then went up on Greene Street as far as the Jewish Synagogue. Turned into Broad Street—came on down as far as Cook's Corner then crossed went up on the same street as far as the corner of Dunham's and Blakely's crossed came on down as far as Cook's corner and then turned into Greene Street and came home. I was so completely exhausted I put on my dressing gown and when Mr Dawson called after tea I excused myself. . . .

The people of Augusta give a very large party tonight in honor of the Washington's birthday the 22 which came on yesterday (Sunday). They invited a company from Columbia [County] which came up on Saturday evening. The company here went over to receive them. They all marched up town dressed in uniform presenting quite an imposing appearance. There was quite a large concourse of persons [illegible] on the occasion. I was *particularly* successful that afternoon. After Martha and I returned home we took a short ride in the carriage carrying Jane Phinizy Cora and Holt with us. After returning we walked up town on Greene Street two squares and returned. After tea we were all sitting quite quietly in the sitting room when Mr Thomas called. I did not expect him to come again this week. He spent several hours until ½ after ten oclock which time I found very pleasant. . . .

The soldiers from Columbia marched to the Methodist Church dressed in uniform yesterday. I attended the Presbyterian church yesterday morning— Pa was there—went with sister A and cousin E. We had a sermon from Mr Parsons on the benefit of the tract society which he represents. In the afternoon Sister A. Brother, Pa and I went to the Methodist Church— We sat quite high up. The same gentleman preached. Selected a different text but preached the same sermon very nearly. I was sitting in the front piazza until tea and afterwards was conversing out in the Piazza for some time with Pa. Came in with an assured and lightened heart with regard to one important subject. . . .

. . .

Tuesday, March 2, 1852   Several rather eventful days have gone by since I wrote last. . . . [On Thursday] afternoon Mr Thomas called and left me a beautiful Boquet which I used at the party that night. It was decidedly the handsomest one in the room. Late in the afternoon I commenced dressing for the party. I wore my white tarleton which fit me very prettily. . . . I went into the supper room with Mr Sturgess and indeed saw more of him that night than anyone else. After supper I was conversing with Mr Evans Mr Whatley and Mr Hews to whom I was introduced by Mr Thomas. Mr Hews' mother died that night while he was at the party. I came home with Mr Thomas, Sister Anna with Mr Dawson Pa with Mildred. I had a delightful walk home.

The next morning I was not up until quite late. I was reading *Ravenscliffe*[12] when I received a note from Mr Sturgess requesting my company to Mamselle Parodi's first concert. I returned an answer in the affirmative. It had so much the appearance of rain I scarcly expected to go but Ma and Sister A went with Pa. Mr Sturgess brought a carriage for me and we rode up together. The rest rode back in our carriage. I had quite a pretty Boquet given me by Mr Sturgess. . . . Saturday morning I received a note from Mr Thomas requesting me to go to [Parodi's] second and last concert with him that night. I did not send an answer until the afternoon. I asked Pa's advice at dinner. He said yes if the weather was favourable which it was not. Mr Thomas called directly after tea but we concluded not to go. He has heard both Parodi and Patti[13] sing in New York and Philadelphia. So he remained here until after ten oclock. . . .

This morning the students graduated.[14] Dr Wynn read the valedictory. Mr Thomas wrote me a note requesting me to go with

---

12. *Ravenscliff* (1851), by Anne Marsh Caldwell.

13. Teresa Parodi and Adelina Patti were celebrated operatic sopranos of the day.

14. The Augusta Medical College, founded in 1829, was built in 1835 on

him.[15] I answered yes if the weather would admit. I then commenced a letter to Fannie Floyd and had written three pages when Mr Thomas called. It was then half past ten. He remained until twelve oclock. It was too damp for me to go to the Masonic Hall with him. He leaves with his father for the country this evening and does not expect to return until Monday. . . .

.   .   .

Sunday, March 7, 1852   I am comfortably arranged sitting by my table upon which my writing desk is lying. In the center of my table lies my Bible a present from Ma Christmas. A vase of flowers (rather withered now) is by me. Near the corner is my large dictionary supported on a History. Several other volumes comprise the articles which are arranged on my table. How delightful I find my room. Liberty to leave the noise and confusion and retiring here indulge in meditation or permit fancy to roam, tinging everything with that elysian hue which "Truth dispels with his rod in disenchanting youth." And how pleasant those day dreams are. To live in a world of one's own. A world created by our own imagination. Ah! Me! I wonder shall I ever cease to take pleasure in this castle building? An occupation which I have always so dearly loved. A Journal—Defined to be a book in which one writes their thoughts and actions. If such be the case this volume of manuscript will only have partially have accomplished the purpose of a journal. My thoughts! Write those! and yet— Is it because I fear to write them? And yet is it pleasant to have our very inmost thoughts exposed to the eye of a careless critic? for how am I [to] know by whose eye this page may be scanned. No! I will continue as I have begun. And yet the temptation sometimes to write the feelings which agitate my heart is almost irresistible.

Yesterday morning I was in the house it having so much the appearance of rain. I was engaged in reading Lippard's *Legends of the Revolutionary War*,[16] a work which I bought in New York and

---

Telfair Street at the corner of Washington. The building still stands and is now the home of the Augusta Council of Garden Clubs and the Augusta Genealogical Society.

15. Jefferson Thomas was reading (studying) medicine at that time.

16. *Legends of the American Revolution, or Washington and His Generals* (1847), by George Lippard.

one which I prise very much indeed. Near dinner I dressed with the intention of going out in the afternoon. While I was dressing Pa came in giving us news which in a moment gave cause for great excitement. He informed us that Bud had fallen in the River and had caught to a ring and thus sustaining himself had screamed until a negro man had come to his assistance. Dear little fellow! Oh! what a very narrow escape. Oh God how I thank thee for the preservation of his life. How uncertain is life and how surely certain is death. Oh Heavenly father I pray thee that I may live in the constant preperation for the world to come. When I look upon my dear little brother the tear of gratitude and affection rises to my eye. As much as we love him we all felt that Pa acted exactly as he should have done in giving him a severe whipping.[x] . . . [Note at top of page: "[x] Pa had positively forbid Buddy's going to [the] river. My mother's heart bids me say that I should not have punished him—Jan 6th 1879."]

·   ·   ·

Thursday, March 18, 1852   No one has called so I can retire early. Yesterday morning I rose quite late and eat no breakfast. Sister and I went out in the street together. I bought me a baraish delaine, the dress, 10 yds costing 4.50. Directly after dinner I had a conversation with Pa concerning an all important subject. It ended *rather* satisfactorily. . . . I then went out in the carriage with Ma and Aunt Lamkin. They were shopping— I stopped at Mrs Luthringer's to know if she had returned from Charleston and brought my crape shawl which I had sent down by her to have washed. Mr Thomas assisted me from the carriage. He is boarding at the house of Mrs Bens and is reading medicine with Dr Dearing.[17] After tea Mr Thomas called and remained until eleven oclock. He gave me a beautiful acorn with a thimble enclosed formed of ivory. Quite a hint to learn to sew. I think I shall improve upon it. I was very much amused at all of them guessing what was in it this morning. Mr Thomas made me a promise last night which I sincerely hope he *will* keep. . . .

---

17. William E. Dearing, a physician, was mayor of Augusta in the 1850s. He organized the Wheeler Scouts, a cavalry company for home defense, during the Civil War.

Monday, March 22, 1852 I have but a few moments since returned from the grave yard where I have been upon a sadly serious business. But to commence and go on in order. . . .

Tuesday morning. I was interrupted last evening while writing. . . . [Sunday afternoon] when I returned I found Ma quite sick. She had been taken while we were at church. We sent for Dr Joe Eve.[18] He came and remained until three oclock [A.M.]. I was up until five the next morning when I lay down on the sofa in the sitting room and slept till after seven. Ma being so ill Sister [Anne] and I remained in the nursery. About three Ma gave birth to an infant boy but mortality ne're gained immortality for he never breathed. Early yesterday morning I arose for the purpose of seeing to breakfast as I now occupy the responsible situation of housekeeper in lieu of Ma. After giving out dinner I was engaged in conversation till near dinner when I dressed for the day. . . .

Although death is at seasons and places solemn yet never having known and loved this child I could not lament it as I would otherwise have done. After returning I took my writing desk and seating myself upon a footstool in the small balcony wrote for some time in my Journal. After tea I intended writing but Mr Thomas called. He remained until after ten oclock. Thinks of leaving off the practice or rather the study of medicine for another year. . . .

. . .

Sunday, April 4, 1852 [at Aunt Lamkin's] Although quite sleepy it is my birthday and I must write. I am now eighteen and my feeling is regret—sincere regret. The retrospective glance which I cast upon the past year presents to my view only a year of great happiness—as unallowed happiness as it is possible to conceive of. . . . My first thought was of my present "beau ideal" when I awoke this morning. The next that it was my birthday. . . .

. . .

---

18. Brothers Joseph and Edward Eve and their cousin, Paul F. Eve, were physicians in Augusta and Richmond County. Gertrude most often refers to Joseph or Edward Eve.

Monday, April 19, 1852 . . . .The day after I returned from Aunt Lamkin's, (which was Saturday the 10th of April) I went out in the street riding and had the pleasure of receiving a bow from Jeff. I bought me a very pretty black lace bonnet with purple and straw colored flowers. In the afternoon Sister and Aunt L went up to Mr King's funeral. I was in conversation with cousin Berry [Clanton] when the bell rung and Mr Thomas called. Cousin Berry soon left. Jeff called to tell me he was to leave for the country that afternoon but would return on Monday. After he left I went up town with Martha Phinizy where we met Mildred [Eve] and Ginnie Coombs. . . . Monday (April 12th) was a day of excitement as it was the day of the election for Mayor. Mr John Phinizy Pa Mr Kitchens Dr Dearing and Mr Phillips were the candidates. Dr Dearing was elected. Phillips received only one vote. In the afternoon of that day cousin Emma Cora and I went down to Tobin's garden for some ice cream. . . . Tuesday Gen Thomas dined with us. I felt quite embarrassed at the idea of meeting him yet when I did so I was perfectly calm and composed. I attended to the arrangement of dinner and sat at the head of the table. After dinner Mrs Clark and Mrs Skinner called. Gen Thomas left soon after. I then came up to sister Anna's room and slept until late in the afternoon. Pa Aunt Sister A and cousin Emma went to hear the Campbell minstrels. I went with Mr Thomas. I was not particularly pleased with the performance. Yet I enjoyed my walk home very much. . . .

.   .   .

Saturday, May 1, 1852 What a beautiful bright May day is this. Rather warm but gloriously beautiful. The type of our sunny climes. Thursday afternoon I had retired to my room undressed and commenced reading when Ace Chapman and Geo[rge] Jones called. I dressed and went in to see them. They remained late. After their leaving I commenced reading again and then dressed for the wedding. I wore a new salmon coloured silk which fitted beautifully. Cousin Berry walked up there with us. He left the next morning for home so we bid him "good bye" there at the foot of the steps. I enjoyed myself very much at the party. When we arrived the ceremony was being performed. We stood in the passage. Dr Carter handed me a chair so Miss Ginnie Moore and I stood up in them so had an excellent opportunity of seeing all that was to be seen. It was a conversational party and quite pleasant. Immediately upon entering the room I saw Mr Thomas. He was conversing with Sallie Adams. I was in conversation with Dr Phinizy,[19] Tom Roberts, Mr Whatley, Mr Evans and Mr Hews. I was with the latter some time promenading. I was then conversing with James Gould when Mr Thomas came up. I was conversing and promenading with him some time. Then Dr Phinizy and Tom Morgan. The latter I went up to the supper table with. Mattie Wilde and Fannie Smythe sang and played on the piano. We left soon after. The carriage was sent for us but sister walked home with Mr Dawson. I with Jeff. . . .

·   ·   ·

Tuesday, May 4, 1852   Susan has not yet finished cleaning of my room as she has been assisting Annie in her search for a diamond ring which she has misplaced. Its having been a present from Aunt Lamkin she prises it very much. Consequently its loss causes her great anxiety. I rose late this morning. The rain of last night has cooled the atmosphere and all things looked revived and refreshed. The last few days have been quite sultry. Holt is much better this morning. Pa handed me a letter this morning. I noticed it was post marked Augusta and opening it and noticing the signature I found it was from ——— A beautifully written letter—Expressive of feelings of deep devotion. I will write a short answer and return it to him as soon as possible—as of course there can be no reciprocation from me.[20] Sarah Blalock[21] has lost her beautiful child Georgia. Sister A went up yesterday morning. Ma sent the carriage in the afternoon. . . .

·   ·   ·

Monday, May 17, 1852   Here I am seated in my room engaged in a new avocation—teaching Mamie and Buddy. I just commenced this

---

19. Probably Thomas B. Phinizy.

20. Gertrude does not identify the writer, and any attempt to do so here would be mere speculation. She had several serious suitors in Augusta as well as Mike Nisbet of Macon.

21. Sarah Blalock was related to the Clantons through the Lukes. She may have been the niece of Mary Luke Clanton and Elizabeth Luke Lamkin, the child of their deceased brother.

morning [and] am quite pleased. I will now hear Mamie's lesson in Geography and proceed. . . . I received a letter today from Leab Goodall five or six pages long. . . . Leab Goodall is keeping a journal which she says "she will give to me when she dies." I have an idea of writing a series of tales. There are several girls I know whom I would make my heroines. I would change their names of course but in their historys there is so much romance that imagination would scarcely be called into requisition for there is so much romance in real life that "Truth is indeed stranger than fiction." Could we but look into the innermost scopes of the hearts of those around us how much would we see all undreamed of now. Could we read the hearts of those who under a calm exterior conceal an anguish too terrible to tell "how many would our pity share who now our envy bear." Mat Oliver as Mat Cameron. Leab Goodall as Henrietta Templeton. Joe Freeman as Lillian Lephi, Bec Lasnette as Fannie St Clair and dear Moll Capers bearing her own name will appear. I commenced the first tale this afternoon, having Mat Cameron as my heroine. I wonder when Jeff will be in town. Oh! I hope tomorrow or very soon. . . .

.   .   .

Sunday, May 30, 1852 Today has been the witness of an unusual pleasure. I have again heard dear Mr Myers preach. And oh! what a round of recollection rushed upon my mind as I heard his familiar voice! I could almost imagine myself in Macon again. The College girls in the Gallery and Mike, Reab and Dick Nisbet together with Ike Wilcox and Bill Roberts sitting on my right. Thursday (May 27) passed and Jeff did not come. I really don't know wether I was sorry or not. Singular! I know I was but we judge of others' feelings by our own and I supposed he would have come, had he wished to. He did not come. So I came to the conclusion he did not want to. After hearing the children [recite] their lessons I dressed and went up to see Mildred Eve. . . .

Friday morning (May the 28) I soon after breakfast commenced a letter to Bec Lasnette. Suspended it to hear the children's lessons. While thus engaged Jeff called. He called for both Annie and I. She sent in an excuse. As he was to call after tea he remained for a short time only. After dinner I finished the letter to Bec. It commenced and rained very hard. Had quite a thunder storm— I have since heard of an accident which occurred. A Gin factory which was in process of erection was blown down killing one white man and injuring one or two negros. Late in the afternoon I dressed up in my new white swiss dress and was sitting out in the Piazzi when Jeff and Dick Taylor of Athens rode by. . . . When I woke this morning I found it raining. During the cessation I went to S[unday] School. There were few at church. I of course was well entertained for Mr Myers preached. The sermon being over he had an opportunity of speaking to me— Wished me much happiness and &c—reminding me very much of my parting with himself and Mr Smith last commencement.

. . .

Wednesday, June 9, 1852 Oh this procrastinating disposition of mine! What will it lead me to— I had no idea of the flight of time since writing last. Monday (May 31st) I wrote a letter to Jule Thomas. On Tuesday June the 1st Pa handed me three letters. In one envelope were the cards for Mat Oliver's wedding with Mr Wood. . . . When I read the invitation to Mat's wedding I wept oh so bitterly. That dear Mat, how sad is the reflection that she is married. . . .

Thursday, June 10, 1852 This is the last night of our stay in town this season. This time next year and what changes will have taken place! Who can tell? Who can look into futurity and tell? But I will content myself. "Sufficient to the day is the evil thing." I will hope on this time next year and I will perhaps be married. Changes take place and perhaps the tie by which *we* are bound will be broken too. Heavens, the thought is unbearable indeed. I wonder if in June 1853 I will be as happy and as free from care as now. How strange the wish we have to look into the future! Which as Miss Landon tells us is so "dark drear and unfathomable." I have recently been reading the works of L E L.[22] What a spirit of melancholy pervades her whole works. I had read them and imagination ever ready had imagined her of a sad temperament that her whole life had been twinged with sorrow. There was one sad remembrance—one haunting thought which spread its frighting shade over all her joys. And

---

22. Letitia Elizabeth Landon, English poet and novelist, wrote under the initials L.E.L.

with her "Love had indeed (to use her own words) turned to dust in touching earth." What was my surprise to hear or read from excellent authority that Letitia Landon was naturally of a very gay, lively temperament. I was disappointed I confess. . . . This morning I don't know exactly what I did do. Ma was busy making a cake for Salina who is to be married tonight. She is staying at Mrs Boggs who gives her a large wedding.[23] She marries Mr Joseph Watts who belongs to Mr Warren. Malonia and Amanda are her attendants. Malonia wore a straw col tarlton and Amanda a white swiss dress. Susan a green barege. They all looked *very* nice indeed. . . .

Sunday, June 13, 1852 Again I am in the country [Columbia County] and oh how cool—how very pleasant it is. I am surprised at my reluctance in wishing to come up. Probably after a while I will again become wearied, find my life here too monotonous and wish for the varied life of a city and as it is I am unwilling to remain here all summer. I wish to travel some where. Perhaps we may spend a month at Madison Springs.[24] I have named our place Woodlawn. A pretty name I think and appropriate. We came up day before yesterday (Friday June the 11th). Early in the morning I was up and busy at work. The waggons were packed and started. Before we left Mr Hinse and cousin Mary called to see us. Also Martha and M. E. Phinizy. I sent Mamie out to get me something to bring up with me. I came up in the Buggy with Pa starting after twelve oclock and getting up here soon after three. Thus selecting the three very warmest hours in the day for our ride. Buddy started in the waggon but joined us on the way and drove almost all the way. The shrubbery has grown very much indeed. We have a very good vegatable garden fine orchard and a very excellent prospect for watermelons. The waggons and carriage arrived late in the afternoon. I immediately commenced my duties of housekeeping which I have assumed for this summer by giving out supper. . . .

Yesterday morning I was up early. Immediately after breakfast donning my bonnet and taking my basket I started to gather squashes beans and &c for dinner. I also gathered cucumbers for

---

23. Salina was a Clanton slave who apparently was "hired out," as was sometimes allowed.

24. Madison Springs near Athens, Ga., Catoosa Springs in north Georgia near Ringgold, and Indian Springs north of Macon were three popular summer resorts of affluent families. They are mentioned frequently in the journals.

making pickles. Then we arranged the parlour and did as much as possible toward the other rooms. I am now in my room, the one Sister A and I used last summer. She has the one adjoining. Yesterday afternoon I gathered some fruit. Co slept with me last night. It was very cold during the night and is rather so this morning for June. In one of the Macon papers I saw an announcement of Mat Oliver's marriage. Well it is over. Mat is indeed married! I cut the announcement out and intend preserving it. This morning I was up later than I was yesterday. Mamie and I gathered plumbs and pears and I added to the cucumbers which I have in brine. How very domestic I am! Quite a transformation really! I have a blank book which I bought which I intend for writing such quotations in as I may like.

. . .

Wednesday, June 30, 1852 Near two weeks have passed and I have neglected writing again in my journal. And now to take a retrospective view. On Friday the 18th we were quite busy, I dressed very carelessly and everything in the parlour disarranged when Ma remarked that a Buggy was driving up to the door. I looked out and saw Jeff in a two Horse buggy with a boy. I hastened up stairs to dress. My hair (quite an unusual thing) was parted in the middle. After as it appeared to me an interminable length of time I came down stairs. Amanda had arranged everything very nice. After dinner we were playing Backgammon and late in the afternoon I rode with him in his buggy.

Early the next morning Ma went up to see Aunty carrying all the children but Holt. Pa left after breakfast and Jeff, Sister Anna and I walked to Mrs Barnes' old spring, getting a sufficient quantity of Ticks. After returning he sat for some time and then left. I was quite unwell all day. . . . The evening we returned home [Sis Anne] and I walked to meet the children. They started school to Miss Holbrook that morning. She is teaching at the "Richmond Academy"[25] this year. We rode home in the waggon and got some wild

---

25. The Academy of Richmond County (Richmond Academy), a school for young gentlemen, was chartered in 1783. The old building on Telfair Street, next door to the Medical College, is today the home of the Augusta–Richmond County Museum.

cherrys. Yesterday afternoon I was reading undressed in my room when Billy Savage came from school with the news that Bud Jimmie had hurt himself. I went down in the carriage for him. On returning home Dr Thomas[26] was sent for who on examining his arm said *two* of the bones were broken and one out of place. He then dressed it. Mrs Heggie has just sent over to invite us to a barbecue to be given at her spring on Saturday.

Friday, July 9, 1852 Never have I found it so difficult to keep up a journal as this summer. Yet why? I cannot complain of my life being so dull—so monotonous. We have been up here exactly one month today and how short it appears. . . . Friday July the 2d was a very warm day. I expected Jeff up but had given up the idea of seeing him. I was seated on one of the posts to the Piazzi when he drove up. I jumped down and met him. After tea we were in conversation in the parlour till late. A little misunderstanding occurred. All my fault though. I made use of some remark jesting, and he looked up with such a look of sterness! It startled me! and for a moment my old feeling of pride o'ercame me and I felt the blood gush to my cheek. I had almost said too much. Thank Heaven! I did refrain and now I love him more, oh how much more than ever. Oh Love thou art formed of such strange contradictions! That one look accomplished so much. I respected him more then than I ever had before. I am so constituted that I *must* respect those whom I love. And I do so respect him. When first entering into my engagement with Jeff I loved him tis true.[27] Yet I did not attempt to analyse my feelings. I loved calmly and was undisturbed by fear till he called for Pa's permission. Until then I never had suspected how much I did love him. I had a short conversation with Pa just before he went into the room and then commenced my agonised feelings. Hurrying up to my own room I only gave vent to my feelings by prostrating myself upon my knees and burst into tears and prayers. Jeff then expected to graduate as an MD. That interview occurred in

---

26. Dr. Thomas was a physician in Columbia County and a neighbor of the Clantons. He was no relation to the Thomas family of Burke County.

27. Gertrude's first reference to being engaged. The understanding probably took place around mid-March to mid-April, when she wrote of her conversations with Pa, of Jeff calling on Pa, and of General Thomas dining with them.

Augusta. Although not a direct consent Pa's answer was satifactory. I did not write this in my journal then for I dared not.

During his last visit Jeff persuaded me to consent to marriage next fall. Saturday afternoon I took a long ride with him. We went out towards Bel Air. The next day we attended church at Abilene. . . . Jeff and I were in conversation all the afternoon. During a dispute between us with regard to the cutting of an apple with one of his knifes he found it that I was obstinate. And as I laughingly retorted I had discovered he was capable of looking very *stern*. Monday morning he left after breakfast. . . . Yesterday we were in town. Did a great deal of shopping preparatory to leaving for the up country. We will go to Madison Springs the month of August. I bought me a travelling dress and elegant thin dress and a rose col' morning dress. Sarah Blalock will make two of them. . . .

. . .

Friday, July 23, 1852 . . . Tuesday (the 20th) was the day of the Picnic. Early in the morning the carriages and buggies came rolling by giving to our usually dull looking road quite a gay appearance. All of them went to the Picnic from here but Bud Jimmie and Holt. We spent quite a pleasant day. I cut out two hankerchiefs and marked a good many clothes during the day. After dinner I dressed and late in the afternoon our party returned with Aunt Meigs and little Joe Mitchell. I took several games of Backgammon before tea. Thursday morning Aunt M left and Pa went to Augusta. I was engaged in sewing some during the day. We expected Pa to return. He did not and Ma moved up stairs. We were all about to retire when he rode up. I inquired of him if he had letters for me. Upon his answering in the affirmative I threw on a dressing gown went down and he handed me an invitation to a party in Athens directed to the Misses Clanton. A letter from Mollie Capers one from Jule Thomas Lissie Dean Leab Goodall. Lissie enclosed in her letter a programme of the concert and second day of commencement. She went to Oxford[28] with Fannie Floyd. Jule wrote me from Indian

---

28. Emory College, chartered by the Methodist Episcopal Church in 1836, and the town of Oxford were founded at the same time. The names were used synonymously. The college was the forerunner of present-day Emory University in Atlanta.

Springs. She thinks of returning home the last of this week or the first of next. Although Jule wrote me a longer letter than usual still it was unsatisfactory. She says that Jeff is enjoying himself but is nearly dead to see me. While I was reading my letters Pa called sister down stairs. Upon her return she showed me a beautiful breast pin he had brought up for *her* and a silver fruit knife for each of us. I had requested him to get the knifes in the morning and was very much obliged for them. I did not retire to bed until after eleven oclock. Quite late for the country. . . .

Something of a tragedy has occurred in our neighborhood recently. Last week Mary Culbreath was spending some time with Mrs Heggie. The latter went to Augusta. Ann Heggie did not return from town that night on account of the storm. Matt did. There was no one in the house that night but Mary and Matt. Taking advantage of this circumstance he entered her room and effected her ruin. Mary sent for Jessie Wood her brother in law. He came and carried her down to Mrs Berry's where she bo[a]rded. On the way she informed him. Her brothers together with Jessie Wood started (fully armed) for him. He got the advantage of them. In a day or two he was in Augusta. Hearing that a large party were in pursuit of him, he by a circuitous route succeeded in getting to Savannah and then took a ship for—no one knows where! It was expected he would carry off his property and being very much in debt his property was levied upon and Ann and her *three children* left without a home! They are now at Mr Berry's. "Truth (is indeed) stranger than fiction."

Thursday, July 28, 1852 I have just finished a note to Aunt Lamkin and Pa has handed me a letter from Leab Goodall containing the regulations of her school. For several days Friday Saturday and Sunday I scarcely remember what I did do. On Monday since Mamie had to [have] her tooth extracted Sister and I went down to Augusta. We had but little shopping to do. . . . Yesterday morning Brother went down with Edmund to Augusta and returned with Pa last night. Dr Thomas has taken the bandage off of Bud's arm but it is not straight so yesterday he called in Drs Dugas, Rosignol, Harris, Jones and &c.[29] They gave him chloroform, it acted as a nar-

---

29. Louis Dugas, Henry Rossignol, Dr. Harris, and Dr. Jones were Augusta physicians. There were two or more physicians named Jones in the area.

cotic and then while he was under the influence of it they endeavoured to pull his arm in place but could not succeed so the dear boy's arm will remain crooked. He cannot raise his hand to his mouth yet he is cheerful and is now engaged in playing a game of Backgammon with Rosey. He will not mind it so much now as he will when he grows larger. How I love him and how dear he is now that he is thus afflicted. Dear brother. I cannot realise it now in its full extent yet I shed bitter tears last night and even now when I think of it the tears will start.

Sarah sent up Aunt Lamkin's dresses last night. Ours *of course* were not ready when she promised them. We will send for them tomorrow. Pa gave [me] a very large trunk with my name upon it yesterday. My band box trunk has my name upon it also. I intend packing up tomorrow. . . .

Sunday, August 1, 1852 Tonight is the last for some time I will spend at Wood Lawn. Tomorrow we leave for Athens and Madison Springs. Aunt Lamkin and her family are down. On Thursday I packed up a number of my clothes in my trunks. In the afternoon I combed my hair and then commenced a game of backgammon. While thus engaged a Buggy drove up. Jeff had arrived— I hastily dressed and came down. He brought me a letter from Jule. She suggested to his flirtation with a widow Grimes. He gave me a long account of her and his adventures up the country. . . . Saturday morning I put on my travelling dress, wrote a note to Jule and gave it to Jeff. He left after breakfast. I will see him at Madison Springs. I must write in a common place style for Sister Annie and Jimmie are conversing here in the parlour and diverting my attention. . . .

Saturday, August 14, 1852 We have been here one week precisely. We left home Monday August the 2d. . . . Reached Athens Monday afternoon. Dressed for tea. Tuesday and Wednesday was at the Chapel [University of Georgia] first with Jake Phinizy of Augusta and then with Mr Hammond a son of Gov' Hammond[30] of South

---

30. James Henry Hammond, former governor of South Carolina, lived in Beech Island, S.C., just across the Savannah River from Augusta. The Hammond family had strong ties with Augusta society. Gertrude probably refers to Edward Spann Hammond. See Carol Bleser, ed., *The Hammonds of Redcliffe* (New York: Oxford University Press, 1981).

Carolina. I formed a number of pleasant acquaintances. Among them Mrs Houston formerly Puss Dougherty. Also an uncle of Bec Lasnette's (Mr Will Hallis). Miss Mary I Harris was in Athens. On Wednesday the students gave a party. The Ramsay girls and Sister A went. I did not but had quite a pleasant evening at the Hotel. Thursday was a long dull day. We came over here [Madison Springs] Friday. Found quite a crowd here. . . .

Wednesday night while engaged in conversation with Jeff I enquired of him where Jule was. He did not know exactly. I soon saw her engaged in conversation and dancing with Bob Connelly. In dancing she ran across the cotillion and only had time for "Howdy Gertrude" accompanyed with a kiss—and thus we met! The night of the Fancy ball passed off pleasantly— I dressed and went up. Mamie looked quite prettily as a Highland lassie. Jimmie dressed as a Sailor. Cousin Emma as a Swiss girl wearing the dress Ophelia Ramsay wore as a flower girl at Catoosa last summer. Dr Hanah of Savannah acted the part of an exquisite to perfection. Johnny Phinizy of Athens supported the character of a countryman equally well—to the annoyance of his family. Dr Reid a gentleman having a face very much resembling busts and pictures I have seen of Shakespeare and weighing three hundred lbs dressed as a Sultan, his children also in Turkish costume. Mrs Reid as an elderly lady. Miss Fanny Lamar wore the very becoming costume of Diana Vernon one of Scott's heroines.[31] Mr Bond of Macon was as much disguised as in fact more so than anyone else in the room. He had several pillows about his person giving him an appearance of much greater rotundity than he possesses. Mr Martin of So Ca wore quite a becoming costume. The goddess of Harvest (Ceres) was personated by Miss Strong. Mr Connelly appeared as a shepperd. The Misses Ramsay and Phinizy Jule and Jeff and Harriet Miller were down here Wednesday morning, the ladies engaged in sewing on Mr C's costume. I have been up to the ten pin alley three times since I have been here. Am not very successful—

.   .   .

---

31. Diana Vernon is a character in Sir Walter Scott's *Rob Roy*.

Tuesday, August 23, 1852 It is now between eleven and twelve oclock. Jeff leaves tomorrow! I cannot realise it. Never before did I part with him with so much reluctance. Never did I know how dear he is! How inseperably my existence—my happiness is combined with his. It is indeed a fearful thing to love. It only appears as a recent thing that I have awakened to know with what an intensity—with what a fervour I love. . . . I went up in the parlour last night. After tea was promenading with Jeff. A little circumstance occurred then which gave me a new insight into his character! . . . Jeff has been down here since the second cotillion— He did not dance tonight, an act of politeness and delicacy fully appreciated by me.[32] . . .

Wednesday, August 24, 1852 Jeff is absent! The polar star of my existence has left. And Oh! what a void is left. . . . Jeff came down for me before I had quite finished dressing. We walked down to the spring. Pa and a Mr Evans were down there so after taking a drink of water we returned instead of taking a seat in the bower. Returned— oh so slowly— Jeff took a seat for a short time in the piazzi and then went up to the house. We had but little time for conversation. After breakfast we assembled on the collonade to see the stages off. The hour drew near and I felt we must part but at last the word good bye is uttered—the farewell kiss for Jule and cordial grasp of the hand for Jeff. I did not hear a word he was saying when he bade me farewell. I was endeavouring to look calm for I knew I was observed. Mr Rolsten of Macon told me I had not a vestige of colour in my face—but perhaps it was imagination. I took a game of ten pins and then walked to the bathing house but did not take the bath with Sister A and cousin Emma. I did not go up to dinner.

.   .   .

Saturday, September 9, 1852 We have been at home one week today and how very swiftly the week has passed. . . . Aunt Paull and Ally are up with us now. Sister A went down for them yesterday. She sent on her white dress, my white crape shawl and both of our feathers by Mrs Luthringer to New York to have them dyed. I also

---

32. Gertrude abstained from dancing in accordance with the tenets of the Methodist church.

sent on a letter to Mrs Holt who is there now requesting her to select some portion of my bridal paraphanalia. My bridal dress—second day dress—bonnet and velvet cloak. Pa gave me permission and with his usual kindness is quite liberal. I expect Jeff will be up soon. I do so much want to see him. Dr Smith has been here this morning. Melvina has been sick. He left me some medicine to take and I will now stop to take some.

.   .   .

Monday, October 4, 1852 Jeff left this morning. He came up late Saturday afternoon and never have I enjoyed a visit more in all my life. Though short how pleasant. As Tupper expresses it "How much concentrated joy in blest love" and oh to love and feel you are loving an worthy object, one worthy of the priceless gem of woman's affections. For several days I have been quite unwell. On Saturday Ma and sister A went down to Augusta. I was not well enough to go. I sent off a letter to Fannie Floyd and one to Lissie Dean, requesting both to act as bridesmaids for me. I rather expected Jeff would be up on Saturday but when Ma returned sister said Jeff was in Augusta but told Pa he would not be up. Pa however mistook his remark for he did come, though late. I had on my Gingham dress but went in so notwithstanding. The next morning it was cold enough for a fire in the parlour. We went to church down at Abilene, and arrived there, just when Mr Collins was half through his sermon. Sister A and I rode together and Jeff in his Buggy and thought me "so cruel" because I did not ride with him. Yesterday afternoon I took a ride with him on our usual Bel Air road. On Saturday afternoon I did a little sewing for Lurany and was wishing for Jeff to arrive all the time. That night he presented me with my engagement ring, a beautiful ring with a cluster of nine large diamonds— Since he left this morning I have been sewing on a blue silk apron— I am writing on the Piazzi and it so dark I cannot see.

.   .   .

Friday, November 5, 1852 We have now been in town some time and yesterday is the first day I have seen Jeff! He has been very ill. I was wondering last week why he did not come up to see me when I received *a letter* (the first) from him informing me he had been very ill for some time. It was the first letter—yet it caused me to shed such bitter tears. To think of his being so sick and I so far away and could not hear from him. Yesterday was an eventful day. A day to break the monotony of everyday life. Mr Jenkins[33] delivered a eulogy upon Henry Clay[34] and a more beautiful speech I have never heard. His style of delivery is so good. Tuesday night (or rather Wednesday) I wrote to Jule. I had been expecting Jeff up and thought if he did not come yesterday he must be very sick.

While over at the City Hall yesterday morning my eye wandered over the vast assembly there hoping to see him but I looked in vain and had despaired of seeing him when to [my] great surprise in returning I was told he was in the parlour. I entered the room and met him looking wasted tis true by sickness but looking very interesting. He left before dinner in spite of my request to remain. While conversing with him I felt that I never knew how dear he was. How much I loved him. I can now understand Mat Wood's love for her husband, who has that fatal disease consumption. Yet feeling all this and endeavouring to suppress the tears that would rise when I thought how much Jeff had been suffering, yet I chatted on gaily as if perfectly composed. Our own native poet[35] of whom every Georgian has so just reason to be proud says

"There are some thoughts we utter not.
  Deep treasured in our inmost heart
    Ne'er revealed and ne'er forgot."

Such has so often been my case.

A Journal is intended for the outpouring of thought and the expression of ones inmost feeling but "there are some thoughts we utter not" either verbally or written and there are some emotions too powerful for words to convey an adequate discription of them. I had almost formed the conclusion to abandon this Journal but I believe I will still continue it although the relation of facts is not very interesting, still as I write for my own amusement I need not

---

33. Charles J. Jenkins of Augusta was a statesman, an orator, and a postwar governor of Georgia.

34. Henry Clay, statesman from Kentucky, was the main force behind the Compromise of 1850, which kept the Union intact for another ten years.

35. Richard Henry Wilde of Augusta, poet, scholar, and statesman. He was a mayor of Augusta and a U.S. congressman.

care. . . . I have been busy since I have been in town selecting and having my dresses fitted. Most of my bridal dresses and &c are bought but Jeff's health being so bad will defer our wedding which will depend upon his recovery to perfect health. I do wish he would get well not that I am *particularly* anxious to get married but then it makes me feel so sad to think of him as suffering— He "hopes I will enjoy myself until he sees me again." How can I? When he is sick?

Tuesday was the day for voting for President for either Pierce or Scott.[36] The third candidate Daniel Webster having died recently. Thus Calhoun, Clay and Webster are gone.[37] The trio have departed and whom have we now to supply their place? Upon whom will the mantle of Webster's greatness fall. "Let us hope (as Mr Jenkins in his speech yesterday remarked) that in a case of great trial some Elisha will appear to ward off all approach of evil." I had hoped Jeff would have been up on Tuesday to have cast his *first vote* but sickness prevented him. But I must now change my dress for the morning.

---

36. Franklin Pierce, president of the United States from 1853 to 1857, defeated Gen. Winfield Scott in the 1852 election.

37. John C. Calhoun (1782–1850), Henry Clay (1777–1852), and Daniel Webster (1782–1852), were the three preeminent statesmen of their time.

3. The Plantation Mistress

Write often for thy secret eye.
—Martin Farquhar Tupper

Sunday April 8, 1855[1] My first Sabbath in my twenty second year! On Wednesday the fourth I was twenty one! I left school when seventeen, spent a most delightful summer after at Indian Springs and Catoosa Springs and often indulge in gay and pleasant retrospection of things witnessed and persons known then. The next winter made my debut in society and although I did not dance and was thus incapacitated from entering into all the excesses of gayety yet I spent a delightful winter as a gay girl of fashion.[2] During this time I regularly kept up my Journal and in that I see many allusions to Mr Thomas and can there read how unconsciously to myself he was quietly laying siege to (as I conceived) my impregnable heart.

After a short courtship we became engaged which engagement lasted until the following December. He was attending Medical lectures in Augusta that winter so I in consequence saw a great deal of him and as "Time flies swiftly when we only tread ye flowers." the spring passed and summer came, when we removed as usual to our summer place in Columbia Co. Mr Thomas then visited me several times and upon one occasion brought me his dagaureotype which I now have. Jule graduated that summer in Macon. He went for her and then they visited Indian Springs— In August our family

---

1. On the first page of this journal and several later ones, Thomas wrote the following quotation from Martin Farquhar Tupper: "Husband up thine ideas, and give them stability and substance, Write often for thy secret eye. So shalt thou grow in wisdom." The words are probably taken from his work *Proverbial Philosophy.*

2. The Methodist church considered dancing sinful. Gertrude never danced, but she did disobey another tenet by attending the theater.

left for Athens and Madison Springs— Soon after Jule and Mr Thomas came up. Soon after returning Mr Thomas came up to see me again and presented me with a most beautiful engagement ring with nine large diamonds which I now wear, and as I write can see the light flashing from it. Our wedding day was appointed for the 25 of November but a few weeks after his last visit to Columbia Mr Thomas was taken quite sick. While slowly convalescing I received two letters from him. In the meantime although our marriage was postponed in consequence of his illness my preperations were carried on, and having engaged Mr Myers to perform the ceremony we were married on Thursday December the 16th 1852 (I have just been interrupted by our cook Tamah who has come in to ask for her ticket giving permission to let her marry Billy Boselair. As a marriage is not an everyday occurrence and they are to be married this afternoon I will stop writing and prepare to go down to the church and witness it.)

Twilight is fast fading away and I find that I have not time to indulge in so minute a retrospection as I had at first intended. The summer after we were married we went North, our party consisting of Pa, Ma, Sis Anne, Jimmie Lamkin, Mr Thomas and I. I have notes which I kept that summer while travelling— Written hurriedly they are of course quite imperfect, yet they serve to recall instances almost forgotten amid the whirl and confusion attendant upon travelling— Pa was spending his first summer at Rowell's a place which he bought from Judge [Wm.] Holt. In Dec of 1853 my darling little boy was born. I was confined with a sickness which did not last very long and the advent of the birth of a son was hailed with a degree of rapture mingled with silent yet fervent thanks to God, the giver of all good things. We at first thought of calling him Edgar Lewellyn, but finally concluded to call him Turner Clanton Thomas for Pa. He is now fifteen months old, and is of course quite a pet. This afternoon his nurse Isabella took him to church. In February of last year we moved down here. We are living near Rowell's and in the summer am only one mile from Ma. We are only six miles from Augusta and in a pleasant neighborhood.[3]

I have not been keeping a Journal since I have been housekeep-

---

3. This home in the country and the slaves there were given to Gertrude by Turner Clanton as part of her dowry/inheritance.

ing but intend endeavouring to persevere in this undertaking. I am writing for my dear little boy and for my children should I have others and in this book they will read, hurriedly recorded a statement of events unimportant in themselves yet they make up the sum of my life as "Trifles make up the sum of human ills."[4] This will at least serve to prove that heretofore my life has glided on smoothly—my barque has glided calmly and swiftly too o'er the sea of life for am I not twenty one? I do not feel old. My feelings are still as gay as bouyant as at seventeen. I am much happier now than then. I have selected my destiny and am content with it. I am fortunate and thank Heaven for it. When I see others so much less happy than I, I am constrained to wonder that God should so bless me. . . .

[Last] Sunday I attended divine service at the Methodist Church and heard Mr Evans in an excellent sermon.[5] After church I partook of the Lord's Supper and was benefitted in an unusual degree. Oh! for an increased degree of Grace to know and do my redeemer's will. To live more as I should. More to the glory of God and the advancement of that holy cause of which I profess to be an unworthy disciple. Sis Anne remained in while this service was being performed. How greatly I desire her spiritual interest. I think she is inclined to take an interest in religion and how fervently do I desire to bring her with my husband to the throne of Grace and pleading only the shed blood of our Lord and Saviour obtain pardon and redeeming love. In the afternoon I attended the upper Presbyterian Church.[6] Sis Anne and Alathea Paull accompanied us. We heard rather an obtuse sermon from Rev Dr Talmadge, the president of Oglethorpe College.[7] While in town Ma decided to give Mary a large dancing party while cousin Emma was at home. A great many invitations were issued, but the evening was very inclement and a

---

4. The quote is probably a corruption of one of the following: "Since trifles make the sum of human things," from *Sensibility*, by Hannah More (1745–1833); or "Trifles make the sum of life," from *David Copperfield* (1849–50), by Charles Dickens.

5. Gertrude usually attended St. John Methodist Church on Greene Street near the Clanton home. She also attended St. James Methodist on occasion.

6. First Presbyterian Church on Telfair Street.

7. Samuel Kennedy Talmadge, then president of Oglethorpe College near Atlanta.

great many of the girls were prevented from coming— Mr Scales[8] and father (Gen Thomas) had their buggy to break and the horses to run away on Tuesday. That night Mr Scales spent here and as our carriage had carried Gen Thomas home, I availed myself of the opportunity and went up to town Wednesday and returned home Friday. Mr Thomas came up the next day Thursday which was the day Mary gave her party. Wednesday was my birthday, the 4th of April.

Tuesday, April 11 [10], 1855 . . . . My domestic affairs in which I take quite an interest and what little sewing I do cause me to have few leisure moments. I have recently added to my sources of occupation in a flower garden. Ma and Aunt Lamkin have supplied me quite liberally with flowers and they seem to be doing well. I am making Turner Clanton a set of undershirts as I am shortening his dresses still more. I bought him a hat yesterday and he goes strutting about largely. I commenced writing this afternoon in the front Piazzi, but stopped to sow some flower seed Aunty gave me. Now I am writing in my bed room. Tamah has just got out supper. Mr Thomas is having some piles of brush burnt, and Turner is in the kitchen with Isabella. . . . Saturday I was busy planting out flowers in my garden and having plants put out in the vegatable garden as it was a good season. Pa came by to see us in the afternoon and left me five very nice Shad. Sunday morning I spent at home, reading. I am now reading the old testament through— In the afternoon went over to see Tamah married and heard Sam Drayton preach. He is one of the most intelligent Negroes I have ever met with, and has a decidedly fine command of language. Dr and Mrs Longstreet[9] Mr [Anderson] Carmichael, Mrs [Robert] Harris Mr Thomas and I beside the Segos were present. The bridegroom just awakened from a sleep he had been taking during the sermon, had his witts (to use an expression familiar to his class) woolgathered and looked quite faint. *He* took the bride's arm and she being taller than he, it looked as if the order of "to obey" should have been changed. . . .

---

8. Julia (Jule) Thomas had married Nathaniel Scales of North Carolina.

9. Augustus Baldwin Longstreet, best known as the author of *Georgia Scenes*, was a Methodist minister and former president of Emory College. He had practiced law in Augusta as a young man and was related to Mrs. Robert Harris and Mrs. Anderson Carmichael.

[Yesterday] While in town Mr Thomas handed me a letter from Mat Wood, formerly Miss Oliver. She is one of my dearest friends. One around whom the closest tendrils of affection continue to twine. I have not seen her since we graduated in Macon very near four years since— And oh what changes since then! Mat married Mr Louis Wood a very handsome man but she knew when she did so that he bore within his system that full destroyer consumption, yet with woman's love, she nerved herself with woman's strength, and in one year after leaving school she married. . . . She still continues to write me and her letters have a more cheerful tone. Yet she still feels the aching void which nothing she says can ever fill. Her little boy "the image of his father" is living—

One passage in Mat's last letter read thus, "Mike Nisbet was in Macon this winter. You know [he] is living in Kentucky now is married and has a little daughter five or six months old. He is as proud of it as he can be." And thus ends one episode in a chapter of romance— With him is associated almost every incident connected with my girlhood. Knowing him as a college boy and as a man, he was one of those characters in whom one will become interested from the raw mixture of good and evil, and yet his was not a character suited to my idea. And although seeing so much of him may have flattered my girlish pride, for what female is unwilling to receive admiration? Yet aside from his diminutive sise, his diss[i]pated habits, the one who could tune my heart to perfect melody and wake within me wild echoes which would sound his name alone—this master mind had yet to be discovered, and I thank thee oh Heavenly father for thy many mercys, but for none do I so sincerely thank thee as for *my husband*. Combining such moral qualitys, such an affectionate heart, with just such a master will as suits my woman's nature, for true to my sex, I delight *in looking up* and love to feel my woman's weakness protected by man's superior strength— Oh my Journal! That friend for a lonely hour. It does indeed seem like one of the quiet joys of memory to again have thee to confide in, for with their thoughts filled with busy care, men are not always ready to enter into all those silver threads of feeling, which make up the poetry of life.

Sunday, April 15, 1855 Since writing last time has passed with a quiet yet soothing monotony which renders life so delightful— But I must recollect I have had more company than usual, for Wednesday Ma Sis Anne and Holt spent the day with me. Ma brought little

Kate,[10] our sweet little sister with her. She is only two months old and is a very fine child indeed. I had a Spunge cake baked for dinner and although I have often made Pound cake this was my first attempt at Spunge. Before dinner we rode over to Rowell's where I gathered a few flowers. As yet the garden looks quite barren. While here Ma cut out a dress for Turner Clanton but in attempting to sew it the next day I found it was too large and am so inexperienced in sewing, and this was the first plain waist I had ever made for him, that I at first found it rather troublesome. When finished I felt amply repaid for my trouble, for it looks very pretty indeed. Thursday Mother [Mrs Thomas] and Mr Scales came up and spent the day with me. He went on to Augusta but returned to dinner. I made my first boiled custard for dinner. It was very nice indeed. Mother assisted me in tearing off the skirts of my muslin dresses and basting the hems. That night I sent them down to Lurany to make for me. I sent them by John whose wife America lives at the plantation, but sent that which was torn off for the wrists instead of the skirt. The next day Lurany came up on Anne (Buddy's little pony) and I rectified the mistake. Mother and Mr Scales left early and Mr Thomas and I then went fishing. Went in the Buggy to the creek half a mile below the bridge where I found a very nice log thrown across a cool romantic part of the stream. I carried *Harper*, as I generally carry a book upon a similar excursion as a "dernier resort," but I soon became quite interested in fishing and was quite successful in the short time I was there, catching three large fish. Mr Thomas caught two. . . .

"The spirit is willing but the flesh is weak." While Miss [Eliza] Logan, the celebrated tragedienne, was in Augusta I yielded to the temptation of going. I heard her in three pieces, *Evadne or the Statue* was the first, then *The Hunchback* and the night of her benefit I heard her in *Dugomar or the Barbarian*. There may be something in the expression "stolen pleasures are sweet."[11] Yet never have those intellectual faculties which surely a good God gave us to cultivate and enjoy—never have those faculties been so gratified, never was there such "A feast of reason and flow of

10. Catherine (Cate, Kate) Clanton, Gertrude's little sister, was twenty-one years younger, the last child of Mary Luke and Turner Clanton.

11. The phrase is loosely quoted, possibly from act 1 of *The Rival Fools* (1709), by Colley Cibber: "Stolen sweets are best."

soul"[12] as in listening to the birdlike articulated sound of Miss Logan's voice in uttering sentiments appealing to the noblest impulses of one's soul, and now when reading a fine sentiment her voice comes unbidden and haunts me—as Carlyle[13] expresses it: "Like the memory of a joy that is past, sweet yet mournful to the soul." Mournful too in more senses than one. For is not dancing and attending of theaters considered the two mortal sins? They are at least, great bugbears with the world generally. And we are commanded "to take up our cross," be self denying—and *avoid even the appearance* of evil! This I have not done. I have violated a promise. It was contrary to the rules of the Methodist church. . . .

. . .

Wednesday, April 25, 1855 Yesterday afternoon I was feeling so badly as to cause me to take Castor oil and laudanum. The effects today have caused me to be lolling in bed and doing little or nothing else. . . . Sunday the baby was still sick and we did not go in town to church but remained at home all day. Aunt Tinsey (one of Pa's servants who is staying at the Rowell Place) came over soon after dinner and I took her through the house to see how the rooms were furnished. She seemed very pleased and said she "knew Miss Gertrude could not pray, that she had everything too nice about her." She then came in where Mr Thomas was laying on the bed and gave us her experience in religion. It interested me very much. Such a mingling of pious feeling and superstition. Soon after she left I was aroused by hearing a knock on the door. I found it was Ma Sis Anne Mamie and Co. Soon after Pa Buddy and Holt came so I had a good deal of company. Pa brought Turner some ice which he relished very much. He also gave him a silver half dollar in order to bribe him to come to him. His Grand Pa Thomas gave him two goats when he was down there the last time. . . .

Friday, April 27, 1855 Mr Thomas has just started in his Buggy for town although it has very much the appearance of rain. I sent a

---

12. "There St. John mingles with my friendly bowl, / The feast of reason and the flow of soul," from *Imitations of Horace* (1733–38), satire 1, book 2, by Alexander Pope.

13. Thomas Carlyle (1795–1881), Scottish essayist, moralist, and historian. He coined the phrase "necessary evil."

note in inviting Sis Anne and the children down to take a fishing excursion with us tomorrow. I am having a cake baked and requested him to get some confectionerys this afternoon. The sickness from which I was suffering Wednesday is rather on the increase today and I have had very violent pains in my stomach and have just taken another dose of Castor Oil and Laudanum. When I was in town on Tuesday I had Sarah to cut me a dress (my half dollar muslin). She will baist it and I will finish it. I am endeavouring to be economical and yet I like to have everything I have very nice and neat. I am endeavouring to cultivate a taste for sewing, for which at present I have rather an aversion. Requiring a bonnet for ordinary occasions I called in at Mrs Hall's to get one and found she sold nothing trimmed for less than five dollars. She also charged 75 cts for a tarleton lining—so I carried it in to Miss Mitchell's. She lined and put a cape on for 62 cts, I finding the ribbon which I bought at Guy's at 37½ cts a yd. The bonnet cost me about 2.62½ and is a very nice one indeed. I had thought I had made [my] selection of summer dresses but Shear has beautiful tissue silks at 50 cts a yd and I selected and bought one. Also bought Turner a summer hat (for dress) and yet it is not very pretty. It cost me a dollar and a half and I think the ribbon too thin.

Yesterday I was sewing in the morning, mending some white jaconet dresses and I had cut Turner out a new purple calico dress when I saw a boy coming on horseback with a note directed to Mrs Col Jefferson Thomas (Mr Thomas having received his commission last year from Gov Johnson.)[14] It proved to be written by Mr Scales, from Mother, telling us Jule was the mother of a fine daughter and telling us to come down soon. Pinck[15] is going to school to Mr Bristo at Twiggs Academy and so are the Harris boys. It was their servant brought the note. Yesterday after dinner we went down to see her. Her child is quite large and as far as I can judge looks more like Mr Scales. Dr Edward Eve was her physician. He called there to see her this morning. I carried down some homespun and got Mother to cut out one pair of drawers and one undershirt for Mr Thomas as I will have to make him some new ones. . . .

Finding writing a delightful employment [while at school] I wrote a great deal and thus followed Tupper's advice which I have upon the fly-leaf— "Husband up thy ideas, and give them stability

---

14. Herschel V. Johnson, governor of Georgia (1853–57).
15. Pinck was the family's nickname for J. Pinckney Thomas.

and substance. Write often for thy secret eye so shalt thow grow wiser." And as he gives his opinion of the "careful penning of a good letter" so do I give mine in favour of a journal. There is nothing better calculated to improve the young, to give their hearts *stability* and order. . . .

Wednesday, May 2, 1855 . . . We took the fishing excursion Saturday as we expected. Early Saturday morning the carriage containing cousin M A Danforth, Sis Anne . . . came by for us. I had a champaign basket with eatables and Mr Thomas and I were ready to join them. I took Turner and Issabella to take care of him. We had a delightful day. . . .

There was a Negro meeting down at church and we hurried dinner to go. We walked down to church and found quite a crowd had collected. Benches had been brought out of the white people's church. I procured a seat in church and heard an exhortation from the Babtist minister Peter Johnson. A very fine looking Mulatto man, dressed very nice, with a gold watch and fob chain. While reading the hymn and his text he would place and take off a pair of gold glasses. He is not so polished nor by no means so talented a man as Sam Drayton. The Methodists and Babtists intend alternating at this church different Sabbaths. So there is a prospect for some preaching. In their exhortations they very often do much good. They appeal to the heart more than the understanding. After an intermission of a short period they were to administer "The Lord's Supper." My seat was very uncomfortable and I was warm, tired and half sick, so I proposed coming home. It annoyed Mr Thomas to leave but I had no idea of remaining in the state of mind I was in then to witness so solemn a ceremony, so we left. . . .

The next day Tuesday we went in town to spend the day. The firemen in Augusta had invited the firemen from Charleston to come up and remain a few days. On Monday they were met at the depot and escorted to the Planters Hotel. Tuesday they marched through all the principal streets in their uniforms with their engines beautifully dressed with flowers. It was quite an imposing sight. They formed in front of the City Hall so we had an excellent opportunity to see them. All the little children and darkies in town seemed to have turned out in honor of the occasion— My pink muslin was finished with the exception of the long sleeves so "making a virtue of necessity" I wore short sleeves. I bought some cord and half doz spools of thread at Grey's and in the afternoon bought some needles and a very pretty calico dress for Issabela at 8 cts a yd. . . .

Thursday, May 17, 1855 A much longer time has elapsed since I have written than I either wished or intended. I have been a good deal from home which has prevented me in a very great degree from the performance of several duties. . . . On Saturday May the 5th Mr Thomas and I rode in town in the Buggy and remained a short time. Upon our arrival there we were handed an invitation to a party at Mr Andrew Miller's given to the bride Mrs John Miller. He married Bec Royals of Burke Co, an old college mate of mine. Since my marriage invitations have by no means been so frequent as before. Married persons seem in a very great degree neglected and we can only wish that more of the costume of the continent as well as the fashion of married ladies taking the lead in society may be introduced among us.

On Sunday the 6th we went in town to church. I wore my new muslin a very pretty thing. We attended the Methodist church and found such a crowd there that we had to take seats in the gallery. We had the (to me) unexpected pleasure of hearing Bishop Pierce preach. He took his text from David[16] and preached an excellent sermon. I remained after church to partake of sacrament. While George Pierce was expatiating so eloquently upon the charms of christian resignation and &c my thoughts would revert to Ella his daughter. A sweeter girl I have seldom known. While in college with her, she Junior while I was Senior, I became quite attached to her. She was quick and impulsive yet with her faults I loved her dearly. Last summer she married a young man by the name of Turner. He was to become a Methodist minister. *Five months and twenty days* after her marriage Ella became the mother of a little daughter who is still living— Such an act required no announcement. What a shock it must have been to the family.

In the afternoon of the same day I went again to the Methodist church and heard Mr Glenn our presiding elder. He preached a regular old fashion Methodist sermon, and I heard the unusual sound of a lady shouting "Glory to God." Mr Evans is trying to get up a revival and has been preaching every night for the last two

---

16. Gertrude obviously means the story of David.

weeks. I have been so busy all day today that I really cannot write more tonight but must hurry to bed and to sleep.

. . .

Wednesday, May 30, 1855 . . . It being very pleasant, after dinner Mr Thomas and I rode down in the carriage to see the Allens. They are up from Savannah and are improving their house to remain in the country permanently. Cornelia Allen went last summer and spent four months and a half travelling in Europe. She has excellent manners— Perfectly easy and with colloquial powers almost unsurpassed. Without being pretty she is charming. There is so much play of [illegible] such perfect enjoyment of life in her expression. I have seen her but this is my first personal acquaintance with her. She keeps a journal— I wonder what kind of an impression I made upon her. Somehow conversing with her gives me a new impulse to study. I must see more of her. . . .

Saturday, June 2, 1855 How beautifully Richard Henry Wilde has expressed this idea

> "There are some thoughts we utter not
> Deep treasured in our inmost soul—
>   Ne'er expressed—ne'er forgot."

And thus it is, there are some thoughts we utter not and not even to you my Journal faithful record of the little events, which make up the sum of human ills, not even to you can every thought be confided—yet there are some moments when I must write—must speak or else the pent up emotions of an overcharged heart will *burst* or *break*. Here can I calm my tumultuous emotions— With a heart throbbing and an agitated form. How can I write? It will suffice— Years hence when glancing over the pages of this Journal, my eye will rest upon this page—landmark of one of the most exciting conversations I have ever held. A conversation which in a moment, in a flash of the eye will change the gay, thoughtless girl into a woman with all a woman's feelings— This page will awaken emotions and cause a heart perhaps grown cold—a heart whose pulses are regulated by the chilling influence (it may be of disappointment) to wonder at the wild tumultuous throbbings of early womanhood— I converse a great deal. I think a great deal— Out of the fullness of the heart the mouth speaketh. There are a few things which trouble me. Unfortunately I am not one of those who suffereth much, endureth much—but I speak unthoughtedly and often regret the hasty impulse— I cannot now write a detail of new events— I could not read— I therefore wrote—

Sunday, June 3, 1855 "A change has come oer the spirit of my dream." Tumultuous emotions have been calmed and I am again in my usual frame of mind and am enabled to tell with a calm frame of mind the events of the few past days. . . .

The record I made in my journal was soon after an exciting conversation. [Yesterday] I dressed late in the afternoon wearing my black silk dress as it was quite cool. Pa, Bud and Holt came soon after and remained a while. I handed them some cakes and just as they were leaving an open carriage drove up the owner of which proved to be Mrs and Cornelia Allen, returning our visit quite soon. I had some cake and wine handed, and enjoyed their visit. Miss Allen was not so interesting as the evening I was to see her. Today we have spent at home. This afternoon I am going down to Mother to remain a few days.

.   .   .

Sunday, June 24, 1855 Today has passed pleasantly. I find it very delightful to go down and hear Sam Drayton preach to the servants. He is a negro of extraordinary talent and cultivation and well repays one for listening to his sermon. This morning I was reading in the Bible for some time. The rest of the morning Mr Thomas and I were laying down in our room. Soon after dinner (just before which I was quite sick) I commenced dressing for church. Isabella carried Turner Clanton and Mamie and Co came down for me and I rode to church in the Carriage with them. Mr Thomas came soon after in his Buggy. Only two persons were immersed and four sprinkled. After a short sermon from Drayton and the administration of the Lord's supper the marriage came off. Pewela looked very well. Amanda has a beau, Studen Washington [Walton], one of the finest looking men I ever saw. Is a barber in town, a widower and has a grown son. Drayton's wife is one of the most ladylike persons I have ever seen. . . . Ma sent me word she had a letter of Mrs LeVert's for me to read and I intended going over after church, but it looked too much like rain. I should like to see that letter. Mrs LeVert is now making the tour of the continent—[17] Nearly two weeks have passed since writing last. In the meantime Pa has moved down and I find it quite pleasant having them near me.

Tuesday, June 26, 1855 Feeling badly I am utterly incapacitated for writing a detail of the occurrences of the last two weeks, even provided I could recollect them all which I cannot. I have had a great deal of sick stomach and headache and find I am again destined to be a mother. Turner Clanton is now 18 months old. The knowledge causes no exhilarating feelings neither do I regret it. Yet suffering almost constantly with sick stomach as I am I cannot *yet* view the idea with a great deal of interest or pleasure. All of the family came over and spent Sunday afternoon before the last with me. In the morning of the same day while laying down in my room I was reading over Journals which I have kept at the respective ages of fourteen seventeen and eighteen. Then I kept notes while I was North last summer. It afforded me a good deal of pleasure and while heaving a sigh for the memory of "joys that are past" many a hearty laugh was caused not only by recollections of amusing occurrences but at my own high flown attempts at eloquence in giving a discription of for instance a moonlight scene. . . .

.   .   .

Monday, July 9, 1855 In accordance with his intention Mr Thomas left for Burke[18] Thursday June the 28th and I spent the time while he was absent over at Rowell's. Having neglected my Journal so much previously I intended improving and carried it over with me in order to write in it while I was over there. Instead of doing so I left it over there the greater part of last week. I had quite a pleasant visit. Amanda assisted me in making a blue mus-

---

17. Octavia Walton LeVert, the wife of Dr. Henry LeVert of Alabama and the granddaughter of Augusta native George Walton, a signer of the Declaration of Independence, was a belle of Augusta, Mobile, and Washington society. She later published her memoirs on the experiences of her European tour.

18. Jefferson Thomas was at this time planting in Burke County, presumably on land given to him by his father at the time of his marriage to Gertrude. Gen. Joseph Thomas owned considerable land in Burke County.

lin dress Pa gave me in the spring. I am quite pleased with the appearance of it. Aunt Lamkin intending to visit Macon during the commencement, Sis Anne wished to accompany her. Pa gave her permission to do so and Saturday the 30th she went in town to do some shopping. I went with Mamie and herself. At the breakfast table I remarked that I only wanted a glass of soda water in town. Just before we started Pa handed me a five dollar bill to buy some soda water he said! I handed Mr Thomas the gold piece Pa gave me [last week] so this came in very good time. . . .

Thursday, July 12, 1855 . . . We heard Sam Drayton preach. Turner wore his new yellow calico and looked very sweet, bare legged and feet ditto. After the sermon while Drayton was calling up mourners Aunt Pink after swaying to and fro fell perfectly flat upon the floor. Several women rushed to her assistance when she rose and commenced shouting. This had such an effect upon Amanda that she went up to the altar. I believe in her for she is not one to act from impulse so much as settled conviction. When she went up I noticed Lurany (her mother) fully expecting an out burst of feeling upon her part. I was inexpressibly touched by her manner, for her maternal affection is the most strongly developed feeling she has. Instead of shouting she raised her hands in such a perfect ecstasy of gratitude, that words were not requisite. While they were praying a low moaning sound would be heard, gradually growing louder and louder until it became a perfect wail— This would be begun by one and taken up by another until it becomes the most awfully harrowing sound I almost ever listened to. I cannot describe its effect upon me. How irrepressible a people they are! How easily their feelings are wrought upon! After church we rode over to Rowell's. . . .

Monday Mr Thomas was in town and sold Bill Avery to Wilson for nine hundred and fifty $950 dollars— We purchased a boy called Henry for seven hundred and ten $710 dollars— It is well Bill is sold for he has been the cause of a great deal of trouble and expense. Mr Thomas was in town the next day until dinner and I was feeling quite unwell all the morning— I read *Harper* and *Graham*. Both numbers are unusually interesting— . . .

.   .   .

Sunday, August 5, 1855 So long a time has passed since writing I am almost at a loss to remember events as they have occurred in succession. . . . I have not had time to write an account of the principal event which has taken place in some time—*I have seen Stephens*—[19] Long wished to see him and to hear him. Had heard him discribed as common looking even worse than ordinary but when he mounted the rostrum and I saw him for the first time! As his diminutive size and person bearing the stamp of a real "Piney Woods Cracker" first dawned upon my sight, what a shock I received.

Sunday, August 19, 1855 It is strange how unwilling for some time I have been to write. It begins to appear in the light of a task— Upon one occasion I had summoned resolution to write but after taking the table (upon which my writing desk usually sits when I am writing) into the Piazzi it grew dark so rapidly that I did not commence writing. After tea something else occupied my attention. I see the last writing I did in this volume was on August the 5th. The day before I was in town to hear Stephens. He spoke against "the know nothings"[20] at the City Hall Park in a speech of two hours length. A free dinner had been provided at the Waynesboro depot to which the ladies were invited. I with my usual curiosity wished to go but was afraid I would meet no one else there. . . . I afterwards saw Mrs Fanning and she wished to go so with Alphonso Walton as our escort and Sis Anne we rode round. Found at the Ladies Depot only a small crowd. As a matter of course Mrs William Eve was there with Eva (who is home during vacation from Georgetown) and Mrs Dr Jones. Ginnie Delaigle who is also home from school North and Miss Berry and Jane Summers, Emma Cumming and Miss Davis, Mrs Glascock and the Setzes and Bignons were the only ladies there I knew. We had a very plain cold substantial dinner— Having an excellent appetite I did justice to all I could get. After dinner Stephens was toasted and rising at the close of a few remarks gave his friends the advice to "Spread themselves"

---

19. Alexander Hamilton Stephens was a U.S. congressman, vice president of the Confederacy, and, later, governor of Georgia. He voted against secession but accepted the majority decision.

20. The Know-Nothing or American party, popular at the time, wanted to keep control of the U.S. government in the hands of native-born citizens.

during the election. He remained with Mr. D'Antignac during his stay in Augusta. Several speeches followed the dinner. One from Mr Owens of South Carolina who is excellent at a stump speech. He was followed by James Gardner and he by Mr McHenry. While the latter was speaking we left. Never having attended a meeting of the kind I was quite pleased. . . .

The previous day I had left Isabella at home to finish a shirt for John and to get her things ready to go with me to Aunt Lamkin's—Returning home Sunday night Mr Thomas noticed the disorder among the books in the dining room and soon after found the key to the sideboard. I was certain of having placed it in the sideboard and locking it up with the other key. Upon looking for it, found it missing— Suspicion fully aroused I inquired of Tamah concerning it and she wished to know "why didn't I leave the storeroom keys with Isabella the day before?" Here was another mystery—which when explained proved that she [Isabella] had taken this key and during my absence Saturday unlocked the drawer in which were the storeroom keys and opening that stolen flour and a bar of soap. These Mr Thomas found among her things and she confessed after first denying that she had taken them. Mercy knows what else she took. Oh I have lost all patience with her— It was too late to make any other arrangement so I took her with me the next day but never expect to take her again for I consider her as one not to [be] trusted in the slightest degree. That day John's wife whom he had had when Coleman owned him came down to see him and wished to persuade us to let him come up to Madison where she lives to see her and still keep her for a wife— Since leaving her John has married America one of Pa's servants and besides the distance is too great for us to allow him to go. I felt sorry for her. She appeared to be a very nice woman and also seemed to entertain a very great affection for John. I enjoyed my visit to Columbia very much. . . .

Monday, August 20, 1855 This morning Mr Thomas rode down in the swamp. Pa has kindly given him as much fodder as he can pull, and last week Tamah and John were at work. Yesterday Sam, Ruffin, Simon and Charles came up from Burke and are at work there now. I was by no means an advocate for their coming on Sunday but Mr Thomas gave them a new hat apiece and some tobacco. They brought the news that Charity has a fine son a few days old. This is the second child born since we have been planting—and I intend keeping a regular list from now out. While Mr Thomas was at the swamp this morning I was working in the flower garden which is almost completely covered with grass. I was compelled to desist in consequence of rain and then was sewing until Mr Thomas returned bringing Holt with him to dinner. Mr Thomas is complaining of headache and Turner is asleep. Supper is not quite ready and I am writing on the table. I have finished reading *Which [or] the Right or the Left*[21] and although I think the character of Samuel Leland overdrawn, yet the object of the author is good and the book turning as it does with sentences of great beauty and wisdom is calculated to do good. The Sunday after returning from Aunt Lamkin's we rode over and spent the morning at Rowell's. Sam Drayton with a number of others took dinner with the servants.

• • •

Thursday, September 20, 1855 I am alone with the baby this afternoon Mr Thomas having gone in town to hear Mr Toombs[22] speak tonight. Election day is fast approaching and political excitement is running high. I today heard that Mr Metcalf had offered to bet five thousand (5000$) that Judge Andrews the know nothing candidate would beat Gov Johnson who is running against him.

Mr Thomas and I were conversing together Monday night and I told him I intended to read Shakespeare and the Waverley Novels[23] during the long winter nights. I have read them before when I was much younger and hardly able to appreciate their beauties so well as I would now. Oh at times what a perfect longing I have for increased knowledge. How much valuable time I fritter away upon things which are useless. I find it very delightful if I can beguile Mr Thomas into a discussion of any literary subject but his extreme taciturnity at times renders that difficult.

This week I have seemed to view things in a bright light. There seems a beautious gush of light on all my being thrown. And the

---

21. *Which, or the Right or the Left* was an anonymous work published in 1855.

22. Robert Augustus Toombs, a U.S. senator from Georgia, was later secretary of the Confederacy before resigning to accept a commission as a brigadier general. He commanded Georgia troops in Virginia.

23. The series of novels by Sir Walter Scott that followed the publication of *Waverley, or 'Tis Sixty Years Since* in 1814.

cause of this is nothing more than the impetus given to thought and action by our conversation Monday night. I intend reading a great deal should I live and improving the talents God has given me. By the way I saw where the good Jean Paul Richter[24] says "we should be interested in human life in every phase as the Turks are said to preserve odd scraps of paper which they find—thinking the name of *God* may be written upon it"— When I read Shakespeare I was in my Junior and Senior class at college— Most of the plays I read with Leab Goodall (Now Mrs Pollock)— In reading a short sketch of William Hazlitt[25] which came out in the July number, I was particularly struck with his expressive and laconic summing up of the characters of the British poets— . . .

Mr Thomas and I rode down in the Buggy to Dr Eve's yesterday. I carried Longfellow's *Hyperion*[26] for them to read and they loaned me the August and September numbers of the *Eclectic*[27] to read— I have been busy sewing all day and have only looked over the contents— Late this afternoon Sis Anne rode up on horseback but did not get down. She was attended by three gallants. Bob Harris Buddy and Holt. We called at the Rowell Place late yesterday to leave Sis Anne three bottles of ale Mr Thomas gave to her. . . .

Friday, September 29 [28], 1855   This is a charming morning. Fall of the year has ever presented to me peculiar charms. It never occasions those melancholy feelings which appear to affect so many persons in connection with it. For the past two weeks I have had more energy "to will and to do" than all the summer. I do not suffer so much from excessive languor and debility so consequent upon the summers and my peculiar state of health. I feel indeed like a

---

24. Johann Paul Friedrich Richter (1763–1825) wrote under the name "Jean Paul."

25. William Hazlitt (1778–1830), English critic and author, wrote *Lectures on the English Poets* in 1819. Gertrude doesn't identify the magazine in which this sketch appeared, but it was probably the *Eclectic*.

26. *Hyperion* (1839), by Henry Wadsworth Longfellow.

27. The *Eclectic* (a literary magazine), which was published in the North, dates back to 1819. It survived frequent name changes. The magazine mentioned by Gertrude was most likely *The Eclectic Magazine of Foreign Literature, Science and Art* (published 1844–98). Later in the journal, Gertrude refers to *The Southern Magazine* or *The New Eclectic* (published 1869–75), which absorbed *The Land We Love*.

new being taking more interest in reading—sewing and everything else. I am having a beautiful calico dress made into a neglige. Amanda is making it for I have no se[a]mstress and knowing so little, and disliking so much the use of the needle, I am often troubled in having my sewing done. Ma however is very kind in having the greater portion done for me. Mr Thomas having had a short crop last year and also having to contend with the disadvantages arising from a new beginning, it behooves us to practice an economy, which is hardly consonant with my nature. Yet to know that my husband was in debt would be even less to my taste. This winter I will need little having to be confined to the house until after Febuary.

When we were first married Pa made an effort to purchase from Aunt Paul her girl Mary— She changed her mind and disappointed him— This winter (or fall) he has offered her one thousand ($1000 dollars) for her—intending to make her a present to me. She has again acted in a manner, singular to others—but strikingly in accordance with her character—and left for Alabama without giving him a decisive answer to his proposition— She expects to be absent several months and I very much question wether Pa will ever become the purchaser of Mary— There are very great objections to the character of this girl yet her being well skilled in the use of the needle would almost conterbalance her faults. . . .

Jimmie Clanton[28] from Alabama arrived at the Rowell Place Sunday and left on the cars in the afternoon. I did not see him but would have been pleased to have renewed the pleasant acquaintance I had with him the summer I was thirteen (I believe). From him I received incalculable benefit. He was in my childish imagination the very embodiment of intellect. His ready wit, cheerful flow of conversation and &c awakened within me a wish to become learned also and to my intercourse with him that summer, do I attribute in some degree the thirst for information which I have ever felt, sometimes in a greater and a less degree. . . .

Sunday, October 7, 1855 Today we have had a cheerful fire burning in my room all day. This has been a beautiful day and I regret

---

28. James (Jimmy) Clanton of Alabama was the son of Turner Clanton's brother, Nathaniel. Later, as a Confederate brigadier general, Jimmy was famous for his raiding exploits.

that we have no preaching, either at Rosney Chapel[29] or at the Servant's church. The servants, Isabella Daniel and Patsey are invited over to Mrs [Anderson] Carmichael's this afternoon by Tina, one of her servants who gives a tea party. I am writing with a very nice pen, Mr Thomas having bought me a very pretty staff and a box containing quite a variety of pens. . . . I was in Augusta the other day and saw *Pencillings by the Way* advertised together with *Pelham*. The first by N. P. Willis, the other by Bulwer.[30] I have long been anxious to see them both and eagerly embraced the opportunity for getting them. I bought the first which is very nicely bound and a very valuable library book. I intend making it a point to buy bound books and then to preserve them to assist in the formation of a library, which I someday expect to have. *Pelham* was in paper cover, which Sis Anne bought. . . .

The next day [Monday, Oct. 1st] Mr Thomas went to the Poor House to vote for Governor Johnson. He was in a real "Know Nothing" crowd, but it is now decided that they are for the time defeated in Georgia—the Democrats having elected their candidate and they have six members out of eight to congress— Stevastopol has not yet been taken. Only some of the towns in the southern part with an immense loss from the Allied Powers.[31] . . .

.   .   .

Sunday, November [early], 1855   . . . On Monday I went in town. Our party being quite large. The week previous Lexius had been removed from the Planters Hotel (where he was hired) to the yard. Dr Jones who was attending him not exactly understanding the case, consulted Dr Ford who immediately pronounced it to be a case of *small pox*, and Dr Dearing the Mayor had him removed to the Pest House. Since [then] two other servants have been attacked with it belonging, the one to Mrs Walton, the other to Miss Bugg. Grif and Warren have also had it and yesterday we were told Jim Luke had been sent to the Pest House with it. All this excited a

---

29. Rosney Chapel was a nondenominational community church supplied by invited preachers and speakers.

30. *Pencillings by the Way* (1835), by N. P. Willis, and *Pelham, or the Adventures of a Gentleman* (1828), by Edward George Bulwer-Lytton.

31. Gertrude is referring to events of the Crimean War, 1853–56.

good deal of uneasiness with us when visiting the yard. We entered on the front side of the house feeling a little queer although every one of us had been vaccinated. I did not carry Turner as he never has been vaccinated although I deem it of great importance and intend having it attended to soon. . . .

When I was in town I bought Turner a very pretty hat which proved too small for him. As I was anxious to have him a new one by Burke Camp Meeting I proposed to Ma going in the next day (Friday) and I accompanying him [Turner]. Daniel and John had to leave early Friday morning in order to meet us on the cars Friday night. In accordance with that arrangement Ma called by for me the next morning and we went in. . . . That was the first day I had ever carried Buddy [Turner] in the street with me, and the little fellow behaved admirably. Coming back he slept most of the way. I had packed my trunk the night before so calling by for Mr Thomas and the trunks on our return we went over to Rowell's to dinner, and soon after in company with Sis Anne we left for the cars. Edmund drove us down to Allen's depot and after waiting for a while we were soon seated in the cars and whirling along in a perfect cloud of dust. After a ride of a few hours we arrived at the depot where we found the carriage and buggy awaiting us. We had sent Patsey down in the carriage to nurse Turner. We took tea that night with Mr and Mrs Simons the overseer who is also a cousin of Mr Thomas— The next day we went to the Camp ground to hear the eleven oclock sermon. . . .

Early the next morning I went round to see all the servants and afterwards gave them all some flour apiece. I had the men's coats made by Tamah and Isabella and was glad to find they fit them so well. Mr Thomas carried down their blankets and shoes for them. Since I was there last camp meeting three of the women have had babies. Maria Jones, Venus, and Charity. That day we attended the eleven oclock sermon which Mr Evans preached at the stand to a very large crowd. We received invitations from Mrs Royal, Mrs Jones, Dr Barton, Mrs Lewis, Dr Douglas and Mrs Ward to dine with them. We concluded to accept of the latter invitation as we were already staying there. After which we took tea with Mrs Jones and left for the plantation. Got our trunks and left for the depot. . . .

Night of the same day. We have just returned from Rowell's where we took dinner for the last time in a long while. Tomorrow they move in town, and the next day Mr Thomas is going to Burke. I think of going in town during his absence. It will soon be so that I will be compelled to remain at home, so I had better go while I can. It was tonight one week ago that we came up on the cars—found Edmund and Columbus at Allen's depot waiting for us. We waited till the cars left and Edmund started. No sooner had he taken his seat than he found something was wrong about the reins. The horses commenced prancing. He pulled the reins and as he would do so the horses would turn. In the meanwhile Edmund called to Columbus to "catch the horses and head them" an order which the latter was too much frightened to obey— I don't know that I ever was worse frightened in my life. Shut up in the carriage, expecting every moment to have the horses dash us up against a tree or break the carriage all to pieces.

The recollection of my situation flashed across my mind. Sis Anne wrenched open the door on her side and jumped out. Hearing my cry of "Oh save my child" she hurried back and threw down one or two steps of the carriage. I jumped out Mr Thomas handed me Turner and then got out himself. All this occurred in a moment the horses having been run up against a tree. Still we did not know at what moment they might dash off. Oh it was indeed a most providential escape. But the reaction of feeling proved too great for me and I burst into an hysterical fit of crying which seemed to alarm Mr Thomas and call forth all the sympathy of his nature. I never loved him better than that night! . . .

After supper of the same day. . . . Mat's brother Charles Sibley has recently arrived at home with his Northern bride. Another marriage is that of Cornelia Allen the night after (Thursday) to Mr Hull of Athens— I expect everything will be conducted on a very elegant style. Her invitations are the most beautifully gotten up of any that I have ever seen. Sarah Twiggs and two other young ladies came around in the neighborhood in the carriage and handed the invitations out from a silver basket, or waiter. I am invited and intend accepting of that invitation if nothing prevents.

A sad occurrence has taken place recently. Mrs Charles Hall formerly Miss Annie Cumming was burned very badly with camphine and yesterday I was in town and upon riding up to Mrs Hall's millinery store I found it shut, with crape upon the door. Upon enquiring of Mrs Boggs I found that Mrs Hall was dead after a week of very intense agony. I have heard several accounts of how the accident happened. The servant girl who was with her died from the effects in a few hours.

I very well remember what an excitement Miss Annie Cumming's marriage created. I was going to school to Mrs Bowen in Augusta at the time and Miss Eliza Bowen assisted them in getting married. He was the eldest son of Mrs Hall the milliner and there are doubts as to the legitimacy of his birth. Mrs Hall had him educated for an Episcopalian minister. Becoming acquainted with Miss Annie he addressed her, their interviews generally taking place at Mrs Bowen's when she (Mrs B) was engaged in school. Upon Mr Hall's proposing for his daughter Mr Cumming treated the proposal with the greatest scorn. They were privately married and it remained secret for near two weeks. I believe they were married three times. Mr Cumming finding how much Miss Eliza was implicated took his children from school, so did Mr D'Antignac and others thus injuring the school very much. Mrs Bowen died soon after—her death no doubt embittered by the circumstances. Since then the Cummings have become reconciled to their daughter although the marriage was a bitter blow to their pride.[32]

.   .   .

---

32. The incident here related concerns the marriage of Annie Cumming, daughter of Henry H. and Julia Cumming, to Episcopal minister Charles Hall. The Cummings were a socially prominent family, and Henry Cumming was a lawyer and important community leader in Augusta. Annie's sister Emily, who was the same age as Gertrude Thomas, married James Henry (Harry) Hammond (the son of South Carolina governor James Henry Hammond) of the famous Redcliffe plantation in Beech Island, S.C.

4. Trials: Life, Women, Slavery

Is it not enough to make us shudder!
—*January 2, 1859*

The first day of 1856 New Year's day! and oh how sad a day has it been— Now I do indeed begin to know what are the trials of life— Within a few weeks past I have become a Mother, and last night about half past ten oclock the little treasure which had been loaned me *for so short a time*, winged its flight to the God who gave it. "The Lord giveth and the Lord taketh away. Blessed be the name of the Lord." But oh it is hard. Nature rebels and turns shudderingly away from the thought that tonight my poor little darling [Joseph] will sleep its first sleep in its grave. The dear little creature whom I loved so dearly and cradling him in my arms would willingly have shiel[d]ed from every rude blast.

Tomorrow night he would have been three weeks old. This was a premature birth, being born two months sooner than I expected. He was very small but it was so perfectly healthy that I had hoped to raise him. Susan nursed him for the first two weeks, and then as it was Christmas week I engaged Mrs Stoy to come and remain with me. On Saturday night we were remarking how well he was looking and after he was nursed he was laid in bed. During the night he made some noise as though he had [phlegm] in his throat— I directed the attention of Mrs Stoy to it and he appeared to be better. I *never nursed him afterwards*.

In the morning after breakfast I took him to nurse and laid him down by me. I thought I had never seen him look so sweet. His complexion appeared fairer, yet he evinced no disposition to nurse. Mrs Stoy took him and immediately noticed how badly he was looking. As she said, "So much weaker than usual." He rapidly grew worse and we sent in town for Ma. Mr Thomas intended going to Burke but postponed it. Oh what a shock it was when he an-

141

nounced to me that he did not expect the baby could live. The dear little darling lingered in the greatest agony till last night [Monday].

Ma remained with me Sunday night. Sister Anne stayed last night and so did Mother and Bob.[1] After supper I slept a while and waking heard the last struggles of the baby— Then followed a silence and I not knowing inquired of Mrs Stoy if the baby was worse— To this she replied "No mam' he's better." I knew he could not live and the answer instantly aroused my suspicion. I instantly asked "Is he dead?" Her answer in the affirmative was received with no loud outburst of grief— I felt that I was in the very presence of the Shekinah.[2] There is something so solemn in the very thought of death yet I felt as I looked upward that now indeed there was a reality in Heaven. The mortal had put on Immortality— Corruption had put on Incorruption and there was brought to pass the saying "Death is swallowed up in victory." He had suffered so much I was glad he was out of pain. Yet tis hard to give him up.

This morning Mr Thomas wrote to Pa to have the grave dug and to buy a coffin. They carried the body up this afternoon. Mr Thomas has not returned yet, and oh how much nearer and dearer do we feel towards each other since this affliction. "Tis in grief true affection appears." I never felt how much I loved my husband as in the last few days. He has shown the greatest possible kindness and sympathy and done everything in his power to alleviate my grief.

• • •

Friday, January 18, 1856 ... This afternoon I have paid several calls. Mrs Harris sent over today to know wether I would accompany her this afternoon to call on Mrs Dr [Edward] Eve and Mrs George Twiggs. We called on Mrs Allen, Mrs Twiggs and Mrs Eve. The two first were from home. Mrs Hull (Cornelia Allen) is living at her father's and her husband is planting at Martin's place. By the way speaking of Mrs Hull reminds me of a repartee given by Mrs King[3] of Charleston, which little Bob Allen told to me. When

---

1. Bob Thomas, a younger brother of Jefferson Thomas.
2. Shekinah is defined as the presence of God on earth or a manifestation of the presence. It is also interpreted as the feminine aspect of God's presence.
3. Susan Petigru King was a talented author with a lively reputation in

Thackeray[4] was visiting Charleston where he was feted a good deal, he remarked in the presence of a crowd to Mrs King— "I understand Mrs King you are a fast lady"— Everyone present endeavoured to suppress a smile while she with her usual vivacity instantly replied, "Ah indeed! It appears we have both been under an erroneous impression. I have always understood that Mr Thackeray was a gentleman." This same lady Mrs Harris was telling me, is indeed a fast woman. Her reputation being anything but unblemished . . . She is however a woman of decided talent being the author of *Busy Moments of an Idle Woman* which I have read. She has also written *Lily* which I have never seen. I was very much pleased with *Peg Woffington*[5] and think the more I read of his works the more I would be pleased with Reade as an author. . . .

Both Pinck and Mamie have left for college now.[6] He is at Davidson College in N Carolina. . . . Friday I went in town. It commenced snowing just before I started but everything was ready and I started. I had a warm brick in the Carriage and plenty of blankets shawls and &c so I was not cold although it was snowing faster and faster every moment. I ordered John to drive round so that I could at least catch a glimpse of the grave yard which to me is invested with so much interest, but the snow and the thick falling tears prevented me from having even that melancholy pleasure. . . .

. . . .

Monday, March 10, 1856 Tonight is Mr Thomas' birth night. He is twenty five tonight. Since supper we have been holding an animated conversation with regard to Mr and Mrs Harris. I was arguing that had I a husband who gambled and drank to excess, that I should spend more and have my expenses more in proportion to his

---

Charleston society. Her husband, Henry King, a respected lawyer, was killed in action in 1862.

4. William Makepeace Thackeray (1811–63), the English novelist, visited and lectured in Charleston and Augusta in the mid-1850s.

5. *Peg Woffington* (1852), by Charles Reade.

6. From 1849 through the mid-1860s, Gertrude, Mary (Mamie), and Cora Clanton and their cousins Emma and Lizzie Lamkin and Lizzie Walton all attended Wesleyan Female College. There was much traveling back and forth amongst the families.

own. I was perhaps wrong yet it is just so. As it is I endeavour to economise in some degree and assist Mr Thomas in disengaging himself from his embarrassments. Fearful that some of the remarks I had made had wounded Mr Thomas' feelings I approached and took my seat near him. Just then he remarked that tonight and not last night was his birthnight as he has supposed. With a heart filled with kind wishes and affectionate emotions filling my thoughts I bent towards him and requested him "to kiss me." He was reading and probably engaged, made rather an impatient gesture and did not appear inclined to respond with alacrity to my request. I drew back offended I confess. I felt the blood rush to my face and tears of wounded pride filled my eyes— I am proud—know and feel it and am sensitive in an exceeding degree. The idea of it having occurred on Mr Thomas' twenty fifth birth night caused within me the feeling that perhaps this might, some years hence, perhaps two or more, this remark might be remembered— It saddened me— I am not superstitious but perhaps someday hence *when I am dead* my child or children may read this, and tell their father, for I know his disposition well enough to know he will never read it. His disposition is not one to love to wander over such mementoes of an absent or dead friend. . . .

Sunday, March 30, 1856 Again a long interval—during which time Aunt Polly Lyons[7] has come to Georgia on a visit bringing her little grandson George Howard. . . . In reviewing this month I appear to have been in a constant bustle of excitement. I have been a good deal in town. The merchants are beginning to receive their new goods. I have bought me a very pretty blue silk and had it made by cousin Mary Ann Cooper. Poor creature. She appears to have a hard time of it— She is nursing Jim Cooper and sewing for a means of subsistence. He has had rheumatism for a long while and for the last fifteen months has been constantly confined to his bed. Since October has only been out of the bed (and then was lifted) twice to have his bed made up— I had rather I believe work for a sick husband than an idle trifling one like Mr Blalock. There is Sarah, sewing hard all the while and he, although in the enjoyment

---

7. Polly Clanton Lyons of Alabama, later of Texas, was a sister of Turner Clanton.

of health and streng[t]h, doing nothing. Standing idle while his wife—a woman—is sewing for the bread she eats— . . .

A jury, whose names ought to be remembered long, have at last decided at Appling court house [Columbia County] the case of Mary Culbreath. I have often heard "Never go to law to have justice done." The summer of 1852 her person was violated by that brute (unworthy the name of man) Matt Heggie. We were then living in the country. It was the summer before I was married I believe. I have not time to relate all the circumstances connected with it. I remember well the excitement it caused in the neighborhood. She was in his house, an equal with himself, a friend of his wife's—everything appearing to plead in her favour. She was at his house. His wife not at home when the deed was committed. The testimony is conflicting, but my opinion is in favour of her innocence *very* decidedly—and oh it does indeed speak little in favour of a woman having a defender for insulted virtue in chivalrous man when such men as Matt Heggie, are permitted to go free, to desolate the life of some other woman. I would sooner trust my self with a wild beast than with a man so totally devoid of all that is noble in man.

Today week ago the 23d of March Jule and Mr Scales were in Augusta. They went in on Saturday and so did we. Mr Thomas has joined a Cavalry company[8] recently gotten up in Augusta and that afternoon they were to have paraded but it rained and prevented them. . . .

Wednesday, April 2, 1856 . . . Yesterday afternoon Aunt Polly and I went to see cousin Eliza Anthony now Mrs Davis Thomas.[9] We went a good deal out of the way and found it a very long, dull road. We found Cousin Eliza living in one of the rudest of huts with a mud chimney to it. Not near so good a house as our kitchen. The house had one room in it, very plainly furnished. She met us with her little girl Artemesia (whom Mr Meigs named) and invited us in. She evidently felt mortified at the extreme plainness of everything— Upon enquiring for the rest of the babies we were shown the infant which is two months old, which she calls after her

---

8. The Richmond Hussars were organized in 1855.
9. Eliza Anthony married Davis Thomas of Columbia County.

mother (Tabby). It is a fine little thing. Her twin boys are not yet two years old and are a good deal alike. One has red hair and the other black. Cousin Eliza has only been married five or six years, and when she did, ran away without her mother's permission. They have moved once in Georgia. Then to Alabama and back again to Georgia. Every time they have worsted themselves. . . . I have been under the impression I was twenty two and that my next birthday (which will be day after tomorrow) I would be twenty three. Instead of that I am only twenty one at present.[10]

. . .

Sunday, April 6, 1856 . . . During my sickness I missed seeing Amanda married. She married the week before Christmas, a barber in Augusta called Studen Walton tho Amanda calls him Mr Washington. She had quite a large wedding. Sis Anne gave her her wedding dress. I, her veil, Mamie her sash— Cousin Emma her gloves and &c. Mr Thomas went up to witness the ceremony. . . . [Yesterday] I walked up to Sarah Blalock's with Sis Anne. She was particularly communicative. Mentioned some instances showing how carelessly her feelings had been trampled upon by people who altho wealthy—had no higher sense of honour than herself— I had never seen Sarah's feelings apparently so outraged. . . .

. . .

Thursday, April 17, 1856 This morning I sent Patsey over to Mrs Harris with a very amusing book of hers I have been reading, called *Widow Bedott Papers*.[11] It is indeed one of the most mirth provoking things imaginable. Some of the Poetry *is sick*. Aunt Macquire's account of A Donation Party and a projected Sewing Sociey are very amusing sketches. The work was written first in detached pieces by Miss Berry afterwards Mrs Whitchers the wife of a minister. Then too I have read *Christine: or Woman's Trials and Woman's Triumphs*.[12] It is something rather different to the usual style— Being

---

10. Gertrude was born on April 4, 1834.

11. *The Widow Bedott Papers* (1856), by Frances Miriam Berry Whitchers.

12. *Christine: Or Woman's Trials and Woman's Triumphs* (1856), by Laura Curtis Bullard.

a very decided woman's rights book advocating women having their perfect equality with the other sex. Some of her arguments were very good indeed. Yet the denoument of the plot was rather unsatisfactory since Christine the heroine marries and then confesses that she is glad that the *tie* of marriage is so strong that it cannot be broken, this too after she has been advocating to the contrary.

It would appear that I have been reading quite a medley of literature for I have also read recently a work called *Caste*.[13] It is interesting altho written by a very decided Abolitionist. The heroine Helen and her brother Charles are educated in a Northern school. Their expenses being paid by some unknown person. At the age of eighteen three thousand dollars was sent to them and then the remittance ceased and furious investigation threw no light on the subject. Charles established himself in the mercantile business and married a young Northern lady. Helen comes South as a governess and becomes engaged to Herbert Warner the son of the family. It is subsequently discovered that she is the child of a mulatto slave (Corilla) and her father is Col Bell a near neighbor of the Warners. I must confess I was sufficiently Southern to think him justifiable in breaking off the engagement but after a great deal of suffering, Herbert finding his happiness to depend upon Helen follows her to Italy where they are married. . . .

Mr Thomas has made quite a bargain in selling his horse Grace. He got a horse and 25 dollars boot. The same horse yesterday he swaped for a very nice one and sixty five dollars boot. I was fortunate enough to find a turkey nest with four eggs in it today. One of them is laying in the turkey house. I now have eighty five little chickens—

. . . .

Monday, [May] 12, 1856 . . . Pa was going to Screvin Co to visit Mobley Ponds. A plantation for sale there. He wished Mr Thomas to accompany him so not wishing to remain at home by myself I stayed in town. . . . [While sewing and conversing at Ma's] we were speaking of the virtues of men. I admitted their general depravity, but considered that there were some noble exceptions. Among

---

13. *Caste* (1856), by Mary Hayden Pike.

those I class my own husband, I staked my own reputation upon his, and [in] that, perhaps acted rashly, but I do not think I did. Were that faith dissipated by *actual experience* then would be dissolved a dream in which is constituted my hope of happiness upon earth. Of course between a husband and wife, this is (or should be) a forbidden subject but to you my journal I would willingly disclose many thoughts did I not think that the prying eye of curiosity might scan these lines—

Monday, May 26, 1856   Today I have been quite busy in finishing cutting out the pants for the men at the plantation. I have sent them their shirts and the children their clothes. Mr Thomas has a fine prospect for a crop this year which I am heartily glad of for several reasons. One of them is that if practicable I would like very much to travel somewhere. I am very well prepared and then too I have no infant and I cannot tell wether next summer I will be so free from care. . . .

. . .

Saturday, July 26, 1856   Again a long interval and I do not think I could summon energy enough to write tonight were it not for a very pleasant ride taken with Turner and Mr Thomas in the Buggy this afternoon and walking very rapidly from the house to gate five times and back again. Indeed, I find this weather very enervating and a slight nausea, consequent upon certain symptoms, adds greatly to my lassitude. Again, I have prospects of becoming a mother and the idea (aside from the fear of accident and the natural shrinking from pain) causes pleasurable emotions. I do not wish an only child, yet I should not object to long intervals. I think Mr Thomas views the subject with the same idea of myself and is gratified at the prospect. I have as yet mentioned this to no one but himself. . . .

Mother has returned from North Carolina much pleased with her visit.[14] Sunday was a week ago, Sis Anne and Mamie went down with us to hear preaching at Union and spend the day at

---

14. Mr. Scales and Julia Thomas Scales settled in North Carolina but visited in Augusta and Waynesboro frequently. Mother Thomas had been visiting Jule.

Mother's. There were fewer than usual at church— The Thursday night before we were at Twiggs Academy to hear Mr Ryarson preach. He was extremely interesting and preached to a crowded house. Mrs Paul Eve was there. She has fleshened out a great deal and is quite fine looking. Mr Thomas was in Burke at the time and I remained at the Rowell Place. Pa had gone down with him to visit his plantation. He was much pleased with the prospect for a crop. Pinck came up Monday and remained with us till Wednesday morning— I had made several unsuccessful attempts to make apple jelly during the week and have become discouraged. Mr and Mrs Hull took tea with me the Thursday night of that week—so did Mamie and Sis Anne. I had invited Mrs Harris but a little Negro boy of theirs who was a great pet was very ill and she could not come. He has since died. Saturday we attended a fishing party.

. . .

Monday, August 18, 1856   . . . Day before yesterday two weeks ago I accompanyed Mr Thomas to Burke to the plantation. His Mother and Brother Joe went with us. We took the cars at McBean Station and having arrived at Thomas Station or no 72, we got off and left for the plantation which was only two miles distant. Daniel drove Mother and I in Mr Chance (the overseer's) Buggy. Mr Thomas Turner and Brother came in the little waggon the latter driving. As the road was slanting and he seated in a chair, Brother Joe lost his balance and fell head over heels out of the waggon. With that exception (which resulted in no injury) we went on safely. The day passed pleasantly. The dinner was very nice. The Negroes appeared to enjoy themselves. Judy and Maria Jones are expecting to be confined in a month or two and in that condition I think all women ought to [be] favoured. I know that had I the sole management of a plantation, pregnant women would be highly favoured. A woman myself, I can sympathise with my sex wether white or black.

We returned on the cars the same afternoon and getting out at McBean rode in the Carriage to Mr Thomas' father's. During the ride had an exciting conversation with regard to women, plantation and &c. All together I was so much fatigued I did not join the party after tea in the Piazzi but retired early. I did not sleep till quite late and early the next morning I found that I was in such a situation as to frighten me with fears of sickness. Coming up home we called by for Dr [Edward] Eve. Nothing that he did (in fact he did nothing) proved efficatious, and on Monday I had an abortion[15]—at two months. I was not very much frightened and have suffered more from extreme debility than anything else. I have been sick two weeks and feel as tho I had been ill two months. During the time I have had a good deal of company and Ma has been very kind in supplying me with grapes, peaches and &c.

On Friday the [8th] Pa, Sis Anne and Mamie left for Indian Springs. Pa appeared to dislike the idea of leaving me sick but called to see us the evening previous and after mentioning to Mr Thomas that he had left him as his agent during his absence, he remarked to him that "as Gertrude wishes to have a Piazzi in front of the house if you will see Goodrich[16] I will pay for it." How delighted I am. Nothing scarcely could have afforded me more plea-sure than the realization of a long cherished wish. Mr Thomas having seen several persons, has contracted with Quinn, White and Co for a Piazzi at five hundred and fifty dollars to be finished in four weeks. Daniel has been sick for two or three days and this morning he has had a chill. Wishing to know wether he has a fever I sent for him to come here. He came, stood up by me, answered one or two questions and then fell backwards, falling and knocking Turner flat on the floor. I expect he fully calculated on quite a scene. Instead of that, I sat perfectly still, rather admiring his skill in effecting it so cleverly— I believe I am very sceptical. He may have been really ill but he has taken no quinine to render him giddy, and his fever was not very high. However I hinted my suspi-cions to no one and am in hopes he will get well soon. [Written above last sentence: "I was wrong. He was really sick as was proven."]

Aunt Caty [Paul] and Althea were out to see Ma and I last week. They returned home Saturday. On Friday night Mr Crum-ley[17] preached at Rosney Chapel. Aunt Lamkin, cousin E, Lissie, Jimmie and William Walton left for Indian Springs last week. Brother Joe and Pinck left a few days after for the same place. They are all at Catoosa Springs now. Left earlier in consequence of some

---

15. Gertrude uses the word *abortion* to mean a miscarriage.

16. William H. Goodrich was the leading builder in Augusta. He probably built the Clanton mansion on Greene Street.

17. William M. Crumley, minister of St. James Methodist Church in Augusta.

cases of scarlet fever at Indian Springs. I have written a letter to Pa, one to Sis Anne and one to Mamie— In consequence of my sickness I have been prevented from going to Sunday school for several sabbaths. Mrs Dugas has an infant, so has Mrs Harris D'Antignac and Mrs Robert Allen. Neither of the latter have lost any time. Lurany has made me a large quantity of very nice brandy peaches and now I am drying some peaches and peach leather. . . . What I have written is from an article in the May No of the *Eclectic* loaned me by Dr Eve. [This last sentence is preceded by two pages on the lost Queen of England.]

This is a beautiful extract upon a theme invested with much interest. It is from a novel called *Ruth*.[18]

"How I wish God would give me power to speak out convincingly what I believe to be His truth, that not every woman that is fallen is depraved; that many—how many the Great Judgment Day will reveal to those that have shaken off the poor, sore, penitent hearts upon earth—many, many crave and hunger after a chance for virtue—the help which no man gives them—help—that gentle tender help which Jesus gave [once] to Mary Magdaline. . . ."

"I take my stand with Christ against the world. . . ."

"Is it not time to change some of our ways of thinking and acting? I declare before God, that if I believe any one human truth, it is this—that to every woman who, like Ruth, has sinned, *should be given a chance of self redemption*—and that such a chance should be given in no supercilious or contemptous manner, but in the spirit of the holy Christ. . . ."

". . . I state my firm belief, that it is God's will, that we should not dare to trample any of his creatures down to the hopeless dust; that it is God's will that the women that have fallen should be numbered among those that have broken hearts to be bound up, not cast aside as lost beyond recall. If this be God's will, as a thing of God it will stand; and He will open a way."

And oh how much of this spirit is displayed by *our own sex*. We who should and could at least pity them—tis a woman who with a Pharisaical drawing of the Robes around them, pass by with a glance of cold scorn or indifference expressive of, Stand aside I am better than thou. After all how much is owing to circumstances and as this, no other endeavours to inculcate them, is a striking

---

18. *Ruth* (1853), by Elizabeth Cleghorn Stevenson Gaskell.

difference between a sin, however great, and habitual sin, and it is often want of charity among men that converts the former into the latter, and peoples the world with outcasts. Oh how many of those women are more sinned against than sinning. I am as strong an advocate for purity, perfect purity in women as anyone can be and yet I think it is time to change some of our ways of thinking and acting— It is a shame that what is considered a venial thing in man should in a worldly point of view *damn a woman* and shut her out from every avenue of employment.[19]

. . .

New Year's Day, January 1, 1857   I had taken up the second volume of Prime's *Travels*[20] intending to while away a few moments in reading it over again, when I recollected that tonight was New Year's night. It would be contrary to a custom continued for many years not to write some description of the manner in which the day has been passed. It has been a very gloomy, dark day, constantly having the appearance of pouring down rain. Mamie (who is spending Christmas holidays at home) had promised to spend today with me. I scarcely expected her, but about eleven oclock Ma and herself came. I had dinner for them, a very nice dinner with dessert of Boston pudding and oranges, figs, raisens almonds and preserves and brandy peaches. I also have a beautifully iced fruit cake, which I had cooked in town last week. I have had a slight though constant pain in my stomach and side today and as everything of the kind makes me uneasy in my present situation I have been bathing with flannel in warm camphor and now feel decidedly relieved. I have been so unfortunate in having a premature birth and an abortion that being in a similar state I naturally fear a similar accident.

---

19. Gertrude's quotation marks in the copied extract are highly inconsistent; unfortunately, this particular irregularity was a habit of hers. Part of the passage has, at times, been attributed to Gertrude Thomas herself. Here I have corrected the text using the novel itself as my authority. The quoted passages are excerpts of spoken dialogue taken from a sequence of several pages. The concluding paragraph does not come directly from the book, although some of the ideas may have been gleaned from the magazine article. I have been unsuccessful in locating the article. Gertrude expresses similar thoughts in the entry of February 9, 1858.

20. *Travels in Europe and the East* (1855), by Samuel Irenaeus Prime.

Mr Thomas has been very busy for the last few days. He has some of the men up from Burke and with the assistance of six of Pa's men with two others, he yesterday succeeded in moving the kitchen. Setting immediately as it did behind the house in an exact cat corner, it was a subject of annoyance both to Mr T and myself— Today he has pulled down the smoke house, and put it up again, so that it can be seen by anyone coming up the avenue. He is straightening the yard and making various little improvements to conduce to the comfort as well as appearance of things. The Piazzi proves a very decided improvement to the house and in time I think we will render our home very attractive. Occasionally when I am in town I think I would be extremely pleased to spend the winters in town, but then it appears extravagant for us to have two homes and plant in Burke besides. I am the more reconciled to a slower but more sure mode of progress when I hear of the failures which are constantly occurring. Mr John Carmichael has just failed for a large amount. So have the firm of Grey Brothers, and within the last week Mr John Moore, and Louis Delaigle.

This Christmas has been unusually quiet. Little or no noise or shooting poppers. We were in town Christmas Eve and the next day. Sis Anne gave us some huckleberries (or whortleberries) and some of the most delightful tomatoes I ever tasted— Fruit and vegatables she put up in cans. Her green peas proved a failure. The recent attempt at an insurrection appears to have created quite an excitement in Georgia as well as in Tennessee where it originated. Never during my life have I witnessed so much excitement from a similar cause. It was discovered before anything had been accomplished in Tennessee. Numbers of Negroes were arrested. Some had their heads cut off. Others were hung some severely whipped. It was well it was stopped before Christmas. So much intercourse as there would have been might have enabled them to organise some extensive plan. The police in Augusta were very vigilant. I have never at any time experienced the slightest fear and pray that that dreadful evil may never be visited upon our country. Today is a striking contrast with last New Year's day. During that day we committed our little babe to the God who gave it, a flower that scarce did bloom ere it died. Today we are well in the enjoyment of life and health. May New Year's of 1858 find us enjoying a similar blessing.

.   .   .

Friday, February 20, 1857 ... Mr Thomas went in town this morning to attend the parade and has not returned yet. He expected to remain and attend a meeting for the practice of sword exercise. He appears very much interested in the [militia] company. Dr Dearing is captain, Tom Stovall 1st and Mr T 2d Lieut. I am in hopes the troop will succeed. At present they number about thirty members, a good many of them from the country. I have been quite busy today having the front garden spaded by Tamah. Irish potatoes planted in the vegatable garden, and onions, peas, mustard, collards radishes and early corn planted down by the strawberry bed. My garden has not had a good fence around it to protect it from the encroachments of the chickens and Mr T has not found time to attend to having it made over yet. All of his attention of late has been given to the front garden which is beginning to fully repay us for our trouble. I was delighted and I must add surprised today to find that some of the rose cuttings I had planted out had leaves on them and a number had budded out. This afternoon as I was just through washing my head (a job I always dread) a carriage drove up and Eliza Kerr and Ady Hall called to see me. . . .

Yesterday I had some apple trees planted out. Some that we bought from a man up the country at the rates of two dollars for twenty five trees which was the no I bought. Among them are the May, Red & Yellow, June, July, Mangham Red Pippin, Ladyfinger, Round, Fastround and a number of others. The earlier kinds I have had planted in the garden so that when they do bear they will be under my personal care. I find my home very pleasant now— The weather is charming and I delight to go out in the yard and garden, notice the many objects of interest and at the same time feel that there is such a oneness of feeling, such a mutual interest in everything between Mr T and myself— In this consists the charm of married life. After the first romance of life begins to wear away it is well for it to be supplied by the rational, calm trusting happiness which we can only feel when we know and understand each other's faults. The only remedy for faults discovered must be *to love them down*, and then what a new tie, what a strong cord of love to bind two hearts together is the birth of a child. I am very happy in the prospect of the gift of another such tie of love and hope that I may do my duty as a mother to the immortal soul entrusted to my care. . . . This spring I will be compelled to remain at home a good deal for I will not only be unpresentable in the street but I will find being in town fatiguing and I am really anxious to be as particular as possible. I have been reading a good deal of late. Interesting and moral toned books but I fear I devote too much time to that particular kind of reading to the neglect of more solid reading. . . .

.   .   .

Sunday, September 6, 1857 . . . Already the changing leaves betoken the approach of fall, that melancholy but peculiarly beautiful season of the year. Earth, air and sky are beautiful, bathed in the roseate hue of a declining sun. The melancholy note of the locusts is the only sound to disturb the silence of nature. Not a leaf appears to be stirring— The grass in the avenue contrasting with the yellow wild flowers, together with the cows quietly grasing in front of the gate presents a scene of quiet rural happiness, the more to be appreciated after an absence among different scenes.

I have other sources of happiness too, for my little daughter, my darling "Anna Lou"[21] is born and now I have an additional cause for continuing my Journal and tis to you my little daughter that I write more especially— Our best feelings are our affections and if happily directed, tis in the development of them that our happiness consists. When I first commenced writing I was seated on the steps in the front Piazzi— Now I am writing in my room. Turner is engaged in some mischief at my side while the baby is beginning to make a noise and let me know she is about. She has not been at all well for several days so I will stop and nurse her—

Mr Thomas has ordered up some of the Negroes from Burke to pull fodder, Pa having kindly given him as much as he can pull. Another, among the many instances of kindness on Pa's part! I had intended when I first commenced writing to begin at the beginning and give a discription of a visit we have taken to Catoosa Springs but will not have time now to mention all connected with it. This is the first summer we have travelled since the year we went North, and the trip was very pleasant, altho Mr T the Baby, Patsey and I all had very bad colds. . . .

.   .   .

---

21. Anna Lou Thomas was born May 29, 1857.

Wednesday, September 16, 1857 Last night instead of writing I was conversing with Mr Thomas in the front Piazzi. I was telling him the history of *Light and Darkness* a novel I read while at Catoosa Springs— It is written by Lissie Petite[22] the authoress of *Household Mysteries* a book I read last winter with a great deal of interest. Cousin Nat Clanton[23] joined us at the Springs this summer having just graduated at the University of Virginia and taken a Northern tour. He mentioned Lissie Petite as having been at Saratoga while he was there and discribes her as being a young and interesting lady, not married. I don't know wether this name is merely a "soubriquet" assumed in writing or not. *Light and Darkness* I object to, and wonder that any *unmarried* woman should write so freely, and express herself, on *certain* subjects so independently. . . . The author [Edward Whitley] has this sentiment in his book [*Knaves and Fools or the Friends of Bohemia*]. "We want men's books. Nobody dare write a man's book—a novel a poem or a memoir— When a man writes he considers what can go into a family—what virgin sisters can read. So because our virgin sisters are idiots we get idiotic books." Now I *a woman* say, "Shame on the man who would write anything which would lower the standard of woman's purity." I should like to know what the author means by *a man's book*? If Paul de Cock, George Sands and the host of French writers, who inundate our country with their sea of licentious literature be not sufficiently coarse for them, what a libel upon womanhood is this George Sands, Madame.

The only redeeming trait is her refusing to sign the name given her by her mother to her infamous productions. What an unhappy prostitution of talent. I am an advocate for novel reading in reason, but for a child of mine I think I would prefer their reading nothing to their having their mind contaminated by this intellectual poison— True there is a good deal of reading which while without improving sometimes increases a love of reading— This I would not object to. I wish my children to have a real genuine love for reading— For a woman especially what a charm there is in a new book— I am of the opinion that too much novel reading is injurious to a mind (and especially a young mind) insomuch as it destroys a

---

22. Lissie Petite, author of *Light and Darkness* and *Household Mysteries*, married Peter Y. Cutler in 1861.

23. Nat Clanton was another son of Turner Clanton's brother Nathaniel.

taste for more abstruse works— I find this too much the case in my own experience. . . .

. . . .

Wednesday, November ——, 1857   It is now twenty minutes of nine oclock. I have been reading over the previous portions of this Journal, reading aloud evidently very much to the edification of Patsey and Henrietta who were listening with a great deal of interest. Buddy is asleep in his crib "Anna Lou" in her cradle and Mr Thomas has gone in town to attend a night meeting of the cavalry co. When he happens to be away I usually employ myself at night in writing in my Journal but oh it has been very much neglected of late. My baby has been so unwell as to engage my attention to the exclusion of everything else. She is now near six months old and is very small scarcely larger than children of two or three months. She has had her head broken out with cold and disordered bowells so that she had not had an opportunity to grow. Now however she appears to be very much better—will smile and notice and sleeps well— The little darling. Oh that God may prolong her life and suffer us to raise her to be a blessing to us. A Mother's love— There is no sounding its depths. Oh how strongly are the chords of affection woven around this precious wee bit creature, this little piece of God's mechanism.

In the last entry made in my Journal I notice my mentioning Isabella's having been sent to Burke. It is a long story— Finding it impossible to break her of stealing we sent her down there—where she only remained a week or two before she ran away. Remained around town a week, was caught and lodged in jail—and taken from thence sick. Was brought here where she has remained sick ever since in Tamah's house— Dr Eve was called in and treated her for typhoid fever. She is a girl of a good many excellent traits and it [is] very much to be regretted that this incurable habit of stealing should prevent one from placing any confidence in her— Yesterday she returned to Burke again as I had no disposition to have her remain here. I have had so many trials with her that with my consent I don't think I shall ever have her for a house servant. I would like her sold and a good steady woman bought in her place. Henrietta knows nothing of sewing altho she appears to be a good disposed servant, never has been accustomed to anything except field [work] Isabella is not suited for field work and yet she cannot be a good house servant while she will impose upon one's confidence by taking any and everything and yet it is strange—that to this girl I have a feeling amounting nearer to attachment than to any servant I ever met with in my life. . . . [Note at bottom of page: "I wonder what ever became of Issabela. She was afterwards sold and I have never seen her since—she must be living somewhere in the world, and perhaps she may be suffering but I scarcely think so. I hope not. Aug 1879."]

Monday, December 28, 1857 We have returned home and are again settled in our little room. Home again! And with what a loss—our little darling, our precious little Anna Lou is dead. Today one week ago she breathed her last. This afternoon after returning home the sight of her cradle—bonnet and every little thing connected with her produced an uncontrolable burst of weeping— I have never since the first night of her death felt her loss so sensibly as tonight. In this room in which so much of her little life of suffering has been passed. I look around and it appears as though she will surely wake up soon and require my care. Oh how closely had the tendrils of affection entwined her around my heart. My child Oh my child how I miss your sweet smile, your little twining fingers as they clasped mine, even your feeble moan of pain expressive of so much suffering— Would to God, he had blessed you with life and health and you were still here to cheer our hearts—
        I had been in town several days when I started to return home the Baby appeared so unwell that I concluded to remain and let Dr Eve see her. He attended on her, applied various remedys—had her blistered and on the Sunday following she appeared to be dying— Dr Eve thought so but during the night she commenced to improve and continued to do so rapidly. Mr Thomas went down to Burke for a few days and during his absence she never appeared to be in better health. She would take long naps—smile and really appeared to be strengthening rapidly. Toward the last of the week she appeared to take fresh cold. Dr Eve was again called in, prescribed the same things. Had her blistered again but all in vain. Monday the 21st she appeared quite sick. We knew that she was very ill. First one of us would hold her and then another on a pillow. Drs Eve and Jones were to see her that morning and left prescribing nothing but nourishment for her. She could be heard breathing very distinctly and painfully with her little mouth open— Mr Thomas took her and said he would rock her to sleep. He did so and she appeared to be

sleeping—breathing much more naturally—Dinner was announced and they all went down. Mr Thomas told me to go down and hurry up "the baby was acting so well he would not disturb her." I did so, and was returning when I met Patsey coming for me. I entered the room hurriedly and Mr Thomas extended to me his hands as cold as ice. I glanced towards the baby— A change had taken place— I thought she had fainted off as she had done once before, and called for wine,[24] sending at the same time for Ma. They all came hurrying up. Ma took the baby from Mr Thomas and laid her on the bed. She only breathed one breath afterwards— Oh it was such a shock— And oh she was so beautiful in death. It was so hard to part with her.

* * *

Sunday, February 7, 1858 . . . We attended church at St John's church this morning. Heard Mr Key preach— Carried Buddy (Turner) for the first time. He behaved tolerably well, tho rather restless, when in placing his hand in my pocket to take out my handkerchief he discovered some money and a marble— Nothing would satisfy him but that I should give them to him. He said he would "just tag a little easy on the floor." I was afraid he would let it drop so refused to give it to him— He insisted and thinking he would have a fine play with me he burst forth into such a perfect peal of childish laughter as caused everyone to turn to discover what was the matter— I sent him out with Cora, who had accompanied us— I am sure I enjoyed the preaching much better after he left, but he is old enough (four years old) to do better— . . .

Pa made me a present of twenty dollars yesterday and the same to Sis Anne. She does not like my receiving the same she does— It is quite natural. I wish Pa would give her a sett of diamonds and Negroes and houses to hire and rent out so that she could feel more independent. Surely I have one of the very kindest dearest fathers in the one world and it does not require such additional proof of love to convince me that I love him oh so dearly. My dear, kind father! My love for him is so intimately blended with the pride I have always felt in his personal appearance that the two feelings

---

24. Probably an ammonia wine, which was widely used as a smelling salts for faintness.

are indissolubly connected— He went down to Baker [County] during the last week to buy a place but did not purchase. Mr Thomas is speaking of buying a plantation of Goode Bryant's but I do hope he will not. If he has any money to invest I wish he would go into some business in town and spend the winters there. I do think I should enjoy town life so much—but that is a "chateau de Espagne" for the future—

Tuesday, February 9, 1858 ... Mother and Mrs Finn (who has been spending several days with her) spent the day with me today— Mrs Finn is seperated from her husband. Here is a sad case. He has been supporting a white woman and a family of children he has had by her, while Mrs Finn has often worked hard to support *him*. I do not know the circumstances— Yet I know enough to think she has acted well—with more independence than most women would show. Mary [Finn] (Mrs Hawkins) is happily married. She has no other children to bind her to him. His own conduct has dissolved all feeling of love or duty and knowing that it is a settled thing with him, that there is no hope of reformation I do think she would have been doing an injustice to herself to have remained with him, as a wife— Yet how often is this done— How often let martyr women testify!

Mrs McDonald of Macon, a lady I knew well when I first left school has recently eloped, leaving her husband, a grown son—and a little daughter for the guilty love of a professed gambler—who leaves a wife and seven children— Poor Mrs McDonald what an awful step she has taken! No excuse— She cannot plead the excitement of youth. What can she say? A query— Why is it that while Dr McDonald would be considered perfectly right in refusing to take his wife back to his home and heart, the wife, the deserted wife of the other party is expected to show her woman's love (or rather her woman's weakness) her all forgiving spirit and receive the wanderer back again? Custom does indeed sanction many a wrong and there is yet great improvement to be made in the code of ethicks by which the life of many persons is to be regulated. But I mount my hobby when I commence on the subject of woman and her wrongs— I am no "Woman's Rights Woman," in the northern sense of the term, but so far as a woman's being forever "Anathema Maranatha," in society for the same offence which in a man, very slightly lowers, and in the estimation of some of his *own sex* rather elevates him— In this, I say there appears to be a *very very* great injustice. I am the greatest possible advocate for woman's purity, in word, thought, or deed, yet I think if a few of the harangues directed to women were directed in a point where it is needed more, the standard of morality might be elevated. So much more than I intended for women and &c. . . .

Today I heard for the first time that Mat Oliver (Mat Wood) was married again. Inquired to whom. Mrs Finn did not know. One more chapter in the romance of that life. What next? God bless you Mat. Yet I never thought that I could hear of so momentous an event in your history and know so little or care so little for it.

Thursday, February 12 [11], 1858 . . . . Tuesday a singular little circumstance took place. A man came here telling me Mr Thomas had met him and sent him here to wait until he returned. He came in at the front gate yet his appearance was so much that of a mulatto I was in a quandary as to "what to do with him." Patsey said she did not believe he was a white. I did not like to insult him if he was, so I told him he could come in to the fire or set out in the Piazzi till Mr Thomas returned. As it was cold, I afterwards invited him in to the fire. I came out and he remained there till Mr T came back when he went out in the yard. Dinner was announced and at Mr T's invitation he came in to dinner. When he took his hat off, he looked more suspicious than ever. Mr Thomas looked at me and shook his head. He then asked him several questions, among them *where they voted* around here? His reply was "I am not a voter!" "You are not of age?" "Yes sir, but the law does not allow me to vote. Does not consider it right I suppose." Mr Thomas made no reply though tempted to order him from the house, but I then asked him, "Is that in consequence of your mother or father?" "My father I suppose?" was his reply— Had he replied the other way I think *I* should have been tempted to have insulted him. As it was, the temptation to reply to him "that the same law that did not allow him to vote did not allow him to sit at a white lady's table" was almost irresistible, but the fact is, I felt sorry for the poor fellow— He may indeed merit the expression of *base born*. . . .

.   .   .

Sunday, November 14, 1858 Housekeeping and married life are not compatible with keeping Journals, and the excessive languor and indisposition I suffer from previous to the birth of my children unfit me entirely for a regular course of writing— I hope I am sincerely grateful to a kind Providence for his many mercys— Again has he blessed me with a little babe and to make that blessing doubly dear, she is a girl—[25] Father in Heaven I pray thee that thou wilt preserve her in life and health, and enable us fully to appreciate the immortal soul thou hast given in our charge— While I write she lies in her cradle the embodiment of health (and to a loving mother's eye) of beauty— I notice my last entry was made last spring while cousin Jane Thomas[26] was with us. She spent the month of April and a few days in May with us. I found her extremely pleasant and had it not been for the excessive nausea I was suffering from at that time I would have enjoyed her visit very much indeed. . . .

About that time Mr Thomas' father was quite sick. Having Dr Park up from Savannah and undergoing a course of treatment. He grew worse and concluded to go on to the Glenn Springs— He did so, accompanied by Pinck. Not being as much benefited as he expected to be, he left for Jule's and was just on the point of leaving there for the springs in Virginia when the inexorable summons came and he was called from us to appear before a Father in Heaven. I had long since dispaired of his final recovery yet the news announced by a telagraphic dispatch was a shock of surprise. . . . Pinck had written before to tell the family "if they expected to see him alive to come on." Mother and Joe went on and had seated themselves in the cars in Augusta when they received a letter stating that he was much better and "for them not to come on." He died on Thursday the 26th day of August. Mr Scales Bob and Pinck came on with the body and Mr Thomas met them in Augusta and went on down home— Mr Scales and Pinck came on out here and I went down with the former in the Carriage.

The funeral notice was given out for eleven oclock but was obliged to be changed to eight in the morning—in consequence of

---

25. Mary Belle Thomas was born September 23, 1858.

26. Jane Elizabeth Thomas, daughter of Judge Grigsby E. Thomas of Columbus, Georgia, was a cousin of Jefferson Thomas. She married William C. Sibley of Augusta in 1860 and eventually, working with Frances Willard, became a widely recognized leader in the Woman's Christian Temperance Union. In later years, Jane Sibley and Gertrude Thomas worked together in the WCTU.

the warmth of the weather. He was buried down at home by the children that had been placed there before. Mr Thomas wrote the obituary notice and has ordered a very handsome monument to be placed over him. At the same time he ordered monuments to [be] erected over the three children his mother has buried and for our two little ones that are buried in town. Our little (three weeks old) boy [Joe], and our lovely little Anna Lou. His mother's place appears to have undergone a change— I have been down there but once since his father's death, and it seemed so lonely— The principal life of the place is gone— He was so lively, so pleasant and appeared so much to enjoy life. I don't think I have ever seen anyone who had the interest of his family more at heart. I always enjoyed my visits most when he was at home, and I dwell with pleasure upon the good feeling which invariably existed between us. It was during one of my visits down there last spring when he was sick that he drew me towards him and told me "To come again my child. I think a great deal of you." Pa has not been well for some time and I fear that when the hour arrives for his summons from time to eternity, he may not be prepared. Oh God incline his heart to serve thee "For what profiteth a man if he gain the whole world and lose his own soul." "The prayers of the Righteous[x] availeth much" but oh I fear my prayers will not be sufficient. [Note added: [x]"I was Pharisaical. I should have said Believers—for I did believe then. 1871."] . . .

Buddy left last week for West Chester (near Philadelphia) in company with Mrs Boullair's sons for school. He will not be home till next fall— Pa says for two years— I intended going on to North Carolina to see Jule last summer but just about [that] time Mr Thomas went on to the north for Mamie in Pa's place. Afterward we concluded to go but Ma advised me not and I am glad now I did not go. I remained at home as quietly as possible attending to having preserves jelly brandy fruit and &c made, and with all my care the baby was born exactly one month sooner than I expected.

Wednesday, November 17, 1858   This morning when I looked out the ground was covered with a white frost. The avenue looked as though it had snowed. I have seated myself to write, very comfortably, but don't know how long it will continue for I hear the baby moving as though she intended waking up. She rests extremely well at night. Generally sleeps in her cradle till three oclock when I take her in the bed with me. I was not expecting to be sick till the last of October and then I wished to be confined in town. Quite to my surprise, my baby was born one month sooner— I was taken sick Wednesday morning (had been feeling quite well previously). Sent in town that afternoon for Dr Eve— As I was and had been in no pain, he returned telling me that although he knew I generally had a very quick time, he thought if I would send for him when I first felt pain he could arrive in time.

Ma, Sis Anne and Mamie had been visiting that morning at Mrs Harris' and called on their return home. Found me sick and Ma remained sending over for Susan and Aunt Tinsey. I rested very well during the night. In the interval, I had had the sitting room arranged for a bed room. Thursday morning September the 23rd the baby was born. I was not in pain more than an hour but it is a fearful agony— "How sharper than a serpent's tooth" must be "an ungrateful child"[27] to a mother. I sent for Dr Eve, but he did not arrive in three quarters of an hour after the baby was born. Aunt Tinsey's presence inspired me with a great deal of confidence. I have concluded to call her Mary for Ma and Mamie and think I will add Isabel for Isabel Morrison (now Mrs Harrington). We will either call her Mary Bell or Mary Lou.

When the baby was four weeks old I spent the day at the Rowell place and was sick all the week after. That week Pa moved in town and as soon as I was well enough I went in and remained several days. I was purchasing black to wear for Mr Thomas' father. Bought a raglan, bonnet, dresses and &c. The change of scene I found beneficial and now feel as strong as usual— We have taken the parlour for our bed room and I find a large room so much more comfortable. I am delighted with the change. Yesterday I finished reading *Yeast* by Charles Kingsley and today have read a few pages in *Tom Burke of Ours* by Charles Lever, said to be one of his best novels.[28]

. . .

Tuesday, November 30, 1858 While I am writing the baby is fretting and Mr Thomas practising upon his voilin. Unless he stop[s]

---

27. "How sharper than a serpent's tooth it is / To have a thankless child," from Shakespeare, *King Lear*, act 1, scene 4.

28. *Yeast* (1851), by Charles Kingsley, and *Tom Burke of Ours* (1844), by Charles James Lever.

soon I cannot continue writing for I do not know what I am doing— I dislike very much to hear him tune the instrument but endeavour to keep my nerve as quiet as possible and say nothing— Last night we had some excellent music from a young man by the name of Tipton. He is hired as a kind of overseer at the Shrivale[29] place. He and Dave Youngblood who drives the waggon camped here last night on their way to town. The former plays reels and a great many tunes remarkably well and has never been taught by anyone. My attention was attracted to his fine forehead (indicating so much talent) but the lower part of the face so animal reminding me of having seen the same thing mentioned with regard to the English poorer classes. What a pity it is that education is not more generally diffused. Burke County is the only place that I have ever heard grown men say "Dis and Dat, and De"—the latter for the— Mr Thomas was in town today. I have been reading for the past few days *Dr Thorne*, and today have been reading Miss Bremer's *Impressions of America—*[30]

Saturday, December 4, 1858 It is the hour of twilight. Mr Thomas has walked up the avenue. Turner has been playing in the yard and has just come in. The baby is asleep. She has had loose bowels for the last day or two and we sent down to Dr Eve for some medicine for her. Had it not been for that and it being so cloudy we would have gone in town today. . . .

On Wednesday the first of the month, Mr Thomas and I went down to attend Mr Dove's funeral. We had a very cold ride. Carried Turner and Mary Bell and took dinner at Mother's. Instead of going to the funeral, she went in town which I was a little surprised at. While they were depositing the body in the grave, the latter caved in and Mr Thomas and a Negro man who was assisting slipped into it. Altogether it was a very solemn scene. Pa came by this afternoon to see us and brought Turner a letter from Buddy. This ink is so pale that I derive no pleasure whatever from writing.

---

29. The Shrival (or Shrivale) place was one of the Thomas family plantations in Burke County.

30. *Dr. Thorne* (1858), by English novelist Anthony Trollope, and *The Homes of the New World: Impressions of America* (1853), by Fredrika Bremer, Swedish writer and novelist.

Christmas Day, Saturday, December 25, 1858 This is the first Christmas we have spent at home since 1855. . . . The Christmas of 1856 we were in town. It was just about the time of the threatened insurrection among the Negroes. Aunt Lamkin came down at the same time afraid to remain at home. I wonder that I felt no more alarm at the time than I did, yet I sometimes think that we are like the inhabitants at the foot of Vesuvius, remaining perfectly contented among so many dangers. Last Christmas we were in town under very sad circumstances—after the death of the baby— This year Ma has a more quiet time.

Sis Anne and Mamie spent today with me. They came down yesterday to attend a fancy party at Mrs Shipping's— After some deliberation we took different characters. Sis Anne personated "Night" wearing a new black velvet dress, low necked and short sleeves, with a black lace veil, with silver spangles— This with her sett of diamonds made a very elegant dress. Mamie wore white satin with an illusion tunic or top skirt, bordered with a broad gilt band. The neck, sleeves and crown were trimmed with the same. She wore her sett of diamonds. I don't believe Mamie has decided yet wether she personated "Norma" or "Evadne."[31] My dress consisted of an alapaca riding skirt with black velvet Basque, Mr Thomas' cap trimmed with feathers—Gauntlets, linen collar and undersleeves and a riding whip—making the complete costume of Di Vernon in Scott's *Rob Roy*. The costume was quite comfortable and they all said becoming— A great many were invited from town but there were very few there. Still the evening passed pleasantly. . . . They had a very nice supper and the band to play for them yet it decided me that I was right in an opinion previously formed, that it was difficult to succeed in getting people out from town, so far, when they have to return the same night. . . .

• • •

New Year's Day, January 1, 1859 . . . While I write the thought comes to my mind that someone of my own loved circle may be taken from me during this year. Oh God in thy tender mercy spare me such woe. Preserve my dear ones in life, health and strength—

---

31. Night was the child of Chaos and Evadne the wife of Capaneus in Greek mythology. Norma is the heroine of Bellini's opera of the same name.

and teach us all to live more for Thee and Eternity and less for the transitory things of earth. I have of late felt much uneasiness on account of both Pa and Mr Thomas' health but infinitely relieved of late neither of them complain so much. Pa is looking much better and Mr Thomas appears to have gotten over an attack of dyspepsia from which he complained a great deal. He also suffered from a singular feeling in his chest creating in my mind great uneasiness, which I carefully avoided letting him see. Thank Heaven he appears entirely relieved of it now. . . .

I have just looked over to see what I had written last New Year's day— That day Mr Thomas' Father took dinner with us! It is impossible to realise that he is dead! It is enough to humble us to think how the world goes on and *will go on* after our death. I sometimes think were I to die tomorrow—or any day soon how little *I* would be missed— For a while—how long I know not, I would be grieved for, but *new ties*—new plans would be formed and I alas! would be forgotten—or only remembered as a dream a shadow— But I do not indulge in a misanthropic spirit in saying this. I know it would be so. Everyday experience teaches me so, but I have no morbid feelings on the subject and mine is not a disposition to picture for myself a gloomy future. Life is very dear to me— I have many ties to bind me to earth, and to the loved ones in my family circle— I wish my children to remember me—and for my girl or girls should I have others, these pages are penned, thoughts carefully jotted down—actions slight in themselves but such "Trifles as make up the sum of human ills" I have recorded— For no intrinsic merit they should be prized but because, Mary Bell, they were written by your mother. . . .

Sunday, January 2, 1859 Today Mr Thomas is fulfilling an appointment to meet Joe at his mother's, and I am at home with the children. . . . Lurany interrupted me just now bringing in Lulah— and giving a new turn to my thoughts— What a remarkably pretty child she is and as white as any white child. There is some great mystery about Lurany's case— How can she reconcile her great professions of religion with the sin of having children constantly without a husband? Ah after all, there is the great point for an abolisionist to argue upon— The idea of such a person as Amanda, raised among the refining influences of a white family knowing but little more of the Negroes than I do—or take another case, a servant educated as in *mistaken kindness* they sometimes are and sold for debt. They are subject to be bought by men, with natures but one degree removed from the brute creation and with no more control over their passions. Subjected to such a lot are they not to be pitied.

I know that this is a view of the subject that it is thought best for women to ignore but when we see so many cases of mulattoes commanding higher prices, advertised as "Fancy girls," oh is it not enough to make us shudder for the standard of morality in our Southern homes? A most striking illustration of general feeling on the subject is to be found in the case of George Eve, who carried on with him a woman to the North under the name of wife— She was a mulatto slave, and although it was well known that he lived constantly with her violating one of God's ten commandments, yet nothing was thought of it. There was no one without sin "to cast the first stone at him," but when *public opinion* was outraged by the report that the ceremony of marriage had been passed between them—then his father was terribly mortified and has since attempted to prove that he is a lunatic—with what success I do not know. He preferred having him living in a constant state of sin—to having him pass the boundary of Caste. I can well understand his horror of that kind of marriage. I can appreciate his feeling perfect antipathy to having negro blood mingle in the veins of his descendants but I cannot understand his feeling of indifference to having that same blood flowing through the veins of a race of descendants held in perpetual slavery—perhaps by other men—

I once heard Susan (Ma's nurse) speaking of her reported father in a most contemptuous manner. Laughingly I said to her, "Why Susan, was not he your father?" "What if he was," she said. "I don't care anything for him and he don't for me. If he had, he would have bought me when I was sold. Instead of that he was the auctioner when I was sold for 75 dollars." She was sold for debt, seperated from her mother and has lived in the yard ever since she was three years old. What a moral! It speaks for itself— And these "white children of slavery" as Miss Bremer calls them lower the tone of the South. They are not to blame. Oh No! They know no incentive for doing well and often if they wished they could not. The happiness of homes are destroyed but what is to be done— There is an inborn earnestness in woman's nature to teach her to do right, but this is a mystery I find I cannot solve— Southern women are I believe all at heart abolisionists but there I expect I have made a very broad assertion but I *will stand* to the opinion that the institution of slavery degrades the white man more than the Negro and oh exerts a most deleterious effect upon our children— But this is the dark side of the picture, written with a Mrs Stowe's[32] feeling—but when I look upon so many young creatures growing up belonging to Pa's estate as well as others— I wonder upon whom shall the accountability of their future state depend—

Wednesday, January 5, 1859 . . . Today has been quite a busy day attending to frying up lard, salting meat and &c. Tom brought ten hogs up last night. The first we have killed. I intend having sausages souce [souse meat] Jelly and &c made. I was fortunate in having so fine a day to attend to it. Altho very cold, the sun was shining bright. I gave it more of my personal supervision than usual. Mr Thomas was in Burke today. Took the cars in Augusta yesterday and will return tomorrow. Today the division of his father's estate took place, Negroes, Land and &c— It is surprising with what perfect indifference I view the accumulation of so much property— I don't believe I am at all mercenary in my disposition. As it is, there are few things I want but what I get. Mr Thomas is particularly liberal in his feelings—and when he has money is always willing to share it with me. Indeed, I have great cause for congratulation in my husband's disposition. He evinces a sincere regard in gratifying my wishes. . . .

I was in at Mr Oates' Book Store the other day and met Mr Nott in there very much intoxicated. He insisted upon treating me to a present, said he loved me— "Some folks he loved, some he did not." Wouldn't allow me to leave the store when Mr Clark offered to see me to the door. He then followed me to the carriage. I was not at all afraid of him. Somehow I never am afraid of a drunken man— I feel a contemptuous pity for them— Poor Mrs Nott! Her three husbands have all been trials to her. Although I spent last night and am spending tonight alone I feel quite calm and devoid of fear. Patsey on the floor and Elizabeth in the chair, are both fast asleep. So are the children and I too will seek the land of dreams for I don't sleep five minutes without dreaming—

---

32. Harriet Beecher Stowe, avid abolitionist and author of *Uncle Tom's Cabin*.

Thursday, January 13, 1859   Today I have been quite busy in the flower garden having John plant out evergreens roses and &c. . . . I haven't felt so low spirited since the birth of the baby— At that particular time I always expect to be more or less nervous— I was tired, and by myself and then I had been in the kitchen where Isabella was. All this conspired to make me feel badly. She looks very badly—poor creature. What a life she must have led for the last four or five months, often without shelter. She was caught Monday night, lodged in the Guard House and taken out and brought home Tuesday— She appears determined not to remain in Burke. I don't know what had best be done with her. She will not stay in Burke. I don't want her here and I dislike very much indeed to sell her to a Speculator. . . .

.   .   .

Belmont,[33] **Tuesday, March 14 [15], 1859**   . . . . Mamie has been spending several weeks in Macon with Floride Williamson and the latter returning with her Ma thought it time to give Mamie a party—[34] So Saturday Mr Thomas came home and told me and Sunday we went in town. . . . The evening passed off pleasantly— The table looked beautiful. The centre ornament was a tree formed of ground pea candy and each sprig loaded with chrystalized fruit. On one of the branches was a bird's nest with two or three eggs— Near it hovered one of the birds, while the other had flown to the top of the tree. The credit of the idea must be given to Sis Anne though Sumerean who put her idea into execution said he had been *thinking* of it for the last ten years.[35] At each end were Pyramids of oranges with candy spun over them. They are lovely—perfectly transparent. They present a beautiful appearance yet they are not lasting. The candy has to be spun just before the supper is announced, and the next morning it had all disappeared. . . .

---

33. Gertrude Thomas named her country home Belmont, for Portia's seat in Shakespeare's *The Merchant of Venice.*

34. This was Mamie's society debut party; she did not return to Wesleyan after the summer of 1858.

35. Joseph Sumerean owned a popular confectioner's shop in Augusta.

[The diary of March 15, 1859, to July 15, 1861, is not among the extant journals. During that twenty-eight-month span, Sister Anne married William J. Vason, an attorney, in 1859, and in 1860 Mamie married J. Pinckney Thomas, a planter and younger brother of Jefferson Thomas. The Vasons lived in Augusta. Mamie and Pinck divided their time between Waynesboro and Augusta. Another son, Jefferson, was born to the Thomases on April 27, 1861.]

Ella Gertrude Clanton Thomas, 1852
(*Courtesy Michael F. Despeaux*)

J. Jefferson Thomas, ca. late 1850s
(*Courtesy Michael F. Despeaux*)

Col. Turner Clanton, ca. late 1840s
(*Courtesy Patricia D. Hulslander*)

Mary Luke Clanton, ca. late 1840s
(*Courtesy Madge Byne Rood*)

173

The Clanton home on Greene Street, Augusta, Ga. (*Oil painting courtesy Madge Byne Rood*)

The Clanton home a few years before it was torn down in 1956 to make way for a modern office building. The three-story, twenty-four-room house was built of brick imported from England and boasted solid silver hardware and doorknobs. (*Courtesy Hargrett Rare Book and Manuscript Library, University of Georgia*)

Gertrude Thomas with Mary Belle (left) and baby Jefferson Davis
(*Courtesy Mrs. James A. Miller*)

Mary (Mamie) Clanton Thomas, early
1860s (*Courtesy Mrs. H. LaBorde
Mathias*)

J. Pinckney (Pinck) Thomas, early 1860s
(*Courtesy Mrs. H. LaBorde Mathias*)

Julian P. Thomas, ca. 1900
(*Courtesy Token Thomas Norman*)

Gertrude Clanton Thomas, ca. 1895
(*Courtesy Virginia I. Burr*)

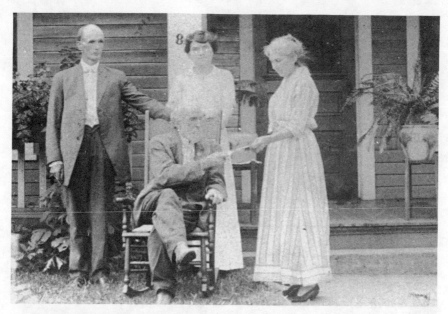

Patrick Farrell, Cora Thomas Farrell, Mary Belle Thomas Ingraham, and
J. Jefferson Thomas, ca. 1915 (*Courtesy Gertrude T. Despeaux*)

Catherine (Kate) Clanton Rood, ca. 1873
(*Courtesy Madge Byne Rood*)

Two children in front of the Clanton home, late 1880s (*Courtesy Reese Library, Augusta College, Augusta, Ga.*)

Augusta Medical College on Telfair Street, Augusta, Ga. (*Photo by Ernest P. Ferguson*)

Civil War powder mill chimney (obelisk) and Sibley Mill on the bank of the Augusta Canal (*Photo by Ernest P. Ferguson*)

Part II   *1861–1866*

5. Days of Confidence

War has been declared.
—*July 13, 1861*

Saturday, July 13, 1861   Events transcending in importance anything that has ever happened within the recollection of any living person in *our* country, have occurred since I have written last in my Journal. Since then *War* has been declared. Our ministers sent North to negotiate terms of peace have been treated with cool indifference. Our forts are still retained with the exception of Sumter. *There* the ever memorable victory was achieved which added fresh laurels to the glory of the gallant little state of South Carolina. Never shall I forget the state of intense excitement which pervaded the city of Augusta when it was announced that the fight was going on down at Sumter. Pa went down to Charleston just in time to witness from the top of the Charleston Hotel, the whole proceeding of the bombardment. It is needless to account the gallant achievment of Wigfall and others or to note the additional honour acquired by Gen Beauregard—[1] So much has taken place since then that in attempting to recall the events connected with the surrender of Fort Sumter, I appear to be endeavouring to recall incidents which have occurred many years instead of months ago— The call of President Lincoln for seventy five (75 000) troops. The refusal of Virginia, North Carolina, Tennessee and Arkansas to comply with Lincoln's call for troops to aid in subjugating the South and the subsequent secession of those states. The removal of the seat of [the Confederate] government from Montgomery, Alabama, to Rich-

---

1. Senator Louis T. Wigfall of Texas, originally from South Carolina, was a zealous secessionist. Brig. Gen. Pierre Gustave Toutant Beauregard of Louisiana, former superintendent of West Point, ordered the firing on Fort Sumter on April 12, 1861.

183

mond, Virginia— The thousands of troops which have passed through Augusta on their way to the seat of war—these and other events of similar importance have occured so rapidly that I feel bewildered in attempting to remember them all— When the fight at Sumter took place I remarked that "if I were not a Georgian I would wish to be a South Carolinian" but the very name of *Georgian* is of itself a heritage to boast of. I have always been proud of my native state but never more so than now. Nobly has she responded to the call for troops. Richmond County and especially Augusta has done much to be proud of. Our city has already sent off ten companys and is prepared to do more—

The Richmond Hussars the only Cavalry co which she can boast of have received orders to hold themselves in readiness to leave— And to this company *my husband* belongs, holding the rank of first Lieutenant and I can write this without one wish to have him remain with me. When Duty and Honour call him it would be strange if I would influence him to remain "in the lap of inglorious ease" when so much is at stake. Our country is invaded—our homes are in danger— We are deprived or they are attempting to deprive us of that glorious liberty for which our Fathers fought and bled and shall we tamely submit to this? Never! My husband will go— My brother Jimmie [Buddy] will leave in the same co so will Jack (Mr Thomas' younger brother)[2] and I am proud to see them exhibit the noble, manly, spirit which prompts them to go. It proves that southern blood has not degenerated in consequence of the life of luxury and ease we have been living. "He is thrice armed who hath his quarrel just"[3] and surely ours is a just cause— We are only asking for self government and freedom to decide our own destinys. We claim nothing of the North but—*to be let alone*—and *they*, a people like ourselves whose republican independence was won by a rebellion, whose liberty was achieved by a secession—to think that they should attempt to coerce us—the idea is preposterous. True, they have a much larger number of men than we have. Yet we are amply able to live within ourselves.

---

2. Andrew Jackson (Jack) Thomas, the youngest of Jefferson Thomas's brothers.

3. "Thrice is he arm'd who hath his quarrel just," from Shakespeare, *King Henry VI, Part II*, act 3, scene 2.

Lincoln has blockaded our ports and has since the 4th of July issued a proclamation calling for millions of dollars and additional men and the North has promised to furnish him the necessary amount of money and men— Indeed we are now in the midst of what all of us have read of—thought of—and dreamed of before, but never realised— A revolution— There are very many I very much fear who do not realise it now. Are not fully awake to the importance of the crisis that is upon us. This war has been forced upon us without reason, without law or pretext unless it is to force us to a state of vassalage—and shall we submit to this? As Mr [Alexander] Stephens remarked in his cotton produce loan speech in Augusta a few days ago— "Rather that all the rivers should be filled with blood and every mountain top covered with the bleached bone of our countryman than submit to them." While I earnestly long for a peaceable solution of this vexed question, I have faith to believe that we will conquor—sooner or later, *it must be so.* Trusting to the God of Battles, I shall see my husband go, feeling that if one word of mine could keep him at home I would not utter it. . . .

Some of our women are emulating the example of our Revolutionary mothers. We read of one lady giving her jewels valued at 1200 dollars, of another giving her diamonds worth 600 dollars, the latter a lady of Columbus Ga— The order is given for sand bags, uniforms and &c and the busy fingers of our women are engaged in the task of love and in an incredibly short space of time the order is filled. Sunday is not excepted but they are busy upon that day too. Georgia has nobly done her duty. Besides the regiment of regulars at Savannah under Col Charles J Williams "Georgia has sent to the field ten regiments of volunteers under Cols. Ramsay, Semmes, Wright, Doles, Jackson, Colquitt, Gartrell, Brumby, Goulding, Anderson, three regiments Independent Volunteers (field officers appointed by the President) under Cols Bartow, McLaws and Johnson of Kentucky two batallions commanded by Majors Villipigue and Hardeman besides two independent companys. There are also in Virginia Georgia companys enough to organise another regiment. So that we have now raised and sent off some 14,000 soldiers besides the regulars. To the brigade of Gen Phillips and the Toombs regiment, the 11 and 12 regiments, must be added Tom Cobb's legion. Col Cobb's independent regiment, Col Hammond's, Col McLain's and Col Underwood's which will increase Georgia's fighting force, including the regulars and Phillips' brigade to near twenty five thousand effective troops."[4] And in case the war continues she will be able to do much more than this—

Belmont, Tuesday July 16, 1861 Mr Thomas [is] in town tonight to attend a meeting of The Richmond Hussars. In my last entry in this book I was so much interested in the political events of the past few months that I did not allude to a domestic event of much greater personal interest to me, the birth of my little Jefferson. Darling little fellow! I have just nursed him and laid him down in such a sweet slumber. He was born on the 27th of April. He was born on Saturday and Mamie's Joe was born exactly two weeks after. . . . We first called our baby my favorite name of Edgar. I have always wished to call a son by that name. After naming for the two grand fathers Mr Thomas next deserved the compliment, but I thought there was no necessity for hastening the period at which he should be styled "old Jeff" and another thing, I do not think Jeff at all pretty and I have not altogether recovered from my girlish admiration for romantic names. I think Mr Thomas appreciates the compliment yet I heard him say to the baby the other day "Poor little fellow it is a pity to call you by such an ugly name."

I had decided on the name of Edgar and we were speaking of him by that name when Cap Stovall called (the day we were moving out of town) to let Mr Thomas know that his company would have to leave in Tom Cobb's legion—[5] Mr T was away from home— After parting with Cap Stovall I went into one of the rooms, seated myself quietly and tried calmly to face the momentous question of Should I be willing for him to go? I rose feeling that it was his duty to go and commending him to the "God who maketh all things for the best," I determined that nothing I should say should cause him to falter. Passing into the room where the baby was I kissed him

---

4. Gertrude was probably reading and copying from a daily newspaper. The commanding officers named, all from Georgia, were J. R. Ramsay, Paul J. Semmes, A. R. Wright, George Doles, John K. Jackson, A. H. Colquitt, L. J. Gartrell, A. V. Brumby, E. R. Goulding, G. T. Anderson, F. S. Bartow, L. B. McLaws, Edward Johnson, J. B. Villipigue, Thomas Hardeman, P. J. Phillips, Robert Toombs, Thomas R. R. Cobb, M. C. M. Hammond, [?] McLain, and W. J. Underwood.

5. Col. Thomas R. R. Cobb (later brigadier general) was the brother of Gen. Howell Cobb, former U.S. congressman and governor of Georgia. Thomas Cobb, a lawyer, didn't enter politics until secession aroused his fervor.

and called him Jefferson for his father and having babtised him with this name under such circumstances I feel that God will cause him to be a solace and comfort to me during Mr Thomas' absence. If the war continues I shall endeavour in my children to find my principal comfort teaching my boys to be proud of their father's example— Turner already shows great military spirit. He is now seven years old. Has been riding on horseback for three or four years. Anne (the little mare he has been riding for the past two years) has been an institution in the family for some years. Buddie first rode her—then Holt and afterwards Turner. His grand pa gave him a very pretty pony called Billy last week. It is amusing to see him on the pony going through the different cavalry tactics. He expresses himself as being anxious to engage in the war—only wishes he was large enough and &c—

On Sunday we sent down to the Rowell plantation for America. She has lost her baby which would have been three weeks old (had it lived) tonight. Pa has kindly permitted us to have her as a wet nurse for my baby. I do not give sufficient milk for him. I have tried cows milk. Then we had a goat. After we moved down here Georgianna nursed him and he commenced to fatten but her baby is nearly a year old and she did not have milk enough for both. My baby's bowels have been very much out of order for the past month but he is much better now. . . .

Sunday, July 21, 1861 For the last few days the most painful anxiety has been felt by the citizens of Augusta and the familys of the Oglethorpe Infantry and the Walker Light Infantry especially with regard to the members of the two companys I have named. We knew them to be under Gen Robert Garnett's command in the northern part of Virginia attempting to crush out the abolition traitors of the Panhandle—we knew too that the Viginia troops they had to aid them were raw militia yet we felt confidence in their acquitting themselves nobly—and so they have. They have fought long and well and when obliged to retreat from Laurel Hill at the last possible moment of safety, so admirably was their retreat managed the pursuers had no opportunity to use their small arms "so well was their rear guarded." . . . Friday afternoon Mr Thomas went in town to attend a meeting of the Hussars. About half past eleven he returned home in a most *joyous, triumphant* state of mind and aroused me with the welcome news that we had *gained another victory at Bull's Run* (about three miles north west of Manassas

Junction) with a loss on our side of 142 and a Federal loss of 986 left dead on the field—[6] The Federalist[s] had been all day burying their dead having sent in a flag of truce asking an armistice which was granted for that purpose— He brought news too that the two companys from Augusta were safe. . . .

I have been so much interested in the war that I have attended to few events of a domestic character. We have been out at Belmont for nearly a month. In looking back to the last winter I recall one of the most pleasant winters that I have spent since I have been married. The house we occupied (owned by Mr Tom Miller) was a very delightful residence.[7] Although rather large with an objectionable front entrance the housekeeping and dining room arrangements were of a very superior kind. If Mr Thomas had not been ordered off we would certainly have kept it for next year but as it is during his absence next winter I expect I will spend my time with Pa and Ma. Col Vason and Sis Anne had their same rooms at the Augusta Hotel and Pinck and Mamie rooms immediately over them. Mr Scales and Jule were also at the Augusta Hotel (where Nat was born)— . . .

Yesterday morning we went over and spent the day at the Rowell place. I was engaged in sewing on my soldiers coat. Saw Mrs Harris' Carriage that had been down to the depot for her. She did not come and speaking of Mrs Harris reminds me of Books. I have read nothing new for some time. The Blockade has prevented the importation of new Books and loyal as I am and wish to be I think that for a time this will prove a serious inconvenience. I do not mean just at present for if we read "the signs of the times" and keep posted in political events we will have little time for anything else—but after the war is over, or if it continues for some time what shall we do for Books? It is true we all have standard books in our library, many of which will repay a second perusal with a more matured mind but our people generally are new to the making of Books and for some time we will miss the delightful pleasure of culling over half a dozen new Books to see which we shall read

---

6. The bloody Battle of Bull Run (the first Manassas), fought in Virginia on July 21, 1861, was the first major engagement of the war and a solid victory for the South.

7. The Thomases, like many others whose primary homes were in the country, rented a house in Augusta for the winter season. The more affluent usually owned two homes.

first— Yet why are we dependent upon the north? The two books which have created most sensation in the novel reading portion of the country for some time have been *Adam Bede, The Mill on the Floss* and *Beulah*. The two former by Miss Evans of England and the latter by Miss Evans of Mobile—[8] and we have plenty of talent lying latent in the South to make for us a glorious name. We have one great drawback—indolence—to contend against. Say what we may it is more this than indifference or anything else which prevents so many from improving their God given talent. Unless urged by the spur of adversity and dependence they are too apt to bury their talent, willing to be entertained but not willing to do anything themselves towards entertaining. . . .

. . .

Tuesday, July 29 [30], 1861   The date of the last entry made in this Journal will be one ever memorable in the history of our Southern Confederacy— Upon the 21st of July was fought the battle of Manassas. But *today* is one still more memorable to me— Today Mr Thomas leaves home for months—perhaps forever! Tomorrow the Richmond Hussars go into camp in Augusta and in another week they expect to leave for Virginia the seat of war. Troops are rapidly being concentrated to enable our Confederacy to follow up the brilliant victory of Manassas. Pinck and Mamie spent last night with us. Ma and Co came by this morning on their way to town expecting we would go on at the same time but there was so much to be done that we concluded not to leave until after an early dinner. Since then Jack has come up. Mr Thomas is asleep now. Jack is resting up stairs. Everything is ready. We are going in town to be with him as much as possible during the time he stays in town. Tamah has gone in this morning. We will carry Patsey, America, Willy, Daniel and Grif— Mr Thomas will carry Daniel with him. . . .

I can scarcely realise that my dear Husband is upon the eve of so important a movement. Yet when I think of it I find the tears roll

---

8. *Adam Bede* (1859) and *The Mill on the Floss* (1860) were written by English novelist George Eliot (Mary Ann Evans). *Beulah* (1859) was by American novelist Augusta Jane Evans, who also wrote *Macaria* (1864).

irresistibly down my cheeks. Many times I have retired to indulge in a burst of uncontrollable tears but I have never but once before him yielded to my emotions. . . . Saturday night he returned from Burke and was telling me at the tea table that that day he had given the Negroes holiday at his plantations in Burke. Upon his telling them that he was going off for such an indefinite time they appeared very much affected. Aunt Patience burst into tears and sobbed bitterly. When the cars came by every Negro from both places followed him and shook hands with him as he bid them farewell— It was too much for me and I rose from the table excited beyond control. Turner joined me and for a time we sat in the front Piazzi, all of us feeling the bitterness of parting— My darling husband how I love him. Oh God shield him in the hour of danger—

.   .   .

Augusta. Saturday, August 11 [10], 1861   Every night this week it has been so warm. The musquitoes have been so bad and I have been so thor[ou]ghly sleepy and tired when night came that I have not felt like writing. Then again Mr T has been at home several nights and of course I could not write then. This morning he took breakfast before I did. I told them when they roused me that I wanted none, so I turned over and took a real good nap from which I woke thor[ou]ghly refreshed. . . .

This afternoon I took May Bell Miller to ride down to the Camp. There was a very large crowd there. All on the three sides of the [Parade] Ground occupied by the Hussars were crowded with Buggys and Carriages, while a good many ladies and gentleman were around the tents. They were practising leaping the bar. They did very well indeed. Yesterday afternoon having been the first time they had practised at all. Beginning with the Captain and proceeding in order of rank, they jumped, some of them going over in gallant style, and other Horses refusing at first to take the leap. Mr Thomas was riding "Stanley" and took the leaps in fine style. It was pleasing to hear as he did so the exclamation from persons who were standing near— "Mr Thomas is a fine rider," "What a beautiful Horse," "The finest Horse in the company and &c-" Stanley is certainly a fine horse. I am now driving the other Carriage Horse (Chester) with a cream col horse which Mr Thomas once used as a Buggy Horse. . . .Late Tuesday evening we rode down to the Camp Mamie and Sis Anne also going— Saw their white aprons given to them and the men engaged in feeding and watering their horses— Ma was quite pleased and that afternoon after we left she & I went round to the South Carolina Depot to see the soldiers take their supper— The ladies serve up a supper gotten up at the expense of the citizens who contribute what they feel able to. They have been doing this all the summer thus entertaining a great many tired and hungry soldiers, giving them breakfast or supper as the case might be. . . .

The next day Thursday I spent the morning at the Masonic Hall lining blankets for the Hussars. I sent down and had two large water melons carried up which appeared to be quite acceptable— That afternoon I had Turner and Mary Bell dressed up nice and took them to the camp with me. It had very much the appearance of rain but I was determined to go for I had heard that *Col Tom Cobb would be there*. I was sitting in front of the tent when Cap Stovall came up and introduced him to me, mentioning my name as "Mrs Thomas the wife of his first lieutenant." I rose and shook hands feeling more pleasure in receiving an introduction to Tom Cobb than any other man in the Confederate States. His name is the synonyme for everything that is upright and noble— Upon his enquiring "if I was willing to allow my husband to go," I replied "Yes, since twas his duty but that I was especialy pleased that he was going in a Legion commanded by Col Cobb"— Mr Thomas just then riding up, Col Cobb went up to him and shook hands remarking at the same time that his was the finest Horse he had seen, adding laughingly that he must not ride a finer horse than the Col. I was amused at Tom Stovall who looking around remarked "My Horse is not here," implying so plainly that if he had been Mr Thomas' would not have been the finest there. Col Cobb gave the men a talk and then coming to the tent where Tom and Bowling Stovall were he took a seat and talked for more than half an hour— He is a handsome man with a pale intellectual cast of feature with a particularly sharp nose which I am disposed to admire. . . .

. . . .

Sunday, August 18, 1861   I have realized one of the most eventful moments in my life— *Mr Thomas has left for the seat of war*— Yesterday afternoon The Richmond Hussars struck their tents and last night left for the Old Dominion. All day yesterday it rained. Mr Thomas had his trunk packed the day before but there was constantly something to be added to it. For several days I had been busy preparing and finishing off. Friday it rained almost all day and the weather was in unison with my feelings— The long suppressed emotion would have vent and for several days I have wept when I would reflect how soon I would be left alone. The company were invited to dine at the Globe Hotel by the hospitable Mr Mularkey but Mr Thomas dined at home. He was copying off his will. His occupation, the rain and the knowledge of the hour that must come completely unnerved me, and when my Husband turned to me to say good bye I could only cling to him in speechless agony— After kissing again, and again the children and bidding the weeping servants farewell, he mounted his horse, in a perfect torrent of rain and rode off to the Camp. . . .

I knew that there was one more chance to see him before he left—the depot. The children had already left so Ma and I rode round to the South Carolina Depot. We found the streets thronged with carriages. The side walks lined with people— Just then it commenced to rain and I never heard rain fall in greater force. We at last took shelter in one of the houses and then Holt brought Buddy to us to bid us good bye— Pa was with Ma and I and as Buddy shook hands with him I saw every nerve in Pa's face quiver and I knew what a struggle it was for him to keep from crying. Bud (brave boy) kissed us and stood the trial manfully—[9] Pa went off and sometime afterwards brought Mr Thomas where we were alone. It was well we waited there for in the crowd we would never have found him. What a thrill of contentment passed through me to see him again and receive the familiar kiss— The supper for the Hussars had been set in the depot in consequence of the rain. We went with Mr Thomas and waited near the door while he pressed through the crowd to procure a cup of coffee. At last he came bringing Mary Bell in his arms and holding Turner by the hand. . . . He did not go with us to the Carriage. Poor darling I know he must have suffered. Seated in the Carriage, sobbing bitterly I heard the cannon firing in honor of their departure and I was irresistibly reminded of the scene in *Fazio* where Bianci exclaims, "My heart! my heart! it is not iron! It breaks, it breaks."[10] I have wept so often

---

9. James (Buddy) Clanton was only seventeen years old and Jack Thomas about the same age when they left for Virginia.

10. From the Italian drama *Fazio or the Italian Wife*, a tragedy by Henry Hart Milman (1791–1868).

and so much today. This must not be. I must endeavour if I can to get rid of this awfully heart yearning feeling which I have. I think of my Husband and miss him so much now, what oh God would be my feelings if I should never see him more!

Monday, August 19, 1861 . . . I wrote to Mr Thomas yesterday and sent to the office three times to have it mailed. Each time the office was closed. Last night I wrote an additional page and this morning another. Every letter to Richmond costs ten cents. A serious drawback it must be to many a poor soldier in hearing from his family. The 10 cts which pays for his letter perhaps deprives his children of bread. Yet what a luxury to hear from the loved ones at home! . . .

.   .   .

Sunday, September 18 [15], 1861 Every moment that I devote to writing is given up to writing to Mr Thomas. I write him everything which transpires and then I dislike to write it over again in my Journal. It seems "like a twice told tale." I commenced to write him tonight but my head swims so that I can scarcely write and I am not in a cheerful mood proper to write. Poor *little George is dead*. He is the only child of Georgiana. Since he has been sick I have had him in the house and have nursed him until he has become an object of great interest to me. Dr Eve was to see him and yesterday I called for more medicine for him. When I reached home tonight I found that he was just dead. Aside from being interested in him I disliked to write Mr Thomas of his death for he has been so unfortunate since he left. We have lost three Horses that I have had to tell him of and I do not wish to tell him of anything calculated to depress him. I received two letters from him last night. He has left Richmond for Yorktown where he will be engaged in skirmish duty for thirty or forty miles around a position of danger without an opportunity of achieving distinction. I have been feeling gloomy all day. . . .

While I am writing the servants are holding misering as they call it in Georgiana's house— They are singing and praying. One of our Horses Henry died a few days ago from a gore received from Reauben a bull of very superior kind. The wind comes to us tainting the whole atmosphere with a most disagreeable odour and compelling one to close the doors and windows in self defence. I feel too dull and bad to connect ideas or guide my pen so I will copy a few lines to wile away time. I do not wish to call America and Patsey in yet awhile. . . . I have just been out in the Piazzi and have been listening to them singing and praying. How remarkably eloquent the Negros are! They can rise and continue speaking for a great length of time without being at a loss for a single word. I was much impressed with the prayer of one of them who prayed for the mistress of this plantation and the absent master. They are now singing "Hallujah praise ye the Lord."

Saturday, October 12, 1961   All of us have some happy moments but in this past week has been crowded enough happiness for a long while. *Mr Thomas is at home*. Oh joyous thought! Oh Darling I never knew before how much I loved you. Absence has taught me the more fully to appreciate your many noble traits of character. I will confide (what may appear egotistical) to you my Journal, that I think that my Husband particularly excels in all those quiet domestic virtues which render home so happy. . . . He is here on business connected with the troop, selling Confederate bonds,[11] purchasing winter clothing and &c— He has only twenty days leave of absence and this week has glided away like a pleasant dream. Mother still continues sick. She has now been in bed or confined to her room four months. She is very much debilitated. . . .

Tuesday, October 15, 1861   I am expecting Mr Thomas every moment from Burke. . . . He has not been very well for the past two or three days, and his Mother's sickness weighs upon his mind. Her nervous organization received a shock when Mr T and Jack (the one her eldest and the other her youngest child) left and next week she will be called upon to give up Bob. . . . I have never seen such a state of things as exists in our country at present. Meat is selling for 30 cts pr lb, and everything else in proportion. Money is very scarce. No cotton selling and as that is the life of our business everything must be at a stand still while it remains unsold. . . .

Sunday, November 10, 1861   . . . My Husband's Mother is dead. She departed this life the 1st day of this month at two oclock in the

---

11. In July 1861 the Confederate Congress authorized $50 million in bonds for war purposes. All citizens, and particularly planters, were urged to invest in the bonds to show their patriotism.

morning— This not altogether unlooked for event is enough to sadden our hearts but there are clouds in the political horizon which add to our depression. The great naval fleet with regard to which so many speculations have been made, has sailed from New York and attacking our coast has succeeded in taking possession of Port Royal [South Carolina].[12] The point of disembarkation is well chosen for their purposes. It threatens the railroad and water communication between Charleston and Savannah, is about seventy 70 miles from the former and thirty miles from the latter city. It is also less than one hundred miles from Augusta. The editor of the *Chronicle*[13] thinks Augusta is in as much danger as any of them if the enemy should dare to leave the seacoast for any distance. "The character of the country between the named seaboard cities is much more difficult for the march of an army than between this point and Port Royal. The first crosses the course of the streams, the last follows them." I have never so fully realised that we are engaged in a war which threatens to desolate our firesides.

Last night a rumour reached us that the Federalists were within 10 miles of Savannah, and that several car loads of women and children had left that place anticipating an attack. God grant ours may be the victory. We lack arms & ammunition. In that respect they have the advantage over us but our men are fighting for liberty and Homes, the Federalists fighting for a name. The Union can *never* exist again. There is one feature I particularly dislike. In their company they have it is reported 1000 Negroes whom they have stolen or who have run away from their owners in Virginia. These they might scatter through our state and do us some harm. They openly boast they have red Zouave uniforms for the Negroes whom they intend forming into regiments when they commence their inland attack. Oh for a whirlwind of destruction to drive from our land the footsteps of the hated foe— Fighting against an equal foe we could conquer or against a greater number but this attempt to arouse the vindictive passions of an inferior

---

12. Port Royal, S.C., was bombarded by the U.S. navy on November 7, 1861. Fifty war ships and transports under Admiral S. F. Dupont sailed into Port Royal Sound. Along with land troops under Union general William T. Sherman, they took Port Royal and neighboring islands where the valuable Sea Island cotton was grown.

13. The *Augusta Chronicle* has had several names since its founding in 1795 but has always familiarly been called the *Chronicle*.

race so fills my soul with horror language fails to discribe it. At the same time that we hear of the successful entrance into the harbour of Port Royal we hear of another success of the Confederate Army in Belmont Missouri— At sea they have the advantage of us but on land we usually come off conqueror—

Mr Thomas has been at home much longer than he expected. The sickness I alluded to in my note of the 15th in the Journal terminated in an attack of jaundice for which he had to have Dr Eve visit him. . . .

Saturday, November 23, 1861   I was interrupted while writing the above by Mr Thomas. It was the last night he was to be at home at Belmont and all my time must be devoted to him. The next day he left home, came in town and Tuesday Nov the 12th left for Virginia again. I accompanied him to the depot and felt as I parted from him in its full intensity the horrors of this unholy war. Oh when will it cease and the dear old ties be again united. . . .

.   .   .   .

Augusta, December 5, 1861   . . . The Presbyterian Church are having a general assembly. The first one ever held in the Confederate States and consequently of much importance.[14] Pa is entertaining two of the ministers. . . . This afternoon Turner came in with a letter from his Pa saying there was a gentleman at the door who brought it and said he was just from Yorktown. I went to the door and found that it was Mr Hatfield. I invited him in the sitting room and listened eagerly as he told me that Mr Thomas was well. What a pleasure it will be to his wife to welcome him tonight. Mr Thomas writes me "that the order now is that 4 men shall [have] 25 days leave of absence at a time. The married men have the preference. Com & non commissione[d] officers also. My turn will come again. Lt Archer is next. Mine next." I have been counting up the time to see how long it will be before he comes. When I think of my dear Husband as being exposed to such hardships my heart aches. He writes me that they have moved from their "comfortable log huts four or five miles below our camp and we have been sleep-

---

14. The first meeting of the general assembly of the Southern Presbyterian church was convening in Augusta.

ing for the past four or five days on the ground under bushes. We sent up for our tents today. We were ordered here at one oclock at night without a blanket or anything to eat—how long we are to remain the Genl himself does not know, at least a month." In the midst of luxury and comfort I often think of him. Tonight it was so bitter cold as I was coming from church and to think that he is exposed to such hardships.

December 12, 1861 One month has passed since Mr Thomas left home. What may not happen in one month more. In these troublous times one can form no idea of what may come next. For several days a fight has been expected at the Peninsular where Mr Thomas Bud and Jack are. I have a triple interest there and watch and wait with such sickening interest for each day's mail. The greatest fire that has ever been know[n] for many years occurred last night. *Charleston has been almost totally destroyed by fire.* It commenced last night at 9 oclock and raged with undiminished ardour all night. The theatre, St Andrew's Hall, several of the churches and many public buildings were burnt, as well as the Circular Church, the Unitarian and the English Lutheran Church. . . . We have not ascertained the origin but it may not have been the act of an incendiary as it was an extremely windy night and may have been a providential yet mysterious act of God. I hope that the Yankees had nothing to do with it.

Friday, December 13, 1861 Tonight we attended an Educational Meeting at the Presbyterian Church where I was very much interested indeed. . . . [Dr Lyon's] object was to found a university of much higher order than anything we have at present where a man might attain a much higher order of intellect (education) than he could obtain in ordinary college course. . . . Just then Mr Richardson of Virginia rose to argue in favour of grammar or common schools. He was answered by Judge Foote of Alabama Dr Thornwell[15] and Mr Bailey the latter the president of a college in Texas. A good many were beginning to leave as they were continuing the

---

15. James Henley Thornwell, a Presbyterian minister, was the acknowledged leader of the Southern Presbyterian church. He was a former president of South Carolina College and a professor at Presbyterian Theological Seminary in Columbia, S.C.

discussion rather long altho I was not weary at all. I hope they will succeed for I have boys to educate and I do hope that we will be enabled to give them that *greatest* of *temporal blessings* a *good* a *thorough education*. The subject of education is to me full of interest. I am inclined to think that we are wrong so far as the education of our women is concerned. It is apt to be too superficial and our young girls leave school *too soon*. The mind should be trained, disciplined for after all it is only laying the foundation. I have learned more than I knew while at school. What I read I derive more benefit from and it is because my mind is more mature. . . . On last Sunday [Dr Palmer][16] preached again. I never saw the Presbyterian Church so crowded as it was. When he preached on Wednesday he confined himself very closely to his notes and appeared constrained. Sunday he dispensed with them altogether and preached a very eloquent soul stirring and gospel sermon. Real Methodist revival sermon— Oh Gospel preaching is the most effective after all— Give to me the preaching that touches the heart. The mind may be edified while the heart remains cold as an iceberg but the "Heart in waking woke the Mind." . . .

The last night of 1861 . . . Tonight since tea I have been reading from one of my note books a discription of my visit to Savannah two springs ago. I recollected that tonight was the last night of the year 1861 and concluded that I would write a few lines. . . . Today I have spent at Belmont in the homely but necessary duty of having meat salted and lard fryed. I was down engaged in the same manner about a week ago. Uncle Sam has great faith in the effect of the moon and willing to test the truth of what I am inclined to believe in myself I did not have as much killed last week when the "Moon was (to use Uncle Sam's expression) on the waste" as this week when it was beginning to fill. The effect which is said to be produced is a shrinking away of meat killed when the moon is wanning and vice versa. I have never seen such a frost as was on the ground this morning between eight and nine oclock. Double Branches had large pieces of ice floating in it nearly an inch thick. I

---

16. Benjamin Morgan Palmer of New Orleans, La., a firebrand Presbyterian minister, preached a Thanksgiving Day proslavery sermon in 1860 that was printed and circulated throughout the South. He was elected the first moderator of the general assembly at the meeting in Augusta.

took Turner and Mary Bell down with me and left Jeff in America's charge. I brought up with me white hyacinths, narcissus and English laurestina.

It would be contrary to custom to omit a discription of how Christmas Day was spent. We all dined with Ma and in the afternoon Ma was sending off blankets to Bud by Express so I wrote a letter to Mr Thomas & enclosed in it. Ma sent some cake and fruits at the same time. The day before Christmas eve the streets presented the liveliest appearance imaginable. The confectionary stores were crowded so that it was impossible to see anything with pleasure. The streets reminded me of discriptions that I have read of the carnival in Rome. There is certainly a striking similarity in the excitement and wild glee of Christmas eve and the particularly quiet manner in which we celebrate Christmas Day making it as the Lent succeeding the carnival. I allude to the white population of course for the servants have a carnival all the time that they are not in the land of dreams during the Christmas week. I think the plantation Negroes sleep a good deal.

I had aided Santa Claus in the purchase of some presents for the children . . . and Ma and I arranged the tables for the reception of their presents. I bought Turner a pistol. His Aunt Anne gave him a knife. His Grand Ma a waggon with two Horses attached that could be wound up and run over the floor, and his aunt Mary a Monkey in a box. Mary Bell had a dining sett of china complete which I bought for her— Grand Ma gave her a ring, Aunt Anne a sett of parlour furniture, Aunt Mary a book and a wooden tea sett. Patsey a cup and I a bucket and a Tin Horse. Patsey also gave her a rooster. For Jeff I had a Hobby Horse which outshone all the toys. Patsey gave him an India rubber dog and Turner bought him a rattle. Mr Scales gave the children one dollar apiece. I sent Lou [Lula Scales] a ring— Gave Cate a tea sett, Holt a pair of ducks and Cora a ring. Ma gave me a handsome sett of mourning jewelry. I gave money to Patsey and America and all the other servants in the yard. I don't know why I am going so into detail mentioning all the toys that the children had given to them unless it is that in counting up the gifts of successive years it may create an emotion of shame that they have preserved so few.

I have often glanced at my neglected Journal and [thought] that I would pen a few lines but it [is] not that there is *nothing* to write but so much that prevents my writing more— Events of such importance are transpiring that the little every day occurrences that make up a day fade into utter insignificance. Every day brings the news of an event which in ordinary times would have startled us and agitated our minds but which from their very frequency have ceased to disturb us so much. . . . Speaking of Christmas Day Mr Thomas writes "I passed yesterday very quietly. We were until dinner getting back to camp from Bethel. We found Mrs Archer here to spend the day with us. We had an eggnog and a turkey for a 4 oclock dinner but I did not enjoy it much. She remained till late but I was rather bored & felt as if I had rather be alone. Today I feel as if I wished this war was over & that I was at home and that every Yankee engaged in it was in the bottom of the ocean." I will say Amen to that wish. . . .

January 1, 186[2] . . . The affairs of the South look more prosperous at the present juncture than at any other period since the commencement of the war. The tide of sympathy throughout Western Europe is decidedly with us. One great advanatage which will be gained by the war is the distinction which will be made between the Northerner and Southerner. We have heretofore been confounded with the Yankees and all that was known of us was gained through the Northern Abolition press. Now they see a united people who in the bravery of their armies and majesty of their cause are making an impression upon the minds of the world. God speed the day when our independence shall be achieved, our Southern Confederacy acknowledged and peace be with us again. I wonder if the Northern people still cling to the delusion that such a thing as our being united with them is possible. So far from it I am inclined to believe that each successive day but widens the gulf between. Each man we lose but serves to render more intense our hatred of the Yankee. Some of them may be sincere in their abolition feelings but what consistency is there in the effort to free one Negro if his freedom causes the death of many whites— Is their love for their Black Brother greater than they experience for their white? Oh they are a miserable fanatic set. . . .

.   .   .

Augusta, February 17, 1862 My pen refuses to fly fast enough to record the thick coming events. Just now we are in the midst of a great crisis. The Anaconda embrace with which Lincoln has threatened us is almost being fulfilled. As he unfurls "his slow length along" we begin to perceive the better his huge propo[r]tions. The

Yankees are upon our coast and his foot prints are upon the soil of almost every Confederate state. We have recently sustained some startling reverses but today we have the news that Fort Donelson [Tennessee] has surrendered and that we have had 15000 of our men taken prisoner. . . . Oh these are troublous times. For two or three weeks an hourly attack has been expected at Savannah. We lost Roanoke Island [North Carolina] and between two and three thousand prisoners. Poor Cap Wise was killed there but in dying called to his men "to fight them on." Last night and tonight there is a meeting at the City Hall to adopt some measures for the defence of this place. The river is now 30 feet high, and still raining. If the Yankees were to happen by an overwhelming majority to take Savannah they could easily run up here as they did on the Tennessee River when they disturbed the peaceful inhabitants of Florence Alabama. For nearly six weeks I have been expecting Mr Thomas home. Lt Archer has returned to Virginia but since the Roanoke fight all furloughs have been revoked. His only chance now consists in coming home to recruit for the Legion which is to be raised to 5000. Tom Cobb ranking as General. . . .

Everything during the winter has been so quiet that I had almost dared to dream of Mr Thomas resignation. While our army has I greatly fear been inactive McClellan[17] has been drilling his men thoroughly and with vast expenditure of money has fitted out a costly armada to send against us who are utterly unable to cope with them on water. During this season of inactivity an apathy appeared to steal over us. Disaffection in some degree began to make its way among our troops, but the reverses we have recently sustained will nerve our men to greater deeds of daring, bind all hands and hearts in a common cause and make us again renew our pledge that we will conquer by God's help.

During the first of the winter I felt unsettled but after Christmas animated by the hope of Mr Thomas' return, and cheered to think that no fighting was going on I began to feel as tho society was not so completely unhinged. I had even commenced the usual winter routine of visiting and was out with Ma paying some calls when at Mrs Governor Schley's[18] we were told by someone that four Gun Boats had succeeded in getting in between Savannah and

---

17. Gen. George B. McClellan was commander-in-chief of the Union army in February 1862. He was relieved of that post in March 1862.

18. The wife of former Georgia governor William Schley (1835–37).

Fort Pulaski. We called on Mrs Boyce and Lamar after that, but "a change had passed over the spirit of my dream"— My heart was no longer in the duty I was engaged in. I was walking up Broad St on my way to the Hall (where I am one of the Directrisses for the Soldier's Aid Society) when my attention was directed to the bulletin board at the door of the *Chronicle & Sentinel* giving information of the taking of Roanoke, the enemy being at Florence Ala and &c— I was particularly gloomy last week caused by the idea that Mr Thomas could not come home and aided by the very unpleasant rainy weather— It is enough to give one the blues of itself without the accessory of defeat and anx[i]ety—

April 4, 1862, Atlanta Geo. Dear old Journal. Welcome again! I assure you I have not forgotten you but during the past month other and dearer duties have monopolised my time. For the last forty days Mr Thomas has been at home and oh how quickly has the time passed. . . . During all this time Mr Thomas has been at home recruiting for the Richmond Hussars. With Corporal Young's assistance he has raised the no of recruits to between 70 and 80. Wednesday April 2d they came on up here where Major Yancey has by Col Cobb's instruction established a Camp of Instruction. Yesterday with all the children America and Patsey I started from Augusta and arrived last night. I was met at the car by Mr Thomas and am now in the Trout House in a very pleasant room. . . . Mr Thomas took tea with me last night and returned to camp. Today we took dinner here. He is the only commissioned officer in the Co and thus the duties fall heavily upon him. After he returned home we remained in Augusta until after the 10th of March when the requ[i]sition for 12000 men was made upon Georgia. That circumstance no doubt quickened the movement of those who volunteered to avoid the draft. . . . It is delightful to have an occasional glimpse of Mr Thomas and feel that the hour of parting has not yet come. . . .

.   .   .

Monday, April 14, 1862 This afternoon Mr Thomas came in and wished to know if I would like to go to see the New Orleans opera troupe tonight. After tea we walked up there but did not go in. I received a letter from Mamie today. She mentions that Pa and Pinck left for Goldsboro [North Carolina] Saturday morning to see

Buddy who has been quite sick. Meal is selling in Augusta for $2.00 pr bushel. Pa has offered in the papers to sell meal at his Rowell Plantation for one dollar to the familys of Volunteers from Richmond and Columbia Countys. Saturday morning two pieces came out about it in the *Constitutionalist*,[19] one of them signed "A poor soldiers wife" wishing to know how they were to get the meal, that the mill was in the country, they had no Horses and could not be expected to turn themselves into beasts of burden, that it would not be cheap at 10 cts pr bushel unless delivered. Now this is en couraging truly. Pa can sell every bushel of meal that he has at $2.00 pr bushel and what reason is there that he should not? but upon such ungrateful wretches.[20]

Thursday, April 17, 1862 Monday night I stopped writing in my Journal and commenced an answer to "The Poor Soldier's wife" who replied in such an ungrateful manner to Pa's offer to sell meal. It was a long reply, fearlessly written and inspired by a womanly horror of such conduct. It is too long to copy into this book. I don't know wether the Editor [of the *Chronicle*] will publish it or not, but if he does not the Editor of the *Constitutionalist* certainly shall. Since I wrote last I have visited the Empire House on Whitehall Street where they have one of the Hospitals and oh such a sight it was. I know I should fail if I were to attempt a discription of it. The night before we visited there three men had died. The wife of one of them arrived the next afternoon but he had been buried before she reached here. She was a plain respectable looking young woman, the mother of three children the youngest of whom was 6 six weeks old. She was giving way to no outburst of sorrow. She could not indulge in the luxury of Grief, but I knew what a desolate heart she must bear under that calm exterior and knowing the value of genuine sympathy I seated myself by her and told her how

---

19. The *Augusta Constitutionalist.*

20. Col. Turner Clanton was generous in his support of the war effort. On September 2, 1861, noting published contributions to the hospital fund, Gertrude wrote, " 'With the card of Miss Catie Clanton $25. With the card of Master Holt Clanton $25. With the card of Miss Cora Clanton $50. With the card of Mrs. Mary Clanton $100.' Pa has been very liberal and has given between 1000 and 2000 dollars to aid the soldier's cause." And on April 23, 1862, "The Richmond Hussars came down yesterday afternoon to give Pa three cheers for his liberal contribution of $500 to them."

sorry I was for her—"that I too had a husband in the Army." Her lip quivered and shaking her head she replied, "You'll lose him I reckon." A few moments after she wished to know "how long my old man had been in the Army?" I had never thought the homely old expression could convey so much pathos. Her name was Bryson. Her husband had left home when her baby was one week old, gone up to Camp McDonald, there contracted measles and removed here where he died. Oh the desolation of that home when she returns to it.

There is much discomfort at the Hospital and to my inexperienced eye a general want of system. The halls were terribly stained with tobacco juice. The convalescents walked through the passages smoking pipes which added to the unholsome atmosphere and there were too many in one room. To a man of refinement and education how horrible the association and promixity of men essentially different from him. No privacy—no seclusion. I verily believe that if I was laid on one of those beds seeing so many around me sick and hearing so much noise I would soon be in the situation they are in. This afternoon as I passed by the parlour door I saw Mrs Jones, Ova and Eva in conversation with two men, one of whom . . . I saw yesterday with about ten more at the Hospital in one room. I was struck with the air of refinement about him then and knew him at once this afternoon. I wanted to go in and shake hands with him & let him know how I sympathised with him, but was restrained by the conventionalism which characterises most Southern women, and prevents them from following the noble dictates of their nature. . . .

.   .   .

Wednesday, April 23, 1862   This I suppose will be the last day of our stay in Atlanta. Mr Thomas expected to have left for Virginia via Augusta last night but the cars could not be procured for the transportation of the troop. . . . Leaving Atlanta entails a seperation from Mr Thomas and how I dread it the "Searcher of all Hearts" alone knoweth. My dear Husband, my own darling—how I shrink from parting with him again. . . .

I have been out several times in the street a good many times on Whitehall the principal street, and have made several purchases. A cap and straw hat for Turner three pair of shoes for Jeff at $1.25 apiece. Black silk thread at 5 and 10 skeins, black flax at 10 cts pr skein. Everything I have bought I gave less for it than it could be bought in Augusta. A good many of the things are higher. I have just stopped to write to Ma informing her that we would reach Augusta tomorrow night. . . . I have been reading most of the day a volume of Bayard Taylor's[21] *Travels* called *The Lands of the Saracen* including his travels in Palestine Syria Asia Minor, Sicily and Spain. . . . The last thing I have seen from the pen of Bayard Taylor (who is a favorite writer with me) has been a discription of Manassas after it was evacuated by our forces. Pity he is a Yankee. . . .

.   .   .

June 2, 1862 "Bless the Lord oh my soul and all that is within me bless and praise his name." Such was the involuntary prayer of Thanksgiving which burst from my lips while writing to Mr Thomas this afternoon. His dispatch had been handed me giving me the welcome news that "The Richmond Hussars were all safe." *The Fight at Richmond* commenced at 12 oclock on Saturday and continued yesterday. Oh what anguish has wrung the brow of thousands throughout the length & breadth of the land— While Mamie has been desponding I have ever felt sanguine that Mr Thomas was uninjured.[22] . . . Wild rumours without the least foundation have been flying about the streets today. Mrs Nichols the wife of one of the Hussars came today to ask Pa what news we had received. She had heard that fifteen of the Hussars had been killed. Another sent to me this afternoon, having heard that twenty five of Mr Thomas' company as well as himself had been killed. Mr Danforth came to Pa this morning having heard that both Mr Thomas and Pinck had been killed. The latter report originating from a servant passing yesterday afternoon and hearing someone crying enquired what was the matter and was told (so he said) by one of our servants, that both Mr Thomases were killed.

Thank God this is not so— The fight thus far has been carried on by the right wing of the army— The impression appears to prevail here that it was not a general fight but was an attempt of the Confederates to cut off some divisions of the enemy that had

---

21. James Bayard Taylor (1825–78), poet, novelist, and travel writer.

22. J. Pinckney Thomas had by this time joined the Richmond Hussars, presumably after the March requisition of 12,000 men from Georgia.

crossed the Chickohominy and were about to establish a new paral-[l]el on the Richmond side of that stream. It is reported that a large body of the Federals are on this side of the crack if so we may yet expect more fighting—and oh God how earnestly I long for a victory and speedy peace.

In a speech made at the City Hall this afternoon in a meeting for the defence of the city I am told Lt Col Rains[23] asserted that in his opinion the war would not last more than five or six weeks longer— If it brings peace in that time and an honourable settlement of difficultys I shall hail it with delight, yea with rapture *but if not* if peace brings in its train dishonourable submission to Lincoln rule and abject compliance with the wishes of his Myrmidons then I say fight on—

"Fight and fight well, strike and strike home" better far better, death than dishonour. The remarkable order of Gen Butler[24] to which I have not referred before has plainly shown the women of the South what they are to expect from men who disgrace the name of man—

It has been reserved for Butler, a Yankee, to fill to the brim the cup of national infamy. He has enrolled his name side by side with the name of *The Cenci*[25] and th[r]ough all coming ages will be branded with the reputation of being the most vile loathsome of all God's creation. "Notice—Headquarters Department of the Gulf, New Orleans, May 15, 1862. General orders no 28. As the officers and soldiers of the United States have been subject to repeated insults from the women, calling themselves ladies of N O, in return for the most scrupulous noninterference on our part, it is ordered that hereafter when any female shall by word, gesture or movement, insult or show contempt for any officer a soldier of the United States, she shall be regarded and held liable to be treated as a woman of the town plying her avocation." Ye Gods shall this man live— It is now the 2d of June and this order was issued 15th of

---

23. Col. George W. Raines of North Carolina, a West Point graduate, had selected Augusta as the most favorable location to build a powderworks factory. Under his direction, Augusta became an important ordnance supply center for the Confederacy.

24. Union general Benjamin "Beast" Butler, so named for his infamous Order No. 28 and for his high-handed rule of New Orleans.

25. A verse tragedy by Percy Bysshe Shelley, written in 1819.

May. Is there not spirit enough left to the men of New Orleans to strike the dastard "to the vile dust from which he sprang."

Beauregard assembled his men and read this order to them and had this appeal made— "Men of the South! Shall our Mothers, our wives, our daughters and sisters, be thus outraged by the ruffianly soldiers of the North, to whom is given the right to treat at their pleasure the ladies of the South as common harlots. Arouse friends, and drive back from our homes the disturbers of our family ties." Almost every paper in the Southern Confederacy has noticed this order and it is said that excitement amongst our soldiers is intense. Had our brave men required an additional incentive for valour they have it furnished in the appeal to protect the honour of their women. Numerous instances have occurred of men attempting to defend their wives subjected to brutal passion, having been shot down.

I have written on copying the order of Butler and the appeal of Beauregard and it is now after eleven oclock. It is raining and my thoughts wander to him from whom they are seldom absent and I wonder where is my Husband? Has the fight been going on today and will it be renewed tomorrow? And I long for morning to come that I may hear the very latest news, and then I shall hope for the day to pass away until the afternoon shall bring me other tidings to satisfy my craving heart. . . .

. . . .

Belmont, Wednesday July 2, 1862 . . . Will you ever forget, Turner, the afternoon that I read the dispatch announcing Mr Hillins' death? It was the certain proof that the Hussars had been in the fight. I had waited patiently all day for Ma to return from town with the paper. Tired of waiting I started up the avenue and saw the carriage drive in the gate. I was too impatient to wait so walked on and met Pa and Ma who were in the Phaeton, Cate asleep on the front seat and Holt on the dickey seat with Palmer. I mantained my composure tolerably until they leaving, I started back to the house with the children. In the wild tumult of that hour my feelings were best expressed in groans. Mary Bell who was walking by me said, "Ma is you sick?" "No Darling" said I. "I am thinking of your Pa in the fight and that poor man Hillins." "Who killed him" asked she and I told her "the Yankees" and in tones of childish indignation she exclaimed against "the Yankees." No wonder that our children will dislike the Yankees. Upon their childish imaginations impressions will be made which will grow with their gro[w]th and never leave them.

Today I was showing a collection of wedding invitations for the last ten years and Mamie asked "Why I was keeping them?" I told her "for the purpose of letting my children's children form some idea of how *Grand Ma* lived when she was a girl." Ma laughed and said that if this war continued "Grand Ma" had probably seen more style than her grand children ever would. Who knows but that this may prove a prophecy? If things continue to be revolutionised as they have been and are it would require more than "mortal kin" to tell what the future has in store. *We* have never had the war at our door yet. Have never been subjected to personal indignity from Yankee Myrmidons and hence have never realised here in Augusta the full horrors of the revolution. I feel bright and sanguine of my Husband's safety. I feel that this great battle certainly cannot last much longer— It is pouring down rain and quite late. Children and servants asleep and for fear that the heavy fall of rain may produce a saddening effect I will close altho I feel in the mood for writing. I haven't a "Gray Goose Quill" but I have a good steel pen equally "the slave of my will" or rather "obedient to my thought" for my *will* would demand that I could convey some faint idea of the times in which we live. But events crowd so rapidly upon us that we learn to wonder at nothing. Even the infamous death of William Mumford[26] who tore down the federal flag which was placed on the Mint House in New Orleans has caused but little comment. I was tonight reading a very interesting account written by a New Orleans (Yankee) correspondent of the *New York Herald*.

．　．　．

---

26. William B. Mumford was hanged by General Butler for pulling down the Union flag that was flying over the U.S. mint.

6. The Home Front

Our prospects are extremely gloomy.
—*December 31, 1863*

Sunday, September [late] 1862   Two months and more have passed since I wrote last and in that time how much has happened both of an individual and national character. To begin with Mr Thomas has resigned his position in the army and is at home again. I am writing confidentially to you my Journal and I will tell you exactly how I feel with regard to this matter. While he was contented, and satisfied with camp life and soldier's fare I never should have been the woman to have urged him to come home, however much I might have missed his society, but when Col [Gen.] Tom Cobb by the promotion of several others over him did him great injustice and he wrote me that "a due sense of self respect demanded his resignation" I wrote him "to come"— Previous to doing so he was ill in Richmond at Miss Lyons' and it was with difficulty that he succeeded in having his resignation accepted. He remained several days in North Carolina with Jule and reached home on the __ day of August. For more than a week he had fever but has gradually been improving altho still suffering a little from dyspepsia but never at any period of my life, not even in the sunny hours of courtship or those immediately after our marriage, have I ever enjoyed such quiet happiness, such perfect enjoyment of his society. I said I would not have recalled him from the service. I say now that I would most heartily oppose his joining again unless the enemy were at our doors. I shall never regret the one year spent in service but I feel that he has escaped with his life— Oh when I think of the thousands and thousands of desolate homes and hearts, of the many bright intellects and manly forms hushed in death I turn to my Husband and thank God that he is home again. Our letters to each other both carefully preserved will form a more perfect journal of my life than this book during the past year.[1] In order to avoid being conscripted Mr Thomas procured in Virginia a man to act as a substitute for him.[2] He is a Marylander and it is fortunate that he succeded in obtaining him as soon as he did as the law on that subject is becoming more and more stringent.

Mr Thomas is one of those men who find their happiness in their homes and he never would have voluntarily left home and family and joined the army or navy making that his profession as so many do. Yesterday he went down to Burke and will return tomorrow. I miss him very much while he is away. This morning I took Mrs Harris in to the Presbyterian church to hear Dr Palmer of New Orleans preach. . . . Since hearing him last New Orleans has been surrendered—he has been forced to leave his home. May New Orleans soon be surrendered and may I often have the pleasure of hearing similar eloquent addresses from Dr Palmer who since the recent death of Dr Thornwell stands without a rival in the Presbyterian church.

. . .

Tuesday, October 7, 1862 I was beginning to be interested in writing last night just as Mr Thomas came home— He was tired and immediately after supper went to bed. I left off writing not wishing to disturb him and lay down but not to sleep. I remained awake for more than two hours. . . . We have just subscribed for the Charleston *Courier* and the Richmond *Examiner* so that with the Augusta *Chronicle* and the *Christian Advocate* we will obtain all the interesting news with regard to the war. Mr Turner is editing a paper called *The Countryman* which I think I shall subscribe for. I was much pleased with his contributions to the *Field and Fireside*, when that paper was first published. We thought of going in town this morning (Mr Thomas and I) but have concluded to go over and see Cora who leaves for Macon this afternoon.[3] Pa is going down to

---

1. These letters do not survive. They may have been lost in the fire that destroyed Belmont in the mid-1870s.
2. At that time it was still legal for a man to hire a substitute to take his place in the army.
3. Cora Clanton was attending Wesleyan Female College.

Dougherty [County] to his plantation and Ma goes with him for the first time.[4]

The papers contain a dispatch announcing the news that "a brother of the guerrilla chief Morgan was killed and a son of George D Prentice[5] mortally wounded." It may not be patriotic for me to be interested in an enemy but that man Prentice through his writings his poetry and &c had taken a strong hold upon my imagination. The Yankees were certainly ahead of us so far as literary attainments were concerned. I suppose one great reason of this was that it was more remunerative to write at the North than the South and we Southern people had for so many years aided in establishing northern institutions to the neglect of our own. Even now when we are waging this terrible warfare our papers have copious extracts from Northern papers. If this is so now, how will it be when peace is established between us? Will we resume the same old relations? Lincoln has at last issued his proclamation for the emancipation of slaves. Will it ever be carried into effect? Perhaps when we are reduced to poverty we may by the spur of adversity be led to throw aside the indolence which is the bane of a Southern people and develop what latent talent may exist among us. That the Northern people are more intellectual or capable of writing better than the people of the South I do not believe— It is only that they are more accustomed to the routine and mechanical part of writing. . . .

•   •   •

Monday, December 29, 1862 . . . The Battles of Sharpsburgh and Fredricksburgh have been fought—[6] Bud, Jack and Pinck have been wounded in a cavalry charge (which must have a seperate account for itself). Pinck, poor fellow is still suffering terribly from his

---

4. The Dougherty County plantation near Albany, Ga., was the largest and most valuable of Turner Clanton's properties.

5. George D. Prentice, poet and essayist, was the editor of the *Louisville Journal*.

6. The battle of Sharpsburg or Antietam, Md., on September 17, 1862, inflicted heavy losses on both sides and ended with the Confederate forces under Gen. Robert E. Lee in full retreat. On December 13, 1862, at Fredericksburg, Va., along the banks of the Rappahannock River, the Army of the Potomac under Gen. A. E. Burnside was repulsed by the Confederates, whose

wound. The others are doing well. Jack with the loss of an eye—
Sometime when I have more energy I will write a full account of
it.[7] I am suffering terribly from nausea and lack of energy—for
the last six weeks I have been I cannot say blessed with the prospect of again becoming a mother— I am too sick and irritable to
regard this circumstance as a blessing *yet awhile*— Jule with Mr
Scales and the children have been making us a long visit and I
regret that during the last two or three weeks of their visit I should
have been rendered by my situation incapable of enjoying their
visit as much as I would have liked— The fact is my nervous organization is so completely disorganized that I require perfect quiet.
The noise of my own children annoys me at times and I feel as if I
did not have energy to raise my head— I think my intellectual as
well as spiritual nature sympathises with this depression of the
body. . . . Christmas has passed again but tomorrow night I will
hope to write again and trust I shall be more in the mood than I am
now.

Tuesday, December 30, 1862 . . . The weather for the last month
has been extremely cold. I don't think I ever suffered more from
cold in my life than I have this winter. Instead of the perfect quiet,
the delightful contentment arising from having little to do except
read and make myself comfortable, I have been in a constant state
of bustle and excitement, not of the most pleasurable character for
nearly every servant on the place has been sick. Tamah has been
sick for nearly two months. First we had Nancy cooking—then she
was taken sick, then Patsey, then Daniel and afterwards one of Mr
Scales' women, Lucy, for awhile. She left the day after they did and
now we are having an extremely inexperienced person, Milly, Patsey's mother, who came up Christmas to make her a visit. Nancy
has a baby two weeks old, a boy.

I expect I am spoilt by the Miller house, for there everything
was so delightfully arranged for housekeeping that it makes the

---

losses were only half those of the Union side. Gen. Thomas R. R. Cobb was
killed in the latter battle.

7. Gertrude never wrote the promised account in her journal, but some
years later she did write a reminiscence that was published (with an appropriate illustration) in a newspaper, probably the *Chronicle*. The story is preserved in one of her scrapbooks.

contrast here more striking. We are using our sitting room for a bed room which makes it comfortable for us when we are by ourselves, but subjects us to great inconvenience when we have company staying with us for we have no sitting room and our dining room is very contracted in its size. I look forward with pleasure to the advent of spring and have quite fully decided that I shall be willing to spend next winter in town in a brick house for it is certainly much warmer. Jack has been with us ever since he came home except a few days spent in Burke and a short time with Buddy Christmas week. Lizzie Lamkin has been spending Christmas with Cora and today Lizzie Walton is there. Jack and Bud, with the girls, were at a sociable at Julia Chew's Friday night.

Cora came very near being disappointed in her visit home for the Trustees objected to their coming in consequence of the small-pox being near Macon, but Pa returning from Dougherty came by for her. She was very liberal in her presents to the children. She brought Cate, Mary Bell and Mary Vason beautiful wax crying dolls such as Mrs Sumerean asked five and seven dollars for. To Mary Bell she brought a China boy doll beautifully dressed and a book. To Turner she gave a handsome book *The Costumes of Different Nations* and to Jeff a jointed dog. His Grand Ma gave Turner an excellent knife. His Aunt Anne a top, his Pa a half dollar, his Grand Pa the same and I a pack of poppers which cost 25 cts. His Aunt Mary gave them a half dollar apiece to buy presents which I think I will put in their money box for them, together with 75 cts. his Aunt Julia left to buy him a present with. Perhaps next Christmas he will be enabled to invest his money more profitably. I was anxious for him to have a new saddle, but there were no small ones in town. To Mary Bell, I gave a tea sett of wooden toys, a doll, alabaster, for which I gave one dollar [and] a smaller one at thirty five cts., both of which I afterwards dressed. Mr Thomas gave her 50 cts. Her Grand Ma a washboard, a linen book. (Aunt Cora's presents I have already mentioned.) Uncle Jimmie gave her a jointed sheep, Cousin Lizzie, a little wardrobe, and Aunt Julia a very handsome box of blocks of alphabet.

I gave Jeff a wheelbarrow at $1.50 and a whistle. His Aunt Anne gave him a jumping Jack, Aunt Co, a jointed dog— I, a dog knife and his Pa, 50 cts. I had forgotten two of Turner's toys—a balloon from Uncle Jimmie and a triangle from Uncle Holt. To Cora, Mr Thomas gave the subscription for the *Field & Fireside* for this year, to Holt a dollar, to Joe and Cate 50 cts. I gave Joe a dancing Jack, but could not find the whistle I bought for him. To little Mary [Vason] I gave a doll, dressed, and to Kate a sett of graces. Ma gave me a handsome Valenciennes [lace] pointed collar.

For the first time, we had a Christmas tree which Mamie, Cora and Lizzie arranged in the girls' room and did not exhibit until the next morning after breakfast very much to the delight of all concerned. Turner was very much afraid Santa Claus would not bring him anything as he has a shrewd suspicion who Santa Claus is. Ma gave us an elegant dinner. For the first time in six years we all assembled at the table together and if Pinck had been able to have joined us the party of sons in law would have been complete. To form some idea of the extravagant prices of things and to compare them with the better times which I hope are coming, I will mention that the apples for the dessert were 10 cts. apiece, the oranges 30 and 40 cts., the icing of a pound cake, $1.50. As to the expense of the various items forming the Charlotte Roose, syllabub and &c, I can only conjecture. The baked and boiled turkey would alone have cost 8 dollars.

This is the last night of 1862 and I might moralize, but will refrain as there is no one to hear it but myself. . . . America, who is sick with a cold, is lying down here in the nursery where I am writing at the desk. Cate and Mary Bell are asleep together while in my room are Turner, Jeff and Patsey. The wind is rising and as its mournful cadence swells around the house I can imagine it sighing a requiem for the countless dead who have been ushered into eternity since this year began its course. For so many years have I indulged in a spirit of retrospection mingled with thoughts of the future, that it has become habitual to wonder "Where I shall be this time next year?" How little I imagined that this Christmas would find me at Belmont—my husband at home, my children all well— my father's family in happiness and health and with the exception of Pinck's illness nothing but prosperity. . . .

.   .   .   .

Thursday, July 24 [23], 1863 Tuesday night June the 23rd 1863 my little Anna—Cora Lou was born— I have just written the name of my little darling in Heaven— The names are so similar I expect I will often make the mistake. On Monday morning Mr Thomas went in town. I was feeling badly and was lying on the couch in the nursery reading an interesting volume discriptive of America by

Charles Mackay an Englishman—[8] The morning was quite cool and we had a fire, the children amusing themselves popping corn. I was taken sick as I always am—in no pain whatever— I immediately wrote a note for Ma and Aunt Tinsey to come over and sent in town for Dr Joe Eve—and if he was not at home Dr Ed Eve or Dr Jones. . . . Dr Ed Eve came about dark just as we were sending for Dr (Edward) Bignon. I was in no pain until about 10 oclock Tuesday night. My mode of being sick certainly has some advantages. It gives me time to prepare and a physician time to be with me— Dr Eve remained all night Monday and Tuesday night going in town for a little while Tuesday morning.

I took cloroform for the first time and was pleased with the result at the same time not altogether satisfied as to its safety— Dr Eve said that I was easily affected by it but he was not aware of the effect that it did exert. Ma who is afraid of it did not apply it as often as he told her to. At one time after a long inhalation everything became indistinct. I appeared to see Dr Eve who was just before me as tho in a dream. Everything seemed dim and distant. I appeared to be floating off— A feeling of lightness which I cannot discribe came over me. At the same time I was conscious enough to tell Ma to "take it away" and then in recovering from the effect I felt just as one does in being aroused from a dream— Its effect in lulling pain is magical and of all the ways to select for committing suicide I should think it preferable— I have read Bayard Taylor's discription of eating Hasheesh and De Quincy's *Opium Eater*[9] but they, neither of them discribe more wonderful things than I have dreamed of and I have never felt tempted to try the effect of any of those magical drugs upon my susceptible system. . . .

Friday, July 31, 1863 While I am writing the funeral services of Aunt Dinah are being performed. For a long time, nearly ever since Christmas she has been complaining, altho never sick enough to be confined to her bed. For some time previous to her death she appeared to be in her dotage, an object of merriment to the children, and a great cause of anxiety to Uncle Sam, her husband, who remained constantly with her. She would watch him closely and as

---

8. *Life and Liberty in America—Sketches of a Tour* (1859), by Charles Mackay.

9. *Confessions of an English Opium Eater* (1822), by Thomas De Quincy.

soon as he left the room would go to the fire or pour water over the floor. She had for a long time been a member of the church and was naturally one of the liveliest old souls I ever saw and an incessant talker in her low country language. During the time of my sickness she was in once to see the baby and appeared interested in it. For some days before she died she appeared to be in a stupor (sleeping apparently calmly) from which it was impossible to arouse her— Last night a great many of the Negroes in the neighborhood were here to sit up. It was late before "they gathered" as Nancy expressed it and late before they seperated. I did not get to sleep until between two and three oclock. Some of the songs were beautiful as sung by some of the Singing School class— The voices chiming beautifully—and to my taste as harmoniously as anything I had ever heard in a concert room. . . .

The pageantry of a funeral goes far to relieve the grief of a Negro in the loss of a friend. They are naturally religious and like all "pomp and circumstance" of a funeral. They are particularly solicitous with regard to the manner in which they are dressed. Poor old Aunt Dinah had a complete suit of clothes to be buried in complete from the white jaconet dress to the new white gloves and stockings which had never been worn. Uncle Sam has a nice suit put away carefully for a similar sad time when he shall be called away— No doubt they often deny themselves comfortable clothing during their life that they may have something to dress their poor perishing body for the grave—

Mrs Harris was telling me of a remark made by Lydia her house servant. After the death of her baby Mrs H found Lydia dressed in black sitting in the room by the baby— Speaking of the funeral which was to take place in the afternoon, "If they all come" said she, "I think we shall have a right nice little *performance*." Lydia was telling me of the baby's death afterwards and said "I hadn't no idea it was going to die. I found its feet was cold and I got up and warmed them but after a while its nose got cold and you know" said she (with a laugh), "there was no way of warming its nose and then I knew it was going to die."

Uncle Sam is our driver. He formerly belonged to Mr Thomas' father who bought him from Mr Trowbridge a Negro trader. He was raised in Carolina and Florida and claims that he had his freedom given to him by a previous mistress and was "cheated" by Mr Trowbridge who took charge of his papers (free papers) and never returned them to him. His story as he told it to me was really interesting. The seperation of his daughter from him and her from her children. But fortunately for them the Negro is a cheerful being. Sitting by the dead body of his wife he told me with a smile of gratified pride that he could mark the initial of a former masters name— WH — and "that is more" said he "than any other nigger in this yard can do." I had noticed that every watermelon that was brought in had some kind of a mark upon it WH similar to this. Noticing them this morning after hearing Uncle Sam speaking of his *writing* I knew that he had intended to write WH and left out one of the straight lines in the H. And yet I had too much respect for the old man's vanity to correct the mistake before any of the servants whom he had intended to impress with the wonderful extent of his "larning" and must do so at some other time.

The Afternoon. Mr Thomas has just returned from town. Today he sold ——— bales of cotton at ——— cts and invested $15,000 in Confederate (8) eight pr cent bonds, telling me when he handed them to me that there was a protection from "the Yankees" in case they came. And it is a source of considerable comfort to me to know that I have in my possession something which can with ease be transported and made useful in any portion of the Confederacy to which I may be driven. The importance of having something of the kind has impressed me very forcibly ever since our fright at the late reported Yankee raid upon Augusta. Charleston is being besieged and has been for some weeks and not withstanding several defeats which they have received and the more recent one at Fort Wagner they still persevere— I have preserved the accounts as they have been published in the Charleston *Mercury*— We are taking that paper now and it is an effort to read it distinctly so yellow brown is the shade of the common paper upon which it is printed. The terms for the daily paper is (20) twenty dollars pr year— This appears high now but when our papers are published at 50 or 100 dollars pr year I will read this with the same smile with which I read an account I had given of some of the items of Ma's last Christmas dinner "given to form some idea of the extravagant prices of things." The oranges I then thought high at 30 and 40 cts went up to 75 and 1.00— This was here. What they were in Richmond can be imagined when a water melon sells there now at 10 and 15 dollars.

Buddy reached home Wednesday July the 30th [29th]. I never was as glad to see the dear fellow before— Dressed in his Lt's uniform he looks well altho much sunburnt and suffering from the sabre cut received on his head in the Brandy Mountains fight and his shoulder is quite painful to him from having been thrown from his Horse in a recent fight. Cora is at home. Mamie, Pinck, Cousin Emma & Lizzie attended the commencement at Macon and met a large crowd there. Sis Anne and Mamie have within the last few weeks left the Augusta Hotel. Mr Metcalf having raised his rent. Mr Wheelock pretended he was going to close the house, "A Yankee trick" Sis Anne said for raising his rent which he afterwards did. Mamie and Pinck have gone down to Burke to remain until Pinck's furlough is out. He has been staying with Ma all the winter until late in the spring when they went to the Hotel for a little while. Sis Anne is spending the summer at the house in town where she is quite comfortable. . . . Pa has very kindly proposed that Emmeline, America's sister (who has a baby a few months old) can come and nurse the baby if Nancy's milk does not agree with her. I sometimes lose patience and think that people who do not have nourishment enough for their children ought not to have them and indeed I have just enough now. Two boys and two girls, a good number if they live to be grown.

During this summer I have been much interested in pasting a scrap book. I have two filled and cannot buy another in Augusta altho I have material enough to fill several more. A great many important events which occur in our country's history I would allude to more fully in my Journal if it was not so much easier a plan to paste the printed account.[10] In writing now I have an eye always to the future when I shall read portions to my children or submit the book to their perusal— I regret now that I have permitted so much of the year 1863 to pass unrecorded. I am without the letters which I wrote to Mr Thomas the year before to assist me in linking the broken chain. Our gallantly besieged Vicksburgh has capitulated— Our invading army of the Potomac have returned. Morgan[11] has not been successful in his raid. Charleston is menaced. Altogether the sky is more ominous than it has been before in fifteen months and yet I am still sanguine. Never for one moment do I permit myself to doubt that all will be well— . . .

---

10. Unfortunately, the scrapbooks from the war years are missing.

11. Brig. Gen. John Hunt Morgan was a romantic hero of the Confederate cavalry.

The last night of 1863 I am more and more impressed with the force of habit— When this season of the year comes around or my birthday commemorates the flight of time, the habit of long years proves irresistible and I find myself thinking of my Journal and wondering how I was engaged this time last year or how I will be engaged next year? And just here I am particularly struck by the entirely unexpected condition in which I find myself— Had someone last Christmas suggested the possibility of my occupying this house we are now living in I should have given a most decided answer "No." . . . This is a fine neighborhood and nice associations for the children. We have a good deal of room but the house is certainly more contracted than I could wish. Carpenters work and painting create a disturbance which is not congenial to my nature. I don't wonder that men have studys which (by the way) I imagine to be only an excuse for making themselves comfortable and being out of the bustle and confusion of the housekeeping department and children. Madame de Stael[12] has somewhere observed the benefical effect of solitude upon the mind adding "it was in the Bastille I first learned to know myself." . . . Tonight I am sitting in the sitting room before a fire which is almost out and the rain which has been falling steadily all last night and today still continues and so easily am I affected by outward circumstances that folding my hands and laying my Journal aside I could look into the fire and listening to the rain drops as they fall, reflect upon the disappointment of our sanguine hopes for the coming of peace with the closing of the year. But I will strive against such feelings and hope that the close of 1864 may find us an Independent Nation upon the face of the earth but while I hope so I confess that there is more hope than trust. Our prospects are extremely gloomy. . . .

Mr. Thomas is the 1st Lt in a company called The Wheeler Dragoons[13] or the Richmond Dragoons, I really cannot tell. The fact is I cannot get up any very great degree of interest in companys which remain about town. This company has been entered for the defence of Augusta for the war and is thought to be the safest to

---

12. Madame de Staël (1776–1817), the French writer, was imprisoned during the French Revolution.

13. The Wheeler Dragoons were a local cavalry unit organized by William Dearing and named for Gen. Joseph "Fighting Joe" Wheeler. Jefferson Thomas was first lieutenant.

join to prevent being sent off. Hence it has a large number of men enrolled upon its muster list. Mr Thomas has been a member of it for some time and thinks the repeal of the substitute law *perfectly right*— As it was in the French Revolution so it is now. The human mind is so constituted that it cannot stand a constant pressure— The war has been going on for a much longer time than we could have thought of and our minds are becoming in some degree accustomed to it— It is in this way that we must account for the gayety which appears to prevail in our town. I hear of numerous partys which are being given and a number of sociables. . . .

We were invited last night to a sociable at cousin Mary Ann's. Lizzie Lamkin and Walton are spending some time with Cora who is spending Christmas vacation at home. Buddy is still at home. They with Ma, Holt, Kate and Jack were there Mamie also. Miss Taylor from Charleston, Alice White, and Miss Mary Evans with Mr and Mrs Wheelock Mrs Berry Mr Estes and Mrs Cormia and Ellen with a few young men were there. Among the latter a young man who cousin Mary Ann says is immensely wealthy—gave Henry Evans $400 to introduce him to a young lady and then gave her two very handsome diamond rings. His name is Keenan but he is not a gentleman "to the manor born" for when one of the girls requested him to hand her a piece of candy last night, he walked into the next room *picked it up in his fingers* and carried it to her— . . . Cousin Mary Ann's refreshments consisted of egg nogg and cake and Confederate candy, very nice. I tried some of it this afternoon and cooking it too much it changed to sugar— She had Confederate almonds (Ground Peas) [peanuts] which it was a humiliation to Annie's pride to hand around—and to tell the truth I was surprised to see them.

I have written on so much that it is now after 9 oclock and yet I have said nothing of Turner's and Mary Bell's party which we gave them last week in lieu of the Santa Claus presents. Mary Bell has been told that Santa Claus has not been able to run the blockade and has gone to the war— Yet at a late hour when I went up stairs Thursday night the night of the party I found that with the trusting faith of childhood they had hung their little socks and stockings in case Santa Claus did come. I had given the subject no thought whatever but invoking Santa Claus['s] aid I was enabled when their little eyes were opened to enjoy their pleasure to find cake and money in their socks— Jeff was delighted— Mr Thomas bought Mary Bell at auction a saddle for which he gave $100. A most extravagant purchase. The same day he bought a hanging glass for $75. Cora gave Cora Lou two pairs of socks.

What boots it now to wonder what the coming year may bring forth? Well for us perhaps that we do not know. . . . But reality calls upon me to look around me, to see our country agonised in a struggle for an existence, and deeper, still deeper settles the conviction that we are upon the eve of some great struggle, the echo of which will reverberate through all time. Fortunately for those who believe in an all ruling Providence we are taught that "he doeth all things well"— I wish I could echo Byron's "What ever tide befall me Here's a heart for any fate"[14] but we do not know the stuff of which we are made until adversity tries us. I have great faith in that innate courage which all women are said to possess when great trials come upon them—providential trials— I write despondingly as to our future but indeed I do not think as a mass of people we fully realise the importance of the struggle in which we are engaged—

. . .

Thursday, February 4, 1864   The realization of a long cherished wish is accomplished and I have seen *Gen Morgan*. He arrived on the South Carolina Railroad and was met by a large crowd at the depot and from there escorted to the Southern States Hotel where he is being entertained by the City. As is usually the case he is entirely different from what I had imagined deferring most particularly in the fact that he is much more gentlemanly in his appearance than I had supposed. I had thought of him as rather a small man, dark hair & eyes rough looking and entirely different from the handsome, light haired, fair complexioned man I find Gen Morgan to be— He wears a mustache and goatee and has a genial smile which irradiates his whole face— Looking at him I thought more of him as the pleasant companion, the lover of a good joke, the graceful man in a lady's parlour—of *this* rather [than] the gallant, dashing, daring noble chieftain he has proven himself to be— A direct

---

14. "And, whatever sky's above me, / Here's a heart for every fate," from Lord Byron, "To Thomas Moore" (1817); Gertrude may also have been thinking of "Let us, then, be up and doing, / With a heart for any fate," from Henry Wadsworth Longfellow, "A Psalm of Life" (1839).

bow from the Gen himself as his open carriage passed ours (as we were sitting in it in front of the hotel) in return perhaps to a glance of undisguised admiration from myself would of itself be something to be proud of—but tomorrow I expect to call with Mr Thomas and see them at the reception which I suppose they will have. . . .

Friday, April 15, 1864 I have to record the saddest event which has ever occurred in my history, *the death of my father*.[15] How calmly I write it and yet I look at the written words and do not realise it yet. Occasionally since his death the idea has obtained an entrance into my mind producing a wild tumultuous grief to be succeeded by a quiet approaching to apathy. I cannot realise it, nor will I until as successive years roll by and I miss day by day some of the loved tokens by which he was wont to express his boundless affection. I will learn that the loss which I have sustained is indeed irreparable. As it is, I expect to see him again. I think of him as being alive, at the plantations—in the street and *cannot* think of him as lying in the cold and silent resting place in which he was placed yesterday— During the winter Pa's health has been very bad but for six weeks he has been confined to the room almost constantly in bed. During the time I was often to see him. My conscience reproaches me that it was not oftener, and sat up with him quite often but was never uneasy about him until two weeks before he died. . . .

Thursday morning I was down to see him and noticed for the first time the jaundiced look of his complexion. He was very sick all morning much nauseated. I think it was the day before that he had Judge [Ebenezar] Starnes to come and see him in connection with an alteration in his will.[16] Thursday afternoon I was at the Prayer Meeting at the Presbyterian Lecture room and went down to see Pa late in the evening. I sat up with Ma the first part of the night and Mr Thomas the latter part. It was that morning that calling Mr Thomas & Buddy to his bedside he told them "that he

---

15. Gertrude's poignant and detailed account of her father's death runs for twelve typed manuscript pages. The portion retained here contains the essence of the ordeal.

16. Turner Clanton, conscious of his critical illness, added codicils to his will on three occasions just prior to his death.

did not think he would live that his will was written, that they must both look after his interest." He especially warned Buddy against gambling drinking and &c— No one was in the room except Mr Thomas and Buddy and both of them were very much affected— Fast Day, Friday April the 8th rose bright and unclouded but it was the saddest day I had ever known for that morning Dr Dugas in answer to Ma's question, told her that there was no shadow of hope for Pa's recovery.[17] . . . At one time he said "I know that I am in a very critical state, there are ninety nine chances against my getting well to one in favour of it"— At another time he said, "If I do get [well] what obligations I shall be under to a kind Providence." And again, "If I do recover it will be owing to kind nursing." He took the nourishment that was given to him as he said "he knew that it was a crisis" and did all he could to summon his failing energys to meet that crisis—

I thought he was doing so well that Mr Thomas and I came up home late Monday morning.[18] He told Mr Thomas "Good night" and to me he said "Good night my Daughter"— About four oclock Ma sent for us to come down that Pa was much worse— I rose, dressed calmly, yet hurriedly while all the while the words "Good night my daughter" rang through my mind as I thought, "Oh God was that a last farewell." Sis Anne met us telling us that he had been asleep for a while. All the night he had been vomiting with actions which had weakened him very much, the powerful opiates which he had taken appearing to have had no effect upon his bowels— The crisis had *come* and *passed* and now we almost knew there was no hope for him, and yet when after breakfast Dr Steiner said to me "Mrs Thomas" and walking out of the room through the passage into the sitting room said to me while tears were in his eyes that Pa could not possibly live more than twenty four hours— the shock was terrible— He said he would advise me to send for his spiritual advisors and offered to loan me the Episcopalian Prayer for the Dying— Sending Turner for it I returned to the room in which Pa lay moaning with pain and found that he had asked where were his children. . . .

---

17. Doctors Louis A. Dugas, Henry H. Steiner, and Lewis D. Ford all attended Turner Clanton during his final illness.

18. Gertrude must have meant "evening," as her mother sent for them again early the next morning.

Soon after Pa enquired for Col Vason who came to him and received a warm pressure of the hand and was addressed in what I understood to be the following words "I leave a large interest here sir, which I expect you to be interested in. I wish you all to live in peace and harmony. May your career in life be happy and prosperous." I was struck even in that hour with the polite expression which he used. Col Vason sat without replying a word when Sis Anne whispered to him to give Pa some assurance when he replied with great earnestness, "I will Col to the best of my ability." . . .

When I went in after his remains were placed in the sitting room on the low french bedstead upon which he died, it having been rolled into that room, I looked at him and calmly commented upon the pressure of the lip. The bright gas light gave a ghastly look and he did not look natural to me— . . . I looked upon Pa as he lay there and thought as I have ever thought that he was the handsomest man I ever saw and that death had never placed his signet upon a more kingly brow. I felt as I pressed my lips to his, that I would like to lay down by the side of him and place my arms around him, to know that he tabernac[led] with us for a little while longer— God forgive me but I was proud of the casket from whence the jewel had departed. He was placed in the coffin but I did not see him afterwards until evening when I was about to come home. I then requested Mr T and Mamie to leave me for a while alone and then kneeling by his side I asked God's guidance for the future.

Yesterday morning was bright and beautiful, the perfect realization of the long deferred spring morning. A large crowd gathered to do honour to the mortal remains of our father. Rev Dr Wilson and Mr Scott officiated in the burial services[19] and all the children gathered in the parlour to pay the sad homage to the best of parents. . . . I do not know what to think. Sometimes I can but think Pa must have had sustaining grace from on high to comfort him. If he did not, then he summoned the energy of his iron will and met the dred King of Terrors with a calmness and composure which approaches the sublime. Perfectly conscious of his impending doom no expression of fright or timidity passed from his lips. He clung to life with tenacity as who does not. He had much to live for— His

---

19. Joseph R. Wilson was minister of the First Presbyterian Church and Mr. Scott, a minister at St. John Methodist. Dr. Wilson was the father of Woodrow Wilson, who was a young boy at the time.

sufferings were great. They caused moans unutterable to pass his lips yet he prayed, "Thy will be done on earth as it is in Heaven" and in God's hands I leave him knowing that a just God must have degrees of punishment as well as reward— His solicitude for his servants was shown in his last illness and he particularly requested that Susan and Uncle Jim should be rewarded for nursing him so faithfully. To Aunt Vilet (the cook) when she approached his bed at one time during his sickness he said "Vilet we have been a long time together. You have been a good and faithful servant but we must soon part"— . . .

I had hoped when I went down yesterday to have found the cross on the grave and was disappointed. I had thought when the coffin was lowered that I did not see it and that it had been reserved to dress the grave— Mentioning my disappointment to Buddy he quietly took from his breast pocket an envelope with a geranium leaf and a small piece of arborvitae and gave it to me— Bless the dear boy. I remember hearing Pa speak of the refinement of taste which prompted some young girl to ask for a flower which decorated the grave of Weston Thomas— How it would have pleased him to know of the genuine love which prompted his Soldier Boy to prise a flower made sacred by such associations. Oh my father. I feel that today has been consecrated to sweet memorys of thee! As I said to thee, so I say now God *forever* bless thee! How delightful the Roman Catholic doctrine which permits one to pray for the repose of the soul of the dead. . . .

. . .

Wednesday, June 29, 1864 I am glad that the funeral of Lt Gen Polk[20] has had the effect of rousing me to write. How often when a train of thought has been passing through my mind I have thought I would like to write that in my Journal but did not summon energy to put my thoughts on paper. I have risen early this morning. Mr Thomas has just returned from Burke. Daniel our Carriage driver has been impressed or conscripted as they call it to work on the fortifications. He drove us to the Sand Hills Saturday morning and

---

20. Lt. Gen. Leonidas Polk, an Episcopalian bishop from Louisiana, was killed in the battle of Kennesaw Mountain, Ga. His funeral service was held at St. Paul's in Augusta. Gertrude attended and described it in great detail.

was impressed in the street after we came home. I could get a substitute for him but as he expressed a wish to go so Turner said I thought I would let him try it a while. They commence work at seven and "knock off work" early in the afternoon so I suppose it has its attractions.

All of the Negroes about town were being conscripted to work on the fortifications here. Great apprehensions being excited about a raid, Col Rains having received and published a letter to the effect that citizens of Augusta (not mentioning their names) had given information to the enemy and were prepared to assist them in case they (the Yankees) attempted a raid. I do [not] know why it was but it did not give me the slightest uneasiness. For several days the Wheeler Dragoons have been impressing Negroes to work on the fortifications at Atlanta. At first the order came for one hundred thousand Negroes and then for one fifth of what each man owned between the age of seventeen and fifty— The Negroes have been greatly exercised thereby— . . .

. . .

Monday, July 4, 1864 . . . Today is the fourth day of July. I had forgotten it until this morning. One of our waggon tires ran off while we were moving and all the blacksmith's shops were shut up when we sent to have it mended. It is warm, so very warm! This is a very disagreeable house to live in—cold, exceedingly cold in winter and hot, excessively hot in summer. I enjoyed the spring very well but none of my surroundings are congenial to my taste. I think I am luxurious in my taste. . . . Were I a refugee I could more willingly submit to the annoyance of an uncomfortable house but there is a great scarcity of houses to rent. I expect I annoy Mr Thomas by my frequent allusions to this subject so hereafter my journal I think I shall tell you when anything worries me for you know it is almost impossible for me not to have someone to talk to. I wish I had a book with a key to it in which I could write what I feel. There is a song "Whisper what thou feelest" and it is just this almost irresistible inclination which I sometimes have to confide in some- one— There are thoughts, doubts, suggestions which present them- selves to my mind. If I could only talk of them. . . .

I find my thoughts recurring to the Catholic confessional (that great repository of secrets) with a longing checked by the idea that these priests are *men*. Again with a feeling of intense relief I think of Mary— Mother Mary! Christ's Mother! and shall I confess it, I almost find myself believing in the intercession of the saints. I am told that "there is only one Mediator, Christ Jesus between God and man," but does our Savior's *Mother* possess no influence upon him? . . . I don't think Mr Thomas understands or is interested in my struggles and trials. He listens sometimes when my "Heart unfolds its leaves" and I read to him some of its pages. Listens, but that is all.

Tomorrow we move to Belmont. I hope I will read something which will strengthen and invigorate the tone of my mind. I wish to read some healthy, strong, sensible, woman's writings— Nothing sentimental or romantic— No strange dream of fiction. . . . Mrs [Susan Petigru] King insists that each household contains a skeleton— Dining one day with Thackeray when he visited the South, a door of the sideboard just behind her would remain open. Jumping up she fastened it by inserting a piece of paper. "Does that door contain your skeleton?" was his enquiry seeing her interest. "Ah" replied she, "that would not contain one half of my skeletons." . . . No, it is the writings of some sensible, practical woman, one who has "suffered & grown strong." . . .

Tuesday, July 12, 1864 This morning I rose with the expectation of going in town. I had rested badly last night and was feeling very dull this morning. Our well was out of order having just been operated upon. A large number of clothes had to be washed and other domestic annoyances conspired to make me cross. Mr Thomas concluded he felt so badly he would not go. I started late. . . . [T]he carriage passed a poor woman and her little boy carrying berries into town. Both were barefooted. I passed them but then told Daniel to stop and invited them to ride with me. With an apology for her bare feet she accepted the offer. As I listened to her simple story, her husband in the hospital in Richmond, one brother killed and the other not heard from, she just from the poor house, having moved yesterday and this morning starting out with berries to sell— As I listened I felt ashamed that the little trials of life should so affect me. I bought her basket of fruit leaving her with a bright smile of contentment upon her face and then rode to the cemetery. Entering the enclosure I knelt by Pa's grave and there besought God's guidance for the future. . . .

A large number of Yankee prisoners were at Allen's station as we came up. Some of the officers were good looking men with beards neatly trimmed and dressed clean but the privates! Such an outlandish set of men I have seldom seen. They were in box cars, some of them with their pants rolled high above the knees, shirt bosoms open to the waist, hair matted, shirts torn across the backs and presenting a repulsive appearance altogether. Yet I cannot have the vindictive feelings I hear expressed. A Fallen captive foe cannot be the object of such feelings. It is for the triumphant foe—when he attempts to lord it over me and mine that I shall reserve my indignant and righteous rage. . . .

Thursday, July 28, 1864 Just after dinner has never been considered a favourable time for the mind to work with ease—but the past week has been so full of excitement that I must no longer refrain from an allusion to some of the events which have taken place. Last Saturday Mr Thomas coming from town brought the news that a battle had been fought in Atlanta and with the triumphant shouts of victory came the sad intelligence of the death of Major Gen William Henry Walker.[21] . . .

As Mamie and I were going from the Catholic Church[22] I saw a portion of the Dragoons going rapidly up the street and heard Mr Thomas' voice as he gave a command but I thought they were being dismissed to meet again as usual. That was Monday afternoon. This is Wednesday. I have not heard from him since. He and I are invited to Mrs Harris' to meet Gen and Mrs Longstreet[23] tonight. We called to see them Saturday at Mrs Carmichael's. I was feeling dull and remarked to Mr Thomas that were it not for telling the children hereafter some personal experience with regard to Lt Gen Longstreet I would not go. . . . I found him to be a good looking man with a pleasant face—fair complexion and what I called heavy black beard and Mr Thomas said was auburn— Mrs Harris said he talked very little indeed but soon after coming in and being seated he changed his seat and seating himself on the teteatete by me continued in conversation until we left. He talks a good deal—in

---

21. Maj. Gen. William Henry Talbot Walker of Augusta was killed at Decatur, Ga., near Atlanta.

22. St. Patrick Catholic Church and First Presbyterian Church were used as hospitals when large numbers of the wounded began arriving in Augusta.

23. Lt. Gen. James Longstreet, the nephew of Augustus Baldwin Longstreet, was from nearby Edgefield County, S.C.

a quiet, low tone of voice. Appears to have no inclination to join in a general conversation or make himself the observed of all observers. . . .

On Monday forenoon Cora, Lila Thomas Mamie and I went round to the 3d Georgia Hospital to carry a lunch to the sick men. We found all the rooms crowded but gave the lunch we had to the patients in St Paul's ward. All of the cots were occupied most of the men suffering with diarrhea and intermittent fever— A young man by the name of Rainwater and one by the name of Dennard, the latter from lower Georgia were the only two we conversed much with. Everything appeared as comfortable as it was possible for a Hospital to be— In the afternoon there was a call in the papers for the ladies to meet at the Catholic Church to render some assistance. Riding there Mamie and I found a state of destitution such as I had read of but never imagined before. Laying on the floor upon beds hastily filled with straw were wounded men, wounded in every manner. Some with their arms and legs cut off, others with flesh wounds, two men in a dying state, another poor fellow with the ever present thought of home mingling in his delirium as he sits up and gathering his coarse shoes proceeds to put them on saying "I am going home, I have a furlough to go home." Soothingly I spoke to him and smoothing his coat his only pillow I persuaded him to lay down. Near the door lay a man singularly ugly at best but almost horrible with the accumulation of dirt consequent upon having travelled upon the cars. All those men had been brought down from the hospital in Greensboro [Georgia] the people fearing a raid. One of the men named Jones on the right hand side of the church was dying. A crowd of ladies were standing around him. One of them asked him if he wished anything. "Nothing" the man replied "except to be prepared to die." During the night the summons came for him, his soul was required of him.

The next morning visiting the church, in the vestibule or piazzi of the church I saw something covered up but did not know what it was until told that the dead man was there. He was resting on a soiled straw bed covered with a common blue blanket with the flies swarming over it. A gentleman (Mr Milligan I think, and by the way the only one who was there paying them any attention) lifted the blanket from off his face remarking "that it was very much such a face as Stonewall Jackson's." There lay the man around whom had clustered all the endearing associations of home. A mother—a wife—a sister had loved him. Perhaps now around the family altar a group of children pray "please bring Pa home safe and well," happily unconscious how he died. God grant they never may know! A crowd of children and servants were around him at times, all privileged to lift the blanket from his careworn but intellectual face—and there he lay unknown & uncared for, prepared for the hasty burial which awaited him. For the weary soul I could not weep but for those who loved him my heart went out in yearning sympathy as the tears (which I was ashamed should be seen) coursed rapidly down my cheek— I don't know where that man's family lives but if I did what could I write them. I could tell them that he was dead but I would not have them know how he died. . . .

Saturday, July 30, 1864 The war is nearing our own door— Passengers from Macon say that it was rumoured that our forces and the Yankee Raiders were drawn up in line of battle eight miles from that place when the train left. The central R Road has been cut at Gordon on Friday (that is last night) and a number of cars burnt— the raiders busy tearing up the track. Buddy left for Dougherty [County] yesterday afternoon and in a note from Ma this afternoon she expresses herself as being very uneasy about him as indeed I am— He has gone right into the midst of them. If not taken by the Yankees he will be impressed into service at Macon—and [h]is arm is not so that he can use it. All is quiet up the road that Mr Thomas is on— I received a note from him yesterday written very hurriedly with pencil dated Madison. A letter from him to Col Rains was published in yesterday afternoon's paper stating that no enemy was there. A large party of raiders were seen in the vicinity of Covington last night. I fired off two pistol shots tonight to keep my courage up and will send Frank in in the morning early to hear the latest news. I don't know how I feel! A strange kind of apathy comes stealing over me as if I knew that *it must come*—that which we had so often talked of—so often jested upon, would soon be a fact that the Yankees would be in our midst and then what? I don't know. Let the future decide.

•   •   •

Saturday, August 27, 1864 I have just finished reading such an excellent piece in an old number of the *Eclectic* April 1858. "A Woman's Thoughts About Women." . . . [T]he fact is I have of late been a martyr to bad pens and indolence and (I might as well admit it) irritability! I wonder if the one was the result of the other. Perhaps so but I am not well really or I would not be so easily annoyed, so nervous, followed by depression. Even while I am writing my pen glances from my hand down the page— When I was writing some time since this happened several times. I suppose it was some nervous contraction of the muscles of the fingers, but I drew a sheet of paper to my side and thought perhaps (I have heard of such things) there may be some spiritual influence wishing to communicate with me. If I could commune with my Father's spirit I would willingly do so. . . .

Wednesday I was quite sick with dysinterry—and was in bed the next day but actual pain I can suffer better than the various maladies of mind and temper which caused me this morning to ask am I a hypochondriac? and then look in the dictionary to find out wether there was really such a disease and if so what it meant? and this brings me back to the article in the *Eclectic* to which I have just referred— An admirable piece probing like a surgeon's instrument to the root of my disease. When I was first married I think I was cheerful and usually I looked at the bright side of everything believing that the best offering we can make to God is to enjoy to the full what he sends of good and *bear* what he allows of evil—like a child who when it once thoroughly believes in its father believes in all its dealing with it, wether it understands them or not. So much was this the case that our family gave to me jestingly the name of "Uncle Michael" an old uncle of Ma's who always looked on the bright side of things, thought his pototoes were the largest, his hogs the finest of anyone else and upon one occasion when his crib, with a large amount of corn was destroyed by fire, consoled himself by saying, "Dad shame my skin if there wasn't a many a rat burnt up in it." . . .

In April I had to record the death of Pa and since then—to you my Journal I must confess to a wild, unsettled, chaotic state of mind through which tonight for the first time I see glimp[s]es of light breaking. The question of "where oh where in the great unknown world has my father's spirit gone?" has tortured me as with the whip of Scorpions. A restless longing to know—to be sure, to have something definite— that spirit which was so calmly conscious as to know that it was raining so short a time before his death. Where can it be? I think that anyone would pity me who knew how I have suffered as with bowed head and clasped hands I have thought on this subject. [Pa's will . . . giving of spirit . . . making a most liberal provision for all of us children but as God is my witness I would rather never of had that additional increase of property if . . . I would have been afraid [of] the knowledge which was communicated at the same time, how hath the mighty fallen! The bright sun which I had worshipped been dimmed! and loved . . . Oh no! but oh it is a bitter cup which my heavenly Father allowed my earthly father to press to my lips and I would not drink it. I rebelled. I . . . doubting everything. I was cold and indifferent to spiritual things.]²⁴ I had no faith in God or man—and yet all this time I have prayed, wildly, earnestly—and then again a mere lip service—my prayers not ascending higher than my head— All this has caused me to be in a highly excited nervous state reminding me more of the state of an opium eater as [Thomas] de Quincy describes it. . . . Felt this while I not only had not the power of execution but the will to attempt— I appeared to be under the weight of an incubus or nightmare.²⁵ . . .

The last page of what I have written I have written tonight (Monday) and I have spoken of the feelings I have had and spoken of them as something past but it was only this afternoon sitting in the Piazzi that as I was by myself these questions and doubts came to me with their depressing effect. Looking up to the blue sky above me I prayed fervently and calling Mary Bell to me I listened to her sweet voice till the evil spirit was charmed away. People in olden times were "sore vexed with a devil" and mine is a want of faith— Tonight I was singing a song which I have heard twice lately, "How firm a foundation." Oh how consoling "As thy days may demand shall thy strength ever be." "That soul though all hell should endeavour to shake. I'll never, no never, no *never* forsake." Oh God help me. I am very weak— Twice tonight while I have been writing

---

24. The square-bracketed lines above have been deliberately crossed out in the journal and some erasure has been attempted, either by Gertrude herself or by someone else at a later date. Nevertheless, the portion quoted here is readable.

25. Turner Clanton's will was a disappointment to Gertrude and Jefferson. They had expected a large legacy. Instead, Gertrude was shocked and humiliated to learn that her husband had borrowed a large sum of money from Colonel Clanton that now became a debt to the estate and the cause of family friction. At the time of his death, Clanton owned six plantations, hundreds of slaves, the mansion on Greene Street, the Rowell summer home, a warehouse, city lots, stocks, bonds, and a large number of accounts receivable. His estate was worth approximately $2.5 million.

my pen has fallen from my hands. Saturday night I could not sleep until I had taken a dose of medicine. It is now twenty minutes of twelve. I am wrong to sit up so late. . . .

Tuesday, August 30, 1864 How differently I feel tonight from last night. This morning I rose at twenty minutes of six and commenced to dress. I felt languid and was strongly tempted to go back to bed— Changing my mind I took a shower bath and rode in a gallop on Horseback up to the gate and back again. All the morning afterwards I was busy straightening drawers and putting things in order— Tonight since tea have been reading the papers. . . . The subject of an armistice is attracting general attention. I do not feel sanguine with regard to it and indeed think that it would be a suicidal move upon the part of our government to agree to an armistice. Our ports would still continue blockaded—we would be denied the privilege of strenghtening our position and Lincoln in the meanwhile would be elected. . . .

Saturday, September 4 [3], 1864 This morning I received a note from Mr Thomas about day telling me that a dispatch had just been sent through him to Gen Wright[26] from President Davis and General Bragg[27] "to send every armed man to Atlanta." . . . Mr Thomas expects he will have to go but I trust that his company will remain for the defence of Augusta. Oh these are troublous times. I leave Belmont not knowing what an hour may bring forth. I carry all the children with me. Fortunately I had intended going in and they are prepared— In case of a nearer approach of the Yankees I will remain in town. I wish to carry something with me and don't know what to take. I will carry the Confederate Bonds and silver spoons and forks. Perhaps the Yankees may make a raid here before I return. For the last two or three days I have felt particularly calm and free from trouble or anxiety. Oh for peace—and still I am not at all excited singular as it may seem, I do not form an idea of what the issue of this fight may be—

.   .   .

---

26. Maj. Gen. Ambrose R. "Ranse" Wright of Augusta.

27. Gen. Braxton Bragg of North Carolina resigned command of the Army of Tennessee in November 1863. In September 1864 he was serving as chief of staff to President Davis.

7. The War Comes Near: Doubting Thoughts, Fading Hope

Oh God will this war never cease!
—*November 21, 1864*

Friday, September 16, 1864 I was interrupted yesterday to go to ride on Horseback with Mr Thomas. After riding up the road and galloping back we rode over to the farm[1] where the Negroes were threshing wheat. I find Horseback riding delightful exercise and very beneficial. One of the Grey Ponys Grace is the most delightful riding animal I ever rode. I feel better than I have been during the summer and this notwithstanding the omminous appearance of our political world. Atlanta is in possession of the enemy and our forces are on the Macon road some distance this side. Last Sunday it was rumoured that Beauregard had taken Hood's[2] place but this has not been confirmed. McClellan[3] has been nominated by the Chicago convention and his letter of acceptance has crushed the hopes of the peace party. Yet I see they are having disputes amongst themselves. I heard the news of the fall of Atlanta and sighed. I heard of the death of Gen Morgan and as my heart sank heavily within me tears, bitter tears rolled down my cheek. I feel his death more sensibly from having seen him and it is so sad to imagine that manly form, that noble countenance hushed in death. It is particularly sad to think that he was betrayed. . . .

---

1. The farm property, sometimes called Yankee Farm and later named Dixie Farm, was adjacent to and north of Belmont.

2. Gen. John Bell Hood of Kentucky and Texas was given command of the Army of Tennessee following the removal of Gen. Joseph E. Johnston by President Davis.

3. Union general George B. McClellan was nominated by the Democrats to oppose Lincoln in the 1864 election.

Mr. Thomas' company still continue in camp at the hill. Each officer stays two days and has to attend drills besides. Mr Thomas left this afternoon. The local troops upon arriving in Macon were ordered back to Augusta. They came back with music and marched up Broad St where Gen Wright made them a speech. I happened to be riding down town when they came in from the cars and could but smile and think of that king who in battle array "marched up the hill and down again."[4] I thought if they had marched in more quietly it would have been in better taste. When our war worn scar covered veterans return, maimed and halt, arms in slings and some with scarce "body enough to cover their souls," they will require no music aside from the exultant shout of a grateful people— Mr Thomas took no share in the ovation as he stopped at the plantation in coming up. I was always puzzled to understand that parable in scriptures when the men who were hired at the eleventh hour received the same hire as those who had borne "the toil and heat of the day." It is almost impossible to avoid judging by the code of our human ethics and I thought it unjust. I was greatly relieved by someone's solving that problem by the statement that this was the *first* call they (the labourers) had received. In the same way I do not like such indiscriminate praise as the press bestows. The idea of praising militia and local troops in the same eulogistic strain as the volunteer organizations! It wars with my ideas of justice— for certainly this was not their *first* call and they went because they were compelled to. Local troops are necessary and while I am glad that Mr Thomas has so comparatively comfortable a position I still am very proud of the time he was in active service— . . .

Saturday, September 17, 1864 . . . How I do wish this war was over. I wish to breathe free. I feel pent up, confined—cramped and shall I confess it am reminded of that Italian story of *The Iron Shroud* where daily—daily hourly and momently the room contracts, the victim meanwhile utterly impotent to avert the impending doom. Never have I so fully realised the feeble hold upon this

---

4. The quotation comes from a song dating from Charles I's time: "The King of France went up the hill / With forty thousand men." The words later appeared as: "Oh, the brave old Duke of York / He had ten thousand men / He marched them up to the top of the hill / And he marched them down again." The verse is sometimes used by journalists as political satire.

world's goods as I do now. I don't think I have ever enjoyed that peculiarly charming season the Indian Summer more than I have during the past few weeks. Looking up the three Avenues and at the Goats Cows and Horses so quietly walking about, listening at the cooing of Pigions, the chirping of the different fowls in the yard— I imagine this contrasted with men clad in Yankee uniform rudely violating the privacy of my home. I imagine the booming of Yankee cannon and the clash of Yankee sabres and I ask myself how soon shall this thing be?? Nor does it require an imaginative mind to foretell such an event but the last page of my Journal must bear no such cowardly record.

I have sometimes doubted on the subject of slavery. I have seen so many of its evils chief among which is the terribly demoralising influence upon our men and boys but of late I have become convinced the Negro *as a race* is better off with us as he has been than if he were made free, but I am by no means so sure that we would not gain by his having his freedom given him. I grant that I am not so philanthropic as to be willing voluntarily to give all we own for the sake of the principle, but I do think that if we had the same invested in something else as a means of support I would willingly, nay gladly, have the responsibility of them taken off my shoulders.

This Journal was commenced July 13th 1861 and I am ashamed that three years of the most eventful period of my life should have had so poor a record but I find that the absorbing theme of war is one to be talked of better than written about and what I write is so commonplace when contrasted with the stirring events to which I allude that I shrink from making a record of them. I have cut out for the scrap books (which I cannot buy) an account of all the important events which have taken place. . . . Again political events have absorbed so much of my Journal to the exclusion of domestic matters that one might readily suppose that I was not the happy mother of four darling children. . . .

Thursday, September 22, 1864 Was it ominous that I should find my pen split when I took it up to write tonight? In these troublous times how superstitious we become. Shall I dare hope that this new Journal which I am commencing will record Peace, an independent Southern Confederacy? Truly the skies are gloomy and the heavy storm appears ready to discharge its thunders in our very midst. Yet how calm, how indifferent we are—we laugh, we smile, we talk, we jest, just as tho no enemy were at our door. And yet the idea has several times suggested itself to me that someday I would have to aid in earning my own support. We have made no arrangement whatever for such a contingency. Gold has increased in value and we have *not a dollar*—and yet I am hopeful of the success of our cause, the ultimate success of our Confederacy, while I do not think it improbable that *we* will lose our fortunes before that final success is achieved.

Tonight President Davis passed through town. I was within ten steps of him which made the disappointment of not seeing [him] greater than it would have been. I had been spending the day with Ma and in coming out home took Mr Thomas to the Waynesboro Depot. A large crowd had collected and were just in the act of dispersing after having listened to a speech from the President. I have always been anxious, very anxious to see him and thought the wish was certainly to be gratified now. The band having just arrived serenaded the President. We waited outside of the car for him to make his appearance again, but he did not. Mr Thomas first proposed going into the car and introducing me to him (he having seen him in Richmond), but at last decided not and I took my seat in the carriage and came on home more disappointed than if I had not been so near him. Mr Thomas was going to Burke and not having on a uniform felt that the President might demur. (I was going to say, if it would not be irreverent, "Friend, where is thy wedding garment?") Mr Fargo remarked to me "that the President was much more infirm—more decrepit than he had expected to see him, yet, when he spoke, there was a great deal of fire and vigor about him." Writing, as I do, for my own pleasure and partly for the benefit of the children, I wish I could record my personal impressions of a man whom I would willingly go to Richmond to see, but I will hope hereafter to see something more of his majesty. Who knows? Revolutions effect great changes and I may yet live under a monarchal rule. . . .

Friday, September 23, 1864 It has always been a source of great comfort to me to express my thoughts in language. Indeed this has often times proven a source of subsequent regret for sometimes to express the idea in homely phrase "I talk too much" and yet I can but think in some cases it is better to talk than to brood over troubles. This morning I read the humble petition of James Calhoun, mayor of Atlanta, E. E. Rawson and L. C. Wells councilmen, imploring Sherman[5] to permit the order for the women and children to leave Atlanta to be revoked, and the reply of Sherman, in which he refuses to comply with that request. A lady remarked of the people of Macon the other day that "they were the most whipped people she had ever seen" but how humiliating it is for us to read of the abject submission and the utter scorn mingled with ridicule with which Sherman replies.

Since reading the paper I have been busy cutting out the winter clothing for the children, everything goes on in its regular routine. The children are playing in the yard. Milly nursing the baby. Patsey washing. America scouring. Nancy cleaning— Tamah cooking. Frank and Wash—Hannah and Jessy playing in the yard.[6] The farm servants all at work and while I have been cutting out, Sherman's letter has been occupying my mind. I had decided that in case of the Yankees taking possession of Augusta I would remain there if I could, but the exiles of Atlanta has taught me that a different destiny awaits me if Sherman reaches here, and that he will do so I firmly believe to be *only a matter* of *time.* Yet Macon and Andersonville appear to be in more imminent danger than Augusta, but to you my new Journal, my new friend I will confess that what troubles me more than anything else is that I am not certain that Slavery is right.

The doctrine of self government I suppose of course to be right and yet our Southern people do not appear to have learned the art, even if they had the right granted them. Where is there more power exercised than is displayed in the manner in which our Gen's are "relieved"? But as to the doctrine of slavery altho I have read very few abolition books (*Uncle Tom's Cabin* making most impression) nor have I read many pro slavery books—yet the idea has gradually become more and more fixed in my mind that the institution of slavery is not right—but I am reading a new book, *Nellie Norton,* by the Rev E W Warren[7] which I hope will convince me that it is right— Owning a large number of slaves as we do I might be asked

---

5. Union general William Tecumseh Sherman.

6. Frank, Wash, Hannah, and Jessy were the children of slaves belonging to the Thomases.

7. A proslavery book, *Nellie Norton* (1864) was written by a Baptist minister from Vineville, Ga.

why do I not free them? This if I could, I would not do, but if Mr Thomas would sell them to a man who would look after their temporal and spiritual interest I would gladly do so. Those house servants we have if Mr Thomas would agree to it I would pay regular wages but this is a subject upon which I do not like to think and taking my stand upon the moral view of the subject, I can but think that to hold men and women in perpetual bondage is wrong— During my comparatively short life, spent wholly under Southern skies, I have known of and heard too much of its demoralizing influence to consider the institution a blessing—

.   .   .

Friday, October 21, 1864   Again Mr Thomas is ordered from home and naturally I turn to my journal to tell you how lonely I feel, and yet Hope whispers with her siren toungue into my willing ear, "He will come again." Last night Cap Kirkpatrick brought an order from Gen or Col Fry[8] commanding all the local companies with the Wheeler Dragoons included to meet today—prepared with sixty rounds of ammunition, rations for two days, blankets, canteens and &c., prepared to go to Macon. We cannot tell why it is or for what purpose they are required. Mr Thomas conjectures for the purpose of going on to assist the militia in taking Atlanta. Cap Kirkpatrick thinks it is only intended by Col [Gen.] Fry as an experiment to test the alacrity with which the men will respond at a moments notice. I am inclined to agree with him and hope now that Mr Thomas will return home tonight. How much I have missed him today. His being in camp is so entirely different from his being at the front. Oh God how we sigh and yearn for Peace, honourable Peace—

I have just paused and with my head bent upon my hand have reflected upon the present condition of our country. The deep gloom which hung over us just after the fall of Atlanta has been lifted from our midst and the movement of Gen Hood has brightened both the army and the people, but we are kept in as complete ignorance of the movement of Hood's army as if they were in the Crimea instead of the upper portion of Georgia. Now I argue unfavourably from this circumstance for I have noticed ever since the

---

8. Brig. Gen. Birkett D. Fry was in command at Augusta.

war commenced that if there is good news we usually hear it soon after it occurs. . . . This morning as I was bidding Mr Thomas good bye we were standing by Stanley and I felt an almost irresistible impulse to press my lips upon the silky hair of the noble creature upon whose endurance so much of my husband's safety depended. As I gently stroked him, Mr Thomas remarked— "We are going to try it again Stanley, old fellow," and I felt almost like whispering to the intelligent animal— "Bring him back safe, Stanley." It would be a brilliant thing to recapture Atlanta. I wish it could be done. I wish Mr Thomas could be engaged in the fight if he could escape safely, but he *might not* and then what? Am I willing to give my husband to gain Atlanta for the Confederacy? No, No, No, a thousand times No! . . .

.   .   .

Tuesday, October 25, 1864   I was in town today and have decided to go in Thursday. Mr Thomas thinks I cannot move without him but I wish to surprise him by having everything prepared for him by the time he comes home. I received a letter from him this morning. He wishes me to send him a few things by Lt Primrose who goes on tomorrow. I will send him a box on Thursday by Sargeant Byrd.

On Sunday I was in town and attended the Methodist Church. Mr Cox preached. I had never heard him before and a more uninteresting sermon I never listened to. The tones of his voice were so monotonous as [to] be suggestive of sleep. In the conclusion of his sermon he had the rise and fall in his voice ending with an en-da which has always been connected in my mind with country preachers. After the sermon Mr Scott "lifted" a collection for the payment of a large debt hanging over Asbury Church. Now I have never been inside of that church and know nothing of it except that it is a Methodist church [and] as such having a claim upon me, but I do very much dislike some of the features connected with the Methodist Church and to none am I more thoroughly opposed than this intolerable begging system. As we do not rent our pews and thus afford ourselves a settled income, this I suppose cannot under the circumstances be very well avoided.

What I particularly object to is the clashing of worldly or money matters with spiritual sensations. Imagine Mr Scott calling like an auctioner for persons in the congregation to rise and make an offer (or bid) of $500 dollars—no one responded then he asked for 300 [dollar] contributions, adding that "he would put his name down for that amount as he was going to give it." Someone had previously given $500 dollars. After calling upon the congregation "to hold up their hands if they would not speak out and subscribe for his call for $200—$250 and $100 dollars—the stewards (Mr Scott among them) proceeded to go through the congregation and collect contributions. While Mr Scott was making these calls I felt heartily ashamed of him, the congregation, and everything connected with it. Ma, Sis Anne, Gen and Mrs Harris[9] were there, besides other persons not connected with that denomination. I felt guilty of a breach of hospitality. As if we had invited those persons to an entertainment and expected them to pay part of the expenses. People were leaving in the midst of it and smiling and shrugging their shoulders— I put down my name for $200 and wished that I could have done more. . . .

This mingling pastoral with steward's duty is very objectiona[ble] in Mr Scott. I would have a minister set apart from everything of the kind. The fact is there are some wants of an aesthetic, refined nature which the Methodist Church in Augusta does not gratify— While I admire religion in any people I prefer to see it mingled with refinement and culture. Our class meeting system is only a bad imitation of the Roman Catholic Confessional. It is not pleasant to discuss the most sacred relations of your life and tell of your various temptations when every word both of yourself and class leader will be heard by a number of curious, unsympathetic listeners. I like organ music too—it adds to the solemnity of church service and does not leave the singing to the whim of a choir who very often dispute amongst themselves— I like the pew system too— It is pleasant to have one's family sit together—and then it gives to a church the advantage of a fixed income to pay expenses— . . . I love the Methodist church—its dear old songs of Zion but it must keep up with the age of improvement or it will not render itself an attractive church to the generation who are coming on.

I have expressed myself freely on several points which I have not before alluded to but have reserved my principal objection to the Methodist Church last. The short pastoral relations— To me there is something infinitely touching in the relations of pastor and

---

9. Gen. Robert Harris of the Georgia militia.

people—when the same minister buried your fathers and mothers—Christened yourselves—Knew you through your childhood and girlhood—united your hand as was your heart with the husband of your youth—performed for your children the same office of christening and acceptance into the church of God as yourself—and will perhaps read for you the solemn prayer which consigns your body "dust to dust—ashes to ashes." How differently could you approach this minister, knowing that he appreciated your trials as he understood your disposition, to a minister who comes among you to remain one—perhaps two years and who as you begin to know each other is suddenly called off and a stranger claims your confidence upon that subject which of all others requires *faith* to elicit confidence. You feel instinctively that you must learn to know your pastor before you talk upon spiritual matters with him— To a man these would perhaps appear trivial objectives but what to a man's nature is sometimes of little importance to a woman's nature forms an essential. As to the creed of the Methodist Church I consider there are good Christians in every denomination—all bound for the same port upon different sailing vessels—

Belmont, October 27, 1864 "Man proposes, but God disposes." I, last night, had some serious reflections upon what I supposed was my last night here for the winter. Tonight I had expected to have been in town, but the rain and Jeff's having a chill causes me to be here instead. I am writing by a small piece of candle which will only last me to write a few lines. Immediately after tea last night, I cut out and commenced sewing on a tobacco bag for Buddy. He leaves for Virginia tomorrow to join his command. I take some credit to myself— My candle just then gave out but it is not nine oclock and too soon to go to bed so I am writing by the firelight, seated on the one mattress we happened to have left here. Grif has just come, having been in to carry Buddy's tobacco bag which I sewed on last night for four hours until eleven oclock and finished today. A very unusual fit of industry for me. Grif had been impressed into the service of some soldiers who wished to find some place to stop at and threatened to shoot him if he did not go with [them]. After taking feed from Gen Harris' field, they stopped at Rosney Church. Grif brought me a letter from Mr Reid of Charleston, enclosing samples of English and French muslins—no black kid glove in the city. I suppose he has no bombazine.

Augusta, November 17, 1864   Three weeks since writing last, my frequent letters to Mr Thomas forming a record of the time since I have moved into town, but I am in trouble and instinctively I turn to my journal. Today I dined with Ma having been out in the morning with Aunty Cousin Emma and Cora. As I entered the house a telagram was handed Mamie who opened it and found that it was intended for me. I read it and then with the foolish remark "I believe I am going to do as I did when the cow ran after me, I am going to cry," I burst into tears. The telagram, dated Macon contained these words "Wheeler Dragoons & self—all well."

This is a dark hour in our country's history. Lincoln has been elected by 300,000 majority and Northern papers say that Sherman is preparing for a winter campaign through the cotton states with five corps, leaving a sufficient force to hold Chattanooga and look after Hood. Sherman some years ago was stationed at the arsenal[10] at the Sand Hills and has been the recipient of hospitality from numerous citizens of this place. President Davis in his message says that we are better off than we were this time last year, but when President Davis advocates the training of Negroes to aid us in fighting—promising them, as an inducement to do so, *their freedom*, and in the same message intimates that rather than yield we would place every Negro in the Army—he so clearly betrays the weakness of our force that I candidly confess I am disheartened. I take a woman's view of the subject but it does seem strangely inconsistent, the idea of our offering to a Negro the rich boon—the priceless reward of freedom to aid us in keeping in bondage a large portion of his brethren, when by joining the Yankees he will instantly gain the very reward which Mr Davis offers to him after a certain amount of labor rendered and danger incurred. Mr Davis to the contrary, the Negro has had a great deal to do with this war and if—but I fear I grow toryish in my sentiments—

Monday, November 21, 1864   Oh God will this war never cease? Will we ever settle quietly in our old peaceful domestic relations? How strange it all seems. Even now I can scarcely realize the state of suspense in which we have all been placed during the past few

---

10. The U.S. Arsenal, located in the Sand Hills, had been seized by Gov. Joseph E. Brown in 1861 and became part of Augusta's ordnance operations during the war. It is now the site of Augusta College.

days. I don't believe I have felt so gloomy at anytime tho as I did Saturday afternoon. During the morning I rode out (Friday), and just as I was leaving the house I received a letter from Mr Thomas written the Sunday previous— Said he "Ah you can form no idea how much I miss you—good bye to you and all my little ones." . . .

Short as the time has been since Thursday, I can scarcely collect the link of events sufficiently to tell how the time has been spent. Oh I remember now that Mr Scales spent Friday night with us. He was taking a gloomy view of our prospects, but he talked just this way I remember one year ago. Then I confess I felt more determined "to do and dare and die" than I do now. Saturday we were busy hauling wood from the depot, Mr Selkirk the agent having been good enough to let me have two car loads brought up. It was fortunate I received it when I did as the trains are occupied now in removing government stores to the exclusion of everything else. It was, as yesterday and today have been, dull gloomy days. The whole heavens overcast with clouds— All nature appearing to mourn over the wretched degeneracy of her children and weeping to see brothers arrayed in hatred against each other. "Man, the noblest work of God."[11] Verily, when I witness and read of the track of desolation which Sherman's army leaves behind them, I am constrained to think that the work reflects little credit upon the creator. I know that sounds irreverent but I sigh for the memory of those days when man's noblest, better nature was displayed, when the brute "the cloven foot," was concealed and I could dream and believe that ours was the very best land—ruled by the very best men under the sun!! . . .

As I walked down the street a hundred and one rumours met my ear. One told me that the Yankees were advancing—another that they were retreating this way, Hood directly behind them. "What," said I, "and Hood across the Tennessee?" "Oh I don't know," was the reply and so it was. . . . I joined Aunty Mamie and Cousin Emma in the carriage. A rain coming up, we drove rapidly home and laughed as heartily as if the enemy were five thousand miles away. And yet that night, wishing to divert my mind I commenced *Beulah* again—read on till nearly nine when a man came bringing me a note from cousin Mary Ann. Dispatches had come

---

11. "An honest man's the noblest work of God," from *An Essay on Man*, epistle 4, by Alexander Pope (1688–1744).

for Gen Evans[12] (who was in the country) and a horse was wanted for the purpose of conveying them to him. The telagram was from Gen Brown[13] conveying the news that the enemy had burned the depot at Madison and were at Buckhead seven miles this side coming down the Georgia road. I furnished the horse and then going up stairs went to bed and read *Beulah* until I finished it between eleven and twelve. This may appear strange but I was not as much frightened when I supposed they were coming towards Augusta as I was when I supposed them marching for Macon where Mr Thomas was. I have never been afraid of the Yankees— I do not dread *personal* violence—and their taking *property* is so small a consideration compared with my husband's life that I scarcely regard it. . . .

. . .

Tuesday, November 22, 1864 . . . I am seated in my low rocking chair before a large oak fire [and] am as comfortable as I ever was in my life— The glowing coals contrasting with the sighing of the wind around the house. The room in perfect order and a keen sense of thorough enjoyment of life pervading my whole nature. All this I see and feel and it is with an effort I try to think that a large force are rapidly approaching us with the intention of devastating our homes. I cannot realise it— I am perfectly calm— Is it trust in God! or apathy which causes me to feel so quiet? If I know my own heart I have faith in God that he will do "all for the best." Poverty is not the worst evil which can befall us. I now realise what I have always thought, that Dr [Benjamin] Franklin was right when he said "If a man (or woman) empties his purse into his head, no man can take it away from him. An investment of knowledge pays the best interest." The enemy can take all else— Thank God they cannot deprive me of education. Ma says she feels as if she would do nothing, make no exertion if the enemy came. True to my elastic disposition I have already planned for the future— but poverty offers no charms to my nature. Indolent, loving a life of luxury, could I be enabled to exert myself? Time will tell—

Last winter I complained of this house. I wish I could be sure of

---

12. Gen. Clement A. Evans of Augusta, who later became a Methodist minister.

13. Probably Brig. Gen. William Montague Browne.

as good a one all the rest of my life— Yesterday morning I received a note from Mamie telling me that it was reported that the government was impressing all the provisions in the stores, adding "excuse this writing. For the first time in my life I have to confess to having nerves and they are a good deal shaken this morning"— During yesterday I packed the camphor chest with such things as I will not require till next spring—thinking I would send it on to Carolina. I was cheerful while thus engaged but coming down and looking into the drawer containing all the cherished mementos of my girlhood and the letters of Mr Thomas and my own—together with my Journal, faithful record of my life since I was fourteen, my courage faltered. I felt as if I was putting away a portion of my life— Tears rushed to my eyes and with bended head I prayed that this bitter blow might be spared me. I could risk leaving silver but those Journals, those letters, those treasured locks of hair I *could not* let them go and I have packed them to be sent off instead of the silver. Mr Thomas will be at home today and he will aid me in deciding— my jewelry—my money—Pa's likeness—his hair and notices of his death I shall secure in some safe place. These latter are the dearest treasures I possess. I received a note from Ma this morning. She says "come down. I don't know what to do. I laugh awhile and cry awhile— The reflection is awful as I begin to realise poverty and starvation staring me in the face." I received a letter from Mr Thomas Sunday while I was at Ma's written at Forsythe during the retreat. He had then been riding two nights and expected to make a stand at Griffin. . . .

• • •

Monday, December 12, 1864 . . . Last night and all day today the wind has been very high. Remaining constantly in the sitting room beside a large oak fire my thoughts have been with Mr Thomas. How cold he must be. He left last week with his company for the purpose of impressing Horses for the government. They went in the direction of Waynesboro. Mr Thomas spent one night at Cotton Town[14] from which place he wrote me an account of the destruction of our entire planting interest in Burke. *Sherman's men visited*

---

14. Cotton Town was one of Jefferson Thomas's plantations in Burke County.

our plantation Monday Nov 28th at the time they burned Waynesboro Depot. Henry one of our Negroes left the plantation Sunday night, joined the Yankees and the next morning conducted them to Cotton Town and showed the place in which Uncle Sykes (our Negro driver) had concealed the Horses and mules. They took such as they wished and having dressed Henry in a suit of uniform they stole Melnott a valuable Horse of ours and mounted Henry upon it. They then set the Gin House and Screw on fire, broke open the overseer's house and committed other depredations. Being very closely pursued by Wheeler's[15] forces they left in the direction of Pinck's Plantation, leaving one man to attend to the entire destruction of our Gin House. This man (the Negroes say) our men killed— During the week we brought up some of our Negro men— Gen Young[16] kindly permitted Pinck to go down.

When our Negros were tempted by the Yankees to go with them they refused with the excption of Henry and proved most faithful—but Mr Thomas writes me that John Boss who drove us for five or six years after we were married has since left. Henry has no ties to bind him to the plantation and has been a runaway from childhood. I know he will run away from the Yankees but John left a wife and child. I have very kindly feelings towards him and hope he may do well while I doubt it. After an enumeration of our losses in Burke, the Yankees having camped there one night burning the rest of our cotton our corn cribs and &c, the letter I have preserved of Mr Thomas' adds "do not let our losses trouble you. It may all be for the best." . . .

My fire is almost out for which I am sorry as I am in the mood for writing for the first time in two or three weeks. What a time we have had! Like the man travelling in search of novelty I have experienced a new sensation— I have been frightened! I look back to that Sunday night Nov the 27th and can compare it to only one night in my life's experience. The night in which after having been away from the children for several nights and Jeff having had croup the night previous, I came up home during Pa's illness and went to

---

15. Maj. Gen. Joseph "Fighting Joe" Wheeler, a Confederate cavalry officer.

16. Maj. Gen. Pierce M. B. Young, a cavalry officer, was probably Pinck's commanding officer. Pinck had been seriously wounded in 1863 while fighting with the Richmond Hussars under Maj. Gen. J. E. B. "Jeb" Stuart.

bed fearing that the summons would come during the night, as come it did, to tell me that he was worse. Just so that Sunday night I went to bed, not knowing but that during the night the bell would toll and the alarm that the enemy were upon us would be given. I was resting with this weight upon my mind when Mr Thomas came up from camp in the middle of the night and requested me to have his rations cooked that he was ordered to leave. I hastily rose and attended to preparing something for him and then dressed as I was, lay down on the foot of the bed to await the messenger he was to send back for his Haversack— Grif coming later quieted my anxiety by bringing me a note telling me "that there was no one there to give the Dragoons orders so the Yankees could not be very near."

The next morning I rose at half past five to go to the Depot to see Mamie and Cora off, having been awakened twice & again during the night by messages from Ma. While I was dressing Mr Thomas returned. I took teaspoons, forks and large spoons with my Pie Knife and thought I would at least secure that much and get Mamie and Cora to carry it to a place of security for me.[17] When I reached the depot I found the cars had left and upon going round home I found all the trunks "and their name was legion" out in the back Piazzi, while out in the front Piazzi were all of them in travelling dress seated in every imaginable position, anxiety depicted upon every face. When they reached the cars Mr Scales heard a rumour that the Yankees were in Carolina and would fire upon the cars, so as they were going without a gentleman he thought it best for them not to go. He also understood that Allen's Depot had been burned. All Burke was on fire and he thought that the enemy would be at Augusta in half an hour and would have nothing to do but walk into it. Just then a gun fired— "That's them" said Mr Scales too much excited to be grammatical "don't you hear them?" I came up home after taking breakfast with Ma and sat down all day and literally did nothing. I was so tired and worn out I felt as if I could make no exertion if the Yankees did come.

Tuesday Mr Thomas invited some gentleman to dine with us. Among them was Col Connelly upon whose staff he had been

---

17. Mamie and Cora were going to North Carolina to stay with Julia Scales, thinking that it would be safer there, and were taking along some of the family valuables.

placed for a few days. Lt Col Moss Gen Baker[18] and a Major and a Cap and another Major all of whose names I have forgotten. Gen Young dined with us too having just returned from a reconnaissance towards Waynesboro. Col Read was to have been with us but came too soon and left. The veteran troops leaving Augusta that evening made them all late so that when we commenced dinner we had lights lit. In addition to Champaigne and &c I gave them several bottles of the wine I had put up for Mary Bell's wedding day. I laughingly told them so adding that I was afraid the Yankees would deprive me of it. Hearing her name mentioned Mary Bell who was on the stair steps said, "Who, Ma, me?" Col Connelly and Lt Col Moss spent the night with us and Wednesday night also. Both Gen Baker and Col Connelly have but one arm. . . .

    .   .   .   .

Monday, December 26, 1864 I am alone tonight. Mr Thomas has gone down to see Col Vason on business connected with an overseer for the Rowell place. The children are up stairs asleep. Tamah is sick. America has gone down to see her mother and Fanny— Patsey has gone to see some of Bob's family up town—all of them trying to pass "a merry Christmas." I have just written a ticket for Daniel to go to a party at Dr Ed Eve's. While writing the idea occurs to me, Shall we have any servants to write tickets for when another Christmas comes around? Since commencing to write I have changed my pen three or four times and this is a poor one. I am sorry I commenced to write in this book for the paper is as poor as Confederate paper— We took dinner with Ma today. Only Col Vason, Sis Anne and her children, Mr Thomas and I with our children. Holt is at home with us spending the vacation of a week. He is going to Mr Carroll who has charge of the University High School in Athens. What a difference in last year's Christmas dinner. Then every member of the family was at home including Pinck who was sick in his room from the effect of a painful wound— Today Ma received a telagram from him wishing to know where Mamie was. He is now at Hardeeville near Savannah. Mamie and Cora are still with Jule. Ma has written for them to come home— Savannah has fallen! Ma is afraid the enemy will cut the communi-

---

18. Probably Brig. Gen. Lawrence S. Baker.

cation at Branchville [South Carolina] and we will be cut off from Mamie and Cora. I think that it would be advisable for them to remain longer as they are certainly much safer than they would be here— To use a phrase which is quite popular when a place is captured I expect Augusta "to go up," namely "up the spout." Can any better proof be given of the effect of revolutions than the fact that I should announce such an expectation with a military slang expression?

The fact is the time and circumstances somehow appears to create a reckless, careless feeling, an impatience to have it over— It is impossible to settle quietly down or form plans for the future when everything depends in a great degree upon the whim or caprice of Gen Sherman. Some persons imagine that Augusta will be the next place which Sherman will attempt to capture. Others that after cutting our communication with Richmond at Branchville he will take Charleston. Indeed I hear that Charleston is being evacuated today, our troops falling back—this report requires confirmation. John has returned to Burke from the hands of the enemy. We have not seen him so know nothing of his adventures.

Yesterday was Christmas Day. Both that and today have been dull, gloomy and cloudy days. In the morning Mr Thomas Turner and Mary Bell and I went to the Episcopalian Church, St Paul's. It was dressed very handsomely— Over the alt[a]r the words "Glory to God in the Highest" were hung, the letters as fresh and evergreen as the sentiment should be in every heart. This was the subject of Mr Clark's[19] text— The music was grand and inspiring. To my taste there is something especially appropriate in the Episcopalian service for Christmas day. It is fitting that the commemoration of our Saviour's birth should be attended with great solemnity. The tones of St Paul's organ as played upon by Mr Illsey thrilled me with such intensity of feeling that it would have been a relief to have bent my head over and in feminine parlance "taken a good cry." I like the Episcopalian Church, the organ the imposing ritual, everything better than I do the preaching— Mr Clark's voice is quite suggestive of sleep and I am now so prosaically sleepy that I can write no more.

---

19. Rev. William H. Clark.

Tuesday, December 27, 1864 . . . A poor old woman named Mrs Welsh came in to see me this afternoon. Her only son is living in Mississippi whom she has heard from only once since the war commenced. Poor old soul. She has a hard time, and yet destitute as she is she is as much afraid of the Yankees as I would be. I told her that I saw no cause for her being uneasy, that the Yankees would scarcely disturb so old a lady as herself.

A refugee lady who lives in a car out at the depot, by the name of Kirksey was to see me a few days since. Alluding to the difference between this Christmas and last she added while the tears coursed their way down her cheek, "Oh Mrs Thomas my husband was such a good man. Every Christmas he filled the children's stockings with something for Santa Claus presents." Her husband was a conductor on the Georgia R Road was taken prisoner and is now at Camp Chase. The idea occurred to me that next Christmas I might be unable to provide my children with Christmas gifts and I placed five dollars in Mary Bell's hand and told her to give it to the lady to buy some apples for her children. I also gave her some potatoes and meat. Her sister Mrs Church I gave a cooking stove. She was out in the cars with three children, having chills nearly every day & no stove in the car. She has been sewing for me for several weeks.

During the conversation with Mrs Kirksey I asked her her maiden name. "Buchanan" was her reply. "What any relation to the President"[20] said I? "He was a first cousin of my father" was her simple answer without appearing to attach any importance to the relationship. She then added that some years ago Buchanan was on a visit to Atlanta stopping at Thompson's Hotel. Her father who was the fifer for a [militia] company was playing in the street. The similarity of name attracted Buchanan's attention—mutual inquiry discovered that they were brothers' sons. Her father invited Buchanan to go out and take dinner with him & he remained with them nearly a week. . . .

Mrs Kirksey is quite good looking so is Mrs Church but the former is a very illiterate woman. "I have a cousin in Virginia but that is at the North isn't it mam" said she. Again she wished to know "if her husband had to cross the Gulf of Mexico to reach

---

20. James Buchanan, U.S. president 1857–61.

Camp Chase?" How extremes meet when one brother's child becomes President of the United States—the other a fifer for a company in Atlanta! . . .

Tuesday, January 3, 1865 Mr Thomas has gone up stairs and I have just finished reading an interesting letter giving an account of the movements of the state line troops during Sherman's march through Georgia. Alluding to the evacuation of Savannah he mentions that after our troops left the city he could hear the shrieks of women caused by the stragglers—the skulkers of our army who had commenced to pillage and destroy. Some of them were shot by the citizens and others captured by the Yankees. "Wither are we drifting?" is the pertinent question asked by the Editor of the Charleston *Mercury* in commenting upon the increase of crime and lawlessness in that city—and this enquiry comes with startling energy from others when the time appears rapidly approaching when we have almost as much to dread from our own demoralized mob as from the public enemy.

I confess to not being in the most enviable, cheerful mood possible. Tonight I have been cutting or clipping as the newspapers term it. . . . Among the fine foreign items, I read with much interest an account of great works which are being done in Europe. "A railway through the alps"— . . . There they are employing their God given intellect to enoble and elevate—to civilize their race—*and we* in God's name what are we doing? Striving to defend ourselves against our brethren who would butcher us—annihilate us if they could— War is a terrible demon. It does not elevate—it debases. It does not lift heavenward—it crushes into the dust. I lose faith in humanity when I see such efforts to sink the nobler better part of man's nature in an effort to exterminate the white race at the South in order to elevate the Negro race to a position which I doubt their ability to fill—

The time will come when Southern women will be avenged— Let this war cease with the abolition of slavery and I wish for the women of the North no worse fate than will befall them. Their husbands already prepare for them the bitter cup of humiliation which they will be compelled to drink to the dregs— General Kilpatrick[21] spent a night in Waynesboro. [H]is headquarters were at

---

21. Union general Hugh Judson Kilpatrick, a cavalry officer.

Mrs Dr Carter's. He demanded that the best bed room in the house should be prepared for himself and a good looking mulatto girl whom he had travelling with him. A seat at the table was furnished her— The officers deferential in their manner to her while thus publicly insulting Mrs Carter in her own house. Lolling indolently in a rocking chair the girl awaits the entrance of the Gen. "What not retired yet Nellie?" is his salutation. "Not until your majesty returns" is her reply— Take *that scene* Mrs Kilpatrick as a reward for encouraging your husband to come amongst us

I don't know why it is but that man Sherman has interested me very much—perhaps it is upon the principle that all women admire successful courage and that Gen Sherman has proven himself to be a very brave man there can be no doubt. Our enemy as he is I can imagine that his wife loves him. A short time ago I read that his baby six months old had died— I could not be glad of it altho his men in their eager search after hidden treasure opened the graves of babys that had just been buried and left the coffins on the brink of the grave. At one time just after Sherman passed through Burke I wrote Mrs Sherman a letter which I intended having published under the head of Personal in one of the Richmond papers— I did not send it and now that I have read of the recent death of her baby I am glad that I did not. Woman's nature is the same the world over. She brooks no rival near the throne (except amongst the [illegible] that strange anamoly of nature). Northern women are colder in their temperature than our warm hearted children of the sun but I know that amongst the jubilee attendant upon her husband's "Christmas present" to Lincoln [Savannah] I could send Mrs Sherman "a New Year's gift" which would dim and make hollow and empty the mirth by which she is surrounded— I do feel very very sorry for her and will not send this letter if I could—

Mrs Gen Sherman— A few days since I read your husband's farewell telegram to you dated Atlanta. Will you believe it? *for a moment* I felt sorry for you. Forgetting who you were and for what purpose he was coming among us my heart went out in womanly sympathy for you. He bids you expect to hear from him only through rebel sources and urged by the same womanly intuition which prompted me to sympathise with you, I a rebel lady will give you some information with regard to Gen Sherman's movements. Last week your husband's army found me in the possession of wealth. Tonight our plantations are a scene of ruin and desolation. *You* bad him "God speed" on his fiendish errand, did you not? You thought it a gallant deed to come amongst us where by his own confession he expected to find "only the shadow of an army." A brave act to frighten women and children! desolate homes, violate the sanctity of firesides and cause the "widow and orphan to curse the Sherman for the cause" and this you did for what? to elevate the Negro race. Be satisfied Madam your wish has been accomplished. Enquire of Gen Sherman when next you see him who has been elevated to fill your place? You doubtless read with a smile of approbation of the delightfully fragrant ball at which he made his debut in Atlanta? Did he tell you of the Mulatto girl for whose safety he was so much concerned that she was returned to Nashville when he commenced his vandal march? This girl was spoken of by the Negroes whom you are willing to trust so implicitly as "Sherman's wife." Rest satisfied Mrs Sherman and quiet the apprehension of your Northern sisters with regard to the elevation of the Negros— Your husbands are amongst a coloured race whose reputation for morality has never been of the highest order—and these gallant cavaliers are most of them provided with "a companion du voyage"— As your brave husband considers a southern lady a fair object to wage war against and as I do not yet feel fully satisfied that there is no danger of a clutch from his heavy hand upon my shoulders, I will only add that intensely Southern woman as I am *I pity you.*

.   .   .

Sunday, February 12, 1865   I am far from well and remained from church this morning altho I should have been pleased to have heard Mr Evans preach one of his comforting gospel sermons. He is our minister for this year succeeding Mr Scott who has been suspended from preaching—[22] This last I must look upon as the most unpleasant week I ever remember to have experienced— The expected approach of the Yankees—aided by the coldest weather I ever felt combined to place me in a truly uncomfortable mood. Unfortunately I have a prospect of again adding to the little members of my household—of again becoming a mother. Happening as it does in these troublous times I am sincerely sorry for it. How differently I

---

22. This is the same Mr. Scott, the Methodist minister, who had earlier annoyed Gertrude with his manner of "begging" from the congregation.

feel from what I did in Nov when the Yankees were expected. Then I had some energy— Now I have none— Then I could rouse myself to meet the consequences— Now I shrink appalled— Gen Hill[23] who is commanding this post issued an order some time since notifying owners of Cotton to remove it from the City as in case of an advance of the enemy he intended to burn all that remained here. Great fears having been apprehended ever since last Saturday or yesterday week—the authoritys have been very busy having the Cotton placed in the streets and all the vacant squares for the purpose of having it burned as soon as the enemy should approach near enough to render it necessary—

Returning from Columbia last Monday after having heard that the enemy were at Branchville, I passed by the deserted Camps of the militia approaching the city and entering Broad Street I was met by every indication of excitement. Companys of soldiers were grouped in the middle of the street, Guns, Muskets, Haversacks and other military accoutrements were stacked ready for the march. All down the street at intervals was to be seen from two to three hundred bales of Cotton packed to burn at a moments notice— Men women and children were gathered at the doors and on the street discussing the latest rumour— All this caused me to feel that the dreaded hour had come but what caused a more gloomy shade than I had previously felt was that the children and servants were busy helping themselves to aprons and sacks of Cotton unmolested by the guard. The militia refusing to go over into South Carolina were detailed to roll cotton (I spelt cotton with a small c I wonder if it is because poor old King Cotton is dethroned).

Arriving at home on Monday found Mr T was in camp but not ordered off as I had so much dreaded. The bell tolling for one oclock just after I came in the house caused me to start with a feeling of alarm. Every new rumour of an inward approach has depressed me more and more— Mr Edward Thomas has a large lot of cotton placed on the vacant lot just above us. Ours was not moved until Wednesday or Thursday morning— For a day or two the first of the week it rained steadily—and has been succeeded by intensely cold weather. We are again dependant upon pine wood (having used up that which we paid $100 dollars pr cord for). Night before last it

---

23. Lt. Gen. Daniel Harvey Hill, later associated with the *New Eclectic* magazine.

was reported that Aiken was in flames—and the Yankees in large force advancing upon Augusta. Yesterday we learned that Wheeler had whipped Kilpatrick back beyond Aiken— This news together with the bright cheering day causes me to feel brighter than I have felt this week altho physically I am far from well having taken cold which has settled in my lower limbs & given me rheumatic pains. Mr Thomas has had neuralgia in his face and a very bad cold.

Yesterday I went up to see cousin Mary Ann. Found her busy superintending the packing of large trunks to be ready to move at a moments warning if the Cotton should be fired and her house endangered— Jake has had ladders made, and has bags attached to poles to dip into tubs of water to wet the side of his house in case of danger. It has been rumored for several nights that the cotton was to be fired— Mrs Stovall has tubs and buckets of water in her attic ready to use. We have done nothing and the only time I have been at all roused is when I have thought that by some extra exertion we might have secured ourselves from such total wreck. I believe the burning of the Cotton is more dreaded than the approach of the Yankees. One thing is quite sure. If it is fired and the wind is high the greater portion of the City will be burnt. The wooden houses certainly and they are occupied principally by persons upon whom the loss would fall heaviest. Gen Toombs blames Gen Hill so I am told and thinks the Cotton should have been removed farther in order to secure the City—but altho the authoritys have been removing it all the week they are not near through yet.

I am fully satisfied as to the patriotism and military necessity which calls for the burning of the Cotton but I greatly fear that in the terrible confusion attending its burning our own people will become demoralised— The mob rule the hour— The Yankees enter and provoked at the loss of the Cotton make it an excuse for sacking the city and then pandemoniam will reign. Again this move may deter the enemy now approaching— Knowing that the torch is ready to be applied to the Cotton and that Gen Hill is a fighting man they may not venture. Indeed those who profess to be informed state that Charleston and Columbia are the present objects and this movement of Kilpatrick's as intended to cover the movements of the main body. By the way I will take this opportunity "of giving the Devil his due." Even Satan is not so dark as he has been painted. Gen Kilpatrick is not a married man as I had understood. He was at West Point with Gen Young. . . .

Wednesday, March 29, 1865 I know I will regret hereafter that I have made no record of time and events which are fraught with so much interest, record of events which are hourly making history— but I cannot. I shrink from the task. At times I feel as if I was drifting on, on, ever onward to be at last dashed against some rock and I shut my eyes and almost wish it was over, the shock encountered and I prepared to know what destiny awaits me. I am tired, oh so tired of this war. I want to breathe free. I feel the restraint of the blockade and as port after port becomes blockaded, I feel shut up, pent up and am irresistibly reminded of the old story of the iron shroud contracting more and more each hour, each moment. I live too fast. A strange contradiction, yet true. A life of emotion, quick rapid succession of startling events will wear upon the constitution and weaken the physical nature. I may perhaps be glad hereafter that I have lived through this war but now the height of my ambition is to be *quiet*, to have no distracting cares—the time to read— leisure to think and write—and study. I have just been reading that sad record of an intellectual woman's life, Mrs Gaskell's biography of Charlotte Bronte,[24] and I do not think that to have been the author of *Jane Eyre*, would I have been willing to have suffered the torments of ill health, extreme nervous excitab[ili]ty and sensitive shrinking from mankind which she endured. . . .

Country glory and patriotism are great things but to the bereaved hearts of Mrs Stovall and Mrs Clayton, each moaning for the death of their first born, what bitter mockery there must be in the words. News reached town a few day since that Frank Stovall had been killed in Florida and young Clayton in Virginia. Thus it is— I strive to get away, to forget in reading or in writing or in talking the ever present, the one absorbing theme of war and thus it is thrust upon me— I make no plans for the future. It is impossible to indulge in golden day dreams. The same temperament which would always as a girl weave bright fancies for her own future, would now in the fullness of maturity shake the kaleidoscope of imagination and view her *children's future*—and "could love fulfill its fancy," would have them prosperous and happy—but instead of lovingly looking forward, I shrink from what I too much fear will prove a reality. I have seen poverty staring me in the face when I expected Sherman in Augusta and our planting interest was destroyed and

---

24. *The Life of Charlotte Brontë* (1857), by Elizabeth Cleghorn Gaskell.

God knows there was nothing attractive in the gaunt picture presented. But even then I nerved myself and was prepared to do something if I could— I believe it was the sitting still and doing nothing which unnerved me more than anything else. I looked forward and asked myself, what can I do? Nothing, except teach school and if I left Augusta nothing to support me with my little ones— If I remained, the doubt as to wether I could procure a school unless compelled to take the oath—and a new idea just now presents itself to my mind. I wonder if I would not be compelled to teach the young and perhaps old ideas of the Negroes how to shoot.[25] I'm sure if their ideas were as contrary as the mind of the teacher would be, the shoots would be decidedly twisted.

How strange I can jest upon this revolting subject but indeed I am feeling so much better than of late that I am altogether another person. During the first months of pregnancy I am always sadly depressed and the body acting upon the mind my whole nature is affected. This time I was congratulating myself that I was going through the terrible ordeal in better style but thanks to Gen Sherman and no less thanks to Gen Hill my nervous system received a shock which was terrible. I was made really sick by the combined prospect of Sherman's visit and the burning cotton. That was a terrible never to [be] forgotten week. . . .

I can better endure accumulated physical torture than mental annoyance. Shakespeare never asked a more striking question than, "Who can minister to a mind diseased?"[26] I have been so sad, unusually low spirited—looking only upon the gloomy side of what, after all as sanguine as one may be is dark, heaven knows. Then I have thought of my dying when the hour of trial comes. Mr Thomas says I always say I expect to die, but I don't think so. I know I have thought of it this time more than usual and if I do die, I hope that my baby will die with me. . . . Upon my honor if I knew that I was going to die I should be willing to write a letter to the future Mrs Thomas advising her—telling her of the numerous good qualities of her husband and pointing her to some of the matrimonial quicksands against which my wayward barque has sometimes

---

25. "Delightful task! to rear the tender thought, / To teach the young idea how to shoot," from *The Seasons: Spring*, by James Thomson (1700–1748).
26. "Canst thou not minister to a mind diseas'd?" from Shakespeare, *Macbeth*, act 5, scene 3.

drifted. Then again how I should like to tell her of the different dispositions of my children—

[Later.] ... Being interrupted to give out dinner I went into the kitchen and made up the first cakes I ever accomplished. I remember trying once before to work up some flour without success— Today the dough would stick to my hands but with Tamah's advice I at length succeeded— The children stood around admiring "Ma's performance" as I cut out men, thimble cakes and &c—but my back ached when I was through and I have seen things I liked to do better. Yet I intend hereafter to do more cooking—make up bread and &c. Once before I had a similar idea and tried to help Tamah in drawing some fish and it was about as hard work as I ever did— ... I will stop now and write off my French exercises— At last I am learning French— For some time I have talked of it, wishing to learn, to luxuriate in the acquisition of knowledge and while away many leisure moments— Now when I study I think it may probably aid me someday in the only plan I can form for gaining a support. The burning of Columbia—the movements of Sherman the reinstatement of Gen Johnston,[27] Gen Lee's[28] having been made Commander in chief are all events of great importance to which I must give a seperate time—

---

27. Gen. Joseph E. Johnston. After he was replaced by General Hood, Johnston was restored to command in the Carolinas in February 1865 by General Lee.

28. Gen. Robert E. Lee.

8. Surrender and Yankee Occupation

We live in troublous times.
—*December 31, 1865*

Monday, May 1, 1865   What a first of May. It had not occurred to me until I commenced to write— Today I have witnessed what I am sorry shall prove our last experience as a Confederate Nation— A riot has taken place in Augusta—an event often dreaded but never experienced before! Soon after breakfast I heard that the soldiers were breaking open the stores on Broad Street and helping themselves— Immediately after I saw numbers of men walking rapidly, some running with large bags bundles and &c upon their shoulders— The bell just now tolls for one oclock. When another 1st of May rolls around, the bell which for so long a time has tolled to remind us to pray for the soldiers and alas by so many of us has been neglected—will toll no more— God help us. As an independent nation we will not exist— The bright dream of Southern independence has not been realised— The war is over and again we become a part of the United States—how united will depend alone upon treatment we receive from the hands of the North. It will prove to their interest to be very discreet for the South will prove a smouldering volcano requiring but little to again burst forth. Treated as members of one family—a band of brothers, *in time* we may have a common interest—but pressed too hard upon, our property taken from us—a desperate people having nothing to lose, the South may again revolt and speaking of revolts reminds me of the riot of today which I had commenced to notice.

On Broad Street the scene of excitement is said to have been intense. Government stores were broken upon and one private tobacco store owned by Mr Whitlock who is engaged to Miss Carine Wilds— The commissary stores were threatened but the timely interposition of a speech from John Milledge quieted them. Gen Wright also spoke to the crowd appealing to their better nature and some of the rioters volunteered to aid in quelling the excitement. I had liked to have said rebellion but rebel is a sacred word now, worthy to be ranked with such words as Home, Heart & Heaven— I know none of the particulars, our part of the town being comparatively quiet but not once during the morning have I experienced an emotion of fear— I used the precaution to have the street gate locked hearing that Horses were being taken as well as provisions. . . .

Betsey went for the afternoon's paper—none was issued and she was told that there would probably be none tomorrow. A black man came by during the morning with strawberrys to sell at 30 dollars Confederate money or 10 cts in silver, then when I proposed buying them preferred meat and would not take the money. I bought two qts of the finest I ever saw from him giving meat in exchange. In market this morning the money was refused, nothing sold except for silver or gold— It is now after dinner— Fanny came up during the morning to tell me that Ma had had her silver put up and the Horses locked up and Miss Mary was not going into the country. Mr Thomas coming in advised me to remain in town. Cousin Jane was cautious enough to secure her s[ilver] pieces. I have 25 cts and one 5 cts in silver—and yet strange to say I feel bright and somewhat hopeful.

The war is over and I am glad of it. What terms of agreement may be decided upon I cannot say but if *anything* is left us—if we can count with certainty upon enough to raise and educate our children I shall be grateful. It is humiliating, very indeed to be a conquered people but the sky is so bright, the air so pure, the aspect of nature so lovely that I can but be encouraged, and hope for something which will benefit us. Upon only one point am I unsettled in my opinion—that of Slavery but more of that hereafter. . . . It is rumoured that two thousand Yankee soldiers will arrive in town this afternoon. I hope I will not see them. When I learn the terms of Treaty offered and accepted I can better determine the nature of my feelings for them. If generous I will endeavour to cultivate friendly feelings. "If dispite is on me thrown I've a soul as hard as iron." I haven't quoted that right but the feeling is the same—

[Monday night.] Mr Thomas has gone out to command his company in guarding the town tonight. A large body is out—fears being entertained of another riot tonight. I was sitting in the Piazzi this morning during the excitement when looking across the street

I saw a large number of men rush up the street towards the Episcopalian church of Atonement and heard them as they shouted. Looking up Greene St I saw a body of men with guns marching leisurely along Kollock St towards the church. I immediately supposed the object was to get to the factory. I afterwards learned that Frank Steiner shot the leader of the rioters which immediately quelled the opposing body. It is reported that a Negro came riding at full speed into town today to George Jackson[1] telling him that a party of Negroes were going to set fire to his house—going to Mr Roberts' he collected about twenty men, Edge Eve among them, and went out. But for the interference of the military Mr Jackson would have hung the Negro— This will prove the darkest feature in the future if the Negroes prove insubordinate.

This afternoon I took Mary Bell and Jeff and rode down to see Buddy— He is sunburned but looks well and healthy. Is glad to be home but like every true man and soldier deeply feels the humiliation of our surrender— Mr Thomas is particularly sensitive upon the subject, expects no good terms & in some degree tonight impressed me with his gloomy views. . . .

Tuesday, May 2, 1865   Seated by the window I look out upon what to me appears a sad commentary, or mockery of the times— The boys in the street playing soldier! Armed with guns and old rusty swords which have been given to them by the Negroes driving the waggons of them which are to [be] turned over to the United States authoritys—these boys unable to see the humiliation of having been conquered are enjoying their sport. "The child is father of the man" and may not their children someday avenge us if we are ruled with an iron rod. Today I heard it rumoured that Augusta is to be garrisoned by Negroes and with it was uttered dark threats if such should be the case. Again I hear that Confederate money is to be worth 50 cts on the $100. Both of these reports are on the extreme and I believe neither of them. Aunty Lamkin stopped in the Buggy with Mr T who was driving her down to Ma's to tell me that Mr Murphy was taking Confederate money selling alapaca at one hundred and twenty five dollars pr yd. the same price as last week. Mr Thomas has a few thousand dollars in Confederate money which he says he will keep to see what will happen.

---

1. George T. Jackson was an Augusta mill owner.

America had a little girl Saturday night. She has been at Belmont for near three months expecting to be confined. Nancy who is here working for us was sick yesterday and today. This morning I sent to Tamah to do some washing. Her reply was that "she was not able"— She is threatened with dropsy and is very little account. Patsey had to go out and wash while Milly cleaned up our bed room and Betsey attended to the baby. Daniel has been in Burke for two or three days and I had Uncle Jim to drive the Carriage yesterday afternoon. Josiah came in during the morning wanting to know if I had anything for him to do. All hired Negroes are out of employment. I told him to work the garden and enquired of Uncle Jim if he ever did any washing. "What kind of washing Missis?" said he— "washing clothes" said I. "Good Lord Missis," he replied "I never wash no close"— I laughed and told him he would have it to do if there was anymore sick ones and had him to mend Turner's waggon.

Nash came up this morning from Belmont bringing me a quantity of strawberrys some of which I sent to Miss Henry, Mary Bell's teacher. I have been busy all the morning. Tamah was picking Strawberrys in the dining room and I doing the active part of housekeeping "putting things to rights" cleaning out drawers, arranging the book case and writing desk, doing all this with such a feeling of perfect satisfaction which only those who have lived in constant expectation of a raid can experience. The day is bright and very beautiful. Nature has donned her loveliest robes. The war is over and I lift a grateful heart to God thanking him for this much and trusting him for the future. . . .

Sunday, May 7, 1865 This morning a large force of Yankees came marching into Augusta the drums beating & colours flying—surrounded by a large crowd of Negroes. We did not get up until late and did not see the first company of them. Patsey said there were 800 of them. After breakfast a number of them marched by here on the other side of the street, two officers riding on Horseback in front. I felt no particular emotion as I looked at them through the closed blinds but when I read the morning paper and saw the reward of $100,000 dollars in gold offered for Jeff Davis with a promise of the money for the captors which the President was said to have with him, *then* I felt that the Philistines were amongst us. Immediately after, I read the general order issued by Gen Smith for the Carolina planters having reference to free labor. Tonight the impression is general that *Slavery* is *abolished*, that *the negroes are free*—that is at liberty, the greater portion of them to plunder and starve— It does not surprise me as much as I expected but I will write again in the morning.

Monday, May 8, 1865 This morning I commenced music lessons from Madam Ballot. Was playing over the *Varsovienne* when in an instant I became faint. The room swam around and I came nearer fainting than I ever did in my life. A glass of water and bathing my face soon restored me to consciousness, but it was some time before I recovered from the effects. I don't know what could have caused it for it was after breakfast between 7 & 9 and I was not nauseated as I so often am. It will not do for me to acquire a habit of becoming faint for I will require all my energy to meet the exigencies of the times ahead of us. The fact is our Negroes are to be made free and a change, a very [great] change will be affected in our mode of living. The news was just communicated to us by Pinck as Mr Thomas and I were riding out in the buggy. Friday afternoon Pinck and Cora in his Buggy overtook us and enquired if we had seen the order from Gen Smith with regard to free labor vis: that the Negroes were to be subsisted, paid six months wages in advance and half the crop made to be divided among them. Contracts to [be] made between negro and Planter—there I have followed the Yankee fashion of naming the Negro first and the Master last. A failure to plant will cause the land to be confiscated. . . .
Hereafter I shall put my Journal in a safe place for I intend to express myself fearlessly and candidly upon all points. Last week was the turning point, the crisis with me. "The flood which taken at the tide"[2] would have led to feelings of union brotherhood and kindly feeling— *Today* I *am more intensely opposed* to the *North* than at any period of the war— We have been imposed upon—led to believe that terms of Treaty had been agreed upon which would secure to us a lasting and honourable peace. The treaty entered into between [Generals] Sherman and Johnston, the Northern President[3] refuses to ratify— Now that we have surrendered—are in a great degree powerless we can count with certainty upon nothing.

---

2. "There is a tide in the affairs of men, / Which, taken at the flood, leads on to fortune," from Shakespeare, *Julius Caesar*, act 4, scene 3.
3. President Andrew Johnson, 1865–69.

Our Negroes will be freed our lands confiscated and imagination cannot tell what is in store for us but thank God I have an increased degree of faith—a faith which causes me to feel that all this will be for our good.

Mr T appeared cast down, utterly spirit broken yesterday when the news first reached him and when I would hint at a brighter sky would mock at such anticipations— This morning while packing the camphor chest I planned a school for next winter and was astonished at the bouyancy of temperament which would permit me to indulge in anticipations founded upon such a plan, but I cannot say "Why art thou cast down oh my soul?" for indeed I am not cast down. On the contrary I am not the person to permit pecuniary loss to afflict me as long as I have health and energy. As to the emancipation of the Negroes, while there is of course a natural dislike to the loss of so much property in my inmost soul I cannot regret it— I always felt that there was a great responsibility— It is in some degree a great relief to have this feeling removed. For the Negroes I know that I have the kindest possible feeling— For the Yankees who deprive us of them I have no use whatever. I only hope I shall see very little of them— Yesterday Mr Thomas unfastened Turner's Battle Flag from the staff and I will put it away as a memento of the time when he was a marker in the Wheeler Dragoons. Who knows, perhaps someday it may be used again. Oh a free people may be won but not crushed—

How differently I feel from what I did last week— On Thursday or Friday I believe it was, Mr and Mrs Evans dined with us, Cousin Mary Ann and Mr Danforth, Ma and Aunty dined with us also. Mr Evans was very despondent, said "it was the greatest trial to his Christian grace" he had ever had to contend with. . . . A few days ago Mr Polk called to see me to return some books I had loaned his wife. He said that Gen Upton[4] was a gentleman, had graduated at West Point. Gen Imboden[5] being in Augusta and anxious to go on to Norfolk wished to have Gen Upton to sign the necessary papers. He requested Jim Dawson to take them to Gen Upton. Upon reading the name, Gen Upton remarked "Gen Imboden! Present my compliments to the Gen and say to him that it would afford me

---

4. Union general Emory Upton was stationed in Augusta to keep order and receive public property.
5. Brig. Gen. John Daniel Imboden.

pleasure to have him call and see me. You can leave the papers until I see him." Mr Dawson complying with his request repeated the message to Gen Imboden who replied "Tell him to go to Hell." Mr Polk thought it was rude. I laughed when I heard it and could appreciate the proud spirit chafing under humiliation— Had Gen Upton signed the papers and then requested the honour of a visit from Gen Imboden he would have demonstrated his right to the title of West Point Gentleman. Just so last night three men all intoxicated passed by, one of them gloriously tight—said he "I told him I was a rebel. I am a rebel now, will be for twenty years, will be for fifty years, will be forever, hip hurra"— "Bully for you" cried the other and with shouts they proceeded up the street. I felt my face flush, my eyes filled with tears and in my heart I echoed the sentiment. Last week I would not have done it— Now I could not help it.

Today I see that Booth the man who killed Lincoln was shot in Virginia. He refused to surrender and was shot—better that than the hangman's cord. I cannot in my heart approve the act which at such a moment, at such a time precipitated Lincoln to eternity but I have no cause to love Lincoln. My womanly sympathys go out for Jeff Davis and I do hope and pray that he will escape. Not to save my right arm would I betray him if I knew where he was and yet I was beginning to think him despotic—

I believe I have less patience with the editor of the *Chronicle* than any other Yankee who ever lived. He is a contemptible scamp and I wish someone would give [him] a good cowhiding.[6] Shielded by the force of Yankees who are here, he throws off the thin cloak he wore before and presumes to dictate to our citizens, cooly telling those who are not pleased "the best thing they can do is to leave"—as if they were not much better entitled to remain here than he.

Last Tuesday night Lizzie Lamkin, Cora, Buddy, Edge Eve, Dr & Hittie Casey with Major Sibley, Cousin Jane and Mrs Wells spent the evening with us. They danced and appeared to enjoy themselves very much. Wash brought us up Strawberrys from Belmont

---

6. Nathan Morse, editor of the *Chronicle*, was criticized by some for supporting the peace negotiations and for criticizing Jefferson Davis, but other southern leaders did the same thing. Gertrude herself expressed mixed feelings about Davis.

every day last week except Saturday when he brought mulberrys. Wednesday Mrs Wells and I called to see Mrs Proctor Gen Beauregard's sister. She is a refugee from New Orleans and is now giving lessons in singing, Cora being one of her pupils. I will ride down to see Ma this evening—

This morning Mr Thomas assembled the servants together— told them that numerous reports were about town, that it was extremely probable that the Yankees would free them, that they would then be obliged to work—that he would have to hire someone and had as soon pay them wages as anyone else and advised them to wait quietly and see what would be done. I have seen no evidence of insubordination, on the contrary they all worked very cheerfully but since his explanation there has appeared a more cheerful spirit than ever. Tamah was really lively while she was sewing on Frank's pants in the Piazzi— Daniel was away during the morning and Mr Thomas was sure he had left but he came in in time to feed the Horses—

Wednesday, May [17] 1865 Excitement rules the hour— No one appears to have a settled plan of action. The Negroes crowd the streets and loaf around the camps and corners of the street, and yet I must do the Federals the justice to add that they keep excellent order so far as my observation extends. One of them has never entered our yard or in passing made the slightest demonstration of disrespect. I see no evidence of disrespect on the part of the Negroes who are here from the adjoining plantations but the institution of slavery is done away with and I think that by next winter white help will have crowded them from all employment. Daniel left, I think it was on Wednesday morning of last week. Took off all of his clothes during the night and left without saying anything to anyone. He is here in town but I have not seen him nor do I wish to do so. If he returns to the yard, he shall not enter it.

Thursday Mr Thomas left for Burke. During the morning I was quite busy. At one oclock Betsey a little servant went for the *Chronicle* as she was in the habit of doing every day and did not return again. I was really annoyed about it. I supposed that she had been met by her father in the street and taken away but when I learned that she had taken her clothes out of the ironing room under the pretense of washing them every emotion of interest in her vanished at once— I found that it was a concerted plan between Sarah (her mother) and herself. The former had been owned by us a year and was dishonest. She was an excellent washer and ironer & was in the yard but this winter she stole a midling of meat and when I discovered it she was sent to Burke. Mr Thomas has never been willing to sell a Negro unless for some very great fault. Sarah had charge of the yard during last summer and I am quite sure took a great many things from the store room. She left the plantation, came up and took Betsey home with her. I felt interested in Betsey. She was a bright quick child and raised in our family would have become a good servant. As it is she will be under her mother's influence and run wild in the street.

Saturday I had my store rooms cleaned out. I never saw Tamah more active and cheerful and I remarked to Mr Thomas when he came home "Tamah has something on her mind. She has either decided to go or the prospect of being paid if she remains has put her in a very good humor." . . . Sunday morning Patsey came in before Mr Thomas and I were up and wished to know "who was to get breakfast—that Aunt Tamah was gone." "When did she leave?" I replied. "Last night" said she. "Very well" I said "tell Nancy to get breakfast and cook until some other arrangements can be made." If any expression of surprise or sorrow was expected by the servants, they were disappointed for none was made by Mr Thomas or I.

While at church, I learned that the jail had been burned the night before and that Lizzie Bridges lost almost everything she owned. Coming home from church, I saw Major Sibley. He told me that Jeff Davis had been captured in Early County[7] on his way to Florida. Mr Thomas and I were resting after dinner when Patsey came running in in great excitement, telling us that a fight was expected down the street that if anyone wished to go down town they must go on Broad instead of Greene St, that Jeff Davis was in town and a large crowd had gathered. *Jeff Davis* in Augusta and a prisoner. This was indeed the crowning point, the climax of our downfall. I buried my face on the pillow and wept bitterly. . . . Mr Thomas and Turner went down to see him and I walked down to Ma's.

Coming back late in the afternoon, I saw a crowd of Negroes (nothing I have ever seen equal to it) running and rushing down Greene St, across the street and coming from every direction, all to

---

7. Jefferson Davis was captured by Union soldiers on May 10, 1865, near Irwinsville, Irwin County, Ga.

see the procession as Jeff Davis was brought from the cars. He was driven down Reynolds Street to the Sand Bar Ferry.[8] I stopped at Dr Eve's and waited until the crowd passed by and felt as if I should have liked to have seen a volley of musketry sent among the Negroes who were holding such a jubilee. . . . Mr Thomas says it was a sad and solemn scene. He lifted his hat as the carriage passed. I don't think that the Federals could have objected to such a display for a man who had been and is so deeply shrined in the hearts of the people. I think the United States made a great mistake in having Davis carried through the Southern States in this way. It will prove a triumphal procession to him for even those persons at the South who were becoming disaffected towards him will have their sympathies aroused and a manly emotion of regret for him will be experienced. . . .

A question has presented itself to my mind. What they expect from those whom they will not allow to take the oath. I understand that the oath is only tendered to those who have not been in service or engaged in blockade running. I heard a gentleman say that he went to take the oath ten minutes after these restrictions had been added to it. Turning to a gentleman near him said he, "How could you take it?" "I took it like a dose of salts," said he "held my nose and swallowed it down." . . . Last Friday night the Yankee gunboats passed by the Rowell place and the soldiers stole all the meat, molasses and chickens on the place. They then went to Mr Ware's [and] took his, besides his watch, spectacles and fire arms with what money he had. Saturday night a large body of them camped in the lower or Jackson Avenue at Belmont—broke open our smoke house killed hogs and &c.

I must not forget to mention one circumstance which touched me very much— Sunday night after Jeff Davis passed through we were seated in the piazzi. Tea being announced to be ready Mr Thomas called Jeff, and added "Come Jeff Davis, we will give you that name. It is all that we can do in honour of Davis." "Very well," said I "it may be so since you propose it." This addition to his name was given under almost as solemn circumstances as he received the name of Jeff Thomas. I jestingly remarked that it might hereafter retard his political progress. . . .

---

8. The Sand Bar Ferry connected Augusta with Beech Island, S.C., just across the Savannah River.

.   .   .

Saturday, May 27, 1865 ... My mind is comparatively relieved
for I, for almost the first time this week, have time to play "the
lady of leisure." Last Saturday I took Cate and the children down to
Belmont. I took Milly to oblige her to nurse the baby to Belmont &
to the Rowell Place. On the way there we met Wash who was walking up bringing up Rasberrys and cherrys. Upon enquiring why he
was walking he replied that Sykes had met him, had told him he
was sick and was going back to Burke and took the pony from him.
I confess it provoked me when he told me of it and I should have
liked to have overtaken him and dismounted him. He was the
driver at the plantation occupying a position of importance especially as Mr Thomas had dismissed his overseer. He was one of the
first to leave seduced as has so often been the case by the wiles of a
Delilah— Sarah wishing someone to bring her baby to town persuaded him to run off with her. Of course as soon as she reached
Augusta and her husband she had no use for him. He had left an
ugly faithful black wife in Burke to follow the more attractive face
of Sarah who is a good looking mulatto or brown complected
woman. Finding he was not met with open arms by his Yankee
brethren as he expected to be he decided to return to Burke but he
certainly will not be placed in his former position for he does not
deserve confidence. The other two boys who left Burke have also
returned.

While I was at the Rowell Place Saturday a number of mules
with Yankee & Negro drivers passed by on their way to the plantation, as I supposed to impress some corn. I was just ready to leave
seated in the carriage with a large bunch of flowers in my hands
when I observed a good looking man dressed in Federal uniform
ride in the gate. He came up to the Carriage and with the usual
sociable inclination of the head addressed himself not to me but to
Uncle Jim. "Jack" said he "in what direction have those mules &
drivers gone?" Uncle Jim replied, and I for the first time in my life
addressed one of the men against whom we have been waging war. I
enquired of him for what purpose they were going to the Plantation
intending to mention to him the depredations committed by the
men from the gunboats. Upon my making the inquiry he replied
"heigh?" I dispair of conveying any idea of the impertinence of the
manner in which this exclamation was made. He did not understand my question but why make such a reply? The instinct of a

gentleman whould have taught him to reply "What did you observe? What was your remark?" How vivid the contrast between his manner and that of a southern gentleman in whose deportment is witnessed that reverential manner towards the sex no where else so strikingly displayed. This man's manner roused all the haughty southern woman and as I looked at him I slightly elevated my eyebrows and threw into my glance an expression of astonishment which *he understood* and with an entirely different intonation of voice he enquired "what I had said?" He then replied "that the men and mules were sent down for the purpose of removing a Battery on the river." Turning from me he addressed himself to Uncle Jim wishing "to know the direction and the distance." I volunteered the information which Uncle Jim was unable to give and with out *one word* of *thanks* or a touching of the cap by way of bidding me good morning he rode off and thus ended my first interview with a Yankee. . . .

Last week someone entered our smoke house by prying the bolt off and took a good many hams. We have discovered no clue by which to detect the theft. I had said to Milly the day before as I was going down to tea that I would give her her clothing and a silver quarter every Saturday night. Just before I went in to tea Sunday night Mary Bell told me that Milly said she was going away. I paid but little attention to it and after tea I told Mr T that I would go up stairs so as to give Milly an opportunity to come down and took the quarter up with me to give to her. She was nowhere to be found. . . . For the next two or three days Cora Lou was without a nurse except the little attention Hannah gave her during the morning. Patsey was so busy that she could only partially attend her in the afternoon. [Cora Lou] fell down several times and yet has her face scarred up from a fall. I succeeded in getting a little girl from the orphans' asylum by the name of Mary Jane Pierce. Her father and mother are both dead. She has a step mother and a little step brother. I am glad she will have no outside influence exerted upon her. . . .

I was out in Dublin[9] (for the first time) twice this week looking for a white woman to cook. I could not succeed but I saw Mary Ann a woman who would have suited me exactly for a house servant and nurse. She was perfectly willing to come but her sister objected

---

9. Dublin was the name given to the Irish neighborhood in Augusta.

to being left alone so much. She thinks she will be able to come to me in the fall. Wednesday I had a woman to wash for me. Hired her for thirty cts a day. I think it probable that she was one of the recently made free negroes. I had no idea what was considered a task in washing so I gave her all the small things belonging to the children taking out all the table cloths sheets counterpanes and &c— She was through by dinner time appeared to work steady. I gave her dinner and afterwards told her that I had a few more clothes I wished washed out. Her reply was "that she was tired." I did not for a minute argue with her. Said I, "If you suppose I engaged a woman to wash for me by the day and she stops by dinner time, if you suppose I intend paying for the days work you are very much mistaken." Turning from her I walked into the house. She afterwards sent in for more clothes and washed out a few other things— So much for hiring by the day.

Monday, May 29, 1865 Out of all our old house servants not one remains except Patsey and a little boy Frank. We have one of our servants Uncle Jim to take Daniel's place as driver and butler and a much more efficient person he proves to be. Nancy has been cooking since Tamah left. On last Wednesday I hired a woman to do the washing. Thursday I expected Nancy to iron but she was sick. In the same way she was sick the week before when there was ironing to do. I said nothing but told Patsey to get breakfast. After it was over I assisted her in wiping the breakfast dishes, a thing I never remember to have done more than once or twice in my life. I then thoroughly cleaned up the sitting room and parlour. . . . In the afternoon I went in the ironing room and in to see Nancy. The clothes were all piled upon a table, the flies swarming over them. The room looking as if it had not been cleaned up in several weeks. Nancy's room was in just the same state. I asked her "if she was not well enough to sprinkle some of the clothes." "No" she replied "she was not well enough to do anything." Said I, "Nancy do you expect I can afford to pay you wages in your situation, support your two children and then have you sick as much as you are?" She made no reply and I came in.

The next morning after Patsey had milked the cow & had fire made in the kitchen, she [Nancy] volunteered to cook breakfast— Immediately after breakfast as I was writing by the window Turner directed my attention to Nancy with her two children, Hannah and Jessy, going out of the gate. I told him to enquire "where she was going." She had expected to leave with flying colours but was compelled to tell a falsehood for she replied "I will be back directly." I knew at once that she was taking "french leave" and was not surprised when I went into her room sometime afterwards to find that all her things had been removed. I was again engaged in housework most of the morning. . . .

I lay down on the sofa in the parlour and slept a dreamless sleep from which I was aroused by Patsey coming to tell me that a woman wished to see me to obtain a cook's place. Delighted to hear of an opportunity I at once engaged the woman to come. She was an elderly mulatto woman named Leah and had been Dr Denning's cook. She told me that "the madam had sent her off to procure a place." That night and the next morning I ate two biscuits which she baked (an unusual thing for me to do). At dinner the next day she baked one of the best plum pies I ever tasted. Mr Thomas returned from Burke at dinner and upon informing him of the case he at once decided she must be sent away. He went out to see her and told her "to go up and see Mrs Denning and bring a note and he would hire her." She left promising to do so and as I expected has not returned, and since then I have been in a state of endurance. I had paid 50 cts to a woman to iron for me Saturday. She knows nothing about the business but I kept her yesterday and today. Yesterday to cook (allowing Uncle Jim to go to see his wife at Belmont) and today to wash. She is totally inexperienced, says she wants to return to her home in Burke, represents that her master lost everything when Sherman passed through Georgia, and told his negroes to go & provide for themselves until his crop was planted and then to return all of which I don't believe—

I told Mr Thomas that I did not know but what we are fighting shadows. I certainly sacrificed a good deal to principle for I lost an opportunity to get an excellent cook at $5 dollars per month and Dr Denning's family will not be benefitted. The fact is that all the best servants belonging to familys we know will be engaged by the low class of people and we will have to take inexperienced servants until we can supply ourselves with white servants. . . . Nancy was the first servant belonging to any of our family who left, and shows a more impertinent manner than any of the others. One day last week she entered Ma's back yard with a Yankee soldier. . . . Hastening to the door of her room [Ma] saw Nancy going down into the basement followed by a Yankee soldier who was just at the head of the steps. "By what authority do you presume to search my house" was her indignant inquiry? "I have none" said he. "I came with this woman who says she left some clothes here." . . . Then continuing her conversation with the Yankee Ma added "What do you expect to do with these Negroes you have freed? Before this war our Negroes were a well contented, happy race of people. You have come amongst us have sown seeds of dissention and deprived us of the right to manage them. Now what do you expect them to do?" "Starve I reckon" was his reply. He then proceeded to tell her that his name was Brown, that he had a brother in the Confederate service, and assured her that she would find white labor much cheaper and better. "I am a southern woman" said she "born and raised at the South, accustomed to the service of Negroes and like them better. That Negro has had time enough to get her clothes" she then added. "Take her out of my yard" and addressing Nancy Ma told her "to leave the yard and never dare to come into it again." Nancy evidently expected to produce a great sensation and awe Ma by the presence of Yankee majesty but she reckoned without her host, and left very differently from what she had expected.

Susan, Kate's nurse, Ma's most trusty servant, her advisor, right hand woman and best liked house servant has left her. I am under too many obligations to Susan to have harsh feelings toward her. During six confinements Susan has been with me, the best of servants, rendering the most efficient help. To Ma she has always been invaluable and in case of sickness there was no one like Susan. Her husband Anthony was one of the first to leave the Cumming Plantation and incited others to do the same. I expect he influenced Susan, altho I have often heard Pa say that in case of a revolt among Negroes he thought that Susan would prove a ringleader. Aunt Vilet the cook a very excellent one at that left Sunday night. She was a plantation servant during her young days and another favorite of Ma's. Palmer the driver left the same morning with Susan, remained longer than anyone expected that he would. He is quite a Beau Brummell as he gallants a coloured demoiselle or walks up the street with his cigar in his mouth. . . . Yesterday numbers of the negro women some of them quite black were promenading up the streets with black lace veil shading them from the embrowning rays of a sun under whose influence they had worked all their life. . . . On Thursday Rev Dr Finch of the Federal Army addressed the citizens on the subject of their late slaves and Saturday addressed the Negroes at the parade ground on *their* duty. I think now they have the Negroes free they don't know what to do with them—

Belmont, Monday, June 12, 1865 I must confess to you my journal that I do most heartily dispise Yankees, Negroes and everything connected with them. The theme has been sung in my hearing until it is a perfect abomination— I positively instinctively shut my ears when I hear the hated subject mentioned and right gladly would I be willing never to place my eyes upon another as long as I live. Everything is entirely reversed. I feel no interest in them whatever and hope I never will—

. . .

Saturday, July 22, 1865 This afternoon as Mr Thomas & I were sitting talking together in the front Piazzi we saw several Negroes enter the gate talking together, others appeared to be coming in after them. It was so dark that we could not distinguish them. "Who are you" said Mr Thomas. "Ruffin, Willie, Tom" and proceeded to call the names of several of the Burke Negroes. "Don't come into the house" said Mr Thomas "What do you want?" "We came to bring you a letter" replied one of them. Mr Thomas walked to the steps took the letter from them & walked into the parlour to read it by the candle. "Where have you all come from" said I. "From Augusta" was the reply given in a rather surly tone. I went into the room where Mr Thomas was reading the note and found it was a summons from the Yankee Cap Bryant[10] in Augusta summoning Mr Thomas to appear before him to answer to the demand of these Negroes for wages. "I shall send these Negroes away from here" said Mr Thomas. "I certainly should not think of doing anything else" I replied. Going out into the Piazzi again we found that the Negroes had gone from the steps toward the gate. When Mr Thomas asked them where they intended to spend the night adding that they were not to remain here, one of them replied "Oh we will stay somewhere" or something like that— As they went off one of

---

10. Capt. John Emory Bryant of the U.S. Army's Freedmen's Bureau in Augusta. Bryant remained in the South after the war and became a notorious Republican leader.

them hollored in what we both knew was intended for insolent desire to provoke. And this too we had to endure. As it could not be resented it was treated with the silence of contempt— And has it come to this—

Sunday, July 23, 1865 We have been out in the country now nearly two months and I have not enjoyed the calm contented frame of mind I had hoped to. It is very much to be hoped we are at the worst of this transition state of the Negroes. If not God have mercy upon us. Sis Anne said the other day that she thought things would go on so until Christmas and then there would be some of this—with a very significant gesture across the throat—

Sunday, October 8, 1865 About one year ago I came up the Avenue & selecting a seat in the Pine Woods I leaned against a tree and read *Nelly Norton* and tried to solve the vexed problem of "Wether Slavery was right?" I came with my Bible in my hand to consult and refer to and hoped to be convinced of what I doubted— I little thought then that the question would be so summarily disposed of in less than nine months from that time. Today Slavery as it once existed is a thing of the past & has no longer an existence in the Southern States.

We owned more than 90 Negroes with a prospect of inheriting many more from Pa's estate— By the surrender of the Southern army slavery became a thing of the past and we were reduced from a state of affluence to comparative poverty—so far as I individually am concerned to utter beggary for the thirty thousand dollars Pa gave me when I was married was invested in Negroes alone—[11] This view of the case I did not at first take and it is difficult now to realise it. But "Each heart knoweth its own bitterness" and I alone know the effect the abolition of slavery has had upon me. I did not know until then how intimately my faith in revelations and my faith in the institution of slavery had been woven together—true I

---

11. According to Turner Clanton's will, Gertrude received $25,000 in property (mostly slaves) at the time of her marriage. Jefferson Thomas was given $5,000 in his own right. There were additional bequests by the liberal father who left each of his seven children the equivalent of $45,000 in property and/or cash, with the prospect that they would inherit more when his estate was finally settled.

had seen the evil of the latter but if the *Bible* was right then slavery *must be*— Slavery was done away with and my faith in God's Holy Book was terribly shaken. For a time I doubted God. The truth of revelations, all—everything— I no longer took interest in the service of the church. From May until July I lived a sad life— Lived with a prospect of again becoming a mother and yet felt no longings—no desire for increased spiritual faith. When I prayed my voice appeared to rise no higher than my head. When I opened the Bible the numerous allusions to slavery mocked me. Our cause was lost. Good men had had faith in that cause. Earnest prayers had ascended from honest hearts— Was so much faith to be lost? I was bewildered— I felt all this and could not see God's hand—

The Negroes suddenly emancipated from control were wild with their newly gained and little understood freedom. Cap Bryant of the Freedman's Bureau aided as much as was possible in sowing broadcast the seed of dissention between the former master and slave and caused what might have continued to be a kind interest to become in many cases a bitter enmity. The Negro was the all absorbing theme which engaged all minds. The Negro and Cap Bryant!— The Negroes regard him as a Savior (They are just beginning to discover the cloven foot).

Someone once remarked of [President] Andy Johnson that "his name stunk like carrion in the nostrils of the Southern people." A strong expression but I know of none which will so well express my sentiments for the man who thus presumes to interfere in our domestic affairs—

Belmont, October 14, 1865 I have just read over what I wrote last Sunday. It appears very contradictory but I will not attempt to analyse it—

I am just now recovering from an illness which kept me confined to my bed for three months lacking one week— I shall always have cause to remember it— On Tuesday July the 25th I gave birth to an infant son whose birth was premature, caused I know by the constant strain upon my nervous system. I gave to him the name of Charley and sighed to think it was all I had to give him. I could not even give him what God's poorest creatures can supply, a mother's nourishment— Poor little baby! He seemed loath to enter upon life's troubled cares and moaned his little feeble spark of life away and the angels took him home to Heaven the next night after he was born— Took him home and I thank God that it is so! Little baby! little darling if I could have you back again I would not. . . .

It has grown late since I have been writing. Everyone in the house is asleep. I am using the sitting room as my bed room and the clock is in the nursery so I have no idea of the time. Alexander Von Humboldt[12] slept only four hours and did his best writing at midnight— I always am most disposed to write at night. I have unconsciously compared myself with the great author of *Kosmos* by expressing similarity of taste. Sleeping but a few hours was a peculiarity of his family which I do not share with him. I have just finished reading the life and travel of Von Humboldt which I find charmingly interesting and instructive.

.   .   .

[Augusta] The last night of 1865 . . . Another Christmas has come and gone and another year has passed. I could bow my head and weep, oh so bitterly, did I permit my mind to follow its impulse & think of the bright hopes which have been dashed to the earth, the sad condition of our loved country, but God disposes of all things and it is too late. I do not know what to think. Sometimes I am inclined to look upon our defeat as a Providential thing and then I grow sceptical and almost doubt wether Providence had anything to do with the matter. Slavery had its evils and great ones and for some years I have doubted wether Slavery was right and now I sometimes feel glad that they have been freed and yet I think that it came too suddenly upon them. As it is we live in troublous times. Lawless acts are being committed every day and the papers are filled with the robberies which are constantly taking place.

It has been raining all day. Mr Thomas left this morning to go to Burke to have a settlement with the Negroes. They have made nothing and he has little inducement to plant. Indeed he does not know what to do and were it not too serious a subject to jest upon I should say he was "waiting for something to turn up" like Micawber in one of Dickens' works,[13] and indeed that expression will

---

12. Alexander (Friedrich Wilhelm Karl Heinrich) von Humboldt (1769–1859), German writer, traveler, and scientist, was the author of *Kosmos* (1845–58).

13. Mr. Micawber in *David Copperfield* is always sanguine that "something will turn up."

serve to convey an idea of the condition of the southern people generally. Until Congress decides something definite we will not know how we stand.

New Year's night 1866 This morning I slept late enjoying a sound slumber made more so by the sound of rain. The sun has been obscured all day. Immediately after breakfast I commenced making preperations for baking cake as I was not at home last week to attend to it. Holt came up to see me and soon after Frank Ford called to wish me "a happy New Year." I had thought of buying a cake but had neglected it. Had I not been so busy with so few servants Saturday I had intended being prepared for New Year's. I came in dressed as I was in calico, wished Louis[14] a happy New Year, apoligised that I was not prepared to offer the usual hospitality and hoped he would call again. Immediately after he left I sent Uncle Jim down to the French Store for an iced pound cake. He returned just as the Bell rung and Dr Ford and Col Clinch called. I told Lucy to place the glasses on the Table and the wine Castors which I had filled and was prepared to offer them Champaigne when they left. I received them in the parlour and invited them in [to the] other room to join me in a glass of cake and wine. I had had the wire on the Champaigne cut and requested Dr Ford to cut the string—

Noticing that he was as I thought meeting with some difficulty I thoughtlessly remarked "What's the matter. Doesn't it pop?" I learned a lesson when Dr Ford remarked "Oh yes I am trying to prevent it." At once I remembered that it was *vulgar* to cause an explosion in opening Champaigne but in our family it has been considered a test of superiority and knowing that Mr Thomas bought this basket as a superior article, I felt that its not "popping" was a proof that it was of an inferior quality. At Mr Scales' the other day he opened half doz bottles and the louder it "popped" the better I thought it was and the cork that hit the ceiling was I thought the best of all— I was provoked with myself the moment I made the remark. It was a little thing in itself but I know of nothing more annoying than to have said or done anything which the most fastidious taste could condemn— Tonight the children are attending a

14. Gertrude obviously meant to write "Frank," since Lewis Ford called shortly thereafter.

New Year's party at Mrs John Stovall's. Turner and Mary Belle. Jeff and Cora Lu have been having a tea party up stairs but are now asleep. I have been talking to Ruffin who wishes to engage with Mr Thomas another year. . . .

.   .   .

Sunday, July 9 [8], 1866   I am waiting at Allen's Station for the cars to come to go on to Macon to attend the commencement. I anticipate a real genuine pleasure in meeting so many old friends especially Dr Ellison whom I have not met since the day I graduated and bid him good bye in college fifteen years ago. My life has been a happy one—truly the lines have fallen to me in pleasant places. I have experienced much love to support me in all trials. In having married the husband I have and in having been the happy mother of children, I feel that I have filled the mission for which Providence intended me. I feel that my nature has expanded, my life has been ennobled and that today I am a matured woman, capable of a grasp of thought and appreciation of nature of which in those earlier years I could scarcely conceive. I am writing for myself and write plainly when I say that the fifteen years which left me a young girl and finds me a matured woman have advanced my intellectual powers. I read and read books which then would have bored me terribly— I think and think boldly, I act—and act boldly as for example my going to Macon without a gentleman to escort us. Cora and I.

The unsettled state of the times and a wish to remain with the children decided Mr Thomas to remain at home. He is the soul of generosity towards me and enters into my pleasure in going to Macon with the greatest interest. I have been reading as I came down in the Carriage my Journal kept during the summer of 1860, at which time the first meeting of the alumn[ae] was held. The war prevented the next meeting in 1863 and now that 1866 has come around we are again invited to assemble, and I am on my way to join them.[15] I am tired of waiting. Cora is coming down accompanied by Turner who has been with his Grand Ma going to school since we moved into the country.

---

15. The following entry, dated July 22, 1866, is a long, detailed report of the commencement and alumnae meeting and reminiscences of Wesleyan days.

Sunday, September 16, 1866 One of our hired girls Martha is to be married today. I have furnished her cards & envelopes to send invitations to a few friends whom she wishes to invite in a more formal style. Most of the invitations are verbal. She has been quite busy during yesterday & today making arrangements for the wedding and has been borrowing different articles during the morning to decorate her room. I gave her a wash bowl and sent her out a wash stand, looking glass, screen for the fireplace and vases to receive some flowers Mrs Harris sent to her. A short time since she sent for me to inspect her room. It really looked quite pretty with its whitewashed walls—wreaths of flowers suspended across the room with a larger boquet suspended from the center. The bed was ornamented with sprays of the wisteria vine wound around the posts. She is a woman whom we have hired during the last two months as a washer and ironer. She is a brown complected woman the mother of two children Jimmie and Fanny. Her husband is in Virginia and has married her first attendant upon that occasion. When she first came here she spoke quite freely of her engagement to a Negro man in Augusta. She soon formed the acquaintance of a man Mrs Harris has for her Carriage driver. It must have been a clear case of "love at first sight."

A few weeks ago with a good deal of bashfulness she requested me to read a love letter which she had just received. Upon opening, it proved to be from Mr William Coles as she terms him. It was evidently of his own composition for after assuring her through the medium of a man who spelt no better than William composed that he loved her dearly and "would always be her faithful valentine" he appointed the 16th of December for their wedding day— "Why he must be a crazy Jack" was her emphatic comment. Just then the children came in and amidst a good deal of laughing and boisterous jokes she left the room.

I thought nothing more of it until a few days after as I was at the Store room giving out something—said she "Mrs Thomas I want you please mam to answer my letter for me." "What must I say?" I replied expecting of course to have to assure him of her regrets—assurances of loving him as a brother &c— "Oh you know what to tell him better than I do" said she "tell him yes." "Why" said I "I thought you said you were engaged to a man in Augusta." "Oh" but then said she in a confidential tone "he's a gambler!"

"Yes" she added "tell him I will marry him on the 16th of October." "But" said I "Martha he did not ask you to marry him till the 16th of December." How confused she looked— A touch of nature makes us all akin and this was real feminine nature— I know she blushed as she turned aside with the remark "Why he must be a crazy Jack"— Willing to relieve her embarrasment and to avoid the trouble of deciding how to express myself in assuring Mr Coles of his successful suit, I proposed to her to give her answer when she saw him again— He came over to see her that night and overcome with bashful modesty she hid behind the door—as she told me the next day—assuring me at the same time they had talked it over and concluded to marry on the 16th of September— I did not ask her how the different arrangement was brought about—

During my married life I have never been the confidant of our servants in their matrimonial and love affairs. Indeed I shrewdly suspected that they would have preferred almost anyone else should have read their love letters and I am quite sure I had much preferred someone else should have answered them. When they belonged to us they all preferred having husbands off the plantations, thought that it was exceedingly hard if they could not marry away from home and yet I have known of a number of instances of men leaving now they are free the very women they were so anxious to have before and marrying someone else. Aunt Clary from the Rowell Place was over yesterday— Solomon has left his wife whom he used to be so anxious to visit and to use their expression "taken up" with Aunt Clary. I asked her "are you married to Solomon?" "No mam" said she. "Is he your sweetheart then?" "No mam" said she. "Solomon won't pay for the license for we to get married and I means to tell him I haint gwine to live long of him no more if he don't"— Poor Aunt Clary. Cap Bryant ought to know of this benighted son of Africa and his philanthropic eagerness to *pocket the license fee* would avenge the wrongs of Aunt Clary. . . .

Monday, September 17, 1866 Martha's marriage took place yesterday. Gen Harris and Joe came over to witness the ceremony. The afternoon was gloomy and having the appearance of rain. Notwithstanding a good many servants came. The bridal party came in through the passage into the front Piazzi where the ceremony was performed by Uncle Kelly Beall— The bride had on a lace veil her hair curled and &c and the groom, quite black, very young and rather good looking held on to the arm of the more composed widow— One of the attendants having failed to come Patsey stood up in her place, notwithstanding her being married and having a child—

The ceremony consisted of part of the Episcopalian ceremony mixed in with the Babtist such as that portion "With this ring I do thee endow and &c." The old minister interrupted the solemn ceremony to cry "order" as rather more confusion was visible than he liked. After incorrectly repeating the Lord's Prayer he made the usual enquiry of William of wether "he would have this woman to have & to hold and &c" to which he responded correctly. Then the same enquiry was made of Martha, who by the way was married as Margaret she having been called Martha "for short." A modest inclination of the head was her reply, but this did not satisfy Uncle Kelly. Determined to leave no loophole for escape "Say yes" said he and Martha promised, a promise to obey, which I know she will not observe— When the question was asked "Who gives this bride away" no one answered— Patsey looked towards one of the groomsmen who said "me." "I" said Uncle Kelly and upon being thus corrected he repeated "I" and the ceremony proceeded—

The bridal party then proceeded to the bride's room while a song was sung as they marched—and other songs after they went in the room. Soon after a table was prepared in the yard and cake & wine drank— Bob brought us some of the cake and wine and we drank the bride's health in a most detestable drink of claret— Fearing that in the confusion they would forget this I had given Gen Harris and Joe some cake and wine— After partaking of refreshments they (the bridal party) played games—one of them was performed by all hands joining in a ring and going round singing. . . .

I have been thus particular in discribing a dance or play which I have often seen the Negroes enter into with such merry hearts. Daniel who is still driving for Mrs Cumming was down at the wedding. For six months after he first left us he never came to the yard but last winter he wished to obtain a situation with Mrs Cumming as a Carriage driver, and Dr Cumming[16] called to see me to know if I could recommend him. I always liked Daniel and spoke kindly with regard to him— He obtained the situation and soon after came to the yard in town. He always bowed respectfully in passing the house but I have never talked with him until yester-

16. Probably Harford M. Cumming.

day— As I saw him leaving in company with some others I called him and said "Why Daniel are you going away with out coming to see me?" He stopped outside of the gate and spoke to me, then turning came up to the steps with his hat off and what I knew so well to be a pleased, gratified expression of countenance that I extended my hand and shook hands with him, a mark of favour I bestowed upon him I remember when he returned from Virginia bringing Mr Thomas' Horses home by private conveyance while Mr Thomas came on the cars. This was the summer they were in Virginia and Daniel having been captured by the Yankees had made his escape and returned to the camp.

Daniel was the first servant Mr Thomas owned— When he was coming to see me in Columbia the summer before we were married he drove two black Ponys which he had named "Abdobella and Anabella." Upon my laughing at the pompous names he changed them to "Beauty and Grace"— A grown servant who had been his playmate in childhood (Morah), his Mother's Carriage driver usually came with him. Upon one occasion I remember Daniel came, a little boy about eleven or twelve years old. When we were married his Father gave him to us to go in the Buggy and yet when the Yankees came Daniel was the first one to leave us and our cook [Tamah] who next to Patsey and John were among the first Pa gave to me. . . .

. . .

Thursday, September 20, 1866 . . . Except my visit to Macon I have had no adventure, nothing but the ordinary routine of domestic life and yet to me it has been very charming— Mr Thomas has not been well during the summer months and has been worried in mind as well as body— The unsettled state of the times, the price of cotton and the freedman have all conspired to annoy him. Within the last few weeks he is in better health and proportionately cheerful—for the one acts upon the other. I have enjoyed better health this summer than usual— . . .

I have been reading of late the proceedings of the political world with a great deal of interest. I was particularly interested in the Philadelphia convention—[17] Mr Thomas decidedly opposed to

---

17. The National Union Convention met in Philadelphia on August 14, 1866, to oppose the propositions of the Radical Republicans—the Reconstruction partisans in Congress.

it. I rather in favour of it but I confess to a feeling of most unmitigated disgust when I read of the South Carolina and Massachusetts delegates walking in the Hall arm in arm. I blushed for the Southerner who would allow himself thus to be inveigled in such a claptrap exhibition. I was in the front piazzi when the papers were brought in. Mr Thomas opened them and commenced to read aloud the proceedings of the convention but when he read the above announcement I did not credit it. When convinced could only shrug my shoulders and say Bah! Mr Thomas indulged in a more expressive but rather stronger expression. Mr Thomas remarked that he took no interest in the proceedings but he reads the daily papers with so much interest I think that he cares more than he says he does.

I read the numerous petitions addressed to Andy Johnson. I will call *him* President and own him—him as such when he releases *our* illustrious ex President. I read the petitions signed by so many names with a flashing eye and throbbing heart which echoes every word there expressed— In one petition written I think by Mrs Downing of North Carolina occurs a sentence, if I remember aright like this "Release to us our beloved ex president and accomplish what you have never yet succeeded in doing—the subjugation of the *Southern women*." Another very to[u]ching and beautifully written petition by Miss ——— of Tennessee signed by thousands of names was sent to Andy Johnson a few day since— One petition signed and written last winter requesting that Jeff Davis be released to us [as] a Christmas present reminded me of Sherman's gift to Lincoln of Savannah as a Christmas present and the letter I thought of sending to Mrs Sherman as a New Year's present in return. Reading that now I can see how my nervous system was completely unstrung—for now "that sober reason has resumed her sway" without alleviating my bitterness for the Yankee nation, I should never think of visiting upon Mrs Sherman retaliation for the enormous crimes committed by her husband—and yet it is hard not to visit upon the individual the sins of the nation.

As an instance last week I was returning with Mary Bell & Cora Lu from a visit to Joe and Bob in Burke— As we passed the bridge at Spirit Creek I saw a Yankee sitting on the ground apparently joining in a lunch with a Negro man and woman who had stopped their cart & Horse to rest. I merely looked at him as we passed and thought the Negroes the most respectable portion of the group— Arriving on this side of the bridge a few hundred yds we stopped under the shade of a tree to take lunch— Uncle Jim took his Horses out and carried them to the creek and watered them. Giving him something to eat having finished, I went with the children to bathe my hands in the water and was stooping over when I heard Mary Bell say in the frightened tones the sight of a Yankee or robber in the country would be apt to produce, "Oh Ma there is a Yankee." I looked and saw a young strong looking man with his pants rolled as high nearly as he could get them above his naked legs, a queer looking cap was on his head and a bundle slung over his shoulder— He muttered something like good morning as he passed and walked on to the Carriage, and taking off his bundle threw himself on the ground by Uncle Jim— I walked slowly back and getting into the Carriage I called Uncle Jim. The Yankee approached the Carriage and asked me "for something to eat." I confess that at the moment it gave me pleasure to tell him "I had nothing to spare." "Well" said he "are you going towards Augusta." "Yes" said I. "Well can't you let me ride. My feets mighty tired?" The absurdity of the request positively amused me. "Why" said I "have you the slightest idea that I would take you in the Carriage to ride with me—and you a Yankee?" He hastened to say he was not. "Well" said I "let me give you a little advice. If you wish much kindness shown to you don't travel through this portion of the country wearing *blue* pants. They are not apt to promote charitable feelings towards you."

Commenting on this afterwards Mr Thomas asked me "if I was not afraid to talk to him in this way?" Why I was no more afraid of his insulting me than I would expect a servant to be impertinent when I addressed him— Turning to Uncle Jim I told him "to drive on" and left the Yankee standing in the road. "When he came up and saw the bread the children had left on the ground" (said Uncle Jim) "he said 'My God have you got bread to throw away.'" That touched me in spite of myself and looking back I saw the man trudging along and then my eye rested on the Basket of lunch which lay on the front seat. It reads like a little thing but it is a part of the religion I have taught our children to dislike the Yankees and were we not drilled in the doctrine "that to give aid & comfort to the enemy was treason." I am afraid during our four years pupilage some of us learned that doctrine better than that other command, "If thy enemy hunger give him bread. If he thirst give him drink"— We stopped to pull up some cedars the other side of Judge Allen's and when the man was passing I took the contents of the Basket and gave them to him, excusing myself even then by telling him he was the first person I ever had to ask me for something to eat and I had refused— I justified myself still farther afterwards by explaining "that what I had refused to *the Yankee* I gave to *the man*." . . .

. . .

Friday, October 12, 1866 October! to me the most charming season of all the months in the year, and yet with a strange perversity I am going to leave the country which is so peculiarly suited for a thorough enjoyment of this month and on Monday we expect to move in town. Mr Thomas has rented the Twiggs house, giving $1200 in gold for it which is equivalent to 16 or 1800 in greenbacks, a very high rent, the knowledge of which tempers my delight in obtaining possession of a house we have been anxious to buy ever since our marriage. Lizzie Lamkin is to be married to Edge[worth] Eve and Lizzie wishes to be married in town. Ma has been in such deep mourning that the idea of having company at her house was not pleasant, so I proposed to Lizzie having a party at our house, with which idea she was very much pleased. . . .

I anticipate a pleasant winter. Turner and Mary Bell will be going to school, and Jeff and Cora Lu when the weather is pleasant will be on the street in front of the door or in the yard in the care of Jane who is growing to be quite useful. Mr Thomas will be at his store[18] and I am almost through the sewing for the winter. I wish to have as few servants to keep employed as I can help and oh how much time I ought to have for what I love best—reading and writing. There is so much need of improvement, I have not yet divested myself of the idea that I may yet have to earn my own support. Just now I am quite comfortable and thanks to my generous Husband have no wish ungratified. I am only afraid he is more liberal than he can afford to be— I have not alluded to the opera which we had the pleasure of attending last week. Mr Thomas and I were there two nights. . . .

. . .

18. As Gertrude had wished, Jefferson Thomas acquired a business in town—an interest in a crockery and porcelain store located on Broad Street and known as Mosher, Thomas, and Schaub.

[The journal for the next two years, October 1866 to October 1868, is missing. In that time, Julian Pinckney Thomas was born to the Thomases on January 21, 1868. Sister Cora married an Augusta attorney, Claiborne Snead, and Mr. Scales, husband of Julia Thomas Scales, died. Although earlier entries in the journal contained veiled hints of financial troubles, it was during these two years that the Thomases' debts and personal problems escalated. In December 1868, Thomas wrote, "For two years Mr Thomas has had this complication of affairs to worry him."]

Part III   *1868–1871*

9. Crises: Race, Labor, Debt

Dark days are gathering.
—*November 29, 1868*

Thursday, October 22, 1868 I have just finished reading the speech of Mr John Quincy Adams[1] delivered in Charleston a few days since. By the request of "the executive committee of South Carolina" this Massachusetts gentleman has been invited to that state to teach the people of S Carolina their duty— I have read both of his speeches & in all due humility, I must say that I can discover nothing in them calculated to do good. He began his Columbia speech with the assertion "that he was opposed to the institution of slavery—that he was a warm supporter of Mr Lincoln & his government." He then adds

"The great desideratum for your restoration to constitutional liberty seems to me to be, first, to deserve and then to obtain the confidence of our Northern communities in your acquiescence in good faith in the results of the war." And again "You people here may be, are different from any people I have ever seen known or read of." Was that intended as a compliment or taunt? Taken in connection with such expressions as the following I am inclined to think the latter. "The union, you had broken," "the constitution you had renounced" "paying in full for the stake for which you had played & lost" "To be sure you had no choice," "a determination never to yield us peaceable possession of the fruits of the war is the crime for which you are suffering politically." I imagine Gen

---

1. John Quincy Adams II (1833–94) was a Massachusetts legislator. He was the son of Charles Francis Adams and grandson of John Quincy Adams, sixth president of the United States.

Hampton[2] & the revolutionary heros listening quietly to this cold blooded man as he utters such sentiments as the above—

The executive committee received a sensation which must have reminded them of the long ago school boy days when they sat with downcast countenances and listened to a reprimand for past misconduct and were promised forgiveness after due submission to "the powers that be." Mr Adams defines the characteristics of the Northern people to be "cold cautious and thoughtful." Those of the South to be "warm impulsive and impetuous," and he was no more qualified to advise us than he was to appreciate, or judge— Throughout the speech there is a self sufficient tone which I confess to quote his own expression causes "a rising of the gorge" as he thus coldly dictates. With me the wounds are too recent— They have not healed sufficiently for the ball, or cause of dissen[s]ion to be probed for— So much for the Columbia speech—

In Charleston he was more considerate, admits that the theory of the present congress is not his, but adds "I came here to learn not to teach. But now after you have told me what you have (with regard to the institution of slavery) I will tell you candidly that you could not restore it if you would." (cries "We don't want to") "Well I know you don't, but still you could not if you would"— Was there not an implied doubt in that sentence? He tells the coloured people, "the people whom the radicals tell us are the only loyal people at the south." "Through no fault of your own, you have no education and no property and besides you have been subjected for a long series of years to a condition of slavery in which you were debarred from some of the most precious privileges of life. This was no fault of yours. It was no fault of the late slaveholders or of the present race of white men but of their ancestors who lived long ago." Why did he not tell them *whose* ancestors were responsible for their bondage?

Warning the Negroes against "Negroes only voting for Negroes" he tells them that "the blacks will be crushed down. It may not be as bad as the old slavery but I think it will be worse." He adds "Inquire who is the best man for the best place"— "It is charged" said he "that some of them (the whites) try to influence their employees by threats of discharge. Is that true?" (cries of "yes

---

2. Wade Hampton of South Carolina, a general in the American Revolution, was the grandfather of the Confederate general Wade Hampton.

yes"). "Well I am glad that I have something that I can talk about at last."

Yes he had at last accomplished his object, worked upon the passions of the Negroes until he had strengthened the enthusiasm for Grant and lost votes for Seymour—[3] . . . I read both speeches attentively and can see no good to be gained to the state of Carolina by them—on the contrary many votes gained for Grant from the Negroes. He tells us candidly "we are prisoners of war. We can do nothing"— Well, we knew this before—& the city of Charleston went to considerable expense to have the idea confirmed by a Northern man. My own opinion is that the South has made sufficient concessions. Let us resolve to do our duty— We need no Northern man to teach us that. With most of us the present duty— the duty of the hour is to provide sustenance for our familys and *avoid politics*. The South has a glorious record. Let us not dim her glory by senseless humiliation. Let us retain our dignity. Zenobia in chains was still a queen—[4]

. . . .

Sunday, November 1, 1868 I have not alluded to the present unsettled state of affairs among the Negroes and white people but it has for some time been a subject of much interest and one of the most interesting topics for conversation. But things are rapidly approaching a crisis. Tuesday will be the day for the Presidential election and the South feels instinctively that she is standing upon the mouth of a volcano, expecting every moment an eruption, and if it takes place then—what then? Widespread desolation in the moral world which will exceed anything ever exhibited in the convulsions of nature. I am writing calmly because I feel calmly— My pulse beats as quietly as ever, indeed I feel stronger than I have at anytime today and yet tonight it is reported that all of the houses in the neighborhood are to be burnt up.

When I commenced writing I did not know this was the night— Mr Thomas was out watching but I did not know where.

---

3. Gertrude refers to the presidential candidates, Gen. Ulysses S. Grant and Horatio Seymour, governor of New York.

4. Zenobia, the queen of Palmyra in Syria ca. 272 A.D., was the subject of at least two novels prior to 1850.

Four or five coloured men came and went into Dinah's room and Mr T went out to find out "what they were after." Ned came in a few moments after and told me, as he sat down on the floor by my side before the fire, "that the niggers out in the quarter were talking about the election, that Mr McDonald made them a speech today at the church & that Uncle Harry said it was all some of them could do to keep from dragging him out of the pulpit, and that they was all gwine to meet at the creek tomorrow night to march to town the next day with uncle Isaiah as captain—and that uncle Mac said if he had a son who was willing to be a Democrat he would cut his throat."

Ned also added that these men said "that all the white folks was scared of the niggers, that Dr Eve's family was moving in town today and that he was gwine to send his things in tomorrow, and that uncle Mac said 'that things wasn't like they used to be, that they weren't afraid of white folks like they used to be and that they was gwine to have fine times, and burn up every house along the road.'" Ned is a black boy about fourteen years old, boasts that he voted the Democratic ticket at McBean. Isaiah and Mac are farming with Mr Thomas on shares— I listened to Ned without being in the slightest degree alarmed. Just then Mr Thomas came in, his coat was covered with cobwebs— "Why look at your coat. Where have you been?" said I. He looked warningly at me reminding me of Ned (for we have perfect confidence in none of them) and told Ned to bring him some water adding to me in a low tone of voice "under the house listening to them." "I would not allow a party of radical Negroes to assemble here" said I. "I would send for Gen Harris and some of the neighbors and if a crowd assembles order them off"— "They are all right" said Mr T "I understand it" and putting on his overcoat he left the room.

A few moments after two little girls, Lena and Minny, came running in the house out of breath and told me that Uncle Bob (Patsey's husband) said "please to tell Mr Thomas to come there"— This was such an unusual proceeding for him to send for Mr T instead of coming that I went to the door and then concluded I would go & see what he wanted. Patsey has been quite sick for the last week. Going into the room I found them in quite a state of excitement— Mr Thomas they said, had told them "that *they* were going to burn the house up tonight and Bob had just come from town and he wanted to understand what about it." Dinah was in the room and Warren came in. He is a very independent, impertinent hand hired to work on the farm— I know he and Bob are both radicals. I took a seat and talked with them awhile, told them that the white people were anxious to avoid a difficulty but that if forced to it they would fight and fight well—that I did not feel uneasy &c. "Well I want to be where Bob is" said Patsey. "I do not wish to be where Mr T is," said I "for I would want him to be in the fight." "Why Miss Trudy[5] would be a good soldier herself" said Bob. "I would not be a good soldier Bob" said I "but I cannot imagine myself as being a coward," and as the idea flashed across my mind of my being a suppliant for mercy at their hands, I felt my face flush and the tones of my voice rang clear and distinct through the room and I felt that I would not be afraid of a legion of them— But indeed I think I have no cause for fear of personal injury.

Mary Belle who had been setting in the parlour with me while I was talking to Ned came running out in the yard and after a short time we came on in the house. Soon after I heard Dinah complaining to Ned & telling him about "telling the white folks everything what is said in the kitchen." I called to her and explained "that Mr Thomas had left the room before Ned came in." I said this to avoid trouble for Ned. He didn't tell Mr T. He told me. I suppose that was a white lie. If so I hope Mrs Opie[6] will forgive me. Soon after, Mr T came in not before Mary Belle (who disliked as she said to leave me alone) had gone up stairs. Of course she told Mary of the excitement without telling on Ned and soon after Mary (who sleeps in the room & is about the age and colour of Ned) came in and said as she was fastening a window "Miss Trudy is the coloured folks gwine to rise tomorrow?" I comforted her by telling her "No" and just then Mr T came in and she went up stairs.

I proceeded to tell him what I had said to Bob. "Yes" said he "I thought you never would get through." "Why where were you?" "Under their house" said he. "I went for the purpose of hearing what plans would be made and was there when you came out and heard every word you said." I laughed right out and so did he as I thought of how comfortably I had been seated and what a tantalising position I had unwittingly kept him in. The house is quite high

---

5. Gertrude was often called "Trudy" by family members and "Miss Trudy" by the family slaves, now former slaves.

6. Amelia Alderson Opie, English novelist and moralist, wrote *A Wife's Duty* (1847), among others.

but of course his position was constrained. "Well you heard me say nothing amiss" said I "except that I would wish you to be in the fight and that I was glad the Negroes were free!" (That is a point upon which Mr Thomas and I do not agree) "That was all right but you told them you would have sold some of them before the close of the war." "So I did" I replied "and if I had told them that I would voluntarily have freed them all they would not have believed me. On the contrary I told them I would have sold them as a plantation to Pinck but would not have seperated them and the house servants I would have kept with me if I had known they would have been freed the next day. The Negroes are not so ignorant as we imagine." "I was surprised to hear you tell the servants that I had told you nothing about the houses being fired in the neighborhood." "Told me when?" I said in the utmost surprise— "Last week, don't you remember that a Negro told a member of the club, adding that he had begged for Mrs Twiggs' and Judge Allen's houses." He had told me, I had exclaimed that "I did not believe it" and had not given it one thought since. Even when those Negroes came and Mr Thomas went out to hear what they were after, I only thought they came to make arrangements for the march to town Tuesday. . . .

We talked together for some time comparing notes and then I told Mr Thomas that I had decided not to go in town. He proposed it to me last week and altho I consented it was against my better judgement. If I were a man I cannot imagine myself a coward and as a woman I dislike to show that I am afraid to remain at home. Indeed I think the women of the country are very wrong in showing this exhibition of fear. I deem it well calculated to encourage evil passions in the Negroes. Leaving home as they do they certainly leave their husbands more free to act in a case of emergency—but by remaining at home they protect their property and awe the Negroes— True the coloured people are not now as they were during the war but we trusted ourselves to them then. Why not now?

Monday, November 2, 1868 It is now late. Since the weather has been so cold I have been sleeping up stairs with the younger children and Mr Thomas and Turner remain in the wing room to guard the place and prevent robberies— I have since tea been in the sitting room with Mr Thomas and the children and he has been reloading his guns. The children have gone to bed and Turner taken off his military suit which he wears today for the first time. It is the cadet dress of the [Richmond] academy. Mr Thomas has two guns and two pistols and as I came on up stairs I brought one of the latter. In my hands I had the lamp, bunch of keys, ink stand pair of scissors to cut Mary Belle's finger nails in the morning and the pistol with the mouth of it towards me. "Take care" said Mr Thomas. I reversed the position, came on up stairs and placed it on the mantle piece and sincerely hope it may have no occasion to change its position again until morning. . . .

Just as I closed this book I was fortunate enough to find a better pen on the mantle piece so I will turn the lamp up throw an additional piece of lightwood and give Mrs Harris' experience of yesterday. Just as the Gen and herself were between the Rowell Place & Mrs ——— they saw a large waggon approaching, four or six Horse team. She supposed it to be servants coming to town but just then Gen H said to her in a low tone "My what is the meaning of this. There must be some news of importance to cause this movement." Upon a nearer approach it proved to be Dr Ed Eve's family and the [George] Twiggs going into town with Willy Eve & Mr McDonald riding as a body guard by the side of the waggon. Exchanging salutations they passed. "Isn't this too bad" said Gen Harris. "I feel as if ——— the Carriage driver is laughing in his sleeve at us." Who is there who cannot understand his statement? Arriving at church Mrs Harris found everyone wearing an excited air. Taking a seat by Mrs Allen, "What is the meaning of all this?" said she— "Nothing except a sensation report of Mr Ben Neely's" said Mrs Allen. . . . Judge Allen made a speech at church in which he severely denounced the attempt to create a panic—said one sensationalist might excite a neighborhood. Mrs H said the Gen also made them a speech. . . .

Just here I must take occasion to say that I do not in my heart wonder that the Negroes vote the radical ticket, and to have persuaded them otherwise would be against my own conscience. Think of it, the right to vote, that right which they have seen their old masters exercise with so much pride, and their young masters look forward to with so much pleasure is within their *very grasp*— They secure a right for themselves, which it is true they may not understand, but they have children whom they expect to educate. Shall they secure this right for them or sell their right away? It is within their grasp. Who can guarantee that they will ever have it extended to them again? If the women of the North once secured to me the right to vote whilst it might be "an honour thrust upon me," I think I should think twice before I voted to have it taken from me. Of course such sentiments smack too much of radicalism to promulgate outside of my own family & though I do not say much, I think Grant will be elected and I don't think if we can have peace that it will make much difference, as he says

"Let us have peace."

Tuesday, November 3, 1868 [at night] Mr Thomas returned from Pine Hill the place he voted at just after dinner. He says there were —— votes polled, all for Seymour and ten or fifteen coloured votes. Gen Harris reports —— votes at the Poor House, some coloured votes and all for Seymour— Late this afternoon Mac returned from Augusta and Mary Bell enquired of him "if he voted." He replied "Yes the republican ticket." "How was everything going on?" "Beautifully mam beautifully," said he throwing his arms about with much energy—

Turner came in just at dark and reported that a riot took place. This was after Mac left I expect. He was at Ma's and all of them at dinner except Cora who was dining with [Mamie]. She came running in crying "that they were fighting at the City Hall and her husband was there." Holt seized his arms and all of them ran into the street to witness the scene. The men were flying in all directions. Turner did not know how it originated but thinks two men were disputing when one of them drew his pistol and this commenced it— The Negroes were up town talking and threatening. Then they started down again. The white men formed in line to check them. The Yankees advanced took position between the contending parties, and the police arrested several ringleaders among the Negroes. Quiet was restored when Turner went up to the Hall and while standing on the railing of the monument, a pistol was shot and [Albert] Ruffin, the deputy sheriff (a southern radical) fell. No one knew who fired the shot. He was taken into the Hall from the yard and died soon after— When Turner left everything was quiet but a disturbance expected tonight but everyone prepared for it—but I do not apprehend it. The sight of a few dead men will calm their excited feelings more effectually than many words. Turner asked Mac tonight "who he voted for?" Mac hesitated. He had forgotten the name. "Who did *you* vote for" said he (he did not know Turner could not vote). "Grant & [Schuyler] Colfax said Turner." "Then I voted for the other side" said Mac and that was about all he knew. He said he voted what they told him to. Mr Thomas influenced uncle Harry to stay at home. He is an old man who cuts wood for us—

Monday, November 29 [30], 1868   Old friend! dark days are gathering around me, heavy clouds obscure my future. Tears gather, it is only with an effort that I prevent them from rolling down upon your pages— Mr Thomas' affairs are so complicated, & he is so depressed "run to death" as he expresses it— For a long time I have known of his pecuniary embarrassments. Within the last two or three days a man who is the agent for a New York company has been in Augusta and it is in his power to force the firm into bankruptcy   I was in town last week and walking up town I passed by the store of Mr Drake, above the Central States Hotel— The doors and windows were closed and upon the door was a card stating that the store had been closed and the goods levied upon by Mr Levy the sheriff. Mr Thomas is afraid that tomorrow he may find his store closed with a similar card upon it. Just above Mr Thomas' store is that of Mr William Jones— His store has been closed and as I stood opposite in Mr Wright's store last week I wondered how long it would be before Mr Thomas' was closed also.

When we moved out from town I was so cheerful—so delighted that we were doing something toward the retrenchment I so much desired. I so dearly love this place and I had thought that in case of our becoming bankrupt that we would still own this home. Tonight Mr Thomas tells me this must go too, that if this was a state court it might hold good but that United States courts are different, that the homestead bill will do us no good— I have heard so much of homestead bills, bankruptcy, state courts and so on I understand nothing of it. I have been so sanguine of at least having a home that when the idea was brought home to me that this place could be taken I was stunned, speechless with astonishment. I suppose I ought to have spoken words of consolation to Mr T. I did not but the tears rolled thick & fast down my face, and all, everything looked dark & dreary. "Will there be nothing coming to us from Pa's estate?" I said. "I am afraid not" was Mr T's reply. "Then what are we to do?" I said. "If I had only taken a second course of medicine" said Mr Thomas— I said nothing but tried to think! tried and tried in vain and the tears came faster & faster.[7] "My children, oh my children" was the burden of my sigh. I looked up and saw Mr Thomas' eyes were filled with tears and somehow the current of my thoughts changed instantly and I spoke cheerfully—& he was

---

7. Gertrude may well have been an influence in Jefferson's not continuing his medical studies. She wanted him to be a successful planter, like her father.

enabled to bid me hope that some favourable turn might take place—but oh old friend this is very trying. I do not know how long it will last but to Mr Thomas the strain upon his nerves & physical system is terrible.

During the past few weeks Pa's estate has been in the hands of arbitrators for settlement and from the length of time they occupy I think they can arrive at no determination. Col Vason & Mr Thomas are at deadly enmity with each other and I scarcely know which to do most, condemn or pity Col Vason for the vindictive spirit he has shown.[8] I looked out upon the bright moonlight night when I came up stairs and I took heart and will hope that things may not be so dark as Mr Thomas thinks they are—

December 3, 1868 . . . Mr Thomas left for Burke yesterday morning but all day yesterday and today I have felt unsettled—as if I was on the eve of moving. Mr T has said all summer he felt as if he was camping but I have experienced an altogether different emotion— now that there is a prospect of this place being taken from us I feel adrift. On Tuesday Patsey left us. She has been nursing Julian and was apparently much attached to him. Her husband wished her to go in town & I rather think she liked the idea but I cannot think she will do as well as she has done with us. We were giving her seven dollars and feeding her nurse & George—& her baby could have as much milk as she wished for it. She had a good room plenty of firewood and only housework to do, with a morning in each week to work for herself. She had no scouring washing or cooking to do for me. To do her justice she was always willing to take the place of the others when called upon and I think studied the interest of our family— With the exception of a few months spring before last she has remained with us since she was freed. I will never be able to offer her as good terms again— Dinah who is with me now is an excellent servant. She has one child two years old and a girl to nurse it. I have been giving her seven dollars to cook wash and iron, and now she does the house work that Patsey did and the washing & ironing for the same price.

When we came home on Friday from town Turner told us that during the day Mac & Warren had moved off— The day before Mr

---

8. The friction between Vason and Thomas was the result of Jefferson's debt to the estate.

Thomas had told them to put up some fencing which wanted repairing. This they objected to, but told him to hire the labour and take it out of their portion of the crop. Their contract engaged them to keep the ditches and fences in order and it is now four weeks from the end of the year. Mr T told them that if they would not work he would not advance provisions to them. He would not pay out money for their provisions and hire men to do their work for he knew that when he settled with them they would be dissatisfied—Without saying anything to him about it they took advantage of his absence and moved the next day. I am not at all sorry—of course it would have been better for them to remain & keep the place in order but if they did not intend to work I prefer their being away.

This was another of the many occurrences which accumulate to annoy Mr Thomas and in Patsey's leaving he feels that we "are quite broken up." While on the subject of servants I will mention that I have a kind very good natured black girl named Mary who nurses Julian and does what the Yankees call "chores," drawing water, making fires and &c. She is about fourteen—Ned is our little Democratic darky—the most utterly no account young gentleman of African de[s]cent that I know—yet his musical genius is something wonderful and his good nature is equally remarkable. Then we have an old man Uncle Harry who cuts wood for three dollars a month, a clever old man very much hen pecked by his wife and fashionable daughter in law who lives at Judge Allen's. These at present comprise our house force but I wish very much I had a Carriage driver—he ought to cut wood & keep the garden in order. . . .

The tournament which took place on the 24th of Nov was a brilliant affair— . . . Cora Lou & Mary Belle and Jeff rode with me together with Sis Anne & Turner Vason. I sent up to ask her & her children to take a seat with me— I intend that the enmity existing between Mr Thomas and Col Vason shall not affect my feelings toward her. Mr T and Turner came up to the race course from here. We had a good stand to witness the riding— . . .

Friday, December 4, 1868   I was interrupted while writing in the twilight yesterday by Mary bringing Julian to me. . . . I attended the Tournament Party & bought the gloves and a yard of illusion for it. Ma gored my blue moire antique & made a sash for it. I wore it surplice with illusion & illusion sleeves trimmed with bands of cherry velvet. The waist was trimmed with wide lame fringe which gave it a very dressy appearance—the latter was Ma's. My hair was frizzed, worn high, with curls hanging below the knot, & dressed with crimson roses. This costume was suitable for a lady on the shady side of thirty. Ma told me she never saw me look better & Holt said, "Sister I would like to know what you are primping & fixing up so for?" but I consider it a duty to oneself to look as well as one can— That is to make the most of the material nature has provided and I will go farther and say that when nature is lacking art should be called into requisition. . . .

December 21, 1868 . . . Mr Thomas made an arrangement with the man from New York by giving him a mortgage upon our lot in Augusta. It has been settled upon the children and I but there is a mortgage upon it for cousin Polly for $5000. As I was leaving for Augusta yesterday two weeks ago Mr Thomas said "Gertrude here is a paper which I wish you to sign." I had my bonnet on just ready to leave. Enquiring what it was I found my signature was required to give away my right to the town lot, that is to allow a mortgage upon it for $2500 for this man from New York— When Mr Thomas two years ago gave cousin Polly a mortgage upon that place for the benefit of the firm I knew that it was gone— Mr Thomas said if this was not done the store would be closed and brought to bankruptcy— I signed it but did not read it.[9] . . . Mr Thomas has been sued by a man by the name of ———— for a large amount for which Buddy is security— He is very uneasy as he has right to be— Oh these security debts. How I detest them. I feel as if I would be willing to break and have it over with but the idea of my and Mr T's family suffering from their kindness to us is dreadful to both Mr T and I. . . .

Belmont, January 5, 1869 My first chronicle in this book of the advent of a new year! I dread your arrival New Year and I greatly fear that ere your twelve months shall have passed that I shall have passed through a fearful ordeal—and yet I read that this time last

---

9. Under the terms of Turner Clanton's will, Gertrude and her children inherited lifetime interests in certain properties—a provision intended to protect them from having their property seized to satisfy Jefferson Thomas's debts. This was the first instance of Gertrude's signing her interest over to her husband, thereby allowing him to use the property as collateral.

New Year's I had the same anxious forebodings—the same terrible anxiety with regard to the future. Farewell old year. You brought me much, very much of care and sadness, but much too of quiet enjoyment for during the past summer and during the Indian Summer my nature was refreshed. My soul had been thirsting, like "the hart which panteth after the water brook." Oh I too had yearned for quiet, for relief from "Martha's trouble" about the cares of this life. Of late these cares have been renewed for I so sympathise with Mr Thomas in his feelings that I am apt to echo his sentiments & they are usually of a most depressing character— Christmas Day he went from town down to Burke & returned Monday very much pleased with his prospects for a new crop! He had made his arrangements, paid off his negroes for last year and engaged them for this. This morning he went down again but I am very much afraid something will have happened to give him annoyance— He has made no arrangements for this place yet.

Having made his plans in Burke for this year Mr Thomas felt at liberty to enjoy himself and on New Year's day he went in town and in company with Buddy and Bill Dortic he went around making New Year's calls. . . . I enquired of him when he came home that night something about what he had seen but all of his conversation was about the Russells.[10] Anna Russell he said looked like a queen receiving her subjects. She was wearing what Mr T discribed as a white silk and Buddy a white satin and Mr Dortic was sure cost 1,000 dollars. It was trimmed with flounces of lace and her hair was powdered. She returned home on Tuesday the 29th and this was her first opportunity of receiving her friends after her return from Europe. She has been away two years. I joined Anna after communion on Sunday and walked home with her as far as Ma's. She was wearing a walking suit consisting of a heavy black silk skirt with half doz flounces, a velvet Paletot fastened around the waist, a band of muslin (white such as Ma wears) around her neck, and a black Bonnet and Parasol, a suit she could have worn in light mourning. She has evidently learned that it is in bad taste to wear conspicuous colours to church.

Mr Thomas did not go in on Sunday & at tea I was laughing and talking about the beauty of the Russell girls Anna especially— "If I had thought of Miss Anna's being at church" said Mr T "I

---

10. Gertrude refers to the prominent Henry F. Russell family.

Crises . 303

believe I would have gone in. You had better look out old lady. I may be wanting a second wife." "Yes" I replied "Anna said she enjoyed your New Year's call, rather longer than are usual with such calls she said but very welcome"— "Hi, what, what's that" said Mr Thomas as he lifted his head from his mustache cup of coffee. I repeated the remark amidst shouts of laughter from Turner who enjoyed his father's discomforture— Mr Thomas has an idea that in all matters of etiquette he is "comme il faut" and generally speaking I think so too. Ella and Julia Russell are also extremely pretty girls and Mrs Russell and Mr Russell very handsome specimens of their entirely different styles of beauty. Mr Thomas said last winter if he was Mr Russell "he would sit in the amen corner every Sunday so he could see and admire his wife and pretty daughters as they sat in front of him," but I expect Mr Russell is like most other men when he goes to church he likes to look and admire someone else's pretty wife and daughters. . . .

I had intended writing of our Christmas dinner at Ma's the Christmas trees, the exceedingly cold weather, the children's presents and &c. I must give Buddy's reception[11] a seperate notice but my fire has gone out and the recent twinges which I have had in my arm remind me that I am no longer "sweet seventeen" but—I had to stop and count up on my fingers. I do believe I am thirty five—dear me I ought to feel older than I do.

. . .

January 28, 1869 Turner is at a surprise party at Mrs Wheelock's tonight and will remain in town. I do not approve of his acquaintance with Ady Wheelock or the idea of his being called a sweetheart of hers. As I said last night I should like to know who was the Mother of the girl Turner married & I don't think Ada knows who was hers. She was left at the Hotel by a person who bore that relationship to her & Mrs Wheelock adopted her— I was told the other day that Mrs W had Dr Zeke a negro dentist to operate on Ada's teeth. The idea of a Negro placing his fingers on a young girl's mouth— The idea is profanation. Appropo Negroes, I was with Jule at Russell's the jeweler a few evenings since and among other pho-

---

11. On December 22, 1868, James (Buddy) Clanton married Lizzie Walton, daughter of Polly Walton.

tographs was a likeness of Fred Douglass.[12] He looks as if he was two degrees removed from the ape creation. I do not believe he has the talent with which he is credited. Mrs Smith who was [is] the sister of Mr Henry [H.] Cumming & sister in law of Mr Gerritt Smith of New York,[13] tells Mrs Harris that all of the letters which purport to be written by Fred Douglass are the production of Mr Smith. Some years ago when Tom Cumming visited at his house he found that every China plate was ornamented with a picture of a negro and the slaveholder with his whip in his hand. . . .

[Friday] when Mr Thomas returned leaving Turner to attend a surprise party at Mrs Nelson's I offered him my place on the sofa. He declined it & after tea seated himself by the fire & taking his pencil & paper commenced adding up who he was owing. I was very much interested in my book but was brought back to the real, the everyday life by that topic & I began to think, "I can retrench in something, what shall it be?" When just then as climax for his desponding moments Mr Thomas handed me a receipt. I looked at it & found it was for a Bagatelle table purchased at Auction for thirteen dollars. It surprised me so that I laughed until I almost cried. Mr Thomas explained that he bought it thinking it would be useful in case he builds a store in Burke. . . .

.   .   .   .

Feburary 7, 1869 I was thoroughly out of spirits last week, dejected both in body & mind. We all have our troubles, our thorn in the flesh but sometimes we are more sensitive to its piercing than others. I wonder too if there is not some truth in the remark that in every house there is a skeleton, some subject which by mutual consent it is best to avoid. I think I have a consciousness of this and when the door opens and I catch glimpses of my skeletons I try not to look but I cannot always help it, even to you my dear friend I must not confide every thought I have. I would like to. I think that it would afford me inexpressible consolation but I cannot. There

---

12. Frederick Douglass was a former slave, a noted orator, and a vocal abolitionist.

13. Gerrit Smith of Peterboro, N.Y., was a wealthy and fervent abolitionist. He was a principal supporter of the fanatical John Brown and may have had advance knowledge of the Harpers Ferry incident.

are depths in every woman's nature which must not be sounded. I have had thoughts which I would not wish my children to know. I have learned that the heart is desperately wicked and wondered that knowing our own hearts as we learn to know them that we are so lacking in sympathy for those who have their trials too. What I have written sounds very enigmatical, does it not friend Journal? But you see I am trying not to express myself too freely and thus fall into the opposite error— When Mr Thackeray was dining with Mrs King some years ago in Charleston a sideboard door flew open. She rose & was shutting it when Mr Thackeray said to her "Does that door contain your skeleton?" "Oh no" she lightly replied. "It is not large enough to contain one half of them." The best plan to adopt is to do as she did. Shut the door upon them and keep it locked—and if sometimes the door *will open*, don't stand to look but shut it quick, and as you value your life don't take anyone with you, no "Sister Anne" as did Bluebeard's wife. All this is nonsense. I will change the subject—

I went in town Thursday to attend a party at Mrs Dr Ford's. Since Christmas a number of ladies have clubbed together to have a party alternating first at one house and then at another— Music furnished and no refreshments. Invitations are given for cold water entertainments or as one of Mrs Cohen's servants said in giving an invitation "dey water parties" and in some cases I expect there is a terrible irony in the remark— I had written Ma the day before to have my dress made for me and when I went in I found Aunt Eliza & herself busy sewing on it. I worked with them and that night had the satisfaction of wearing it. It was my purple silk, each width turned, made surplice in front, with apron front and a Pannier. Lizzie Lamkin (Eve) and Ma both said it was becoming and the former said "she never saw me look better in her life." Even Mr Thomas admitted when questioned that I looked "very well."

It was a bitter cold night. I wore my heavy sacque with crimson opera cloak thrown over it and crimson opera cap. As I left the room I took in my hands a crimson feather fan. As we left the door a gust of wind nearly took away our breaths and just then Mr Thomas saw the fan! "Good Heavens" said he "what do you want with a fan. Do hide it." I was so thoroughly chilled that I was tempted to follow his advice and left it in the dressing room. Later in the evening I enquired of him "if [he] had noticed any fans?" He replied "No" and I then showed him half dozen which were held in the hands of persons near us and then explained to him that a fan was considered an indispensable article of a ladies toilette at a party. But aside from its giving tone to my dress I really did not care for it and only reminded Mr Thomas that he must not infringe upon my perogatives. . . .

I had a pleasant time as I generally do at parties. During the evening a quadrille was formed for the old people. Dr Ford (Dr Dasy)[14] wished me to dance with him but I was amused in looking on. Dr Lewis Ford danced with Mrs Gen Wright who was the prettiest lady in the room. Dr Henry Campbell danced (for the first time he said) with Mrs Ford, Gen Wright with Mrs Butts & Dr D Ford with I have forgotten who it was— Gen Wright came up to Mrs Butts & I & knelt upon the floor and wished her to dance. She refused & turning to me he said "It is not worthwhile to ask Mrs Thomas. She always refuses to dance with me but we Methodists are coming out" said he. "We are having tableaux at the theatre, organ music and concerts charging a dollar at the door and so on."
. . .

•   •   •   •

Monday, February 15, 1869 . . . Saturday I was visiting. Called to see Mrs Allen, Twiggs, Bryan, Coe & Neely. In the afternoon I went to see Mrs Shackleford and Mrs Shoop. Very well for country visiting. I drove or rather Turner drove the new Mares which Mr Thomas bought last week. They match and drive well together and I am very proud of them for our "old rips" as Turner called them were a sight sad to behold— I have seen Mr Thomas stand beside them this summer and say "Did I ever think I should live to see myself brought to this?" A love for Horses is a passion as deeply woven in Mr Thomas' nature as his love for—whom, shall I say— for—himself? . . .

Saturday night I was very uncomfortable and Sunday morning I found that I was covered with crimson blotches which were painfully irritating. In attempting to walk from one room to another I became giddy, my head swam, everything became dark and I groped my way to the sofa. On Friday morning I had been similarly attacked but not so severe. I came up stairs took a bath and went to bed & have not left my room since. The eruption has not disap-

---

14. Lewis DeSaussere (Dasy) Ford, father of Lewis Ford.

peared but I am relieved of the headache and nausea which I suffered so much from yesterday— I did not send for a physician but consulted a medical book and sent to town for medicine. I am drinking sarsparilla also which I am not sure does me good. Saturday morning Reauben, our bull entered one of our stables and gored one of the mules so badly that she died in a short time after. Since Christmas, he in the same stable gored a mare and caused her death. Today Mr Thomas sawed his horns off.

Sunday, February 21, 1869 Since I wrote last Monday night I have been very sick. That night I was very sick and the next morning had a chill. The night before I sent for Mr Thomas before I went to bed to show him how my arms neck & body was broken out in scarlet blotches. He insisted upon another dose of sarsparilla. I took it & in a few hours woke up in so much pain I sent for him again and consulted him if I should take an emetic. I did so and was so sick the next morning I sent for Dr Eve. He came but I was not relieved until a late hour in the day. The next morning Mr Thomas and Turner went in town. Dr Eve came again and found me with another chill which was followed by high fever, which lasted all day. The large quantity of quinine broke my chill but I suffered very much from the effect of the Morphine.

Morphine always has an unpleasant effect upon me. I would lay perfectly quiet upon the bed, *knowing* that I was there and with my eyes shut I would see a succession of pictures as in a panoramic view, some of them lovely, other[s] hideous. In one case as the view was presented the appearance of a panorama was so true to nature that the picture or frame was pulled back to make the picture complete, exactly as in the shifting of scenery. Sometimes the frame is pushed back to enable the edges to meet, this being done and a few seconds allowed to look upon it, the picture would glide by to be succeeded by others. The beautiful face of Mrs Tom Beall glided by me and while I would willingly have looked longer, it slowly faded from my view to be followed by Lurany one of our servants, both of them are in the spirit world, and of neither of them have I thought or spoken in weeks. Lovely unknown countenances would be presented to my view and as I looked upon them suddenly they push out their tounges and looking like demons would advance towards me. All this would take place while Mr Thomas and the children would be sitting by the fire. . . . I have been better yesterday and today altho not well enough to go to church this morning to hear Mr Hard preach. . . .

. . .

Sunday, March 7, 1869 . . . I am disappointed tonight. I had expected Mr Thomas but he did not come. He left on Tuesday night for Burke & Savannah. He wishes to make arrangements for receiving his supply of provisions from Mr Stark[15] & hopes to secure a tenant at his plantation which will enable him to get his provisions and &c at less cost. . . .

This morning I went in town to church. Hunter drove the Carriage. Ben still continues sick and I am afraid will never recover. I think and fear he has consumption— Jeff went with me and we were both very, very, cold. Mary Bell met me looking very sweet and pretty dressed in her crimson dress, white hat trimmed with crimson, white plush sacque and coloured kid gaiters, with crimson gloves, bow for the neck and hair of the same colour as were the cuff buttons she was wearing. Every article she was wearing except her dress had been given her by Ma, except the gloves which were a present from Aunty. Ma is sending Mary Bell to dancing school and Buddy gave her fifty cents to go to the circus the other night. I am very, very, much obliged but I wonder if persons whom we are owing do not think us extravagant when they see me dressing myself and my children so much. . . . Mr Wright is preaching against the Catholic religion, very unwisely if he would allow me to advise him. The greatest benefit next to praising a book is wholesale abuse of it and the same rule will apply to religion. . . .

May 3, 1869 Today is Monday the beginning of a new week and celebrated in town today as the 1st of May. . . . I had thought of going in town with Turner tonight to witness the celebration as Kate and Mary [Vason] took such conspicuous parts in the ceremony of crowning the queen, but I am not in harmony with such scenes of merriment.

The crisis—the crash has come at last. Mr Thomas has had a sheriff to take possession of his store and on the eleventh of this

---

15. W. H. Stark, Jefferson Thomas's factor in Savannah, Ga.

month his goods will be sold at public auction. Ah me, ah me! Can you wonder that I have not written oftener during the past two or three weeks. For two years I have watched a death struggle, have heard every sigh, every groan, have seen the anguished brow, the convulsed lip—have seen *the mask* off, and have known that my husband's affairs were terribly involved, have known too that we were living beyond our means and have been utterly powerless to avert the blow which I knew was coming— I felt when our house was mortgaged to cousin Polly that it never would be ours again. I knew when I signed away my right to it a few months ago that I was only retarding the crisis which has come now. But what could I do! I am glad it has come.

"An[d] it were done, it were well it were done quickly."[16] We would have been infinitely better off had it happened two years ago. The debt which now hangs like an avalanche above us would not have reached such magnitude. There would have been some prospect of freeing ourselves. Poor dear Buddy. His generous act of endorsing for Mr Thomas will involve him in trouble. Ma blames him that he did not require collateral or security from Mr Thomas, but I blame Mr Thomas more. Yesterday for the first time I was confidential in talking with Ma with regard to Mr Thomas' business. "I have thought at times that you knew nothing about it" she replied, "that you did not know how much he was involved"— "Not know of it." Heavenly Father! Thou knowest, and thou alone, how much I have known of it—*how* the knowledge of it has deepened the lines upon my face—furrowed my brow & aged my heart. I think I could have borne the loss of property and cheered my husband and toiled by his side but the knowledge that Buddy will lose so much by him paralyses me. Pinck and others have mortgages which will in some degree render them safe but Buddy has nothing— "Not know of it." Oh my God! I have been so proud a woman. What have I done that I should be so punished? My life, my glory, my honour have been so intimately blended with that of my husband and now to see him broken in fortune, health and spirits.

---

16. Loosely quoted from *Macbeth*, act 1, scene 7: "If it were done when 'tis done, then 'twere well it were done quickly."

Monday [Tuesday], May 4, 1869   I have written very little of late. It soothes me to write but I do not wish to record all I have felt during the past few weeks. Mr Thomas' extreme depression of spirits, joined to unusual irritability reacts upon us all. Turner, dear, brave, good boy stands erect by his father's side, his confidant, his friend, bearing on his young shoulders the weighty knowledge of our embarrassed situation. He never murmurs—never complains that he has little spending money—that he has been taken from school and is assisting in ploughing—driving waggons and other farm work. He has little time for reading of which he is so fond, but seizes every opportunity to do so when it does not conflict with his work. Mr Thomas was complaining of his having a book a few days since. He was reading on the load of fodder as it was being drawn home by the mules. I said nothing but greatly prefered that he should have been holding converse with an intelligent author to the illiterate Negro who was driving— Every spare moment he has, he indulges himself by stretching at full length on the shucks in the corn house and reading, sometimes newspapers, sometimes novels. I am not afraid of the latter. He encounters enough of the real, hard, practical side of life in his everyday experience to counteract the effect produced by novels. . . .

I have borne a brave front as Ma's remark "I thought you had not known" would prove, but I am a coward where public opinion is concerned and where honour is involved. I was in Augusta last week, went in the Carriage. We are ploughing our Carriage Horses but they are in good condition. Hunter was driving, true, he is a field hand (I have no driver now). He was well dressed and so was I. Altogether I was ashamed to drive down Broad Street and would not go by Mr Thomas' store— The goods have been levied upon— but the doors have not been closed and yet everyone must know of it. I bought me "a love of a bonnet" for eight dollars and a dove coloured barege for which I gave 35 cts pr yd. The bonnet is of the same shade of Neopolitan straw, a pattern hat and bought from Mrs McKimmon who like myself "has failed." My bonnet and dress were bought with money which I had saved by selling some of my last summer dresses, in part payment of the servant's wages—and yet I was ashamed to buy them.

I don't think I am morbid and yet last night Turner went to the party. I do not wish to cloud his young life. I told him to wear a small Diamond pin in his bosom— He objected because "sister had worn it." I did not urge it for I thought "people will notice it and think I had best sell my Diamonds and pay my debts"— I wonder what Buddy will allow me for my Diamond pin in part payment of what we owe him? It was Pa's gift to me but I must not let Pa's boy suffer. I will ask him. Ma says I am singularly short sighted in money matters. I believe I am, but I do believe in trying to pay one's debts and that is the reason I wish that ours had not accumulated to such an extent. . . .

It is night now and since tea I have read that notice which I so much dreaded to see in this morning's paper had I gone in town— and I read it like I read the invitation to "the friends and acquaintances" of my Father to attend his funeral at a stated hour upon a certain day. I read it as I read the other. I was obliged to know that it was so and yet I could not realise it. . . . I will get the newspaper that I may make no mistake. It is headed "U N States Marshall's sale" but the words which follow are "I have levied upon as the property of Mosher Thomas & Schaub" and then follows a list of furniture shelving crockery and &c— Turner Jeff and Julian, my three boys remember that your father tried and struggled very hard to avert this public sale and if anything I have written appears to reflect upon him I did not intend it. I have been very sorry to see the debt accumulate so largely for I hope I am not requiring too much of my three boys when I tell them *to pay their father's debts* and I hope before I die that I shall have the satisfaction of knowing that we owe no man anything.

I have not alluded to my having received the Road Place and four town lots as a portion of my share of Pa's estate.[17] If I knew that Mr Thomas would be permitted to retain his other places and we could obtain a support from them I would be willing for Buddy to take the Road Place and keep it until we could pay what we owe him— I will be satisfied after a support for my family for all I have or can expect to have to assist Mr Thomas in paying his debts. I wish I had more to aid him.

Friday, May 7, 1869 . . . I had expected when I commenced to write to have a quiet time. Happening to look up just then through

---

17. After five years, this was only a partial settlement of Turner Clanton's estate. Gertrude was born at the Road Place and had a special feeling for it, though it was the least valuable of the Clanton plantations. Her receiving it probably took into account Jefferson's debt to the estate.

the open window I saw Cora Lou walking behind a crowd of little coloured children and heard one of them in peremptory tones order her to go back. Mary, Julian's nurse a black girl almost fourteen replied "Let her alone. Let's see what she will do." Here was a case for my interference but no enquiry of mine could make any of them confess what I had just heard except Lina, Diania's nurse the only one who ever receives punishment. The influence of little negroes I have always considered hurtful and we try to have as few as possible. There are three now in the quarter and Diania's nurse and baby make five. With the two Marys I feed and clothe. To distinguish them from each other I proposed to call one Mary & the other Maria, but Mr Thomas objected. We distinguish them now as Mary Clark and Mary Young.

I remember a few years ago that it was an uncommon thing to hear a servant addressed by any other title than that of their master. I do not remember the "ontitles" as they called them of more than half dozen servants we owned before the war. "Trimmings to his name" & "handle to his name" is another favorite style of alluding to their titles— . . . My cook is called Cornelia Shelman and she is the most utterly worthless of all the indolent race— Since breakfast she has added the crowning annoyance of impertinence to her other aggravations and I have dismissed her. I have told her to go home two or three times before but this time I think I will insist upon her leaving. Her father whips her so much and so often I do not like to complain to him. . . .

The moral character of our Negro race is so low. Their standard of morality has always been low but that was not their fault. Some might say that the fault is with them now and not with us. Very true, but as we have assisted in retarding their moral development as a race heretofore, we ought now in justice to assist them in their efforts to do right. We show them so plainly we expect nothing from them. We place no high stand point for them and urge them to gain it. The majority of us expect no more virtue from our Negro men and women than we do from our horses and cows. This may appear plain language— A book has been written of late to prove the Negro a beast signed Aeriel. I did not read it for I was told it was infidel in its teachings. . . . Just here the idea occurs to me that if virtue be the test to distinguish a man from a beast, the claim of many Southern white men might be questionable to the claim of "Man made in the image of his maker" but this is a digression.

I am led to this train of thought by the circumstance of Diania who is living with us. She has been with us since the 1st of August. In January Hunter (Ben Hunter) made her a visit. Mr Thomas hired him & they have been living together as man and wife ever since. That is occupying the same house but neither pretending to claim the other as husband or wife. Diania has been very anxious to have him marry her to which he consented but a great obstacle was in the way. She was married in the summer of 1865 to Gen Hutman's butler or one of his house servants and seven or eight months after gave birth to a boy, whose father was a coloured man and married to someone else. She remained with her husband a few months longer when he left *her* for someone else— Now, she wishes to marry Hunter thinking she will claim him by a greater right than she does at present. I told her she ought to obtain a divorce from her husband and then she could marry Hunter. She went in town, saw Mr William McLaws who told her "she would find it expensive procuring a divorce but not difficult, that it would take time and money but that if she would give him ten dollars and her husband ten, he would write them off a paper which would divorce them." Diania concluded she would avoid the expense and together with her husband signed a paper promising to have no claim on each other.

Armed with these credentials Diania thought she would marry. . . . But just here a rival appears upon the stage of action. . . . Her name is Emma a tall, good looking, brown skinned woman who dresses well and wears a string of very large beads around her neck. . . . [Hunter] went to see her and Diania went after him, told him to come home which he refused to do and did not return until the next morning. She is very confidential and I felt sorry for her until I saw her that day walking with him and as loving as ever— I made some remark about it and said "we ought not to allow them to live together." "I hope you won't interfere unless you wish to deprive me of two excellent hands" said Mr Thomas. "Why Ma" said Turner, "None of them are married who are living in the yard, neither Mollie or Mary Hall are married to their husbands and some man at Mr Robinson's claims aunt Mollie as well as the husband she has here."

Friday, May 14, 1869 . . . I am willing for the children to enjoy themselves and was pleased to have Turner attend the picnic and the party tonight but I shrink from going in town— I am glad that the children having measles will be a good excuse to account for my absence. I would not like them to know the real reason but I wish the nine days to have passed which people will take to discuss our failure! I was reading the *Chronicle* yesterday evening—and I read that attention was directed to the sale of glass ware and &c at the store of Thomas and Schaub "where goods were being sold for half price." I felt my face flush, and I did not recover from it for some time. I have always thought that next to meeting the eye of an offended Jehovah was the terrible ordeal of encountering the gaze of the multitude when our short comings our misdeeds are read out of the book of Judgement. No wonder for the cry for "the rocks and mountains to cover us." Mr Thomas went in the first day of the sale (Tuesday) he has not been since— . . . I am so proud I would dislike for anyone to suspect how much my pride has been mortified— I know many persons who "roll as a sweet morsel under their tongues" the misfortune of their neighbors. . . .

Just as during the war when I fain would think of something else and could not, so now my mind involuntarily returns to the sale. It will be over with this week I hope. Mr Thomas is interesting himself in his farm and I think will be more cheerful after the affairs at the store are closed— He was undecided what to do. At one time thought it would be better to buy the office furniture and try to borrow money and rent the store or rent the store and sell goods on commission. I opposed it for two or three reasons. 1st he has no money to buy goods, and it will not pay to borrow and pay interest (that will ruin anyone at the rate we have been going on) 2d the goods sold on commission would not pay for the rent of the store and the hire of clerks. 3d & by no means least, I would not keep the store where I had been sold out. "The very place to remain" Mr Thomas added but he has dissolved copartnerships, published a notice to that effect but what there was to dissolve is more than I can see. What the future has in store for us God only knows. I do not feel quite so desperate as I did last year when I did not expect anything from Pa's estate. I will at least have a home. I was born at the Road Place. . . .

Aside from the great trouble, I have had minor troubles which are by no means small in their effect upon nerves & temper— My cook Cornelia Shelman (isn't that a pretty Name?) I wish you could see her. A stout black woman about twenty two years old without a perfectly whole garment on—a waist of one kind, skirt of another and as Lizzie Lamkin says "body and soul coming apart." Well, Monday her month was out and I told her I would have no use for her longer. That morning she broke open the potato house and took out a good many. . . . Tuesday I hired a woman by the name of Hannah. She has a husband and several children but she only has a little child three years old with her. She knows, if possible, less of cooking than Cornelia. Her biscuit & waffles & batters are spoilt with sour yeast and the rice, onions and vegatables with salt. This morning after breakfast I was in the yard—went into the kitchen to see if it had been cleaned up. None of the dishes had been washed and in front of the fire was my new cook fast asleep. . . .

. . .

June 1, 1869 . . . As soon as the storm was over we walked out to witness the effect. I then returned and was sewing on Jeff's pants, but my quiet was disturbed by Diania and Hannah quarreling in the yard. The latter had accused Diania of taking potatoes from me and Diania stood at the door of Hannah's room a few days since threatening to have a fight with her. I did not interfere then for some time nor did I this afternoon until Diania still talking in a very loud excited tone told Hannah "she cared no more for white folks than she did black ones. She would take one to the court house just as soon as she would the other" and alluded to Hannah's mistress "as poor old white folks." I thought it was time to interfere then and told Diania she must hush talking so. To this she paid not the slightest attention and repeated the same thing over again. Mr Thomas coming out into the piazzi told Diania she must not talk so but this appeared to infuriate her the more and she raged for some time longer for the edification of the farm servants, threatening "to take Hannah to court and &c"— "You brought it all on yourself" said Mr Thomas to me. "Why did you interfere? I can do nothing. I can dismiss them or shoot them but nothing more"— I had requested no assistance from him but I thought and still think that Diania or any other servant should be reproved when indulging in such loud impudent talking unchecked by my presence, for she knew I was in the hall where I could hear every word she said. As he says "What can we do?" . . .

. . .

10. Conjugal Discord

And my nature, never gentle, becomes indignant.
—January 9, 1870

June 19, 1869 ... I am worried about a paper I signed the other day, this time not without reading what I signed. It was a lien upon the crop in Columbia [Road Place] for $800 and a lien upon the crops in Burke for any reasonable amount. This is done in order to procure provisions to run the plantations this year. Mr Thomas had requested me to carry in the paper and have two persons to witness it. This I had done but two of the gentleman of the family were not at Ma's at the same time & it had not been done— On Monday at her request I rode in the carriage (after signing my name to both papers) to the store and acknowledged before Mr Murphy and Cowling my signature. They acting as witnesses. That night when I came home remembering Ma's warning to be careful how I signed papers in Mr T's embarrassed situation or I would lose the little sum I had settled upon me, I asked Mr Thomas if his crops in Burke were levied upon as his store had been could not his factors in Savannah fall back upon the crops in Columbia? He said "No" but that he would consult his lawyer he had not thought of that. He said so & I was satisfied until tonight I enquired of him if he consulted Mr Shewmake. He replied "No" but that he asked several men & they said a lien upon the crop would come in before any other claim. "Were those men lawyers?" said I. "Were they any better qualified to form an opinion than yourself?" "No" he replied but that Stark (his factor) would be a pretty fool to advance supplys without knowing what he was about knowing the condition of his (Mr T's) affairs.

I might render my Journal much more spicy were I to relate conversations verbatim but I omit the garniture with which Mr Thomas clothes most of his remarks to render them emphatic— Alas, a habit into which he has fallen since the war, and in which

317

he bids fair to become the character for whom Bill Arp[1] advertised a few years since. I was not and am not satisfied. If Mr Thomas has his crop levied upon have not I risked the small sum my children have left. I am willing to do all I can but I cannot forget Kaolin.[2] All I ask is to be safe—and cling for their sake to the little I have left to clothe & educate them with. Those men did not know the condition of Mr Thomas' affairs as I do. Sometimes I ask myself am I right to express myself with regard to my husband's pecuniary affairs as I do? But no one will read this book until all the incidents to which I refer will be of the past, and my children will know that I tried to act for the best.

Mr. Thomas' prospects both in Burke and Columbia are encouraging and on this place he is doing well. If he is permitted to retain his planting interest he may yet do well. He is asleep now. He thought I did not have confidence in his judgment, and I would have been better satisfied to have been sure I had acted right. He would not consult with me and in self defence I will talk with you and I have my reward. I am reminded of the story of the man who married a woman with 60 cts and he only 50 cts and he vowed she had been throwing up the odd 10 cts to him ever since. I hope I do not illustrate that woman in the persistency with which I cling to and do not wish to lose the little I own. Most men dislike to admit that their wifes own anything. It is all the masculine "my" and "my own" which they use and in polite circles it would be considered in bad taste for a woman to say "my plantations" "my horse" "my cows" altho they are really as much her own as the dress she wears.

I heard one of the farm hands illustrate the idea forcibly a few days since. She (Mollie) wished her account seperate from her husband's so she would know how she stood. "What's mine is mine," she said "and what's tother folks is tother folks." "Robin" (her husband) she said "liked to buy too much sweet things, too much sugar and such like to put in his belly and I likes to put on my

---

1. Charles Henry Smith, a writer for the *Atlanta Constitution*, wrote under the name "Bill Arp." He became popular during and after the war for his humorous way of expressing southern sentiments.

2. Kaolin is a fine white clay used in the manufacture of porcelain. Deposits were being worked in the Augusta area and Jefferson Thomas had invested heavily, through the purchase of stock, in one such venture—probably related to the business of his store.

back." This she said and proved herself a true woman. As I laughingly told some gentleman the bill securing a married woman's property had been passed now that most of the women in Georgia had nothing to lose—like locking the stable door after the Horse has been stolen. Mr Thomas is very liberal—inclined in some things as I tell him to be extravagant. He trades with the servants at the plantations for chickens & eggs— They send me a good supply of butter and with an excellent vegatable garden & fruit pastry for dinner fried chicken for breakfast—teacake for tea we are quite comfortable. I would like to sell the vegatables but there are so many in market. . . .

Sunday, June 20, 1869 This morning after giving out dinner I assisted Diania in dressing Mary Bell, Cora Lou & Jeff to attend Sunday School. Hunter who has been engaged to work on the farm during the week & drive on Sundays had gone to town when I ordered the carriage without notifying any of us. I called old uncle Robin who was in the quarter. He came to the door stripped naked to the waist— I told him to get the carriage. I suppose it took him some time to complete his toilette for when the children were dressed the horses had not been harnessed. There was nothing to do but to have the children walk to school or arrive there too late. Mr Thomas is so much afraid of losing some of his hands, for they are difficult to obtain that he will tolerate some things which I will not. Implicit obedience and the utmost respect I require from those I employ about the house— I am polite & demand the same. I always try to pay promptly and require that a positive order I give shall be obeyed. I am fortunate in having obtained a good cook. She came Thursday June 10th and it is refreshing to have someone who understands her profession. Hannah is attending the dairy. We have four little calves born within the past six weeks but we will have to dismiss her. I am sorry for her. She has a child two years old & expects soon to have another. Her old mistress has her eldest child. Diania went in town with me taking her little boy whom she leaves with a married coloured woman whom she calls Miss Green. . . .

.   .   .

June 26, 1869 . . . I have indulged myself in more leisure than usual since my return from Augusta & spending several days with Ma. A coloured woman a very bright mulatto is living in the neighborhood with Mr Towns who rents a portion of Mr Ware's land. She sews beautifully & has been making some of Jeff's jackets. She returned the work a few days since by her little girl & said she could not finish it. I was not at home but Hunter said because the little girl's father was sick. The child is very bright & there was only one inference. I do not believe she said it nor do I think he is her father. She bears too strong resemblance to someone else. I asked aunt Lily a few days ago if Mr Towns was well, wishing to send more sewing. She did not know but said she saw his children at church Sunday. This relationship is so common as to create no surprise whatever. I have never met with an educated coloured woman before this one. She belonged to the Sniders of Savannah & was bought by their daughter Mrs Dawson just before the birth of her second child. She sent to me a short time since for the newspapers to read as she was "so lonely." She had told me that she had read a great many novels. I could not understand before why she used such good language, rather high flown but well expressed. She spoke of young mistress as "dying just as she budded into womanhood." I sent her a magazine to read for I felt sorry for her. I have always thought education a questionable blessing for servants during slavery times.

The laws of our state permit Negroes to vote & hold offices but forbid their marriage with white persons. I sometimes think I am ahead of my time—that my ideas are more liberal, more advanced than they ought to be but blood is blood and I predict that in the next generation, that which I confess to me would be a stigma of disgrace will then be no especial drawback in matrimonial alliances. The bright mulatto man & especially woman who has coursing in his or her veins the blood of the first men in the South, first in talent. I don't say anything about the morality side of the questions. I am handling the subject fearlessly as a great social problem. I predict that these persons never having known the weight of bondage & having received the equalizing influence of education will be received socially into some familys. I make this prediction because already I see social equality between our uneducated women & our late servants, & I see the contrast between black as well as mulatto women who have (without the education of books) been trained under the most refined associations. I am forced to see the difference between them & some white help I have employed. It is for this reason I would cry aloud for education for our children thorough and complete. What was it but blood &

education which gave so much power to Aaron Alpeoria Bradley[3] in our late legislature? Sometimes I think our people are blind. They do not see the hand writing upon the wall. There must always have been a strong affinity for the two races or else as one of the same members enquired last year "why so many ring streaked and striped among our (the black) colour?"

The boys of our country poor as well as rich must be educated, must have instilled and ever kept before them the idea of social & mental superiority & this must be no imaginary idea of caste but a real, substantial fact. I commend industry but parents are making (many of them) a great, a very great mistake in having their boys descend too suddenly to the rank of the day labourer. Boys who were born heirs to thousands plough daily side by side with the Negro who perhaps works for his victuals & clothes. Commenced early and continued can this go on without degradation? I have seen that it requires three generations to make a gentleman. Can this white boy with the aid of hereditary antecedents accomplish nothing more than the one beside him? What are his talents for—? Let this continue—& while he follows the plough, his education totally neglected, permit the mulatto boy, perhaps his father's son by a woman a shade darker than *his* mother, let him receive an education, common or collegiate and where will caste be then in the respective influence those two men will exert, each voting each holding office?

I look around & I see worthy men who talk about their sons being indispensable in the field, "hands are so scarce" and to obtain a hand the boy's head suffers and he grows up an ignoramus while negro women toil and strive, labour and endure in order that their children "may have a schooling." "What a man puts into his head" Dr Franklin tells us "no one can take away from him." For this reason I again repeat, our children, the children of the country should be educated. We have the superiority of race by nature & education. Let us see that we maintain it and then all laws concerning marrying or giving in marriage will be useless. As it is the law is almost an insult to Southern woman. I know that what I have written will appear inconsistent. I do not allude to society as

---

3. Aaron Alpeoria Bradley was a controversial black politician elected to the Georgia legislature. He operated a shoe repair shop in Augusta for a brief time.

it now exists, but society as it will exist hereafter unless we interpose the strong barrier of education. If instead of legislating and making laws prohibiting the white men from marrying the coloured woman & vice versa they had made more liberal laws for educating the boys of our country then there would have existed no necessity for the first prohibition. No fear that the men of the South will form alliances with the Negro women in marriage *as they now are*— There may be some isolated instances as indeed there have been of white women but they were the dark spots upon the sun, so isolated as to form no opinion from their actions. Educate our boys & all will be right. Our girls require no training. Natural feminine instinct will be their guide, as it ever has been.

.   .   .

August 7, 1869 An eclipse of the sun is taking place! That announcement is important enough to give it a line for itself especially as astronomers tell us that a similar event will not take place in one hundred years. . . . Just after, Turner came into the room, "Oh Ma" said he "come out and see the eclipse, hurry. Where is a piece of glass to smoke?" I left my work and went into the back yard where I found all the servants wondering and exclaiming. The surface of the sun was dark and across it was gliding something like a cloud—a few moments after it was the distinct appearance of a new moon and gradually the moon grew larger and larger at one time having a halo of yellow and at another time of blue immediately around it. Smoked glass was in requisition among us but I must confess to being disappointed. . . . "Look" said one of the negro men interrupting uncle Robin "look at the moon. She is laying flat of her back." I looked and found she had altered her position growing larger and everything growing lighter. I came in and commenced to write but could not see the lines very distinctly. I went out into the Piazzi again and was struck by the peculiar light like sulphur thrown over everything. Cora Lou and Julian and M Belle's aprons were perfectly yellow. Julian was playing in the yard with an empty ale bottle trying to fill it with dirt. He is now eighteen months old. I knelt by his side and told him to look at the sun, but he was too much interested in his bottle. Dinah said "the strangest part to her was how people could tell it was gwine to take place" and I could but think so too. . . .

At night. . . . Yesterday I cut out a muslin and today a calico by the princess or gored pattern and have nearly finished both dresses. The long seams are nicely adapted to the machine. . . . I think of going up to see Aunty & cousin Polly next week. My relatives are practical common sense honest people and they will approve of my trying to make my own dresses. It is a very good thing this talk about the approval of one's conscience but approval of someone else helps to shed additional light upon one's pathway. Mr Thomas never praises. I wish he did. Now in this matter of the dresses I told him what I had done not expecting one word of commendation, nor was I disappointed for I did not receive one word of approval— I have learned not to expect it but to do him justice neither did he have the slightest objection to my having it or any other article made out and will if he has the money pay for it without one word of complaint. . . . Mr Thomas is more liberal than he can afford to be and it is just there that I do not think he appreciates my puny efforts at trying to stop the floodgates of debt with which I feel that we are contending. But I do not think that he is the man to appreciate a wearied woman, wearing a faded calico till she can afford a better one, so much as a gay woman, fashionably dressed in clothing for which she is owing the money they cost. . . .

Saturday, September [25], 1869 Holt wrote Ma Aug 20th telling her "this will be my last letter to you before sailing. I sail tomorrow at one oclock on the *Lafayette* one of the French Atlantic steamers. . . . As soon as I arrive upon French soil I will telagraph you and as soon as I am in Paris and recovered from my journey I will write you a long letter and you all must write to me *very very* often."

Dear darling Holt. I look upon his signature N Holt Clanton and I press my lips to it and think perhaps I may never see it again. His letter was dated Aug 20th and today is Sep 25th. He ought to have reached France Sept 1st and we have heard nothing from him since he sailed—no telagraph no letter, and yet last Tuesday night as I lay awake in bed I thought Holt's spirit communed with mine, and told me he was in the spirit world. "Sister" said he "I come to you because I know you have more faith than any other member of our family. I died two weeks since as I was on the steamer." "But Holty" said I "why have we heard nothing of it?" "'The Captain did write Ma but he was obliged to wait until he reached Havre before he could mail the letter" was his reply. "I have seen Pa" he added. "He is in a lower sphere and I expect to see him again but I have seen nothing of your children or Sis Anne's. I suppose they are in a higher sphere." I enquired, "Are you happy Holty?" "Well" said he "I am in a new country. You know I started for a new country and this is nothing more."[4] . . . I called Mr Thomas and enquired when Sis Anne had heard from Holt thinking [if] a dispatch had been received from Holt to Ma she would have received it during Ma's absence in New York. Thursday I went in town and enquired of Sis Anne. Nothing has been heard from him. Col Vason said "Holt was too sensible to telagraph when it was so expensive, two dollars a word." "But Ma gave him the money for that purpose" said I. He insisted "Holt was too sensible," but he could dispatch one word "Safe" and save a world of anxious thought. . . .

I have neglected writing in my Journal during the past few weeks. I am going to be confidential with you dear friend and tell you that for some time past I have hoped to write and publish something of what I write and in that way some of the time I would have given to you has been monopolised by other writing. I wrote a story founded upon real life and after it was written called it, *How One Woman Loved.* . . . The story written and the momentous question of a title having been decided upon and the labourious duty of copying on one side in strict accordance with newspaper rules & then I had to decide what editor I should select to publish it. *The Land We Love* has recently been united with the *Southern Eclectic* and I thought I would have it published in that magazine. . . . I sent the letter and the story, placed a post stamp upon both and neglected to pay for return postage. I sent them and then waited.

A few weeks passed and then one day Turner coming home handed me a letter and one to his father. Upon the envelope of mine was written D H Hill. At no time when a young girl have I felt more emotions upon the receipt of a letter. Making some excuse I rose and leaving the hall went into the wing room and opening the letter read— Charlotte, N[orth] Carolina— Mrs J Jefferson

---

4. Gertrude Thomas showed an unusual preoccupation with life after death and the spiritual world, especially after her father's death. She sought answers from diverse religious doctrines and from the writings of Emanuel Swedenborg (1688–1772), the Swedish philosopher and theologian.

Thomas, Dear Lady, It always pains me to disappoint a true Southern lady, but the *New Eclectic* publishes only selected matter. I
have been sending the military pieces and have no other editorial
connection. My colleagues are so afraid of offending the Yankees
that I have now nothing to do with them. The mss is at your dis-
posal. With great respect D H Hill. . . . I wish Gen Hill had told me
candidly what he thought of that story. As an editor he could judge
if it was worthy of publication. As he has no interest in the editorial charge I do not know that he read it for my handwriting will
daunt most persons I am well aware. I do not think I am cowardly.
If the surgeon's knife is necessary I could nerve myself for it and I
would be glad of an unbiased opinion from a good judge but I expect
then I would write because I could not help it, but then I would
forego the wish to publish. . . .

January 9, 1870 Reading over old Journals to me is sad work. It is
holding "the mirror up to nature" and there I see much reflected
which is discouraging and depressing. When I was younger I was
constantly promising that I would live better, do better, endeavour
"to be up and doing." Of late years I notice I promise less. Warned
by sad experience I cannot trust myself. I have learned how frail I
am. This is well if it does not degenerate into indifference, and oh
my Journal this is too much my present condition. I appear to be
fast becoming a fatalist. I often think "What is to be, will be." I am
sceptical and indifferent to religious interest. . . . I find that I cannot confess even to you my Journal without condemning Mr T. I
must say this much, that habitual profanity consequent upon loss
of property has become a sad habit with my husband. Perhaps I
ought not to mention this but if I could learn my children how
terrible it is in its consequences I would gladly do so. Having said
this much I can better explain that the Heavens are so far away and
can I say God too near? It is impossible for a person with my reverential ideas to hear the name of God profaned so constantly without great pain. Alas I fear I am becoming accustomed to it and as I
do my reverence for God lessens and my ideas and faith become
bewildered. I remonstrate but in vain. And my nature, never gentle,
becomes indignant & I am no meek and lowly disciple but like
Peter am hot headed & say words for which I am sorry. . . .

The clouds gather around us and betoken a heavy storm. Mr
Thomas is again worried terribly about his property. Cousin Polly
(Mrs Walton) has levied upon his house on Greene Street through

her agent William Walton. . . . Mr Thomas thought he could make arrangements to pay the interest and after the note Mr T wrote him I think Mr Walton's conduct was singular, to say the least of it. Granting that Mr Thomas had not paid it, it would only have been deferred one month. By a singular coincidence I remember that when Mr Thomas wrote his will just before leaving for Virginia, having a large property to dispose of he requested me to select Mr Walton as my legal adviser. Mr Walton was one of the arbitrators in settling how Pa's will should be decided. I am not apt to forget my obligations to Mr Walton. So the Greene Street house has been levied upon for $5000 dollars. Well I expected nothing more. I sit and talk with Mr Thomas and try and cheer him taking care not to worry him by saying "I told you so" but what can I do? I particularly wish that Buddy should not suffer. My theme is unpleasant, my fire is going out. I am cold and disheartened. Mr Thomas went down to Burke today & the children are asleep. I can neither look backward or forward but feel that I am drifting wither I know not.

Monday, January 10, 1870 . . . I wonder if we will ever live to know this feeling of freedom [from debt]. I greatly fear not. Mr Thomas is too much embarrassed but I have three boys to whom I leave this request, *pay your father's debts.* For myself I could be content with very little. Pinck and Jule are in some degree secured by a mortgage upon the plantation in Burke, but aside from the Kaolin stock which is worthless, Buddy has nothing to secure him. I pressed, urged upon Mr Thomas the necessity of giving him or Mr Rowley to whom the money is due, a lien upon the crop made in Columbia and endeavour to make our support out of this place and the farm. Mr Thomas says it will not support us. I know it will or rather I will make our expenses so small that it will be enough for us.

I have read a great deal of a woman's endurance under pecuniary trials. A great deal of romantic, beautifully written sentiment about cheering a desponding husband, soothing his dejection and &c. I wonder if it ever occurred to anyone to realise or imagine how a proud woman feels under such circumstances? A woman who is identified so completely with the interest of her husband that his success or failure is hers. True, men have the world to face while woman may stay at home and become morbid in indulging in mortified pride. Men go out into the world & endeavour to retrieve their loss & come home depressed dejected and irritable, glad of a safety valve for the annoyance of the day. They come to wifes who have been fretted with careless servants and crying children, fretted by little worries while the ever present thought of debt is pressing like an iron weight upon them. They come expecting to find a soothing welcome, gentle words and loving glances, and here dear Journal I try to do my duty. I have a bright fire, do my best to have tea ready and a fire, to have the children taken to bed directly after tea knowing how essential perfect quiet is to tortured nerves. Know this as only a woman can know I have the will to do this but my cook had tea late and this was annoying to Mr T and seating himself in an attitude of abject dejection his head aching if a child touches his chair & so nervous that the least thing annoys him, Mr Thomas presents an appearance well calculated to try my nerves.

Tea over & the children in bed we commence upon the one theme of business. I listen and when I would urge some step being taken Mr Thomas complains that my manner is too decided. Like Byron I imagine he likes "a low sweet voice in a woman." I am here all day. I see how idle the servants on the farm are but what can I do? If I tell him it worries him and causes him to indulge in some expressions "both loud and deep." He begs me not to interfere and I try to obey him & be indifferent. If the corn crib is exposed, if the hands remain longer than they ought at 12 oclock I try not to let it annoy me, but I can't help begrudging them the allowance which they so promptly claim and think that it lessens our chance to pay our accounts.

It is now the 10th of January. No arrangements have been made either in Burke or Columbia for a new crop. The negroes refused to contract before Christmas and again in Augusta on the 1st day of Jan. Last year they worked for a third of the crop in Columbia and fed themselves. This year they require us to feed them and give them a fourth. Mr Thomas had a terrible cold almost amounting to pneumonia last week. . . . Yesterday Mr Thomas left for Burke. I tried to dissuade him but he said he had lost so much time by being sick. "Well, go to the Road Place" said I. "It is more important that that place should be cultivated and a good crop made than in Burke. You are sure of that place." "No" he replied "Let them wait. They would not sign when he wished them to" & sent word to them he would be up there some time last of the next week but told them to go to work today. I do not expect they will do a day's work until he does go & they may leave and engage with others. We cannot afford to be independent of them for labour is so scarce particularly in

Conjugal Discord . 327

Columbia. I wish sometimes that such matters did not annoy me but I appear to see so clearly when things are wrong that it is impossible to resist telling Mr Thomas—not in a fault finding manner. I never attempt the slightest interference. I only advise him and this I seem to be unfortunate in my manner of doing. . . .

Talking one day I said to Mr Thomas "that he ought not to have involved Buddy without securing him in some way." His reply was that "I found too much fault when he had done his best." "Bear with me" I added "and remember that I have never complained *of you.* There are enough to do that without my being one of the number." So instead of talking to others and annoying Mr Thomas with the troubles of which my heart is full, I have recorded more confidentially than usual the trials which torment me. I have not written much during the winter because I had nothing pleasant to record. I have been very very busy during the short December days cutting & sewing, just as busy as I could be. . . .

When Ma went North she brought the children and I some very nice articles of dress. I sent by her for an alapaca walking dress and then afterwards let Ma take it so that I could buy Jeff a handsome suit. . . . I have a great dislike to being thought extravagant and would often like to explain "Good people, Ma gave me this." My 25 cts worsted & 15 cts calico are all the new dresses I have bought this winter. Ma bought me a Brumond, Cora Lou a hat & Julian one. All the children are fitted up for the winter & I feel that I can rest from my labours for a while. I have written until I am relieved of my depression in some degree and will stop.

Thursday, January 13, 1870   I had just taken my seat intending to write having a good fire and Mr Thomas & the children asleep when I heard Ned calling to tell us that someone was at the front gate. . . . "Who is that" I said. "Don't be afraid mam I will not hurt you" was the reply. The idea of being afraid had not occurred to me. "I am not afraid" I replied "but who are you" for I had discovered from the uneducated tones of the voice that she was no guest of mine. Coming into the Piazzi she enquired if Mr Thomas was at home. I told her yes that he had gone to bed but I would deliver her message. "I wish to see Mr Thomas" she replied "I ought not to tell you." In the moonlight I could not tell wether she was a white or coloured woman her face being concealed by a cra[c]ker bonnet. "What is your name" I enquired. "Louisa" was her reply and then I knew that she was coloured but her answer had excited my curiosity as was natural and I again enquired "what she wanted with Mr Thomas." "Oh it is dreadful mam" said she. "I don't think I ought to tell you." By this time I was quite decided that she should and I replied "Just as you please but it is cold out here" making a step to enter the house. "So it is" she said and then added "I had just as well tell you." . . .

Poor creature, her history is that of many of her sex as well as colour, a case of disappointed affection—of slighted love. "Hell hath no fury like a woman scorned" and here was another illustration. "Oh Mrs Thomas" said she, "You do not know how things are going on at the Rowell Place." She then proceeded to relate that Mr Morris was always drinking, the Negroes supplied him with whiskey and that yesterday he was so crazy that he had to be pulled out of the river by force. That night he had cursed and abused her, had thrown her furniture out of the window and all this she could have stood but there were witnesses to it. Mr Morris is farming on shares with Holt and Kate at the Rowell Place. The woman was very much excited. I know that her motive was revenge and yet through all her talk she tried to excuse him. She said she was bought by him and had been living with him ten years. I expect she came between his wife and himself and tonight realises in some degree the feeling she has caused or rather been made to cause. I think he is a widower, a man of common origin and but little education. The woman's reluctance to tell me arose from her not knowing how I would receive the news of her connexion with Mr Morris.

This relationship is so common as to create no emotion of surprise. Her information amounted to nothing more which she gave to Mr Thomas. Her object being to induce him to prevent the negroes from selling whiskey to Mr Morris, or a blind impulse to injure him in some way. He has one child a little girl, "And oh Mrs Thomas" she said, "He ought not to keep that child on the plantation. It ought to be at school. I nursed it. I love it & do the best I can for it but I am coloured mam." The woman has gone now and I told Mr Thomas that such things as this made me shudder when I look into the future and see white women and mulattoes prove rivals unconscious though the former may be— Education will but intensify the tropical, passionate nature of the coloured woman and the South may witness more instances such as Mrs King records in "Lily."

.   .   .

Saturday, January 22, 1870 . . . Ma sent me a letter today Kate had received from Holt. He is still in Paris & expected to leave on the sixth of this month for Switzerland and Italy. He has now been four months in Paris. Urging Kate to study and be the flower of the flock and bright one of the family he adds "no very difficult task if you but apply yourself and improve your opportunitys but you will meet a bright and formidible rival in Sis Trudy. You will find her a host within herself *and to pass her you must study*. She is one of whom any family might be proud." Dear Holt—like rain upon the thirsty soil fell your kind and flattering opinion. It was pleasant to read such an opinion expressed by my young brother. But very greatfully I appreciated the tender expression "dear Sis Trudy." Holt is usually chary of terms of endearment which causes me to thank him the more for this. I expect I am morbid but my pride has suffered greatly of late. With the exception of this expression of Holt's I have met with no expression of sympathy from one member of my family. None of them have been to see me. Ma and Sis Anne have no Carriage. . . .

Thursday, January 27, 1870 Reading over what I have written I have the conciousness of knowing that I am morbid. I know cousin Polly has a right to what is owing her, but her having advertised the house has caused others to present their claims and caused Mr Thomas great anxiety of mind. I have been sick with terrible cold for the last two weeks. Several days I was in bed from which at times I almost wished I would never have to rise again. One morning Mr Thomas was leaving for town utterly unable to know what the day or hour would bring forth, what new execution would be levied. Coming to the side of my bed he kissed and bid me Good bye and left. "Oh Pa! Pa!" I thought "if you were living this would not be so. You would help us with your good judgement, or cheer me with some kind word." As I thought of him I burst into tears and wept such tears as relieve the pressure of an overburdened heart. I think I am like my father in many things, in none more so than in my quiet indomitable pride—that pride which would make me "suffer and make no sign."

And now my Journal let me tell you a strange thing which happened a few nights since. Before I went to bed I knelt and prayed earnestly to God to help Mr Thomas, to show him some way to relieve himself of the terrible oppression of debt and while I prayed I thought of Pa, and I asked God if spirits were permitted to visit their friends upon earth to commission the soul of my father to commune with mine that night. I hoped that in the quiet watches of the night Pa would come to me and tell me what was best for us to do. I rose, took paper and pen from the desk and seating myself by the fire I thought if Pa could only guide my pen and give me his autagraph I would instantly recognise it. I had heard of such things as one's feeling the pressure of the invisible hand which guides the pen. I felt nothing of the kind. My pen glided on and made the signature of T Clanton but I am almost certain I had no spiritual assistance. . . .

. . .

March 6, 1870 That day the 1st of Mch the first Tuesday in the month Mr Thomas rode in town. I remained at home and determined I would not take time to think. I went out into the vegatable and flower garden and had beets planted and a hedge of flowering peas prepared leading from the wing room. I tried to interest myself but the thought would constantly occur "Now at this hour, the announcement is being made that"— What shall I say? Not that my husband has failed for that was known last summer when the goods were sold at the store, but this was an additional calling of the public to notice our degradation, perhaps that is too strong a word, but *Oh it is humiliating*— Ma consoles me by telling me that "we are not the first, or only people who have been advertised by the sheriff." I know that, but it is little consolation to a person terribly deformed to know that there are some cases in the world as bad & perhaps worse than his own. . . . We have enough left yet of this world's goods to keep hunger from the door and my boys will certainly be able to support themselves and aid their sisters. If Mr Thomas was more hopeful it would infuse new life and vigor into our little family circle. . . .

. . .

Belmont. July 30, 1870 This is Saturday. The farm hands are taking holiday for the purpose of attending a picnic to be given by the col Babtist church. . . . I gave [Charlotte] a white dress to wear and a ribbon for her sash. America is with us now, and she had her daughter, Fannie, dressed in a new white swiss dress with several small ruffles on the skirt. . . . With Mary Belle and Cora Lou I went down to the church to hear Fannie and Charlotte repeat their pieces. At the church I found a large no of servants. The young people were nicely dressed and engaged in singing and dancing. At the church we were met by a coloured man who invited us to go into the church. Soon after the Carmichael girls came.

The dancing on the green continued and our presence did not apparently have the slightest effect in abashing them. Among the dancers I recognised many of Pa's and our old servants. This is the first meeting of the kind I have attended since their emancipation. The different societys composed of three Sunday schools marched into the white people's church and had prayer alternating with singing. A bright mulatto mentioned as Mr Randolph was from Augusta as the superintendant of one of the schools. I have heard persons when talking about the intelligence of the coloured race, attribute all the intellect they possessed to the white blood in their veins. In this case two of the children were very bright, the children of Mr Ware who for years has lived with his slave Mary, a bright mulatto woman and with her has raised a large family of children. Mr Ware was of good family, with good blood and talent cultivated by education to transmit to his children but the other two children were black and the little boy one of the brightest children there. I do not intend that he was of the thick lip, African type, like Milly Ann Johnson, his sister was more in that order, but a black boy with regular features and slight form. One of the brightest intellects I have ever seen among the coloured people was Sam Drayton who used to preach down at this same church, and he was a black man.

After the coronation and speeches from the Rosney Sabbath School, the man they called Mr Randolph addressed the audience. . . . "My friends this is a great thing, this coronation. A few years back and such a thing was unheard of among you. If any of you had dared to crown a queen as you are doing today you would have been striped and not your back only but from your head to your feet, is not this so my friends?" "Not that I know much of it myself" he added. "Now there are many kinds of crowning. Some crown a queen & some of us a president. Now who knows, the way things are working some of you may be crowned President of the United States some of these days." My Journal you have known me for a long time. You can understand *my* sentiments, comment is unnecessary and yet that negro as he took his seat and with an air of importance glanced over toward where we sat had sense enough left to know he had gone a little too far. There was no smile upon our faces but neither was there the slightest indication of anger. He with his sentiments was infinitely too contemptible for anything else than an apt illustration of the idea "that a little learning is a dangerous thing." Previous to this we had openly smiled and expressed our admiration of his singing. After this we contented ourself with ignoring him altogether. . . . We were invited to remain to dinner but did not.

My impression was that notwithstanding the time which has elapsed, and the advantages which many of them had had an opportunity of receiving, the Negroes as a class have made little progress. The Stokes children were the exception and the only ones aside from some of the bright mulattoes who evinced talent in the slightest degree. I do not think it is because they are incapable of being educated, instinct and knowledge makes me reject the Aerial doctrine but I think it is because "the blind are leading the blind." The teachers know but little, and they have no instructors aside from the coloured and Yankee teachers, and the latter seldom teach in the country. . . . Mr Thomas and Jeff remained to dinner with Mr & Mrs C[armichael] and their children. They had a seperate table and were treated quite hospitably but to my taste it is pleasanter to confer than receive a favour from an inferior. Mary Belle was telling me that Nancy and Tamah were both of them there. . . . [Nancy] has been up to see me several times and has sent her children up when I always give them something. She has a daughter named Ella Gertrude for me. . . .

.   .   .   .

Monday, August 1, 1870 . . . I am tired and worried and not in an agreeable humour. I was thinking of resting on the bed by Julian and trying to sleep, but just then I saw my open Journal, just as I had left it and thought I would continue to write. I do not like to record my dull heavy moments in my Journal. I would like for it to record nothing but brightness and sunshine, but life is made up of light and shadows and my own is not an exception. . . .

I well remember going to the rink to witness the skating with the consciousness never absent during the morning that everyone who looked upon me would remember that a few days before, at the market, my husband had had his property sold by the sheriff— and I well remember that never had I looked brighter or jested more merrily, while secretly I writhed in mortified pride. The first bitter agony is over and now I, yes I must be candid, I forget it, at times.

You ask me am I a better woman for this chastening. I answer, No—at heart I am rebelious still. Yet, in my own conscience, I think a great deal of what we call bad luck is bad management.

. . . .

August 29, 1870 Our camp meeting is over! And I feel that it has been a success. I am truly grateful for an increased desire to be more religious, to pray and read more, to strive more earnestly to subdue the quick temper which is my besetting sin, and I am doubly grateful that Mr Thomas has evinced a sincere desire to become a Christian and has signified it by going up to the altar "to be prayed for," thus showing that he wished a change of heart.

On Saturday afternoon for the three oclock sermon an elderly man with a long grey beard arose and selecting his sermon he proceeded to tell us the plain duty of parents and feeling the spirit himself, he was enabled to kindle a corresponding sentiment in the heart of his congregation. And no wonder that when the call came for those who wished to try hereafter to be more faithful as parents, more guarded in the example they presented to their children, no wonder that crowds assembled around the altar to pledge themselves to the effort of living better fathers and mothers than ever before. I say it was no wonder and yet it was a joyful surprise to see Mr Thomas leave his seat and approach the altar. I went too and silently lifted my heart to God to bless him and me too— That night when the call was made Mr Thomas knelt at his seat. He did not feel as much as he expected to and indeed I do not think the minister did either— . . . Mr Rush [a minister] reminds me of Dr Lewis Ford of Augusta, altho his social advantages I imagine to have been inferior. His long gray beard, the shape of his head and the general appearance are similar, altho Dr Ford parts his hair in the middle and wears it quite long. I was also reminded of Major Dickinson when such expressions as "Father Intellect" and "Father Nature" would occur in the sermon, the expression sounding very much like [Emanuel] Swedenborg—of whom both Dr Ford and Major Dickinson are disciples— . . .

That night (last night) Mr Parks preached a plain practical sermon. It was followed by an earnest soul stirring inspiring exhortation from Mr Potter. . . . Mr Thomas went up again— . . . [W]aiting until another prayer was offered and almost everyone kneeling I went over to where my husband was kneeling and whispered as I sank on my knees by him "Mr Thomas" and placed my arm around his neck, but what could I say. I who was no better than he? Silently with uplifted heart I remained by his side for a few seconds then I whispered, "I am going now. Pray on, and we will both try to be good," and pressing my lips to his cheek I returned to my seat to join my petition with those who were praying around me and my prayer was, "God be merciful to me, a sinner," for well I knew that the best prayer I could make for my husband was to try and be better myself. . . .

Saturday, September 3, 1870 Dear Journal I have good news for you and but little time to tell it in. I am going North! Think of it. It has been seventeen years since I was there before. . . . The boys, Turner and Jeff will remain with Mr Thomas at home. Cora Lou will stay with Cora, and Jule and Mamie will take charge of Mary Belle & Julian. It has been nearly two weeks since Ma made me very happy by telling me that she would take me North with her. "It was a very good time for me to go," she said "I had no young baby and Julian was old enough to leave." I think she decided to go as much to give me an opportunity for going as for any other cause, and I know my thorough enjoyment of the trip will fully compensate her for the expense she incurs.

Kate is going on to Georgetown to the Convent. I do not know wether I am pleased with the idea or not. I approve of the seclusion in which the scholars are kept & know from experience that it is an admirable plan for a young girl to have none of the distracting influences of parties concerts & &c when she is at school, but the religion! . . . The sad news of Joe's death [Mr. Thomas's brother] and the busy time preparing for Camp Meeting has prevented me from telling the pleasant news before, and during the past week I have been busy preparing the children to leave home. . . .

Washington, September 6, 1870 The ride on the Potomac river this afternoon has given me the most exquisite pleasure. Seated in the bow of the boat, we glided up the river and I felt as if I was in a scene of enchantment. There was scarcely a ripple on the surface of the water which was so beautifully clear that I could but be struck with the contrast between it & the muddy, sluggish streams of the Savannah, Congaree and others which I have seen. The scenery on the river is beautiful and my feelings were in unison when the bell tolled twice as we passed by the residence of Washington, but the view of Mount Vernon is unsatisfactory and obstructed by the growth of trees. . . .

I have given prominence to the ride on the Potomac because I enjoyed it so thoroughly. Since yesterday morning we have been riding on the cars having changed three times. The ride from Richmond was dusty. The whole country having the appearance of having suffered from want of rain. We looked forward to the boat as a "Haven of Rest" and were not disappointed. . . . As the dome of the Capitol came in sight I thought, "How beautiful" and then I thought "how little cause we Southerners have to glory in a place where such humiliating laws are enacted." No I do not love Washington, or its Capitol and yet I am glad that its buildings were not destroyed.

Someday my children will take pride in it. History does but repeat itself. It was only a few days ago that I read that the Bourbon Princes had offered their services to Napoleon[5] to fight for France, that Victor Hugo[6] was wearing the uniform of the Guarde Mobile, all uniting for France— I thought that sufficient time had not elapsed since our revolution to make the majority of Southern men willing to reunite with Grant & resist a foreign foe. So long as negro soldiers guard and Negro men make laws for us just so long will the feeling of resentment linger in our minds. Arriving at the wharf we took tickets for the Metropolitan Hotel and are now in two very pleasant rooms adjoining each other.[7] It is late altho the noise of carriages rattling over the macadimised roads of Pennsylvania Avenue can be distinctly heard. . . . As I entered the hotel a crowd of association arose in my mind. I remembered Pa was with me upon every occasion when I had been here before. And I well remember Henry Clay who was rooming next [to] us at the National Hotel. I listened to him coughing during the night and the next morning I looked upon him with intense interest, fully aware that I was looking for the last time upon one of the mighty men of this country. . . .

---

5. Louis Napoleon Bonaparte III, emperor of France 1852–70.

6. Victor Hugo (1802–85), eminent French poet and novelist. He was exiled by Napoleon III for his antiroyalist political writings.

7. Aunt Lamkin and Lizzie Lamkin Eve were in the party as well; they made up part of a larger group from Augusta.

Wednesday, September 28, 1870 . . . While I was in New York I had no time to write. When I was not on the street or visiting some place of amusement I was in our room where the sound of conversation would prevent me from collecting my thoughts. It was a vain hope to expect that Ma and Aunty would go to sleep before I did, for they can sit up half the night and talk but I was so tired that it was a relief to rest. . . . How great the contrast between this life and that! I ask myself the question, which do I like best? and I reply, "I like both and enjoy both but it is from contrast." I like the whirl, the busy active life of a large city. I like the opera, the theatre, the concert, the lecture, the study of the human face—but then again I like the quiet of a country life in which I have time to commune with my own heart, to remember what I have seen and gather strength from communion with nature. . . .

Thursday, September 29, 1870 I seated myself with the intention of trying to collect my thoughts and as Tupper advises "to give them stability." I had intended to write, but there are so many recollections which come crowding upon my mind, so many events to record, so many impressions to note I scarcely know where to begin but I believe that my interviews with Dr Foster the spiritual medium and my visits to the church of the Spiritualists strike me as being the most novel entertainment I enjoyed while I was in New York.

I had seen Broadway before, had visited Niblos', Walleck's and other theatres . . . I had listened to the magical voice[s] of Patti and Parodi before I heard Madomoiselle Carlotta Millson fill Steinway Hall . . . but never before had I been so near the confine of the spiritual world as when I visited this mysterious man who either by some powerful legerdemain or witchcraft placed me in communication with my father. You know my Journal, for you do but represent in some degree an inner self, how I have longed to know where he is and what doing. . . . I have heard Pa say that if he thought he could communicate with my Grand Father or Uncle that he would meet them at any hour of the night whenever they might appoint. So too would I and the intention was formed and fully matured that I should seek out a powerful medium when I visited New York.

In company with Fanny Casey, Lizzie Eve and Cap Morgan we visited Dr Foster who lives on 4th Street, the number I have forgotten. Upon entering the room up stairs we found a large man with fair complexion and smile or smirk upon his face which made him look silly. His eyes were blue and his form indicated a lymphatic temperament. "Dr Foster," said Cap Morgan, "we have called to receive from you six dollars worth of information about the spirit world." Fanny and I seated ourselves by the table, a round table of ordinary appearance while Lizzie and Cap Morgan took seats on a sofa where they could observe all that took place. Forgetting that I was to pay for the time employed I entered into a talk with Dr Foster concerning his belief, he assuring me "that he believed in the mediation of a Saviour," when a warning glance from Cap Morgan suggested to me the object of my visit. We wrote off the names of our friends with whom we wished to communicate. Mine were "my father Col Turner Clanton, my baby Joe, Joe Thomas and Anna Lou." . . .

I had seen and heard just enough, Fanny's experience being more remarkable than my own, to make me wish to see Dr Foster again. I persuaded Ma to go, and Aunty Lizzie and I accompanied her, he demanding five dollars if others were allowed to remain in the room with her. As Ma was afraid to see him by herself she agreed to this. Ma was quite systematic, had me to write off a number of questions before we went there. . . . "Holt Clanton is in Paris and doing well," was the next remark and [he] handed Ma an unfolded paper which he had just taken up from the table. She opened it and read, "Where is Holt and what doing? . . .

I had reserved one question to which I wished a written reply. It was this, "Can Gertrude write well enough to make it profitable & for what paper?" To this the reply was, "She can" but he added "the hour is out now and my time is limited." "I wish I could ask one more question" said Ma. "The spirits have left. The influence has passed from me now" was his reply. . . .

Friday, September 30, 1870 . . . Lizzie Clanton said when she heard I was going North "she congratulated me & condoled with Mr Thomas" not as one would naturally suppose on account of my absence from him, but jestingly alluding to my well known propensity for talking a great deal. Some member of the family expressed the wish that Holt would not return from Europe at the same time I did from New York, or we would not give each other an opportunity to relate our experience. "Gertrude will out talk Holt" said Ma "& make one imagine she had seen more in New York than he in Europe." . . .

I have told them of my ride on the Potomac, my visit while I was in Washington to both the boys' and girls' school at George-town, my ride by the White House & view of the Equestrian statue of Gen [Andrew] Jackson, our visit to the Patent office, and the Smithsonian Institute, our visit to the Capitol, our survey of the Senate Chamber & House of Representatives, our ride that night (after bidding Kate good bye) on the cars, my moonlight view of Baltimore and Chesapeake Bay. I did not tell them how "Maryland, my Maryland" echoed through my mind, recalling reminiscences of that never to be forgotten glory when we dreamed and thought we had a country of which we could be proud. I was aroused from this reverie by the tones of a woman's voice imperiously demand-ing a seat on the cars & during the altercation which followed I was forced to regret that this first specimen of a "woman's right woman" should have been shown to me in Baltimore. . . . I intend if I can find time to write out a minute account of those visits which in the above pages I have merely alluded to.[8]

.   .   .

November 13, 1870 The fair in Augusta has taken place. The tournament is over and Turner, my gallant boy had the honour of being the successful Knight. He rode as "Henry of Navarre."[9] His costume consisted of a black velvet jacket and short pants the lat-ter finished with a fall of lace a wide Honiton collar a black felt hat and the white plume of Navarre, fastened by two silver stars. A bright coloured cravat with a very handsome sash of Lizzie Clan-ton's completed his costume. Not forgetting his spurs which were formed of a portion of the band around the first shot which was fired at Fort Sumter.[10] . . .

---

8. In the entry for October 2, 1870, Gertrude wrote that she attended "the church of the spiritualists" at Apollo Hall on two occasions while she was in New York. She found the speaker eloquent and added, "I could not if I would and I do not know that I would if I could, note all the new startling doctrines he advanced."

9. "Press where ye see my white plume shine, amidst the ranks of war, / And be your oriflamme today the helmet of Navarre" from "Ivry: A Song of the Huguenots" (1824), by Thomas Babington Macaulay.

10. According to a family legend, Turner Clanton brought home the band when he returned from Charleston following the firing on Fort Sumter. The spurs, decorated with silver dollars, are presently in the possession of a great-great-grandson, Michael Frederick Despeaux.

With the children Mr Thomas and Sis Anne I had a good view of the Knights of the Tournament. . . . The trial of skill commenced and ended and we could not tell how Turner stood. Mr Thomas was more excited than I ever knew him to be before in all my life. One moment he would say, "Turner is in for one of the prizes" and then again, "No Turner is outside." I told him "do to keep quiet," and summoned my strength to conceal my own disappointment and cheer Turner in his. . . . When it was at length announced that Turner had the first prize I could scarcely realise it and we were at too great distance from the stand to hear the judges' decision. I heard Bob Harris tell someone "Turner Thomas has the horse" and I enquired if it was really so. He replied "yes" and the tears of gratified joy filled my eyes but I was quiet with it all. The Knights rode by amid the applause of the crowd and Mr Thomas called out "Let me congratulate you Turner" but I had not read the announcement on the board and even then I could not realise it. I had never imagined Turner would get the *first prize*. I knew he was a good rider but he was so much younger than the other Knights. In the midst of my joy came the thought, "Oh ye of little faith." I had not had faith to believe altho I had prayed for his success. The mare Lady Arlington was valued at ($500) five hundred dollars. As Turner said that night in his boyish way, "Well, I am five hundred dollars richer tonight than I was this morning."

We all witnessed the race and returned to a five oclock dinner. Mrs John Thomas and Mattie (her daughter) with Gen Scales[11] dined with us. Hon Barnes Compton of Baltimore, the orator of the day before was invited by Mr Thomas but had a previous engagement. They were at Princeton together. He said in his speech "that during the war all Maryland on bended knees prayed 'God save the South' and since the war all Maryland on bended knees prayed 'God bless the South.'" "I don't believe that is Compton" said Mr Thomas. "The Compton I was at Princeton with was a tall fellow with long hair and this man is a fine stout good looking man." Afterwards in talking with him, "I see you still wear pump sole Boots" said Mr Compton to Mr Thomas. I smiled when he told me and thought of "the master passion."[12] . . .

---

11. This General Scales was not closely related to Julia Scales, if at all.

12. Gertrude used this term often. It possibly comes from *The Master Passion; and Other Tales and Sketches* (1845), by Thomas Colley Gratton.

11. Infamous Tuesday

I get bewildered.
—December 5, 1870

Belmont, November 29, 1870 How shall I begin this new Journal. . . . For three years I have been wearing sack cloth and ashes and how much longer it will continue I cannot tell. The last page of the book I have just finished closes with a record of Turner's success at the tournament and a thanksgiving to God for the gift of my noble boy. I would not dim that account with one shadow of care and did not mention what I then knew—that Mr Thomas' plantations in Burke were advertised. The advertisement is posted up on the opposite side [page] as it appeared in the Waynesboro paper.[1] My poor, dear Husband! how he has tried to avoid this publicity, both by advertising in Waynesboro and, having the names J J and J P Thomas when they never sign their names in any other way than J Jefferson and J Pinckney Thomas, as if everyone who reads it will not know who the man is who is advertised. After legal advice was obtained it was thought best for this notice to be be given to secure Pinck and Jule from loss. . . .

Forrest[2] was to have been in Augusta the week after the fair. I had never heard him, was anxious to have Turner go and appointed Thursday night to go. . . . Ma was out when I reached town. My

---

1. The newspaper clipping includes two notices headed "Sheriff's Sale" and dated November 1, 1870. One advertises an 800-acre tract of land in Burke County (Buckeye Land) "in favor of Julia E. Scales, Administratrix of Nath'l Scales," and the other advertises 1,050 acres (Cotton Town) "in favor of J. P. Thomas" and also "in favor of The National Bank of Augusta vs Mosher, Thomas & Schaub, makers and J. P. Thomas endorser. Public sale to be held on the first Tuesday in January, 1871."

2. Edwin Forrest (1806–72), American actor.

face was paining having had neuralgia for a day or two but I was quite determined to go. Late that afternoon Ma came in from the street. Mamie said something about Ma's accompanying me. "I cannot go" said Ma. "Money is too scarce and you ought not to go Gertrude. I have heard bad news this afternoon." I thought she referred to the advertisements of the Burke plantations. "Anything about Holt?" enquired Mamie. "No" said Ma. "Rowley has advertised Buddy's (Jimmie's) lifetime interest in the papers." Without one word I bent my head and again took up the cross and since then have staggered under the load, looking with blinded eyes to the right and to the left for help, finding none, finding one gleam of light through the thick darkness—a feeling of joy that Buddy's is only a lifetime interest, or having owned all he would have lost all.[3] . . .

"Buddy must be paid. He must not lose by us." This has been my constant theme and until I see some plan made towards accomplishing it I will never be satisfied. Mr Thomas tells me that he (Buddy) has paid Mr Rowley the interest on the note and thus postponed the sale, even that is a relief but my subject is too sad. I cannot write about it any better than I can talk about it. . . .

Wednesday, November 30, 1870 . . . I am sitting by the window and unconsciously as I gaze my fretful, peevish, temper changes and Mother Nature comforts her loving Daughter. "You felt just this way two years ago she tells me and yet you have had some happy moments since." How selfish I am to be writing in this strain when I have so much for which to give thanks. Have I not *my children*? But this is an unshared joy with Mr Thomas who while he loves and will take care to the best of his ability of these I have, has so morbid a dread of our having more mouths to feed, and little feet to cover that he chills my womanly heart and makes me untrue to my better nature.

I have never been so much opposed to having children as many women I know. Turner's birth was welcomed as in the natural course of events. Before his birth I made no little garments of love,

---

3. The lifetime interest clause applied to the inherited properties of all the Clanton children. It was Turner Clanton's intention to preserve the properties and leave something for his grandchildren.

weaving into their making bright dreams and fancys, but I remember that I talked a great deal to Mr Thomas of my expectations. When my baby was first placed in my arms, I had no sudden rush of motherly love and appreciation of my responsibility as a mother. I thought not of the immortal soul entrusted to my care but "what a funny little creature it is" was my first thought, and altho I loved him very dearly (how dearly I love him now, God knows and he alone) I did not love him as a baby as I love Julian. Nor has any baby I have ever had so deeply stirred the deep fountains of my heart as this little baby, who has come since our change of fortune, since Mr Thomas has thought we had children enough. The little baby who in my great anxiety to avoid adding to Mr Thomas' expense I scarcely provided clothing enough for a change.

Sometimes I do not know if I do right in acting as I do. For several years I have practised close economy and of what avail is it? Last winter Turner was out of school and among all my troubles none worried me more than to see him engaged in work which any Negro could have done as well. This winter he is in school, attending the [Richmond] Academy. Mary Belle is going to Mrs Robinson, both of them staying with Ma, who charges them no board. My dear darling Mother. . . .

.   .   .

December 5, 1870

Sheriff's Office Waynesboro Ga. Dec 1st 70

J Jefferson Thomas
Dear Sir

I hereby notify you that the lot and entire portion of property claimed, and held by yourself, in the county of Burke, lying and situated in Burke Co. Ga. at and near Thomas station on the Augusta and Savannah Rail Road, consisting of 1200 acres of land more or less together with the entire crop of Corn, Cotton, peas Cotton seed and other produce on the different places of yours also the entire stock of Horses, Mules, hogs, Cattle, Goats, Oxen, Carts and Waggons, plantation tools and &c that could be had or found as yours was yesterday levied on by myself under an execution issued from Richmond County Superior Court in favor of W W Montgomery as Receiver *all of said property will be sold* at Sheriff's sale 1st Tuesday in January, 1871 before the court house door in this town of Waynesboro Burke Co Ga. if not settled for by that time this December 1st 1870.

Edward Byrd, Sheriff B C[4]

I have copied this off so that I will the better impress it upon my mind and then I sent the letter to Ma to read and in my note to her I asked this question "Did *you* know of this execution?" I have not heard from her since. In the interval I can do nothing but what I am compelled to. The clothes were to be sent to the washerwoman's the starch and soap measured and sent to her and then a night shirt to be baisted for my totally inexperienced girl Diana to sew on, then dinner to give out and all this while my heart is throbbing with wounded pride and affection.

The other day I bade Fate do her worst and verily she appears to be accepting the challenge—but I did not think that the next turn of the wheel to which I am bound should be given by my own sisters and brothers, and now I do not believe that they realise what they are doing. In settling with Pa's estate Mr Thomas was owing them I think four thousand dollars.[5] Why this was so I do not know. He was owing some of it to Pa before his death and he was expecting a large legacy when the estate was divided and used some of the money of the estate. For this he is to blame but far be it from me to judge him harshly. There are enough besides to throw stones and blame without my joining them. . . .

If I could but infuse into Mr Thomas the sentiment which I feel so intensely, "Twice [Thrice] is he armed who has his quarrel just." Armed with this panoply I could see my way clearly before me, but these settlements & mortgages confuse me and the homestead act while legal, is humiliating.[6] . . . I am writing this for you my boys, and your mother must do herself this much justice. I did not approve of Buckeye Land and Cotton Town being settled upon me in lieu of the interest of the money of mine which your father

---

4. This additional levy on some of the same property differs from the earlier one in that it includes the land and every single asset connected with it. Attorney W. W. Montgomery was receiver, acting for the estate of Turner Clanton.

5. Accounting records of the estate suggest that Jefferson may have owed more than Gertrude thought.

6. Under the Homestead Act of 1868, Mr. Thomas could designate one of his properties as a homestead, thereby making it not liable to seizure for debt.

had used, simply because I think I ought to have helped him pay his debts—and I must also tell you that in agreeing to this arrangement, it was only because Mr Thomas thought that keeping the place for me he would be enabled to pay something he was owing. Nor have I for three years felt that I had any more claim upon it than any other place in Burke, nor have our family been benefited by it in the slightest degree. . . .

By the laws of Georgia what a woman has cannot be taken from her for the debts of her husband and he as her trustee is responsible for the interest thereof. Mr Thomas had the interest of a large amount for me in his keeping for years and the first debt he owes is to his wife and children— Every improvement in Burke, the building of the quarter and gin house was made by the money derived from the interest of the property Pa gave into his charge for me and my children— In taking this view of the case I thought I could see a certain degree of justice in my claiming what was in a very large degree my own, and thinking thus I consented to the deed being drawn up, simply turning it over to Mr Thomas to pay his debts with it, if he could.

This place I regard differently. It is settled upon me and the children in lieu of certain Negroes Mr Thomas sold during slavery belonging to me. We are told that it will be contested. When it is we will defend it if we can pay for the defense. Mr T tells me that I must get bond—bond means security— Does it not? Well if it does I won't get it, for I am determined that I shall not increase my obligation to anyone. But now comes another thought. Mr Montgomery in levying upon the Burke places has stopped all the operations of the plantations. No cotton is being picked out, none being ginned. Mr Stark our Factor in Savannah has advanced supplys and paid notes, depending on this year's crop to pay him. Cotton is selling at 15 cts and farmers realising no profits and Mr Thomas has not sent him enough to compensate (himself) for the advances made. . . .

It is now after dinner. I suppose I ought to be sewing. I cannot, it would be torture to me. Somehow it comforts me to write, more so than to talk. Dear silent friend you are almost invested with life as I record upon your unsullied page the sad hopes which are disappointed and you do not tell me that it is my fault or when I indignantly exclaim, tell me that it is my misfortune. Nor when as I sometimes do, I indulge in hopes for the future you do not point out to me its impossibility and remind me what a Sisyphus stone I have undertaken to roll when I hope to aid Mr Thomas in paying his debts. Turner my son you will be seventeen next Friday the 9th day of December. You are young my child and the golden cup which was held to your lips when you were born has been overturned and not one drop scarcely left for you to drain. When Pandora's box was opened Hope remained and now my son, if Hope and Energy are yours you may yet accomplish much. I have often asked you to have an aim in life. Let me give you one. Assist your father to pay his debts. Is the burden too heavy for your shoulders to sustain? I will assist you and as years roll on your manhood will develop and your shoulders grow stronger and Jeff and Julian will be growing up and let us will it, and it can be done. God help us. Am I wild, am I visionary that I write in this way? . . .

I am waiting while I write to know if my mother sanctioned Mr (I have almost forgotten the man's name) Montgomery's levy upon the little Mr Thomas has which he can call his own. There are eight legatees[7] for it to be divided between, not a very large amount for each one. I do not know, but I think if I know my own heart, that I would have spared one of my own sisters' husband this humiliation, for that sister's sake, but they say I am romantic, perhaps I am. I know it is legal. I do not forget that. But this is against all nature. I get bewildered. . . .

At night. After writing this afternoon, I tried to sew and could not. Sam came from Augusta and brought the papers and a note from Ma. I will copy it— "Dear Gertrude Your letter makes me very sad. You know you have your Mother's warmest sympathy in your behalf. If I could I would have it otherwise. I was ignorant of the execution in Montgomery's hands. Of course you have an interest in that claim. I regret and am pained to see Belmont levied upon in the morning's paper. I had hoped your home would have been left you. Turner will do as you requested. Lou came last night. Jule and Lou Kettles came to meet her. All well. With much love, Yours affectionately, MMC." I read that note and had scarcely realised the idea that Ma was ignorant of Mr Montgomery's execution before my eye was rivited upon the lines below and my eye took in the fact of what my senses could not grasp, that my home was levied

---

7. The eight legatees were the seven Clanton children and their mother: Anne, Gertrude, Mamie, Buddy (Jimmy), Cora, Holt, Kate, and Mrs. Mary Luke Clanton.

upon. Belmont, the home upon which we have bestowed so much labour and love, the flower garden with its beautiful arch and often the subject of praise with Pa. But this did not occur to me then. I took up today's paper and glanced impatiently over the lists of sheriff's sales to find Belmont. At last I read at the bottom of the page. Shall I copy it? Perhaps so. I cannot too fully take in the idea

Richmond County Sheriff's Sale
Will be sold on the first Tuesday in January 1871 at the lower Market House in the City of Augusta within the legal hours of sale, the following property viz
One certain tract of land known as Belmont situate lying and be-ing in Richmond County containing ninety acres more or less; bounded on the north by Yankee Farm, east by the Savannah Road, . . . William Doyle Sheriff, R.C.

Well I have written that calmly, only pausing once when the tears blinded me, as I wrote Belmont, the beautiful name of my home, and once again, to listen, when I wrote the unaccustomed word, "fi, fa," to listen to a chorus of ha ha's which rymed in my ears as if bidding me join them in the ha ha's and "I told you so," of my dear five hundred friends who today have discussed me and mine. . . .

This morning at one time I thought I understood the senti-ment of "Though thou slayest me, yet will I trust thee," and to some question Mamie asked me the other day I answered, "God and I understand each other." It was an irreverent expression of Faith, but this afternoon I could not see at all, and somehow I wanted Pa worse than I did God & I stretched out my arms and called him. Perhaps tonight in the land of dreams I may see him and hear counsel from him. I know I have wept and then had my heart so wrung for Turner, my dear boy. I do not know that his education can be continued, and yet it ought to be, and it must be for this year at all events, the year of 1871. . . .

. . .

Belmont, December 12, 1870 As I write this name, the name of my home I am forced to think, How long will Belmont be ours? And I remember the fact of its being named for the Residence of Portia in the *Merchant of Venice* and like her home, it is ap-proached by three avenues—[we] named the centre one for "Lee," the upper one, "Jackson"[8] and the other which commands a view of the church and has a winding path is called "Beauregard." In my Journals I have often alluded to the pleasure I have derived from the quiet beauty of the scene when I have been sitting in the front Piazzi looking at Cows, Goats and Horses, as in the distance they grased upon the carpet of living green, which as far as the avenue extended was spread on both sides. Not very romantic "Cows Goats and Horses" in lieu of deer grasing in the park, but there was one element which was mingled in the impression, *possession*, and I know the difference *now*, when I look out upon the same view, with the same animals, and realise that important element is wanting. I think I never realised how my affections were entwined around this place as when I expected Sherman and I am daily and hourly reminded of that time. I am afraid I am sadly impatient.

A few days ago I could see glimpses of light, rays in the darkness by which I am surrounded, but just now, just at this moment in which I write I feel a strange apathy, a don't care sort of feeling, like I would drift upon the current, the faster the better, in other words a feeling of relief that the time for those sales was approaching nearer and nearer. I think I shall feel relieved when I am cut loose from them. They have been weighing Mr Thomas down for some time, borrowing money with large interests, and never being able to pay interest much less principal. What troubles me more than anything else is the fact that Mr Thomas cannot decide where to take a homestead. If in Burke, Pinck (and when I say Pinck I include Mamie) will suffer, unless Mr Thomas can get Mr Stark to pay the bank and thus relieve Pinck. Having done this Mr Thomas will be obliged to mortgage the homestead and borrow money from Mr Stark at 20 pr ct interest. The land is valued at ten dollars per acre. Granting that the homestead act gives him five hundred acres, that will be five thousand dollars and upon that the first year he will be obliged to give one thousand dollars interest, besides the hire of his overseer, the latter charging in all probability as much as he does now for both plantations—and upon one thousand dollars I could support our family for the year, or if necessary upon the half of it. If he can procure a homestead here we have a home provided for us. I think I never before realised the beauty of that word home,

---

8. For Gen. Thomas J. "Stonewall" Jackson.

not even during the war, for I would then had I been forced to leave, have carried with me Confederate Bonds, but I forget. They would have been useless. . . .

I think I was very foolish last month to make up beds and wash soiled dishes. I began seriously to think that it was in very bad taste to have three meals in one day and wondered at the rapidity with which my homely but necessary duties followed each other and if I had dessert, or the plates were changed, seriously considered the subject in a new light, as so many more dishes to wash. Then I complained if a knife or spoon was used by Mr Thomas, if not placed in its proper place and one night when washing some greasy plates with an instinctive shrinking from my unaccustomed work, I told Mr Thomas that I did not think he had any idea how troublesome it was. "Well" said he "Why do you do it? It is only because you cannot hire anyone else." and this was my appreciation. I thought I was economising, until I could hire a good servant and then I wished to teach Jeff and Cora Lou and save their school bills. I did not answer, for Mr Thomas knew as well as I my motive and also knew that I could hire Anna, who had several times applied. But she was not only inefficient but dishonest. I did not answer but I washed no more dishes and Anna would have been sent for next day had not Diania come. My Husband never praises and in this expression his character may be summed up. While I am like a plant constantly reaching forth for sunshine and warmth, and that by the way is a very trite comparison, but I have often been struck by it. . . .

I am here reminded of a verse in an old album which I will look in the bookcase for. If I do not, it will haunt me with its half remembered cadence.

"A boon, a talisman Oh memory! give
To shrine my name in hearts where I would live
            Forevermore.
Bid the wind speak of me, where I have dwelt.
Bid the streams, voice of all my soul hath felt
            A thought restore."

Mike Nisbet wrote that verse, and memory exerts her talisman, and bids the air speak of him, and the gallant friend whom I used to know so well and like so much is remembered and not forgot. And wife and mother as I am I can pause to give a sigh to the memory of one who loved me when I was a girl, and long since has passed to "The shores, where tideless sleep the seas of time."

Holt, darling Holt where are you today? Are you living, or are you too passed away? I suffered so much last spring when I thought you would not perhaps return again and now this long time and again we are left in doubt and suspense. I have allowed my pen to wander as it would today— Mr Thomas believes in "dolce far niente" sweet to sleep[9]—and can throw himself upon the bed and soon forget for the time his cares and rise refreshed. I cannot and when at night I close my eyes, my dreams are often troubled, a reflection of my waking moments. But I do thank Heaven that I can sometimes find comfort in writing and often in reading— My thoughts have centred now upon Holt. When I visited Dr ——— isn't it strange I have forgotten his name [Foster], he made the spirits tell us Holt would be home in November and I never wish[ed] for a more striking proof of our earnest gropings after glimpses of the future than was shown by our whole family—for they all believed and wished to believe that we had heard from Pa, and when Dec 1st came and without Holt, the disappointment of not seeing him made us doubt all the rest of what we had been told.

Only one dispatch has been received in Paris since the siege began,[10] so we are informed and that by Mr Washburne, the United States minister. Ma has written him. Numerous letters have been sent out from Paris by Balloon and Doves, the Germans training hawks to destroy the latter. I will hope Holt will try and get home by Christmas. But if he never comes— But he will I know. I feel that he will.

As I contrast my occupation of today with Mr Thomas' my conscience reproaches me. I have been pleasantly engaged and in writing have succeeded in diverting my thoughts from the one thought while he has been in town all day trying to make some arrangements for us. He has the brunt to bear while I can remain at home. My children my little darlings. Mother wishes she could do something for you. If necessary she would die for you but that would not enable you to live any the better. Time will tell.

---

9. *Dolce far niente* means "sweet to do nothing."

10. Gertrude refers to events of the Franco-German War, July 1870–May 1871. Beginning on September 19, 1870, German troops laid siege to Paris, which surrendered on January 28, 1871.

Wednesday, December 14, 1870 I was busy all day yesterday. Made an under shirt for Mr Thomas and cut out four aprons for Julian & three night shirts for Turner. Cornelia Shelman a coloured woman came to see me in the morning wishing to be hired for the next year. "Miss Trudy" said she "I wants a gored dress. How much will you charge to cut out this one for me?" producing from under her shawl a bundle of thin narrow worsted goods for my admiration. "Five dollars," was my reply, and then added as she looked astonished "I would not do it for that Cornelia, and indeed I have no time just now." I merely named that price because she asked me "how much I would charge," glad of an excuse to refuse. Had she asked me as a favour I would have disliked to have done so. Her mother is a good se[a]mstress, often being employed by me to make the children's garments, after I have cut them out. Cornelia was married last summer and I gave her her second day dress, but did not cut it out or make it for her.

The servants are such improvident creatures, they will often spend a large amount or "take up" as they call it, most of their months wages in buying articles of dress, if we will sell them, but I have never learned to bargain and trade with our old servants. Aunt Lily (Charlotte's Grand Mother) came to buy a white dress for one of her daughters to be married in. "How much does you ask for it" said she as I gave her one which I would not have sold. "Nothing. I cannot sell a dress to you aunt Lily" said I remembering while she was expressing her gratitude that her mother was the first cook Ma had when she was married and that she with her family had been so faithful and worked so hard for us all her life. Poor soul. She is living at the Rowell Place with all her children and grandchildren except Charlotte and the other day her house (belonging to Holt) was burnt up. . . .

Well I am worried. I do not know what to do. Mr Thomas advises my claiming the stock and lands in Burke after the mortgages are paid and I do not wish to do it. He may do as he pleases & will of course, but I have an individuality of my own and I cannot sue for the interest of money a large share of which I had the benefit of before the war. I talked with Mr Thomas last night and tried to persuade him to give up Burke and let it go as far as it would toward meeting his liabilities and take a homestead here and try to raise the mortgage upon the farm. He says that Mr Stark may come back upon the other trust property which I have if he does not claim Burke for me, and oh how it worries me. This morning I knelt and prayed God to help me to decide what was best to do. . . .

Mr Thomas has been in town every day this week. Yesterday he was in consultation with Mr Shewmake and Gen Wright, and today he has gone in to secure their services. I expected him to say something to me this morning after my telling him last night I was unwilling to claim what he wished, but he did not. As he left I told him "not to make arangements binding me for that I thought it was wrong." He answered that "he did not know what he would do." I am so much afraid that Mr Thomas will involve himself in law and spend the little we have left. . . .

At night. I was sitting before the fire tonight with Julian in my lap telling the children the story of Joseph and his coat of many colours when Turner came. He rode down on his Horse which he won at the tournament. He has been trying to raffle her but has not yet succeeded. When Turner comes he brings light and comfort with him. Mr Thomas came soon after and brought kerosine and a can of oysters. The large lamp required filling. It was Turner who quietly attended to it, filled the lamp, trimmed the wick and placed it on the table. The oysters were to be opened and the sardine knife is missing. It is Turner who steps out and in a few moments returns with the can open, and when they are cooked serves them, I am confident reserving for himself the smallest share. He told us all the news about town, trying to remember everything which he thinks will interest and brought to me his report book which speaks well for him, and I in turn tell him of what I have been reading and love to see his countenance brighten as he listens. "I got your note on my birthday Mama and thank you for it," said he. I gave him one dollar tonight. When I was his age how differently I was situated. I remember how much I spent when I was in college but I cannot say I regretted it. My allowance was only such as was suitable to a girl of my expectations. My dear generous father! . . .

I read over the first page of what I have written tonight and so great faith have I in a turn of "Fortune's Wheel" that I will take care of this book and when my eldest grand son is seventeen, I am going to make him a larger present than I did to my son on his birthday, if I live and I may live that long. . . . Why I am growing old despite myself. Hitherto I have contented myself with writing for my children and now I am writing for the grandchildren, for "the generations yet unborn." Heigh ho! I think I had better leave home and get out of my channel of dull [carping] thoughts and go to some of the weddings. . . .

Monday, December 19, 1870   Friday Dec 16 was the anniversary of our wedding day and we both forgot it, and indeed I had not thought of it until I commenced to write and penned the date of today. Our thoughts are with the present and so absorbed as to lose sight of the past, and the future is so obscured we can catch but brief glimpses of it in the heavy cloud which hangs over us. But this morning, I feel brighter and better than I have in some time— Mr Thomas goes in town with a paper signed by both he and I relinquishing all claim to the plantations in Burke with the stock and &c upon it. I never signed my name more willingly in my life much more so than if I had been signing it to a claim for the amount left in Burke after the mortgages were paid, making my claim for the amount as due me for the interest on the property Mr Thomas had in his possession during the time we have been married. . . .

But this arrangement to give up all in Burke without a claim and try to compromise suits me infinitely better, but I am afraid it is done too late. Those men who have executions will feel safe and will probably refuse to compromise. Aunt Lamkin told me that she thought Mr Thomas ought to take a homestead and if he cannot make this arrangement I suppose he will do something of the kind. I sometimes wish I was like other ladies and not burdened with my husband's confidence in money matters. I think how much care I would be spared, but then I console myself with the idea that I am what every woman should be—his friend and counsellor, never loving him better than when the day seems darkest, and duty hardest. . . .

I was in Augusta on Saturday, rode directly to Ma's, taking Cora Lou with me and remained there until the afternoon when I went with Mr Thomas to see Mr Kerr.[11] I found Aunty and Mamie with Ma. . . . I do not think I am envious, but my pride suffers when I think of my children as the poor relations of the family. I have eat so little "umble pie" that it tastes very bitter to me. I think it is best for me just now that I remain at home (I wish I had a home) for "out of the fulness of the heart the mouth speaketh." I said at the dinner table Saturday (Ma was out of the room) that I should like to be off in a new place, far off from anyone I knew, that I had become accustomed to never seeing my relatives for unless I

---

11. Mr. Kerr, sometimes spelled Carr, was one of several lawyers with whom Jefferson Thomas dealt in Augusta.

sought them I never saw them. "If your idea is to avoid seeing your relations," said Mamie, "I should think it would be easy enough to do." She spoke truly. I would only have to remain at home, but I answered "that anyone who could not understand my motives for wishing a change of scene must be dull of comprehension." I don't think Mamie has understood the art of "put yourself in his place." To do my sisters justice, I think they would have appreciated my irritable state and soothed me with a kind word, for Sis Anne and Cora are very kind in their manner. Ma is very kind, but what can she do? I thanked her the other day for having Turner and MBelle with her. . . .

December 30, 1870   Since I wrote last the time has passed swiftly. Mr Thomas left Tuesday Dec 20 for Savannah to see Mr Stark and returned Thursday evening. He had not been able to accomplish what he had wished and I felt my heart give a quick leap for joy while I felt that I was perhaps not sympathising with him as much as I ought but I had not forgotten the large interest which he would have been compelled to pay. On Wednesday night Mr Thomas had a letter sent to him through Turner. I opened it and read it three times over, while such a feeling of disappointment came over me that I know my countenance betrayed it, as looking up I caught Turner's glance directed to me. It was from Mr Miller[12] who was instructed by the National Bank to respectfully decline Mr Thomas' proposition for a compromise. That night and the next day I was very sad and could not conceal my disappointment. In the afternoon Turner and Jeff went in town in the little waggon and took a Holly tree to Ma for a Christmas tree. It was quite cold and they wrapped up warm and the only bright feeling I had enjoyed during the day was the emotion of love and pride with which I bad them good bye as with merry laugh and cheerful talk they left to assist St Nicholas in his Christmas frolic, but I could not sympathise with their joy. . . .

Tuesday and Wednesday the 20 and 21st of December the election took place.[13] . . . All the negroes in the neighborhood marched in procession to Augusta (or most of them) to vote for Daniel Hor-

---

12. Andrew J. Miller, another Augusta attorney.
13. In the election of 1870, the Democrats scored a decisive victory in

ton for the Legislature. He is the man who wrote us a note last summer inviting Mr Thomas and Mr Carmicheal to attend a barbecue they gave. He is a respectable, well behaved brown skinned man but not exactly qualified to make laws for me or mine. When the Negroes reached Augusta they were ordered to stack their arms outside of the City. The election proceeded quietly. The white men and coloured Democrats going in the front door and depositing their votes and the Radicals coloured going into the City Hall from the back door. I don't know how the white radicals go in, from the front though I expect. Bill Hall ran an independent ticket. Col [Claiborne] Snead was elected, much to Cora's joy who laughingly talks of running him for Governor. I can thoroughly appreciate Cora's pride in her husband. . . .

The next morning Friday the 23d of December, I was aroused by the glad shouts of the children at "the snow the beautiful snow." The trees were covered with the snow and the ground was carpeted several inches thick with its warm covering. . . .

Sunday [Saturday] afternoon the Christmas tree with its red berrys was placed in Mamie's room, and the children were summoned to receive the gifts of the merry season. Turner headed the list of grandchildren. Rebe Vason stood at the other end of the row. Julian was in my lap and would not stand with them, but when a horn was handed to Rebe Vason and she blew it, he slipped down out of my lap and said "Me wants one too," and took his place with the others. He was very much pleased with his Dancing Jim, Noah's ark, Whip, Horse and &c. Mary Belle said she had given to her everything she wished. She is the most contented person I have seen for few so nearly attain to satisfaction. . . .

Turner had money and cravats and &c and Jeff and Cora Lou were remembered. I gave MB a card picture and frame to give to Ma and Mamie Cora and Sis Annie surprised her with a black silk suit and I enjoyed her pleasure without one morbid feeling of wounded pride because I had not been invited to join in making a gift which I could not afford. So much for the softening influence of Christmas. After all it was pleasant to be one of the home circle and realise as I did in those little gifts of affection that affectionate hearts had been

---

both houses of the Georgia legislature, reclaiming the seats of the Radicals who were elected in 1868.

thinking kindly of me. The next day was Monday [Sunday], Christmas Day.[14] Twenty one of us sat down to dinner. Buddy and Lizzie were away with their baby, so was Holt and Kate. . . . Ma & I drank Holt's and Kate's health in a glass of wine, as in low tones we hoped that Holt would be with us when we again eat Christmas dinner.[15]

. . .

.   .   .

14. Christmas Day was on Sunday. Gertrude's account is a little confusing.

15. Holt Clanton died in Paris in 1871; the exact date and circumstances are unknown. His body was returned to Augusta for burial in the Clanton section of Magnolia Cemetery.

12. Jefferson Davis in Augusta

I am writing History for you my children.
—*May 27, 1871*

January 2, 1871 ... ... I left [Julian] sick in bed this morning and rode in town to sign a duplicate of the claim bond which was sent to Mr Stark last week. Mr Thomas was afraid that it would not arrive in Waynesboro in time and requested Mr Carr to draw up another. . . .

How I disliked to go and leave Julian but I must not seem negligent of Mr Thomas now when he is so much troubled. Turner drove me in company with Jeff in the Carriage and as our Horses looked so badly we got out on the cross street, and Turner and I walked to Broad Street. Mr Carr did not have the duplicate drawn off. Major Carr had rheumatism so that he could not use his pen. What could I do? I wrote Mr Thomas a letter, remained at Ma's a few moments to do so. While there the procession of coloured people passed up the street. They were celebrating their emancipation.[1] I had forgotten it was the day, indeed I had forgotten that it was the new year until Gen McLaws saluted me on the street with "Happy New Year." I am not so morbid as I was but this is not a Happy New Year to me. I do not generally go on the street on New Year's Day but have usually remained in doors to receive calls, but today I was not a fashionable lady but a business woman— I am afraid I am becoming cross when I remember how changed everything is, and that I must guard against. . . .

I do sincerely sympathise with Mr Thomas in this loss and mortification of spirit. Knowing him as I do I can understand how humiliating it is but the sale over I think and hope he will feel

---

1. President Lincoln issued the Emancipation Proclamation on January 1, 1863.

357

better— I had wished that he should have nothing here to trouble him but Young has moved today and Edmund and Mary expect to go tomorrow and Sam was missing this morning and Uncle Robin whom he thought he had engaged for this year has not come back. These are hands he had last year (just passed) and he has made little or no effort to secure them for another. Young was the best man he had on the place and I am sorry he has gone. Edmund will be no loss. He is indolent and impertinent at times. Diania (Young's wife) is cooking and milking for me. She gives us breakfasts at nine oclock and dinner between three and four and tea proportionately late. . . . When one servant leaves a place they use their influence to prevail upon as many of the others to go as they can. Mr Thomas has hired a white man Mr Simmons and he told Turner that Edmund compelled Sam who is only 14 years old to leave this morning. He left before his month was out. Mr Simmons is at present the only man or boy on the place in our service and he has a chill every other day since he has been here. . . .

January 8, 1871 Since writing last Julian has been very sick. Coming home from Burke Wednesday night, Mr Thomas found him with high fever and together we nursed him. Perhaps it was a fortunate thing for Mr Thomas that he had something to engage his mind, for he was terribly disappointed at the result of the sale in Waynesboro. The two places sold for but little more than the mortgages, Jule buying the one for $4000 and Cotton Town selling for $6000 and something. Some of the land which Mr Dye promised to give 10 for he bought for $5 (five) and Pinck also bought some of the most valuable land Mr Thomas owned for 5 dollars per acre. Mr Thomas wished the Cotton Town place sold altogether and had made arrangements with the sheriff to have this done, but Mr Dye and Pinck said, "no sell it seperately" and it would bring more—it was done and they bought it. . . . I warned Mr Thomas against Mr Dye and begged of him to secure some written promise of what he would do. When he Mr D found out that we had no claim until after the mortgages were paid, I think it was then his object to buy the place for as little as possible and all his promises amounted to nothing. After the sale Mr Thomas wished to make some arrangements about renting the place, trusting to his promise to allow him to redeem it and Mr Dye asked him 20 bales of cotton rent and "hoped he would someday be able to pay him the three thousand dollars he was still owing him," and for which Joe's estate was security.[2] . . .

Sensitive, as was natural under the circumstances, Mr Thomas alluded to Pinck's laughing and jesting with a group of men who were discussing the sale while he was suffering so much mortification. "Take care, Mr Thomas" said I "how you talk. You may be mistaken. Do not prejudice me against Pinck or anyone else, for you know I am not capable of disliking a person one day and hobnobbing with them the next." On the contrary if I think I have cause for blaming anyone for the want of consideration for me I do not take the trouble of telling them so but I *do not forget it*. "Did you have no one to fall back upon that day?" said I, for man as he was I knew he required sympathy. "You took dinner with Jule, did you not?" "No," said he. "I was in no mood for dinner." "But she invited you, did she not" said I? "No" said Mr Thomas, "but if I had wanted to have gone she thought I would have done so."

Persons differ in their ideas but I should have acted differently under the circumstances. Mr Thomas now wishes to set aside the sale made to Mr Dye and this Mr Kerr tells him he can do. Mr Thomas says he requested several persons not to bid and that he could have taken out a homestead and &c. How it will end I cannot tell. Suffice it to say that the old worry is renewed which I had hoped would have been ended with the sale, and the strain on Mr Thomas' mind continues, and Mr Thomas expects me to sign another paper complaining, and &c. This I particularly dislike to do and will not promise until I know what I am about. . . .

Last night every servant on the place was going to the "sitting up" but I requested my housegirl to remain and she is very obliging and slept on "a pallet" in my room.[3] Charlotte is not with me now. Edmund & his wife are still with us and a little boy called Nat. Mr Simmons left Tuesday without a word of warning. After all when I

---

2. The complications of Jefferson Thomas's debts are impossible to follow clearly. In addition to mortgages to his brother and sister and his implication of Gertrude's brother in a large unsecured note, he owed factors, banks, businesses, and various individuals. He owed the Clanton estate and incurred some obligation to the estate of his deceased brother, Joe.

3. A custom from slavery times, when it was common practice for servants to sleep in the room with children or the mistress.

judge from my experience I like the coloured servant better than the white, from the latter I expect more and am invariably disappointed. . . .

I have been thinking this morning of the wild tumult in my heart the other day, when through my mind there came a doubt if Julian would live. Mr Thomas appeared to think him very ill and said so. I sat cold and motionless. I did not rise from my seat, and I know my husband thought I was a careless mother as he busied himself in preparing some medicine. I did not pray, but into my heart there came a wild longing to wrestle with the grim angel Ayreal for the life of my baby. It was not until he called me that I went to the bed and lay down by him. "Mr Thomas" said I, "if God takes my baby from me I do not know what I will do." He did not understand me. I lay down by Julian and taking his hand in mine I felt how entirely helpless, how utterly impotent I was to keep him from drifting from me, and unconsciously with my thought I tightened the clasp upon his little hand.

It was not long but it seemed an age that this defiant spirit continued, and then my over burdened heart was relieved by tears. Julian is better, much better. He has had no fever yesterday or today and I am grateful, truly grateful but in my own consciousness I realise that I was not willing to say, "Thy will be done" had that will required my baby, my darling to be taken from me—

.   .   .

Monday, February 13, 1871 . . . "Gertrude" said my mother to me a few days ago "What do you do at home every day? I should think Cora Lou and the children being in town with me you would have a great deal of time to sew." I hung my head convicted, then rallying said with a smile, "I made Jeff's coat." "But on your machine you could have made that in half day" said Ma. I was sewing on the one I made two days, and an ugly thing it is, made of Jeans. "Do you spend all your time reading?" "Oh no mam," I replied. I then mentioned clothes mending, stockings which I had darned, store room cleaned up, Beaurea[u]s, Wardrobes and &c kept in order and so on adinfinitum, but I did not tell Ma that a good deal of time was spent in writing in this journal & making copious extracts into my note books. Why? Because as I said before I am not confident if I am employing my time profitably. I think so at times but I do not like to talk about it.

Let me tell you something my Journal. I wished to subscribe for something to read, so I sold a mourning dress (an old Bombazin) for four dollars, and a calico for two, adding one dollar to this, I subscribed for *Appleton's* journal which comes every Saturday, and *Harper's Monthly*. . . . I receive *Arthur's Monthly* in lieu of *Once a Month*, which I subscribed for last year and owing to only three numbers being published I receive this in place of it. I still receive *The Children's Hour* for Mary Belle, and *The Working Man* for Turner, a monthly which like the *Hour* is edited by Arthur,[4] the two cost $1.50. Thus you will see I have invested eight dollars and fifty cts in magazines. Am I extravagant? I have bought one pair kid gloves and one pair gaiters for myself since Christmas and paid 1.30 for sewing for the children. For that amount I had four aprons, two pair pants, and one pair drawers made for Jeff—the prices fixed by the seamstress who was glad to be employed at her own home. Would I have been more in the discharge of my duty making those articles than reading and studying? Perhaps so, if I cannot make my present employment of cultivating my mind yield an abundant harvest. . . .

February 17, 1871 . . . I do not know that I have realised it perfectly, but at times I feel that I am the better for the chastening which I have received, but I will not boast. I am afraid of myself. Why? Because today Mr Thomas expects the claim for this place [Belmont] to be decided. He left home this morning for Augusta where court is in session, to appear as a witness to testify that this place is settled upon me and my children in lieu of Negroes he sold before emancipation, belonging to us. And this is why I am afraid of myself. I am not sure that I will be willing to submit without murmuring if the case is decided against me. . . .

I have two natures which war with each other. I am fond of society, the hum of conversation, the sound of music, the poetry of motion in the dance. I thoroughly enjoy a crowd, but there is another nature which pleads for quiet, leisure to read, to write, to reflect, to ponder upon life with its aims and end, and the two natures conflict. When I am in town my thoughts are distracted and it is only here in the country at Belmont that I can learn to know myself. . . . I have been wishing to tell you of the masquerade

---

4. T. S. Arthur, editor of *Godey's Lady's Book* and other magazines.

ball which took place at the opera house on the 7th of Feb. . . . I had my choice to remain at home, go in the dress circle and pay the price of admission or accept of my invitation. I selected the latter horn of the dilemma and dressed in Domino I went with Edge and Lizzie [Eve].

In the afternoon Sis Anne came down. She was going too. Seeing me baisting some wide Valenciennes lace on my purple silk she said how handsome it was. "Why where did you get so much Valenciennes lace from?" "I haven't been poor always" said I with a smile which told how well I was learning to hide the wound my pride had received. The scar is growing less plain, but the wound is there, and I wince every now and then when it is carelessly touched. Not that Sis Anne would for one moment inflict an annoyance upon me. I know her too well for that. A nobler, better woman God never made. . . .

That night it rained very hard but with the storm cover on Edge Lizzie and I left to go by cousin Mary Ann's to show Alice [Danforth] our costumes, but it was raining so hard we concluded to go directly to the opera house and let Edge go for Cora and Sis Anne. . . . In another moment I was for the first time in my life in the green room of a theatre. I wish I were an artist that I could transfer to canvas the sight I beheld. . . . Sitting by the stove resting her feet near it to dry them was Marie Antoinette. She was dressed in a blue moire antique silk, trimmed with ermine, a top skirt of rich lace, handsome jewelry and everything complete about her dress. Near her stood the embodiment of the French tricolor, while Wanda a beautiful peasant made signs of wonder and admiration. Other characters were in the room but what was strangest of all was the silence! Everyone was afraid of betraying themselves by their voice and nothing was said except in whispers. . . . Madame [Octavia Walton] LeVert came in a few moments after. I recognised her dress, a handsome white merino, elaborately trimmed, which I had seen her wear several years ago when we were invited to meet her by Mrs William Eve— She was low neck and short sleeves. They were pretty enough to show but she must be fifty— . . .

. . . .

Thursday, March 9, 1871 The scenes have shifted. Again I am advertised in the daily papers and—but oh the subject is so painful I dislike to talk about, or write of it. Today a sale of the Cows, Mules,

Horses, Ploughs, and &c takes place at Cotton Town. "All sold by consent of parties as the property of J J Thomas, . . ." I think of Mr Thomas, and my heart bleeds for him— How proud he was of that plantation. I had no love for Burke but I am sorry for him— I may be a strange woman but I do not dislike the loss of property as much as I do the fact that it is my own family who are having my husband sold out. . . . This time one year ago Cousin Polly had the house sold at the market at Sheriff's sale. Has it only been one year ago? It seems as if it might have been ten years ago. I have no bitter feelings for her. She acted legally—and I have only to remember that through my husband, her daughter is threatened with bankruptcy.[5]

Last night I wrote this note to Ma. I will copy it. "Dear Ma, I have been mending Turner's coat. The children are asleep and I have my thoughts to keep me company—and such thoughts. I have read that advertisement and I have been trying to remember if in reality or fiction I have ever known of such an unnecessary humiliation being forced upon a woman, who staggering beneath her cross, has this bitter cup pressed to her lip by—her sisters. I shall never forget how I suffered when I read that advertisement in November. Monday night I read it again and again I wept bitterly. Tonight I read it & remembered that you said 'Mr Montgomery was acting legally.' The proceeds of the sale will not benefit the family as there are older executions. As there was *nothing to gain* my humiliation was unnecessary. One word from Sis Anne or Cora and the others, and it would have been prevented. Mr Thomas did ask Col Snead, and he refused, and I only regret that the Sheriff's notice did not state for whom Mr Montgomery was Receiver."

"I suppose they thought they were acting legally, forgetting that there is a higher law and another tribunal at which to be judged. 'In as much as ye did it unto one of the least of these little ones ye did it unto me,' but I am no peti[ti]oner for mercy from my family. Sued by my mother, my sisters and brothers, Mr Thomas' sister and brothers, with Stark's lien for which I am responsible added to it, I rebel and turning to my children for comfort, I think they too may sue me someday. In the midst of my troubles I remember and am glad that we took no homestead in Burke for then

---

5. Polly Walton's daughter, Lizzie, married James (Buddy) Clanton.

Mamie would have suffered. When told that Gen Johnson said that we could recover from Pa's estate by sueing, I refused to make the attempt, for in my Journal I had recorded Pa's dying charge to us 'to live in harmony,' & Col Vason's promise of 'I will Col to the best of my ability.' When I see Pa and he asks me, 'What about Jimmie?' I will tell him, I *did not forget*. Yours Gertrude." . . .

Tomorrow my husband will be forty years old. However much the world considers success the test of merit, it is not always so—Mr Thomas has no extravagant habits and looks after business when he is home. He will not have so many distracting cares now, and he has commenced farming here, but I am terribly afraid the crops will be levied upon before the end of the year. I have given a lien on the Mules in Columbia to run that place, and a seperate lien on "ten head of Cattle, four head of Horses, 2 waggons, one carriage and one Buggy." for the sum of six hundred dollars for this place. The arrangement could not be made without its being run in my name but if this place is levied upon why will not Columbia and the houses in town be responsible for it just as I am now responsible to Mr Stark.

Ah my Journal in my effort not to reduce my children to beggary (for I know it will take more to run this place) and my wish to oblige Mr Thomas I have a hard time. I can the better understand the state of Mr Thomas' mind by the great anxiety I feel. Talking with you has done me good. I wish now I had written to you instead of writing to Ma last night. It may annoy her and she is very kind. . . . A few more turns of Fortune's wheel and I will be at the bottom, and *there I will not remain*. I only hope I will go up as fast as I came down. I met Major Dickinson at church that Sabbath. He believes we will be paid for our servants. If one word of mine would restore the institution I would not utter it. Better have debt to encounter than slavery, but I would be very glad to be compensated for the loss of ours, to receive the moneyed value for them. . . .

. . . .

Saturday, March 18, 1871 . . . For the past week I have felt little like writing. You remember I wrote Ma a note and the next morning expressed my regret at having done so. Spoken or written words are important in the effect they produce. Ma answered my note and told me that she thought I was indulging in wrong thoughts and doing my family an injustice. "I write" said she "with the purest motives of kindness." I will not copy her note else it might prove one of those things which having written I should wish undone. Her letter was like a surgeon's knife, beneficial but painful, showing me that there were two sides of the question I had been discussing.

Mr Thomas came home from Burke on the 10th his birthday, and brought a shad with him, the only one we have had this season. I had intended having oysters for him but used the shad instead, arranged the table with my coloured cloth, cut glass and silver with a handsome vase of white spirea and had Mary Belle to place a boquet of flowers by Mr Thomas' plate. Tried to show him that we had loving hearts and sympathy for him in his trials. Unfortunately he is in such a state of mind he does not appreciate it. . . .

. . .

Monday, April 10, 1871 . . . Tuesday the 4th was my birthday. I was thirty seven years old! . . . . My birthday was spent in visiting. I am driving the sorrell mare and Lady Arlington (Turner's prize horse). I persuaded Mr Thomas to accompany & with Cora Lou we called to see some of our neighbors. . . . At Mr Little's[6] as we passed we found Mrs Allen, having a picture of the house taken. As we stopped before the door Mr Thomas remarked that he did not wish the carriage included in the picture and I laughed at his Master Passion Pride which will never desert him. You remember dear Journal, that our pheaton like its mistress is not as youthful looking as it has been. Yet the springs of life are yet vigorous and I might add the tounge, like that of its mistress, as long as ever. Excuse me dear Journal for lapsing into slang, an error you will admit I seldom commit.

At Mr Little's we found the family with Mrs Brewster and her two sons, Mr Knapp and Mr Miller, all Northern people. Wine and cake were offered and accepted. Mrs Allen and Bob Allen from Savannah were there. During the visit Mrs Little said to me, "Mrs Thomas are you interested in the subject of Henerys?" Quick as thought I ran over the Kings of England to Henry the 8th, but so quick is thought that I was enabled to remember that it was hen houses to which she referred as I replied "that I had tried to be, without being successful." No allusion to the subject had been

---

6. The Fred Littles were northern people who had moved into the neighborhood.

made before the question she asked and I know no one who speaks of a hen house as a Henery, altho I have often read of them. Indeed I am not sure I spell the word right. We were taken out into the yard and shown in the yard a house made by Mr Little.

The view from the rear of the dwelling is beautiful. In the back Piazzi was a long table with carpenters tools and considerable disorder. Mrs Little made some allusion to it, and by way of making conversation, I said to Fred Little "I suppose your father is fond of that kind of work?" "Oh that is his trade," was his reply. "There is nothing about carpenter's work or blacksmith's work that he does not understand." On one side of the Piazzi were bars of country made soap, placed to dry in the sun. Of course all depends upon taste but had I seated myself in that Piazzi to enjoy the view, or with a book to read, those tools and that soap would have prevented my enjoying either the one, or the other. I do not object to country made soap. It is very useful, but the harmony of the view was destroyed.

The Littles appear to be wealthy and the boys are gentlemanly in appearance. One of them a fine performer upon the piano and melodeon, and they are sociable. There is another family the Wilsons, to whom I have referred before. They are Northern and very common. I did not attend the club meeting at their house and would not have called the other day but Mr Thomas said "it was best not to slight them." . . .

At night. I stopped writing this afternoon to go up stairs and select some summer clothing for the children to have done up. While I was up stairs Turner returned from Augusta on Horseback to spend the night as Mr Thomas is in Columbia having left home this morning. Calling to one of the servants to ask some question I heard him reply "Yes" in reply. I looked out. "Who was that answered you then Turner" said I? "Henry," was his reply. "Henry" said I, "When you reply to Turner you must be more respectful." To this he replied that he was willing to say yes sir to Mr Thomas but not to boys of his size.

I came down stairs and told Henry that I was very well pleased with him, but that there was a distinction to be made between Turner and Charley Hall (one of the servants on the farm) and it must be made. He replied that he could leave and continued talking in this way for a while. "Henry" said I "you have said enough and you must stop. I repeat to you that while you are in our employment you must reply respectfully to Turner or leave. You can do as you please, but I should tell you the same if you were the only servant to be hired in the state." I told him this and came in. I do not know wether he will go or stay. I should prefer his remaining for hands are scarce but respect is a quality I demand from servants even more than obedience. I can over look neglected work but cannot tolerate disrespect.

Turner is kind and good. If a horse is to be saddled or harnessed he assists & it is not appreciated. Almost the only time I ever knew him to lose his temper with one of the servants was last summer when he thought he heard one of them speak disrespectfully about me when I had given an order. The servants are very tenacious of their honor. They all call Turner "Buddy," the old name every one of our own servants have addressed him by ever since his birth. They are willing to compromise by calling him Buddy and Mary Belle "Sissy," to avoid speaking as Master Turner or Miss Mary Belle, for that would be too submissive to please them. . . .

Alluding to disputes with servants, last year we had a difficulty with old uncle Robin, and Young (a man much younger) who had taken away Uncle Robin's wife. When I looked out I found the old man on the ground and Young choking him. The servants ran in to tell me that "Young was killing old uncle Robin." I came out and called to him to stop. To this he made no reply, except to continue to strike the old man. To my repeated call he paid no attention. I walked rapidly to the quarter, only a short distance, and again repeated my order to Young. (Mr Thomas was from home). The old man was struggling for breath, and Young so infuriated with passion, that he did not regard me in the least. The frightened Negroes many of them men, not pretending to interfere except by begging Young to desist.

"I will put a stop to this" said I, all the indignation of my Southern nature aroused. "Ned, go in the house and bring me the gun," and while he ran for it, I walked up to Young, and placed my hand upon his arm. "Young, don't let me speak to you again. Let uncle Robin go." He obeyed, and they both struggled to their feet and it was fortunate that they did so before the gun came, for I don't know what I would have done with it if Young had not obeyed. For I do not know how to shoot a gun. I was telling Ma of it afterwards and they thought I ought not to have interfered and wondered I was not frightened. I am glad the two men are not in our employ for they were constantly quarrelling about Mollie.

Last summer Mary Hall lost her baby a few weeks old. Of course it was made the occasion of a solemn sitting up. Mr Thomas loaned Edmund (her husband) a mule and he extended the notice near and far. Night came and the negroes gathered in large numbers and songs, prayers, and exhortations were engaged in. The singing was beautiful and we were lulled to sleep by the harmony.

In the middle of the night we were suddenly roused by a tumult and hastily rising and opening the door Mr Thomas found that Young and Uncle Robin were engaged in a fight just outside of the room in which lay the dead baby they had been sitting up with. Mr Thomas called the old man, and the singing was suspended or had been by the fight. Young went into his house for his Pistol, a splendid one, swearing loudly that he would kill Robin. His wife tried to dissuade him. "Let me alone. I'll kill him. I'll kill him if God spares me" said he.

The yard fence and gate connects the yard and quarter. Uncle Robin had taken refuge with Mr Thomas in our back Piazzi. The moon was shining brightly and I could see distinctly from the wing room. Infuriated with rage Young rushed towards the gate to enter the yard to attack the old man, who cowering with fear was sitting on the steps at Mr Thomas' feet, who in his shirt sleeves and pants stood in the Piazzi. "Don't come in that gate Young," said Mr Thomas. "If you do I shall shoot you. I give you fair warning and call on those negroes to take witness of what I say." Young had prudence enough to stay outside. Mr Thomas told Uncle Robin to go to his house but he was afraid and spent the rest of the night in the Piazzi upon a carpet we gave him. The quarter was filled with Negro men, Mr Thomas the only white man on the place. He went to bed and told them to "sing on" and again we were lulled to sleep by their music. . . .

Reading over what I have just written one would suppose both Mr Thomas and I were on the Ku Klux order, but those were the only times during the two years they remained with us that we had any trouble with them and then I was always trying to protect old uncle Robin who rewarded us by taking pigs, chickens, and so on ad infinitum. So did Young and it was proven on them but what was the use of dismissing them to engage others equally dishonest and perhaps not so good field hands. . . .

Belmont, April 12, 1871 Tonight seven years ago my father died! Oh my father! My father now, as then I long to know where you are! I saw the bright and vigorous will give way, and I have never doubted the immortality of the soul since, but how I have longed to know more of the spirit world, have yearned to pierce the wall which divides, to catch a glimpse of Pa's face to hear one sound of his voice. How I have longed to do this God only knows. Somehow tonight I feel that I am nearer to a knowledge of spiritual life than I have been. I thought I realised that Pa's spirit was conscious of my wish to see and talk with him, but when I drew a newspaper to me and with my pen attempted to write, my hand remained motionless. I uttered a silent prayer that God would help me but my pen did not move. Perhaps the margin of the newspaper is a poor place thought I, and I placed my hand upon the blank leaf of this book and enquired, "If there was a spirit present?" but my pen did not move.

My eyes dim with tears when I think I shall see Pa and my children. Oh my darlings! Ma is very kind to Mary Belle and relieves me of a great deal of the care of her. Perhaps in the spirit world my three children have met Pa, Gen Thomas and Mother. How they will love my children because they are ours. . . . Tonight the anniversary of Pa's death I promise myself that I will read and reflect more upon the Swedenborg or Spiritualist faith, because the little I know of that doctrine comforts me more than any other I know and confirms some ideas I have formed. . . .

.   .   .

Thursday, May 4, 1871 I am alone tonight with the exception of Jeff, Cora Lou and Julian. Lizzie a little coloured girl is sleeping in the house. I had expected to have attended a club party at cousin Jane Sibley's, but my house girl and cook wished to attend a wedding of Laura Shelman's, a friend of theirs and I have had no alternative but to remain at home and take care of the children. I persuaded Mr Thomas to go in town and thought at the time that the mother of my house girl would spend the night in the yard to take care of Nellie's baby— After he left I learned that both Milly and Nelly with their babys and nurses were going to the wedding. . . .

Yesterday Mr Thomas loaned a young white man a waggon and mule to move up here to work [on] the farm. Last night he did not come and this morning Mr Thomas became uneasy about him and thought he had taken the mule. After dinner he sent Mr Morris to find him, who reported that the man was seen about twelve oclock today moving to town and passed by here with our waggon. Mr Morris followed him and they both came back tonight, the man having moved into town. I see little difference in white or coloured labour. Mr Morris broke his contract but concluded to come back after leaving us and hiring to Mr Carmichael. Burton, a mulatto man, working on shares left two weeks ago without one word of warning, nor have we heard from him since. Mr Thomas was very much pleased with him. Edmund Hall moved his wife and himself a few days after and Mr Thomas does not know where he is. He signed a contract but if forced to come back he cannot be compelled to work & Burton and himself have very nearly taken up enough flour, tobacco, syrup, cloth money &c to pay for the time they have been here. Under the circumstances the loss of three hands who have contracted with him is quite disheartening to Mr Thomas. . . .

I do not often complain to you dear Journal of my domestic annoyances. Sometimes I think it would perhaps be better if I did and kept a record of the trials to which Southern housekeepers are exposed. When I complain to Mr Thomas he tells me "So much for the blessings of freedom!" not knowing that in his reply he gives me comfort instead of dissatisfaction. I never liked extorted love or labour. I wish the former to be voluntary, and for the latter I wish to give an equivalent. I have the satisfaction of knowing when I am not pleased with a servant that I can look out for another. What I wish now is a sober respectable white woman or coloured who will find it to her interest to take an interest in pleasing me and interesting herself in my chidren.

Saturday, May 27, 1871   I am writing History for you my children and your mother tells you now of her interview with the man whom she "most delights to honor"—tells you of our President Jefferson Davis, dearer far dearer now in the hour of defeat than he was when chief magistrate of the Southern Confederacy. How I sympathised with our fallen chieftain in his degradation when he was taken through our streets closely guarded, no woman in that hour of peril daring to wave her handkerchief to him to make sign of sympathy—and men so crushed by defeat that the close[d] carriage passed by crowds who dared not cheer him for fear of sharing his fate. We could do nothing else for you my President and we did all we could. We named our boy for you, our boy who during the first year of the war I never dreamed of calling for our successful chief, but we felt honoured in identifying ourselves with him in his change of fortune.

I read of his incarceration in Fortress Munroe [Virginia], sighed, hoped and prayed for his release, taught my children never to omit the prayer of "I pray God for the release of President Davis," echoed Mrs Dunning's beautiful petition when she prayed "that Johnson would give to us Jeff Davis back again, release him for a Christmas gift and thus accomplish what he never had done, the subjugation of the Southern women." When at length hope deferred had made the heart sick, the glad tidings were flashed through the country "Jeff Davis has been released," I thanked God and wept for joy and Horace Greeley[7] is one Yankee for whom I retain a warm place in my heart. What ever the motive I thank and honour him for that one action which enobled his life, going security for our President.

I was at a club meeting at Dr Edward Eve's on Thursday night conversing with Mr Duncan.[8] He quietly remarked that "Mr Davis was in town." "What President Davis?" said I, in tones of glad surprise. He told me "yes." "I shall certainly go in in the morning," I added, "and take Jeff with me." Later in the evening we were conversing in a group consisting of Mr Duncan Dr & Mrs Eve, Henrietta, and others when someone joined us to whom I told the good news and there was a ring of exultation and pride in my voice as I told that Jeff Davis was in Augusta. Looking up I saw that Mr Brewster one of our Northern neighbors was seated near me. He changed countenance, but what cared I as I added, "How anxious I am to see him. I so honour and reverence his name." Mr Duncan added that "Mr Davis owed the estimation he was held in by the Southern people to his long imprisonment." This piqued me. "You must admit that he paid a high price to obtain this admiration?" "Yes" he admitted "but that Jeff Davis ought to thank God for his being taken prisoner. Had this not been the case he would have gone down to his grave unhonoured by the Southern people." "Why Mr Duncan I am astonished at you" I replied, "but I confess I cannot argue cooly with you. I can well imagine that his imprison-

---

7. Horace Greeley, editor of the *New York Tribune* and an active politician, had campaigned for Davis's release from prison and was one of several prominent signators of the bail bond.

8. Mr. Duncan was one of several ministers who preached at Rosney Chapel.

ment endeared him to the 'dear daughters of his people,' as he calls the Southern women. Mr Davis had faults, as who has not?" . . .

Yesterday morning Turner rode in town and Jeff and I went in the Buggy. We were going in town hoping to see Mr Davis. The morning was beautiful and as memorys of the past, the Confederate past thronged through my mind, they were softened by the beautiful presence of nature. Jeff and I talked and sang snatches of little songs and as we passed through Double Branc[h]es watched the little fish as they glided past and my heart had a singularly uplifted feeling and an ever present sense of God's goodness. . . . Driving to Sis Anne's I made my toilette after reading that President Davis would have a reception from 12 till two oclock, and in company with Turner, Jeff and Mary Vason we called at the Planters [Hotel] between 12 and one oclock.

Col Snead met us at the door and we waited a few moments until a party who had been introduced finished their conversation. "Is that President Davis?" I enquired as I saw a gentleman bow in reply to an introduction. "Yes wouldn't you have known him by his pictures?" "No" I replied "he is much better looking, younger looking." Just then the President turned and Col Snead introduced "Mrs Thomas, President Davis, Mr Thomas Miss Mary Vason." I shook hands with him and for the moment forgot all else in the great content of an accomplished hope. Drawing Jeff to me I introduced him as Jeff Davis Thomas. He took Jeff's hand in his, drew him closely to him, and held him there with his arm around him. "I cannot tell you Mrs Thomas how highly I appreciate this compliment." My heart warmed at his reception of Jeff and I added "Perhaps you will understand Mr Davis how dear *you* are to the dear daughters of your people as you so gracefully termed us, when I explain that our little Boy was named for you the afternoon you passed through Augusta a prisoner. We could do nothing else to express our sympathy and we honoured ourselves in naming him for you." "My dear Madam" he replied, "I appreciate the compliment so much the more." We continued the conversation a few moments longer but during that time soul had met with soul and I think I understand his character better than I did before.

We withdrew to permit other introductions and as I stood and contrasted his erect figure and graceful carriage with men who were introduced to him I was *proud* of our President. He is so quietly elegant, so perfectly self possessed, not handsome but bearing about him that unmistaken air of a gentleman, without which the handsomest face would have no attraction for me. Mr Davis wrote his autagraph for Jeff. The card bears on it this inscription "For Jeff Davis Thomas—Jefferson Davis." During our conversation Mr Davis remarked to me "that he had great faith in the Southern women, that they would train the boys right," he added placing his hand upon Jeff's head, "It will come out right. I may not live to see it, but it is not in the nature of God to allow the best people he ever made to remain permanently under the rule of the meanest people he ever made." That remark gave me the key to understand why it was that it had not for one moment occurred to me to render the homage of kissing his hand as I had the night before said I would be willing to do.

President Davis was the courtly, elegant gentleman but not perfect. He has strong predjudices as that remark indicated, but he is mistaken. We are not the best, nor are the Yankees the worst nation God ever made. . . . I shook hands with him and we left hoping that this was not the last opportunity we should have of meeting our President. I have had no president since then and until a Southern man, not a radical presides in the White House I will acknowledge none. The bone of contention, the Negro Slavery has been removed and all may yet be well. . . .

Belmont, May 28, 1871 . . . A few nights since, the question was discussed "If we should be willing to live our lives over again." Almost everyone was willing to make the experiment. . . . Mr Duncan said "he would be willing," but no I believe I would not be willing to be a baby again, but if with the light of my present life to guide me I could begin over I would be willing to make the experiment. "You would be willing to begin again at seventeen would you not Mrs Thomas?" "No" said I "for then my troubles began" at which they all laughed but I continued, "Is it because I have more faith or is it my dislike of monotony which causes me to say that I would not be willing to live my life over again— No I have faith in God's law of progression and I believe that I shall have a higher development when I leave this world"—

We continued the conversation for some time but I have continued the train of thought since then. I believe in all ruling Providence and am willing to trust him for the future. I know that in a few weeks important law suits have to be decided. I know how much of my husband's affairs are involved, but this does not trouble me as once it did. Is it faith? or is it a belief in fatalism? I think the former, for at times my heart overflows with love to God and I am happy, very happy notwithstanding all this. My children are a great comfort to me. I love my husband and I love all God's creatures. . . . Turner is seventeen. Mary Belle will be thirteen in September. Cora Lou eight in June, Jeff was ten last month and Julian is three years and six months old now. . . .

[A significant journal—the one covering the period from June 1871 to December 1878—is missing, perhaps destroyed later because of its dark, unhappy content. It was a troubled period. During those years two children were born to the Thomases, James Clanton in October 1872 and Kathleen in January 1875. Brother Holt died in Paris in 1871, Colonel Vason (Sis Anne's husband) died in 1873, and sister Kate married Henry Rood in 1875. A crushing blow in the mid-1870s was the loss of Gertrude Thomas's beloved Belmont. According to an undated, unidentified newspaper clipping in one of her scrapbooks:

> Captain J. J. Thomas' residence, on the Louisville road, six miles from the city, was destroyed by fire yesterday afternoon, together with all its contents, including furniture, books, silver, etc. Loss fully $8000—no insurance. It was caused by sparks from the chimney. A servant girl saw flames and raised the alarm. Capt. Thomas, Turner Thomas and neighbors tried to extinguish the fire—the roof fell in in about 20 minutes. The family was in residence, but escaped without injuries. Ten acres of wood caught fire from the burning residence and all the timber was consumed. A heavy gale of wind was blowing at the time. . . .

Gertrude later wrote that her living-room furniture was in Augusta at the Clanton home at the time, which may explain why the earlier journals were not burned. She also mentions her piano as being at a sister's home. After the fire, the family moved into a farmhouse on their Yankee Farm property, which formed the northern boundary of the Belmont property.]

Part IV   1878–1889

13. Schoolteacher and Breadwinner

Keep me from the sin of envy.
—*August 10, 1879*

The Farm, The last night of 1878   I have been reading over my last Journal, reading the record for the past three years. I was eight years writing that book and this one has been bought for months. There have been times when I have thought I will begin my new Journal and I have had a disposition to shrink from making a record of my life. Tonight I am grateful to a merciful Providence for his goodness to me. I had forgotten until I read it tonight that one year ago tonight I had written "The absorbing thought is how shall we live? If I can succeed in procuring a situation, this time next year I shall be earning something for my children. My heart turns to Macon and I wonder could I get something there?"

How strange life is. Mrs [Anderson] Carmichael is dead and for two months past I have had charge of the county school. Some other time I will tell how it was brought about. I am grateful and contented that I have an opportunity of adding to the comfort of my family. Dear Mrs Carmichael. How little I thought one year ago that tonight the rain drops would be falling upon your grave. I drew up resolutions of respect which were read before the Sunday School of which she was superintendent and they were afterwards published. It is quite late. I do not know how late for the two clocks are out of order.

Wednesday, January 1, 1879   Again time has rolled around and another year has begun. I know that I will be more constantly employed than heretofore, that I will not be mistress of my own time but with that thought comes the reflection I shall be profitably engaged. A few weeks since I was reading in Holmes 2nd Reader, a pretty little piece of poetry about the chickadee-dee—the robin enquires of the former if she "never grows weary of working

377

for her little ones?" The reply of the Chickadee-dee is that "*Love gives a zest to labour.*" I have thought of it so often since I read it and my own heart beats responsive to the same sentiment. A few days since I gave Jeff fifteen dollars to buy him a suit of clothes. He bought the suit for eighteen dollars. He did not buy them before he had felt the need of them. He has been going in town to Mr Neely this winter.[1] He did not attend school last year. . . .

Mr Thomas went up to the poor house to vote for county officers. If I could have cast a vote it should have been for Charley Sibley for sheriff. I have remained quite closely by the fire. I have cut out and made for Kathleen a dress and tonight worked the button holes. Cora Lou made Kathleen a pair of cotton flannel night drawers this morning and one pair yesterday. She did not use the machine as it is out of order. I worked the button holes in the pair she made yesterday. . . .

This New Year finds me more contented than the two last years. Taxes are still to be paid, debts are pressing but I am more sanguine. I shall hope to write oftener. My mother and family are all quite well. Cora lost a little baby last summer but the Friday before Christmas she gave birth to another little boy. My husband and children are well (except Jeff). May another New Year find our link unbroken. I sometimes think the greatest change may be for Mary Belle—dear bless my child!

Saturday, January 4, 1879   Mr Thomas said to me the other day "Gertrude if you expect to teach school you ought to improve your hand writing." Indeed I am very concious of my deficientcy in that respect as well as in arithmetic. I have had so little experience in that branch of knowledge since I left school that I feel that if I had more advanced pupils it might be necessary for me to study too, as it is none of my pupils are farther advanced than fractions.

Today is holiday. I am not so wedded to my new profession that I do not welcome Saturday with as much pleasure as either of my scholars. I am writing in the school room. Since we have been living here Mr Thomas had an old barn in the yard moved up, improved and made into a wing room which joined on to the end of

---

1. Benjamin Neely was principal of the high school in Augusta. He was named superintendent of schools in 1880. The Neelys were neighbors of the Thomases.

the back piazzi. The room has for the past two years been used for my kitchen. When I first commenced teaching school on the 1st of November I taught for two weeks in a room out in the yard while this room was being ceiled over head and on the sides, and window sash put in the three windows. A window fronting the public road has been cut down into a door giving an entirely seperate entrance from the front of the house. . . .

On last Monday night Turner and Mary Belle were at a party at Mrs Anderson Walton's which they enjoyed very much. Mary Belle wore a handsome dress Ma ordered for her from New York last summer. This week Ma is having made for her an evening dress which she will wear at a Sans Souci at Mr John Clark's next Thursday night. During the winter Mary Belle has been receiving a good deal of attention from Mr [W. N.] Mercier. He is a widower with two children. He is a fine looking but quite large gentleman. He claims to be thirty four. What I like most about him is that he is reported to be a reliable business man. He is engaged in the cotton business. I like his healthy, strong, manly appearance and apparently cheerful disposition, but I have wandered off from the subject of my school.

For the first month I received thirty dollars. I will not draw my second month's salary until next Saturday. I expect to be paid for wood which we have furnished. My stove and eight desks and benches were furnished me by the county. I borrowed from Aunt Lamkin 20 dollars during the holidays, fifteen of which I gave to Jeff— I gave two dollars for a pair of shoes for myself—paid Ma one, gave MB one to pay for the Sans Souci entertainment (The girls of the club pay the expenses) and bought with the other Canton Flannel for Kathleen's night drawers. I would like to keep an account of my expenses this year. Last night Ma sent me five gallons of kerosine. I will notice to see how long it will last. During the last two months I have had twenty scholars but they do not come as regularly as they should. I had a new scholar the other day Ada Sharpton, a niece of Mrs Neely's. . . .

.   .   .

Saturday, February 8, 1879 . . . The last week has been cloudy and I have been very far from well. Indeed the last month has been a sore trial of patience with me— One month ago I was in town. I was owing Aunty twenty dollars I borrowed from her to buy Jeff's clothes. I paid her, bought a dress for Cora Lou of worsted to mix with a blue silk which Cora gave her. I gave $1.50 for it and engaged the making of it with Mrs Marsh for $3.00, bought two white table cloths for 3.25—trimmings for Cora Lou's dress for 84 cts, bought pins four papers for 10 cts, hair pins five papers for five cts, 10 cts candy, 10 cts dried figs (I don't know when I ever bought any before). Paid for the cleaning of three pair of kid gloves 25 cts, 15 for the cleaning of a lace tie, a tea pot for thirty five cts, 10 cts at St James church which I attended Sunday morning. Everything is so low that a great deal can be bought for a small amount of money but oh the scarcity of money— The war times was nothing to it.

I had reserved five dollars to pay Miss Sego. Before the war she loaned Mr Thomas in good faith thinking it a safe investment a small amount. I do not know how much exactly but it was money for which she had sewed. When he failed her money was lost in the general loss.[2] I have always felt that she should be paid but how could I pay it? I had hoped to give her five dollars every month now that I had commenced keeping school. I called to see her, gave her the five dollars, found her sick and promised that Mr T would send her a load of wood, which has not been sent yet. I have given her money before when my children were wanting clothes. . . .

Tuesday, Turner and I went in to attend Watterson's lecture at Masonic Hall.[3] I enjoyed the lecture, the first entertainment I have been to in Augusta this winter. Tickets were 50 cts apiece. I came home to Ma's in good spirits, told Ma to be sure and wake me so that I could get out home in time the next morning. Very early Ma called me. I rose instantly and commenced dressing. Rising, Ma came to the fire place and taking a seat by the fire said to me in a low tone, "Did you know that your place in Columbia has been levied upon?" I did not, but was not surprised, and told her so. I knew that Mr Thomas had had part of the money to pay the taxes but he had used it to keep his name from being protested in bank, a note with Turner's signature and mine upon it. "What can I do?" said I in reply to Ma. "I know Mr Thomas hasn't the money nor

2. That Jefferson Thomas borrowed money from Miss Sego (or Seago), a seamstress and neighbor, before the war seems to confirm the presence of a bad habit that only became worse in the postbellum years.

3. Henry Watterson was a popular lecturer. He was editor of the *Louisville Courier-Journal* from 1868 to 1918.

have I. I could pay it with the money from my school." "I will advance it to you" she said "but you must pay it back." "Of course," I replied. "I would rather you would loan it to me than give it to me.". . .

I told Mr Thomas and if I expected praise, commendation or anything of the kind, then or since, I was disappointed. Not one word of anything of the kind, and this when I know he dislikes an advertisement of that kind in the papers almost as much as I do. Well, a portion of it has been paid. . . .

. . .

February 9, 1879 Today is clear, bright, cold, and beautiful. . . . Situated as I am I have no pleasant church relationship. I have no driver and the carriage is so shabby that I never use it except to drive me to Ma's and then it is put in the stable and never driven on the street. Jeff or Turner have driven me this winter when I go in town or to church out here. Occasionally we get one of the tenants to drive but not often. As the carriage has a dickey seat I do not like for Turner or Jeff to drive or have the Horses to take out or hitch up at Ma's stable. The consequence will be that I shall cease to go after a while in the carriage. I have only taken Clanton and Kathleen to town once this winter and that was Christmas.[4] . . .

Last summer at a meeting of the Grange I read an essay which I had written on Ceres, Pomona, and Flora, the three patronesses who preside as officers over the grange.[5] It was afterwards published in the grange paper with a very complimentary notice. I also wrote an account of the Horticultural society and read it at one of our meetings. I have sometimes thought that I would copy something from my old Journals and see if I could get it published—not for fame, alas! for money. I am so afraid of becoming morbid. There are so many things I could so enjoy—travel, lectures, society, fine dramatic performances, and this life of self abnegation is so trying. If it were voluntary—for some good cause but I deny myself because I cannot help it and I do not deceive myself. I know I deserve

---

4. Clanton was six years old, Kathleen four years.

5. Ceres, the goddess of corn or agriculture; Pomona, the goddess of fruits and orchards; and Flora, the goddess of flowers. Both Gertrude and Jefferson Thomas were active in the county Grange.

no credit for it for were it in my power I would tomorrow have a well ordered home in which I could entertain my own and children's friends. Ah it is— Well, well, I ought not to complain. . . .

.   .   .

The Farm. February 28, 1879   I am writing for the *first* time *with* a *pair* of *eye* glasses. Sis Anne gave them to me. I find that I cannot see to read at night especially the local column of the *Chronicle* and *Constitutionalist* which is printed in very fine type. I am writing in the school room, in the afternoon. It is a bright cheerful room at this season of the year. The week has passed pleasantly. Teaching has been less labourious. I think it has been greatly owing to the strength which a trip to town imparted to me. Last Saturday in the small spring waggon Jeff Cora Lou Julian and I went in to see Ma.

Aunty's carriage was before the door. I accepted a seat with Ma and herself and Cora Lou and I rode up town. It may be foolish to admit it but I do not like to walk upon Broad Street. I have always been accustomed to driving and it is the only way I like to go. . . . I drove up town went to Richards' dry good stores, bought nothing, saw some pretty chromos one representing Miriam and Moses, then drove to Anderson's where I bought some remnants of calico for three and a half cts per yd. The best calicoes are selling at four and five cents. . . .

.   .   .

May 7, 1879   I commenced this school this winter as an experiment. I thought I would try it and if I was not pleased I had only to give it up. I intended if possible to continue it during the year. A remark Mr Wiggins made expressed I knew the sentiment of many of my neighbors. "I know" said he "Mrs Thomas will not continue the school. She wasn't raised to work and she will grow tired of it very soon." I am told that the schools will close for this term at the expiration of this month and what are my feelings with regard to it? Instead of being glad, delighted with my holiday, I am sorry that my school will not be continued through June. I am really heartily interested in my school. And the income I receive is so welcome to me.

It is so pleasant to work for my children and thus procure them the clothing which they require. I had intended subscribing for magazines, buying an oil cloth for the hall or passage, having it papered as well as this room. I had wished to buy a bed room sett and I had tantalizing glimp[s]es of a personal indulgence in buying an Encyclopaidia but I will not be able to gratify my wishes. Aside from six chairs for which I gave five dollars and a tea sett of China I have bought nothing but clothing for the family since I paid the taxes on the place in Columbia. I sent home a good portion of the money for February to Mr Thomas to settle with the hands. . . .

Thursday, May 8, 1879 Mary Belle and Cora Lou have walked over to see Ada Robinson one of my scholars. She has been absent from school for several days on account of sickness. One of my scholars left during the last month. His father moved to town. His name was Green Daniel. He was a bright pretty [boy] but extremely restless nature. His sister Rosa and himself reduce my school to twenty two. I count Kathleen but she is only an alphabet scholar. The Richards boys are absent two days in the week. They go in town and sell strawberrys. Joe & John Johnson and John Keener do not come regularly. They have to remain at home and assist in the farm. I expect I have an easier time because I have fewer scholars or they come so irregularly during the past month. But I really think I would prefer to have them come regularly because I am interested in them and wish them to learn. . . .

.   .   .

August 9, 1879 I have been quite unwell during the last week and just as nervous as I could be. I wonder if the poor women who are thought to be cross are altogether responsible for it. I know there are times when every nerve appears strung to its utmost tension and every noise annoys—when all I wish is perfect quiet. How I wish I had a large bed room with everything in order. I think that it would assist in making me well if my sense of order was not so often disturbed. . . .

.   .   .

August 10, 1879 I was cross yesterday when I wrote the above and not altogether well. Ah me how I do try to keep from complaining when I am fretted. I do not like to write about the little ills which fret me. They would appear so trivial. Last night for the first time in my life I prayed "Heavenly Father do pray keep me from being covetous. Keep me from the sin of envy." I searched my own heart and I was ashamed of myself. I must say this much in defence. I can stand poverty for myself but oh my children! Mary Belle is twenty years old. A pleasure she will have now would be enjoyed with a zest no aftertime can bestow upon it and I so much wished her to travel. I so much wished her to go North with Ma or to Catoosa Springs with her Aunt Mamie but I could not afford it. Pinck is in Atlanta this summer, a member of the legislature from Burke. "A host in himself" as a newspaper correspondent said of him. On Friday Aug 1st Mamie went up to Catoosa taking with her Joe and her four little children and one nurse. . . .

Ma left for Bridgehampton [New York] to join Kate on Wednesday Aug 5th 1879. I never missed her more and she is to be gone three months! And I do not think Ma is as well as she has been. She appears feebler. My dear mother who has always been so strong, strong in every sense of the word. Next year Kate is coming home and glad as I will be to have her with us again mingles the sweet thought that never again while we live will Ma and I be parted for so long a time. Mary Vason went up to Catoosa with Col and Mrs Stovall, Mrs Dr Phinizy and Mattie. She left the last night of July and next Thursday Sis Anne goes to the same place with the rest of [her] children—Turner and Rebie. I think of Mary and Mattie having so gay a time and I do so wish Mary Belle could have gone. Jane (Mrs William Sibley) is also at Catoosa.

I do not care particularly for myself. I know I cannot go and I am content. I read "sweet are the uses of adversity" but I do not realise it. I shall have to strive hard or I shall be soured instead of sweetened when I reflect how much my children are debarred from. They may not be thrown into quite so much dissipation, so much temptation when they are forced to see so little of the world's gayety but I must not write in this way. . . .

After dinner. Oh what supreme folly it was for me to write what I did this morning but I am not a wise woman. I cannot always confine my thoughts within the bounds of reason. I dream dreams and build castles occasionally even now, but they are for my children. I am realising that I am growing old and for me old age has no terror. I was very much impressed by something I read a few days ago from Victor Hugo who acknowledged that passing from thirty nine to forty was the most trying time of his life. "Forty years" said he "is the old age of youth while fifty is the youth of old age." I was forty five my last birthday.... Notwithstanding my having kept a Journal for some time past I am apt of late years to be a little uncertain with regard to my age. This is not an affectation as one would suppose but I scarcely give the subject one thought from one birthday to another.

I have only one dream for myself. Someday to visit Europe. I scarcely think I shall go. Ah well as Dr Deems tells us "wait until we have our wings." Now does not that seem like the very quintessence of folly for a sober middle aged woman like I am to yet have way down deep in her heart the thought that someday the dream of her life should be realised, that before her enraptured eyes should appear Italy, Paris and London and I know what spot would be most dear, the city where Holt lived and died.... It is absolutely necessary for me to remember how much I can buy for the family to give me courage to take charge of the school for another year. I wish, how I wish there was no necessity for it. Listen dear journal I will tell you what I will tell no one else. I do wish I could do without teaching school next year. There! I have told someone and no one reads my Journal. When I think of ten months to listen to such small children and such restless little ones read in the 1st and 2d reader! When the time comes I will find strength for it, but I did not realise how tired I was until the vacation came and the grand finale, the Pic Nic was over.... I had it at the Clanton Summer House (or Rowell Place) had the Grange tables carried over and all the school contributing we had an excellent dinner....

Sunday, August 17, 1879 ... My head aches and so does my face, and so does my heart. It is not the cook's sickness or my own, that is a small matter, but all my life I have tried to make the best of things, hide from outside persons, even from you my Journal anything which would not reflect credit upon my family. Either I have grown more careless or Mr Thomas more reckless for alas the worst state of things prevail. He has taken his name from the church book and profanes God's name constantly— There are times when my own faith fails. I do not know in whom to trust, to what to pray. I cannot write of this, indeed I ought not. I could stand it if it was confined to one room, only to my hearing but alas when children and servants prove no restraint!

Years ago Gen Thomas said to [me], "What would you do Gertrude if Jefferson were to get drunk?" "Lock the door, stay with him and try to keep anyone from finding it out," was my instant reply, given with so much energy as to create a smile. I used to hear Mrs D—— laugh and tell of her husband's foolish speeches and actions when he was intoxicated. I wondered then, I wonder now how she could have done it. From this degradation I have been mercifully preserved but I cannot, I cannot become accustomed to profanity. Sometimes I almost wish I could, but I cannot, I cannot. To me God is so real, so sacred. I am intensely reverential. Poor pitiful worms as we are perhaps we are not judged so harshly after all.

.   .   .

Sunday, November 16, 1879 Clanton is dead! Oh my God how strange it sounds. Clanton my bright, beautiful boy. Where, oh where is he? I saw him die. I saw him after he was dead, but oh darling I want to see you *now, now*. Oh Lord will I ever get used to this yearning, this craving to see my child, to put my arms around him and have him nestle to my side? . . . I stood by his grave last Sunday morning for the first time since he was buried. I went by myself. I wished no one with me. I walked on and on until I entered the gate and then standing by the violet covered grave of my child I felt farther from him than I have done since he died. What! Clanton, my bright boy who could (altho only seven years old, a few weeks before) ride on horseback or drive a buggy. Clanton who had so much life, so much vigor, *he* buried there underneath all that earth. Oh, no, no! My God it is enough to make one cry out in utter despair.

I stood and looked, then I knelt and tried to have communion with my child by prayer. All in vain. No gleam of comfort came. I walked around for a while and read inscriptions on other graves. I was trying to find some balm for my weary, hungry soul and thought, "Others have lost children. I know I am not the only mourning mother." . . . That afternoon Sis Annie and I went down to the burial services of Mr Bothwell. As I stood looking at a grave in the next section I read the name of the first Mrs James Lamar, the wife of the Christian minister. On it was this inscription, "She is not here. She is risen." *There* I found the message I had sought for all the morning. Clanton is not in that grave, his soul which left that body which we buried has been born into a new existence. But oh my boy, my boy what would I not give to see you now. Help me oh my God!

Friday, December 12, 1879 ... It is late but I must write that again pecuniary troubles have come upon me and again I am advertised in the newspapers. There is a column and a half of the newspaper. I do not understand all of it but this I do know that I am to have my lifetime interest in Pa's estate sold to settle a debt due by us to Jones & Norris. I also know that there are several debts of a similar character which will have to be settled in exactly the same manner.[6] I also know and have been conscious all the while that we have been defending the case that it was a just debt. Having received the goods for the plantation we ought to have paid for them. Having signed the papers I should have been responsible for the debt. I cannot plead that at anytime I have been ignorant of the risk I ran in signing papers. As to wether I ought to have signed them that is not the question involved.

I have been feeling better than usual this afternoon. I have been unwell all the week. By the way I am at a critical period in a woman's life, a time when if physicians tell us right the purchase of my lifetime interest might prove a bad speculation. I have been nervous and my strength has been tried by teaching this week. A comfortable fire was burning in this room and seated in a large arm chair I stretched my feet towards it and rejoiced that it was Friday— I should have rest for two days, rest for the brain and body— I never knew the meaning of the word before. Julian came in and I read to him story after story from a specimen number of *The Youth's Companion* a Boston paper I had sent for. About twilight Mr Thomas came in and found us all around the table reading, Mary Belle Cora Lou Julian and I. Throwing a newspaper upon the table with an oath "There," said he "is that notice."

Without a word I glanced at the first page of the *Chronicle* and read among the decisions of the Supreme Court in Atlanta Dec 9th the following— "J J Thomas Trustee and Gertrude Thomas vs Jones & Norris, Complaint from Richmond." It was a column and a half

---

6. By 1879, Gertrude Thomas had signed away her lifetime interest in most of her inherited properties. Turner Thomas had also signed in some cases.

long. I did not understand all of it but calmly read on and on until it was finished. When I read my name published as Gertrude Thomas I nerved myself and read on. When in conclusion I was referred to as Mrs Thomas, my lip quivered and I felt my eyes fill with tears. The names of my six children were published as being interested. I thought they had forgotten Clanton and then I thought, How strange that they should have known that he was not with us. The one supreme thought when I had finished reading it was joy that Pa's will will hold good and that the property was secured for the children. My lifetime interest may be sold but something from the wreck will be saved for them, and oh my father! do you, can you know how grateful, how very grateful I am to you for this provision of your will. . . .

December 17, 1879 Clanton has been dead two months. One month after his death I wrote of him in this book. I had been prevented from going to his grave before by Cora Lou's illness. She was very sick for two or three weeks after Clanton died. Dr Baxley was attending her and we were very anxious for her. The night Clanton died I wrote Ma a short letter in which I told her of his death adding— "Oh my Mother pity me. If you could only see my pretty little Clanton." The day after he was buried I wrote the following letter to Mary Belle.[7] I have wished to but have not had the nerve to copy it. I will now for I wish to preserve the memory of my child among his brothers and sisters. . . . This is my letter to her dated

At Home—Octo 16th 1879

Dear Mary Belle—
    You will have received my letter telling you of the death of our little darling and I know you will yearn to hear something more of him. . . . Mr Thomas went to Columbia to the plantation Friday [October 10th] and took Julian and Clanton. They kissed me good bye in the school room and I moved my seat so as to catch a glimpse of them when they drove off. It was my last view of Clanton in health. They returned late Saturday night. He

---

7. Mary Luke Clanton had taken Mary Belle to New York. Until a few years before her death, Gertrude's mother continued to make annual pilgrimages to New York, accompanied by one or more of her daughters or granddaughters.

had been sick in Columbia that morning and it was raining a little that night when they came back, altho they had an umberella
and oil cloth to protect them in the spring waggon. I did not
think he was very sick. I went to hear Mr Smith preach at
Rosney Chapel Sunday morning as he was a guest of ours. I remained from Sunday School with Clanton who still complained
of his head. I rubbed it and that night we gave him quinine.

The next morning I went into the school room leaving Cora
Lou with him. He sent for me during the morning. I came in,
kissed him, cheered him by telling him that Mama would rub
his head all the time at recess. "You know I must go back now
darling" said I, and left him with Cora Lou. "Well" was his reply
and that one word of *uncomplaining resignation* has haunted me
ever since. . . . When I came in again he *did not know me*. Oh
my God that is so hard. I was teaching other people's children
when I ought to have been with my own child. Mr Thomas was
busy at the gin house. As soon as he came in he saw the change.
(Still did not call me.) Soon after dinner he was taken with
spasms. When Dr Ed Eve came he placed Clanton under the influence of chloral. His spasms were checked but that night we
thought he would die. The Dr remained all night. He continued
very ill all the next day— . . .

He died calmly, his little mouth wearing a grieved, pitiful
look, like a little baby, and Mary Belle in that supreme moment I
called aloud "Anna Lou take care of my child," and thus I
charged my angel child to take care of Clanton. And then a great
quiet settled upon me for a time. I had no time to grieve then. I
laid out his clothes, the little puffed bosom shirt among them.
Shedrick's mother (Eliza) and Mollie sat up with us and Eliza
dressed him with Mr Thomas assisting. He insisted that I should
not. The neighbors were very kind. . . . Cora and Mamie came to
the funeral. Hammond and Flady were two of the pall bearers
and Flady carried one of the funeral notices around. Fanny Mc-
Coy & Nannie Richards made wreaths. Mamie brought a cross
and wreath and Mrs James Miller had one at the cemetery for
me. . . . Do not grieve too much for him. He loved "big sister"
and Grand Ma too. Go out with Ma and use your opportunity for
seeing New York. You may never have another opportunity. You
will miss him more when you come home than you possibly can
now.   Good night.
    Lovingly Mama
PS Your letter to your Papa was received Tuesday just before
Clanton's funeral, so you were with us in spirit. I will save for

you a few of the flowers which were in the wreaths. I have a flower pressed which he had in his dear little hands.

At night. . . . Mary Belle and Mr Thomas went in town Monday. He returned leaving her. She will make Cora a visit and remain in town for several weeks. With the exception of a week spent in Beech Island with Celia Lamar she has been at home since her return from New York. Mary Belle enjoyed her visit to the North very much. Ma did not tell her of Clanton's death or show her the letter I wrote to her until the day before she left for home. She attended no parties or theatres and places which would have shown a disrespect for his memory but Ma thought it was best not to tell her.

December 18, 1879 . . . As I read the piece from which this verse [a Christmas poem] is quoted I wept for I thought of Clanton. Oh if I could but "see the radiance of the crown upon his dear brow." If I only knew that he was happy. You were so small, so shy, always clinging to Mama and afraid of strangers. Do you miss me darling? Oh my pet, my pretty, pretty little boy. Mama yearns so for you. Sometimes I hold out my arms and try to clasp Clanton to me. Again I listen for a sound of his voice. I look at Kathleen and I try to catch some glimpse, some expression to remind me of Clanton. She told me the other day, "I am faid I cannot remember my brother Clanton" not knowing that her mention of him proved that she had not forgotten him. Clanton would have been seven years old on the 16th of October. . . .

He was very anxious for a birthday party. He remembered the party I gave Julian last year. He had never been at one before and that with Ma's Christmas dinners, the Grange and my school pic nic were the only feasts in which my little Clanton had ever enjoyed. I am so glad of every little pleasure which I was enabled to give him. I am so glad that God gave him to me. For seven years he was loaned to me— There have been times when there was an expression in the beautiful eyes of my little boy which only I understood. Oh God Thou knowest and only Thou what a blessing that angel child was to me—

Wednesday, December 31, 1879 The last night of this year! Tonight there is a party at Ma's given by a club of young men of Joe [Mamie's son] and Jeff's age. Ma invited me to go in but I thought that it would not be showing a proper degree of respect for the memory of Clanton for me to attend. Indeed I did not care to go while I did not object to the children being present. Turner Mary Belle Jeff and Cora Lou will be there. We sent Julian in this afternoon with Cora Lou's dress, a light buff bunting trimmed with black velvet. He went against his will for he would have preferred to have remained and played with his goats and his new waggon. He drove Traveller in the buggy so that Turner could have it tomorrow when he makes New Year's calls at Summerville.

I have been reading since tea a book called *The Banker's Daughter*,[8] a very sprightly story and the first novel I have read in a long while. Mr Thomas and Kathleen are asleep. Dinah Hunter moved down to cook for me today. I am writing these common place ideas instead of indulging in reflection upon what the past year has brought for me but I dare scarcely lift the stone which has been rolled over the sepulcher of my buried hope. Last year I wrote "May another New Year find our link unbroken." The greatest change has been for Clanton. He was so anxious for a party when his birthday came around. When it did come he was in "His Father's Kingdom." Dear little Clanton took his Christmas dinner in Heaven but if he knows anything of earth he knows that he is not forgotten. My first thought on Christmas morning was of him. Nor did I forget his Christmas present for while I bought toys for the others I had Turner to buy me camellias for him and the morning after Julian and I went to the cemetery and arranged a vase of flowers—white hyacinths, daffodils and camellias. I remembered how he always loved flowers. I wonder if they have flowers in Heaven? . . .

· · ·

January 2, 1880 . . . The *Evening News* of Wednesday contained an account of the names of the ladies who would receive on New Year's— Among them was that of Mrs A C Vason and Miss Vason on Washington Street. They would receive assisted by Miss Mattie Phinizy Misses Lucy and ——— Dortic and Miss Anne Twiggs. I had thought Mary would have requested Mary Belle to receive with her and this official announcement that she did not do so *cut me—*

---

8. *The Banker's Daughter* (1878), by Bronson Howard.

Yes that is the word. Cut as well as grieved me. I suppose I ought to be above such things. I was thinking of this but reading and striving to forget it when Mr Thomas came in, impatient and worried and by a few words having no reference to what I was already thinking of succeeded in placing me in a most unenviable mood.

I could not sleep well. I was already worried and in the middle of the night sleeping with Kathleen (there was no one here but Mr Thomas and herself and he was in the next room) I thought of my children's future and silly woman that I was I cried because I could not give to my children the advantages of society and comforts which money alone could procure for them. I must do myself the justice to say that I should not have cried because Mary did not invite Mary Belle to receive with her. I hope I am not so foolish as that but I have had so much to try me of late. I try to bear a brave front, to suffer and make no sign but that sale will have to come off soon and Mr Thomas' gloomy forebodings are well calculated to try sterner nerves than I possess and—

Yesterday after dinner Mrs Nixon and her son called to see us. Mr Thomas was resting on the bed, said he felt too low spirited to see anyone so I received them alone. I had a piece of fruit cake which Sallie Richards gave me for a Christmas present. I had that handed with an egg nogg which Dinah made. . . . Turner is on the jury. Jeff is staying with Ma. He is clerking for a Chinaman by the name of Loo Chong. It was the only situation he could obtain. He only gets a salary of three dollars a week. What a change from Athens College [University of Georgia] to which I had so fondly hoped he could have gone this winter. Ah me! Mary Belle and Cora Lou are both in town. The former has been spending some time with Cora— Lizzie Colquitt a daughter of Gov Colquitt[9] has been making Cora a visit. She took dinner at Ma's Christmas, the only stranger present. I have been reading during the afternoon a novel Mrs Sharpton (Mr Neely's sister) loaned me called *Sowing Wild Oats*.[10] I have had strawberrys and onions planted in the vegatable garden today.

---

9. Alfred A. Colquitt, governor of Georgia (1876–82).

10. Probably a translation of the German novel of that title by Gustave von Moser; the book was later put into dramatic form as a comedy in four acts.

January 12, 1880 Last week I had a very small school and I was worried by it.[11] Today I have a new scholar with the promise of several others. The weather has been very warm but two or three days last week it rained. This morning there was every appearance of rain which may have been the reason why the Boggs and Richards children were absent from school. The four Neely children were absent from school two days of last week and I wrote to Mrs Neely to know why it was so? She wrote me that Mrs Sharpton Mr Neely's sister had not decided what she would do about returning to Carolina and that Mr Neely wished the children to go to her. I will copy from her note. "You will understand how we feel and not feel that it is any want of love or respect to you believe me. Your most affectionate friend Eve N"—

I did not answer this note for I do not understand the motive exactly which prompted their action. I have striven conscientiously to do my duty by the children and I have earnestly requested the cooperation of the parents. I have written to Mrs Neely several times urging her to buy the children books and have them study at home. Allen Neely has been without an Arithmetic Spelling or Reading book all winter. Johnny has had no book of either kind. Bessie has been without slate or pencil or a reading book until the last few weeks. Johnny has come to his reading class often without looking at the lesson. I have borrowed for Allen and taken a great deal of pains in instructing him. Within the past two or three days I hear incidentally that Mrs Sharpton will return to Carolina. I have decided that if either of the children return to me they must be provided with books. Ada Robinson has not been at school during the past week because they expected to move into the city but they have decided to remain.

Sometimes I have thought I would give up the school or be glad of an excuse to give it up but I will not be compelled to give it up if I have to import children into the neighborhood or hire them to come. When I give up the school I shall do so voluntarily. Mr Neely would have been glad to get it for his sister and Mollie Richards

---

11. Gertrude was often concerned about the small attendance at her school. Although a certain number of students was requisite to maintain the school, her salary from the Richmond County School District was not based on the school size. In Georgia, each county formed a school district.

made an effort to defeat me last winter after promising me that she would not do so.

. . .

Monday, February 2, 1880 Saturday night I spent in town. Ma was sick that day. That night I dreamed of Clanton. I remember the dream because Ma called me and awoke me. Said she, "I am sorry to disturb you." "I am glad you did" said I "for I have just had a dream of Clanton and now I shall remember it." I have observed that the impression is stronger under such circumstances— This was my dream— I thought I was here at home that I was just entering the Piazzi door of the school room having called the children in from recess. As Arthur and Flady and the other little boys came running in I heard a familiar voice and turning, among them I saw Clanton. "My darling is that you?" I said and approached him. He seemed shy and just as I would walk towards a bird which at my approach I would expect to fly, I advanced to him for I was conscious that it was my child in the spirit and not in the flesh which I beheld—

Nearer and yet nearer I went towards him and then placed my arms around him and lifted him as I did when he was my baby boy. Closing the school room door I walked up and down the Piazzi talking to him in a perfect delirium of joy. "Are you glad to see me darling? Isn't God good to let you come darling? Say amen Clanton." This and other things I said to him and he nestled up to me and with his head resting on my shoulder he said "Amen." Clanton was seven years old, looked exactly as he did while living, yet I bore him in my arms with perfect ease. I took him by the hand afterwards and we walked into the school room, seated him by my side, handed him a book to look at the pictures and while I did this I thought, I wonder do any of the school children see Clanton. I suppose they did for in my dream one of them asked if that was not Clanton? I replied yes—commenced to hear a lesson and turning just then—he was gone. For a moment I was sorry. Then I thought, "It is all right. He will come again" and just then Ma awoke me— and now I think, "it is all right he will come again."

14. Businesswoman

I am a public woman now.
—*March 25, 1880*

February 3, 1880 Saturday Jan 24th Julia Scales, Lou Jackson with her two children Mrs Price with cousin Jane [Sibley] and three of her children came down to spend the day. The carpets, hall and stair oilcloth were down, shades hung in Mary Belle's and my room the yard in order and everything looking as well as I could make it—but the day was gloomy. It was quite cold and the sun under a cloud until after dinner. I did not allude to my new carpets and preferred that they would have thought that I had had them for some time. To persons accustomed to such things they are nothing. It is only when they are deprived of them that they appreciate them. The plastering has been mended. Some of our chromos which were given to us at the fair last year have been framed and hung.

Altogether I have felt more like old times during the past month. Dinah my cook is a treasure. I believe she likes me and she mingles with her service so much interest in my welfare that it touches me. There is a scriptural saying, "How hardly can they that have riches enter into the Kingdom of Heaven" but I think that it is infinitely more easy to be amiable when one is rich. Of all things to try one's temper commend me to the everyday taking care of "wherewithall shall we be fed." Perhaps persons who have never been accustomed to anything better are satisfied with the position in which they find themselves but to me bare floors in winter—windows without shades—and broken plastering are trials much more irritating than loss of property. They are constant, unending in their annoyance, the more so because I feel that I ought to be above such trifles. Loss of property, public advertisements are terrible. They hurt me like the sharp thrust of a dagger but after it is over I brace myself. The wound heals over leaving a terrible scar, it

395

is true, but these other trials are like I should imagine a shirt of hair to be, a daily torment—

I do not think even my own family know how I have felt my change of fortune. I think I have borne a brave front. My parlor chairs are Rosewood with coloured brocatelle upholstering. Some of them broken. For the first year or two after the fire we did not have enough chairs when we had much company without using six unpainted wooden chairs with leather bottoms! How proud I was when they were painted a dark brown. When Belmont was burnt the parlor furniture was at Ma's, fortunately. The piano was at Sis Anne's. Bailie's bill for the carpets oil cloth three rugs was only fifty four and seventy five cts. I wish Rudolph the man who lives with us to paint the inside of the house.... I was notified of a meeting of the Memorial Association[1] today but could not attend even if the day had been better. . . .

Tuesday, February 17, 1880 Just after writing this date I opened the almanac to see how long the month lasted, in other words how many school days there was— I find that the end of the month is next Sunday week. I will have eight more days before I earn enough to finish paying Bailie's bill. The first payment of $25.00 was made last Saturday. This morning I sent 10 cts for a three months trial of *The Cricket On The Hearth*, 15 cts for three months trial of *The Literary Guest*, papers I saw advertised in *The Home and Farm*. I also sent 60 cts for six months trial of *The Sunday Gazette*. A specimen copy of it was sent to us and it was excellent. I sent $1.25 for two Japonicas two Azalias and Sweet Chesnuts which were advertised at 40 for $1.00. I do not expect they can be very large.

I am so anxious to subscribe for *Scribner* or one of the higher class magazines but cannot now. I have sent on a week or two since for *The American Agriculturist* and *The Farm and Home* both papers for the price of one, but have not received either of them yet. I am saving five dollars of my January money for a particular purpose. With the Feb money and wood money I wish to have some dentist's work done. Mr Thomas received $165.00 dollars rent a

---

1. Gertrude Thomas was an enthusiastic member of the Ladies' Memorial Association of Augusta, which was founded in 1868 to honor the Confederate dead and erect a monument in their memory.

few days since as rent for a portion of the Road Place. We bought a carpet for Mary Belle and Cora Lou's room. I think the cost of it was $12.00—also bought a sett of furniture for $38.00— The sett in their room will be placed in Turner's. . . .

My school is progressing well. I have twenty scholars with the promise of several more. Two little German boys came today. Johnny and Willy Barldosky [Boldoski] I believe that is the way they spell their names. They are nearly as large as Julian and they do not know the alphabet well. Yet they are bright intelligent boys. Charley Wheeler who has been coming only a few weeks begins to read well and Charley Wiggins reads very well indeed. There is something in the contact with their fresh pure young spirits which compensates me for the drudgery of teaching. It is pleasing to watch the gro[w]th of their little minds and strive to brighten and stimulate them as they try to learn. . . .

February 21, 1880   Today is Saturday. I wish to talk confidentially with someone and why not with you my Journal? I wish to write for some paper or magazine and I particularly wish to make it profitable and I do not know 1st if I know how to write well enough, and 2d wether I can persuade an editor to publish what I write. I am confident that I could furnish articles which will interest if I can but succeed in having them printed. I have just told Channy my washer woman to go and make me up a fire in the school room (promising her that I would give her some potatoes for doing so) and then I will take my book and papers in there and if I am not interrupted will write. I had intended taking a holiday today but Mr Thomas was late in leaving for town. I sent by him for specimen copies of *Arthur's* Magazine and *The Children's Hour*, magazines I took when we were living at Belmont. Also sent for specimen copies of *Peterson's* Magazines enquiring what their club rates were? I wish very much to take *Scribner* or one of the four dollar magazines.

After Mr Thomas left I assisted in assorting the weeks wash. Then combed and brushed Kathleen's hair telling her while I plaited her hair the story of Joseph, Moses & Daniel. All of them she delights to hear. Afterwards I gave out dinner and then I could have found enough to do to keep me busy for a week. There are new socks, sheets and napkins to be marked and I hesitated and thought, ought I to write or would it be best to mark those articles?

And I decided while I have leisure that is a quiet time I will write. It is absolutely essential for me to be in a particular mood to enjoy writing and I can mark clothes under any circumstances. . . .

The window by which I am sitting, the desk at which I write are the same as they were when I sat here four months ago and wrote that sentence, Clanton is dead! I did not understand it then. I do not now. A few nights ago as I sat in the sitting room I heard Mary Belle singing and playing on the piano some of the songs she used to sing last summer when Clanton was here. He dearly loved music and they reminded me of him. I was reading a daily newspaper, tears rolled down my cheeks and going into the next room I knelt by the side of the bed. I cried with stifled sobs, "Oh my boy! My precious little darling." I reached out my arms in impotent, yearning wish to take him in, to clasp him to me. I laid my head down where his dying head had rested—all, all in vain was the effort to bring myself into communion with him. There are times when I wish I could believe in Spiritualism. . . .

Afternoon. This morning I was writing an article on the country and the lessons taught by nature. I read a portion of it for the Grange last summer but have never had it published. During the time I was connected with the Grange I wrote four articles or essays as we called them which were published. Three of them were on housekeeping and one on the three Patronesses Ceres, Pamona, and Flora. I was Ceres. The articles were published in *The Planter and Grange*. This year that paper which was published in Atlanta has been consolidated with two others and is now called *The Dixie Farmer*. The name is a talisman conjuring up thoughts of a time very dear and sacred to us all. . . .

. . .

March 11, 1880 As I was writing this date this morning it suddenly occurred to me that yesterday was Mr Thomas' birthday. He was forty nine years old. I was sitting by the fire place soon after when he came in to tell me that Mr Morgan a white man who has been living with us during the last month was moving. . . . Remembering that it was Mr Thomas' birthday as he was walking across the room I said, "Come kiss me," when I intended to tell him of what I expect he had forgotten, his birthday. He slightly hesitated, shook his head but instantly returned bent down and pressed his lips to mine, meeting with no warm response for a change had come over my mind. I did not want the kiss then for I had noticed the hesitation. I wonder if women ever get too old to be sensitive. . . .

After dinner today two women called. They were Gypsy women who wished to sell lace. They were the first ones who had ever been to see us altho they called last year at Mrs Keener's and she gave them two hens for telling her fortune. Mr Thomas met them and invited them into the parlor When I went in I found two women. The younger one apparently twenty five with fair complexion blue eyes and hair of perfect blond. A few straggling locks fell on her shoulders and her hair was banged. Her figure was good and she did most of the talking. She wished to sell lace and trade for corn. Her lace was quite pretty she asked 1.50 a yd for. She was anxious to tell my fortune. "Step aside with me for a few moments" said she "and I will tell you a few words." Cora Lou coming in, she was anxious to tell her fortune. Willing to amuse Cora Lou and without the slightest faith in the woman I consented. She said Cora Lou must step aside with her and I told them to come into this, the sitting room.

I had no faith or curiosity and did not care to come and remained in the other room conversing with the other woman whom I had heard called Margaret. She told me that she was not a Gypsy—her father and mother were Irish that she and her brother (who was the husband of the other woman) were born in England. "Do you like this kind of life" I enquired. She replied "No" that her father and mother were both dead. She looked much more like a Gypsy than the other for she had dark hair, eyes and complexion with beautiful strong teeth. Not at all pretty but honest and reliable looking. I would be willing to hire that woman and feel that I could trust her. Mr Thomas was not willing to let them have a bushel of corn for the lace and fortune so I gave them a half bushel of corn and a blue delaine dress for about two and a half yds of lace two inches wide and the fortune telling. . . .

It was raining when they left and the fair haired woman seated herself to drive without a bonnet although she had bought three beside the one she wore. I enquired of her if she would not be more comfortable during this rainy weather in a house than tenting— "No" she replied "I do not feel at home in a house." "When I was a little girl," said she "a lady in Washington city who kept a large hotel wanted to adopt me. She said she would educate me and have me learn to play on the piano but I did not want to stay." She said in reply to my allusion to her hair that "she did not like light hair but that her husband did." . . .

March 25, 1880 . . . My first thought after dinner today was I will only have tomorrow and three more days of next week and one more month will have passed. I shall have made thirty five dollars. It has come to the point that I count the weeks and calculate how I can best spend the amount made. With twenty more dollars and seventy five cts of last month's salary I finished paying Bailie's bill. I presented a wood bill for three months for ten dollars and finished paying for a sett of furniture for the girls' room. I do not know that I have mentioned a man rented some of the land in Columbia Co and paid something in advance. We bought a ten dollar carpet and a forty dollar sett of furniture. I then had five dollars left and oh how anxious I was to subscribe for some magazine— but I could not. Fortunately Carolina Carter (a coloured woman) brought me five dollars and seventy five cts which she had made by selling some old dresses and hats and I was enabled to send on an order for seven dollars a few days ago. I subscribed for *Scribner's* Monthly, *Peterson* Monthly (for Cora Lou) *Youth's Companion* (for Julian) and *The Cricket on the Hearth*, the latter is a story paper for $1.oo pr year.

I wrote off an article which I called "Letters from the Country or Lessons Learned from Nature" and sent it to *The Dixie Farmer* writing to the editor that I would like for him to publish it and furnish me with a year's subscription for it. I have not heard from it yet. Two weeks ago I wrote an article with regard to the improvements on our chapel, signed my name Mrs Gertrude Thomas and it was published in the *Chronicle* and *Constitutionalist*. I am a public woman now—would like for the patrons of my school to have an idea that I am capable of writing an interesting article. I have interested myself in copying an extract from my Journal giving an account of my interview with our President Mr Davis. I think I shall send it to Gen Evans[2] who published the *Georgia Advocate* in Atlanta. I am very much obliged to the editors of the *Chronicle* for publishing pieces which I have written but when they do so they

---

2. Probably Gen. Clement A. Evans, who became a Methodist minister after the war. He had served as minister in an Augusta church.

act from a spirit of courtesy. I would have them publish them because they are proud of them and prize them.[3] . . .

.   .   .   .

April 5, 1880   This afternoon I was looking over my writing desk and in one of the drawers I came across this on a scrap of paper. "Is God as high as that hickory nut tree?" "Ain't he all over the sky?" "How did he make people?" "Who made God?" "Oh I know, the spirits." One day last fall before Clanton died, I was sitting in the front Piazzi and Clanton standing by my side asked me the questions I have written down. I hastily wrote them down intending afterwards to write out an account of our conversation. It was never written but the piece of paper recalled it all— Yesterday I heard Dr [Robert] Irvine preach at Rosney Chapel. I remembered that the first sermon Clanton ever heard preached was at that same church. I wrote an account of it in my journal. As I listened to Dr Irvine I thought with a strange thrill of awe, "Clanton *knows* all that Dr Irvine is trying to tell us." And yet I cannot imagine my little boy as having developed into such wonderful knowledge. I am more disposed to think of him as learning day by day like my little scholars. . . .

Yesterday was my birthday—I was forty six years old. Tomorrow our four houses are advertised to be sold as a Trustee sale. I have signed my right in them away—so has Turner. We have all done the best we could. I am tired now—

.   .   .   .

Saturday, May 15, 1880   . . . A few days since I read a notice of Dr Henry Campbell of Augusta. It was copied from a Richmond paper. The writer alluded to Dr Campbell's maternal grandfather Mr Eve who is buried in the Cottage Cemetery [nearby]. He wrote the epitaph for his own tomb in which he said that his life was a failure.

---

3. The brief entry following this one, dated March 26, 1880, is deleted here. It began with two questions: "I wonder sometimes what I am writing for? Who will take an interest in reading my journals?" She then wrote of ordinary daily matters.

Tomorrow I will go over and read it. . . . The writer of the article on Dr Campbell said that in the grandson the talent of his progenitor was having its thorough development. That Mr Eve who thought his life a failure has other instances of transmitted talent among his descendants. He was the father of Dr Joseph Eve of Augusta and Dr Edward Eve of this county.[4] . . .

Reading that article aroused a train of thought which I have often indulged in. If we transmit certain qualities to our children how much it behooves us to "look well to our ways." There is a satisfaction in the acquisition of knowledge of itself. How much greater will be that pleasure when we realise that it will have its development in our children and children's children. Ah me I see what I am after. I am beginning to realise that I will never accomplish anything and with that hopeful element of my nature which causes me to find comfort somewhere, somehow I do really believe I am looking forward to some child or grandchild in the future accomplishing what I have failed to do in this [life]. Shelley has somewhere said

"I vowed that I would dedicate my powers
To thee and thine; have I not kept the vow?"[5]

Those lines express devotion to beauty but they aptly convey my devotion to my family. To my children I dedicate my powers such as they are. When I die I shall cry Have I not kept the vow? Now my duty is to teach school. If a higher field of usefulness is intended a way will be made for me. Of this I am sure so I go on my way content. I try to do the duty which is nearest and I often wonder that I am no more fretted than I am.

Mr Thomas thought that he had made arrangements with Loo Chong the man Jeff is clerking for to supply him during this year but he tells him now he cannot. Mr Thomas has gone in today to

---

4. Joseph Eve, the father of Dr. Joseph A. Eve, Dr. Edward Eve, and Mary Eve Campbell, claimed six or more doctors and a poet among his children and grandchildren. Dr. Henry Campbell, his grandson, was a renowned physician and surgeon. Joseph Eve was also the uncle of the well-known Dr. Paul F. Eve of Augusta and Nashville. Joseph Eve's self-composed epitaph appears in *Memorial History of Augusta*, by Charles C. Jones, Jr., and Salem Dutcher (Syracuse, N.Y., 1890).

5. From "Hymn to Intellectual Beauty," by Percy Bysshe Shelley (1792–1822).

make some arrangements. I have not forgotten that night in December last when I prayed "Oh pitiful pitiful One have mercy on me." Months have passed and a respite has been given. I have signed with Turner my interest in one of the houses in town (or more if necessary) away. They were advertised but not at Sheriff's sale and not one bid was made. Now Mr Thomas is endeavouring to sell one of them at private sale.

A few days since, Mr Montgomery as Receiver of Pa's estate turned over to the legatees a small amount from Gas stock which had been sold. To me he gave one hundred and 40 or 50 I do not know which. This I gave to Mr Thomas to pay Mr Miller for Jones & Norris but reserved ten dollars of it for paying for the girls' dresses. Now that Mr Thomas has no account or arrangements made I expect he will have to use it for supplies for the farm. It has been sixteen years since Pa died and his estate has not been settled. It was on just such a bright beautiful spring day as this sixteen years ago that he died. I wonder if Pa and Holt and Col Vason and Clanton (and my little ones) have seen each other. I wonder oh I wonder in "endless mazes lost." . . .

. . . .

Wednesday, May 19, 1880   Ah me I feel so tired! Such a heavy dull feeling. . . . Looking from the window across the garden and orchard I see the dense pine forests of Belmont. How often I have sat at Belmont and wondered and struggled to break from the fetters by which I felt bound. Can I ever forget how I felt day after day expecting a visit from the sheriff to levy upon my home? . . . Instead of praying and trusting I grope about and think, Is there nothing I can do?

I said the other day in conversation with Mr Thomas "that I could not suffer a pecuniary loss to trouble me now as once it did." At Belmont I received my babtism of suffering. I wonder tho if a man does not have to brace his nerves anew every time he goes into battle? I know that to me, the inaction—the expectation would be more tantalising than the realisation. And all this writing brings me back to the one thought. Another sheriff's sale— My lifetime interest this time and then what? This is what Mr Thomas asked me when I tried to lift my feeble protest relying on God's care for me because I trusted him. And so the trust property was signed away—advertised as Trust Sale and not one bid made for it. I was perfectly willing that the Rowell Swamp[6] should go, but that is to be mortgaged for this year's supplies. I am willing for anything, everything to go if I can only have a home however humble, and I will teach, write, or do anything I can but Oh I do wish we could settle something. I can make no plans, however humble because of this sword of fate which hangs over my head. . . .

Julian came in a few moments since. Mr Thomas has given him six rows of cotton. He will hoe them he says and have the money to spend as he pleases. He has hoed two rows and coming in looked so bright and animated. Seating himself in the window by my side and swinging his feet to and fro he talked of his plans and I am never so busy that I cannot stop and listen to him. A few days ago I read to him the bet I made when he was a baby, that someday he would be a great man, because as Elsie (his nurse) said "he was born in hard times." It was amusing to hear the tone of his voice as he said with a sigh "I am twelve years old and I have done nothing yet." Yes you have Julian, you have been a joy for your Mama ever since you were born. . . .

June 23, 1880   Today is Cora Lou's birthday. She is seventeen and my birthday present to her was a fan for which I gave one dollar and twenty five cts. My young daughter has had very few luxurys lavished upon her during her brief young existence. . . . If ever I become a rich woman and can dress my daughters as I would like I very well know that I will not receive greater satisfaction than I do now when I study and plan to know how far one month's salary will go towards buying what I most need.

For Mary Belle and Cora Lou I have bought black buntings apiece at 25 cts pr yd. Three yds of black satin trim each at one dollar per yard. They are made with Basques, top skirts and the front of bottom skirts shirred with the satin. They were made for me by Mrs Allen at two dollars and a half apiece— I am compelled to give my sewing to third class manteau makers because I cannot afford to pay first class prices. Aunt Lamkin gave Mary Belle a black velveteen skirt and I bought her a light spring Polonaise of coachman's drab trimmed with silk to match and Miss Lewis made it for three dollars. Cora gave Cora Lou a black velvet skirt and a

---

6. Gertrude inherited sixty acres of river farmland on the Rowell place from the estate of her brother Holt.

light brown Polonaise to wear with it. So both of my daughters have two nice suits apiece. Their bonnets I gave four dollars apiece for. For the price they look very well. I think Cora Lou looks like I did when I was a girl. She is very bright and looks quite as well and prettier than I did with tissue silk and summer silks which cost much more than I have ever given for her a dress. Besides all this Mary Belle and Cora Lou can cut out and make a muslin and calico dress for themselves and understand perfectly what they are about. . . .

At night of the same day. Kathleen is playing with Minnie Lee a little coloured girl. Mr Thomas has not returned yet. When I was in town a few days ago I subscribed for three months to the *Young Men's Library*. It was only seventy five cts and I will enjoy reading books with large bold type for my eyesight has failed so that I use my eyeglasses almost all the time now in reading or writing. . . .

And now I am going to write what I term a case of answer to prayer. I do not know what others would call it. For several months Mr Thomas has made effort after effort to make arrangements with the various city merchants to advance money or supplies but in vain. I do not know why it was so for certainly the security offered was sufficient, a mortgage on the Rowell Swamp land. Week after week he would go in town hoping to make some definite arrangement but without success. One night about one month ago I knelt and asked God to help me and I felt led by the Spirit to write to Mr Howard. I had told Mr Howard that I had written to him without consulting Mr Thomas. The next morning I thought I had best tell Mr Thomas of the note I had written. "I wish you would not send it" said he. "I have seen him several times." "You think I had best not?" said I and I did not send it but tore it up—

The month passed on. From week to week we did not know how the farming operations would be carried on. Mr Thomas applied to Ma for assistance, very much against my wishes but she did not wish to run any risk. Mrs Tubman[7] was applied to but she was not willing to make the arrangements— It is humiliating for me to think of such things, much less to write of them. Saturday

---

7. Emily Tubman, the widow of prominent Augusta citizen Richard Tubman, was a wealthy businesswoman, philanthropist, and society matron.

before last I was in town. Twenty dollars of my month's salary was given to buy provisions for the Negroes in Columbia.

Monday Mr Thomas came in to try again to make arrangements. I was going up to Dr Winkler's [a dentist] with Cora Lou. As I was walking up the street I lifted my heart in prayer to God to help me and again I thought of Mr Howard, but I could not go around on the street his warehouse was on. As I passed Mrs Tweedy's I saw Mr Howard standing on the street in conversation with a gentleman, a way was clear before me— I told Cora Lou to go in at Dr Winkler's and then without one moment's hesitation I returned and interrupting the conversation, said to Mr Howard "May I speak with you for a few moments" and walking a few steps off I told him how much I wished to make an arrangement to supply us this year. He told me to request Mr Thomas to call upon him that afternoon and the arrangement was effected.

He charged us eight per cent and I am *truly grateful*. Nothing more has been heard from Jones & Norris.[8] I do not know what will happen next Tuesday. I am waiting to see for if my life interest is sold out next Tuesday I will not enjoy having an exhibition for my pupils as I would like to do. School will soon be over.

Dixie Land, June 28, 1880   I think I have at length decided upon a name for this place. I think Dixie Land will be a pretty name and the associations with the name are very dear. Before the war this place was called The Yankee Farm when Major [William] McLaws lived here. During the war, we left off the Yankee name and I tried to have it called Dixie Farm. I believe I think that is a better name now for it than Dixie Land for it is literally a farm—on both sides are cotton fields and in front a piece of ground which during the winter is always green with oats or some green crop. When that is cut off peas are sown broadcast, and at times they look beautifully as the light and shadows of a midday sun pass over them or their leaves stirred by the wind show alternate shades of silver and green. Maria Lou Eve[9] says I am the only person she ever saw who pos-

---

8. On May 18, 1880, Jefferson Thomas had received this note concerning a large debt: "Dear Sir, Your proposition of 29th ult is declined by Messrs Jones and Norris. My instructions are that the execution must proceed immediately. Yours truly Frank H. Miller Attorney."

9. Maria Lou Eve, a Georgia poet, was the daughter of Edward Eve.

sessed the magic power of extracting sentiment from an ordinary field pea. . . .

I was feeling quite unwell all last week. Notwithstanding I had a compliment from Mr T yesterday so instead of feeling blue I ought to be bright. "I received a compliment from your father yesterday" said I today to Turner. "What was it?" said he "that you looked particularly well when you came in church?" was his reply. "Why did *you* think so?" said I. "Yes mam" was his reply— "Well if you thought so, why did you not tell me?" was my reply—and this I said not from a spirit of vanity but it is so pleasant to please those we love. Mr Thomas' compliment was this "After all those black lace veils are great things—they hide all the ugly and bring out all the pretty." "Don't you wish you could wear one?" said I. "Yes" said he, "for you look better than I ever saw you." I laughed and suggested that when his eyes become inflamed he could wear one.

. . .

Dixie Farm, August 6, 1880 At no time of my life have I felt more debilitated than during the past month. I can compare my feelings to nothing else than the wretched days of early pregnancy. I have made no record of the time for two reasons. First and best reason I did not have the requisite amount of energy and I do not care to write when I feel so dull and I may add cross for it is best to leave no record of such days. There has been no day during the time I have stopped teaching when the thought of beginning again was not extremely distasteful to me. I shrank from the idea with perfect aversion—for I so wished to be perfectly quiet—where I would hear no sound, no school or farm sound for the one was as distasteful as the other. I know now that what I required was change, perfect, complete, radical change. Oh how at times I wished that I could be transported (for like the impotent man at the pool I was too helpless to make the exertion to go—in other words decide, buy a ticket and go of my own accord) to some place on the seacoast where the only sound I would hear would be the ocean wave as it dashed against the shore—

I am better now. I tried quinine but it did me little good. One day last week I had a terrible attack of sick headache which lasted two or three days. Mary Belle left with Pinck and Mamie for Catoosa Springs on last Friday one week ago. She was very busy preparing before she left. The sound of the sewing machine was another thing which while absolutely essential disturbed me. Some other time I will tell more about her dresses. Jeff has been out home over the past two weeks. He has had quite a gay time since he has been out. I took two of Tult's liver pills Saturday. I think that they did me good. I would like to try some tonic. After all I do not believe I can write. I am too dull. I am very anxious to hear from town, to read the papers and hear from that poor man Dr Tanner. I wonder is he dead or alive. If he does succeed in getting through the forty days what will life be worth to him? Digestion ruined, constitution broken down of what avail the notoriety which he has gained? I wonder if he wishes to establish the idea that the spiritual part of one's being gains the ascendancy when we abstain from food? Kathleen is asking for something to eat and I must attend to the material cravings of her little body.

August 16, 1880 Just as I wrote the above date I remembered that I had neglected to write down the amount we have drawn from Mr Howard. I do this in order to have it act as a curb upon me if I feel disposed to spend too much money, launch out into some additional extravagance. Since the 15th of June we have drawn upon Mr Howard for $390.00 dollars. We borrowed $600 and we owe Loo Chong about $250.00. I do so wish we could have something left over to pay what we owe. I had a dentist's bill at Dr Winkler's to pay of $25.00. That I have paid for with my last month's salary. We have given Mary Belle this trip to Catoosa which I would have felt unable to do if I had not expected to take charge of the school again next year. . . .

Dixie Farm. September 2, 1880 I believe that this is the first moment since I closed the school the last of June that I have thought of resuming it with a feeling of pleasure. I have shrunk from it with a morbid fear of taking up my cross. I have thought "Is there a necessity for this trial of my time, patience and strength?" And all the while I have been unwilling to give my own consent to resume the duty of keeping school. I knew that we needed the money I would make, but I was selfish and unwilling cheerfully to place myself in harness again. As the time draws nearer somehow, I know not how, the prospect does not seem so dull. I say I do not know, yes I do. I remember yesterday I was worried, a reaction from Mr Thomas who was fretted about something. I found that I had lost my self command and going into the parlor I knelt and prayed

God for self control. Since then I have felt better. How I wish I could walk through life with a consciousness that my Heavenly Father takes care of me.

Dear Journal, I have always tried to talk confidentially upon one subject with you. I have told you how I have hoped, dreamed, yearned to write for the press. Well this summer I had thought to have written, looked over old Journals, pasted in scrap books and possibly written something for publication. Instead of doing so I have been so unwell for weeks at a time that existence seemed a burden. I had no energy or strength for anything beside reading a few novels and always ever present was the consciousness that I was trying to shirk the responsibility of taking charge of the school again. I can do better work I thought than teaching little children their alphabet and taxing my nerves to hear reading lessons in 1st and 2d readers. This is what I thought and what was the result— I have done nothing. So thinking it over I expect that I had best do the nearest duty I am competent for, I am interested in my little pupils. When I commence teaching I expect I will have the daily bread given to me which I may require. . . .

.   .   .

Friday, September 24, 1880 Cora Lou returned yesterday. Mrs Sweegan and Helena drove down with her. Helena and Cora Lou have had their pictures taken together cabinet size. That is the first picture Cora Lou has ever had taken. She is sitting in a swing (a new fashion) and Helena standing by her side. I am feeling quite unwell today. Next week the 1st of October comes on Friday— I cannot take pleasure in looking forward to taking care of the school. I try to imagine what I can get. I remember that I wish a head board for Clanton's grave and that is the only way I know of for getting one. Yet I would not be greatly surprised if I resign the school before the time comes. If I could only control the swamp and rent it out but this Mr Thomas is unwilling to—

Turner is away from the river swamp and oh I am so glad, so glad. He is in business at Roberts and Co and receiving forty dollars a month. There was something so degrading in the association with the negroes and the camp life he led while farming there. Now he associates with gentleman and will receive remuneration for his labour. He is staying with Ma. Jeff's salary has been increased at Loo Chong's.

Wednesday, September 29, 1880 I am still undecided about the school. I cannot decide what to do. I have been trying to persuade Mr Thomas to consent to rent the land we own on the river. Turner is away now and we could rent it to Mr Keener or probably to Mr Carmichael. Somehow I cannot help feeling that we ought to make a support independent of the river swamp place. We own the plantation in Columbia. The four houses in Augusta, this place and Belmont.[10] I have proposed to Mr Thomas that I teach and pay the drygoods bill of the family and some of the current expenses and try to make a support out of the other places and if we can rent the river swamp let the money go towards paying the mortgage on this place or some other debt but oh it seems to worry him so and then I get fretted. . . .

Mary Belle had invited Lena Shewmake to spend the night with her and had invited Fanny McCoy to tea. Mr Ingraham[11] and Mr Lamar were invited to tea and spend the night. The former came and remained all night. They both spent the day with us Sunday and went to church in the afternoon. Mary Belle also invited Mr Walker, Mr Phil Schley and Mr Slidell and Gwinne Nixon. They all came but in detachments. . . .

. . .

Friday, October 1, 1880 My prayer of yesterday is answered. My way is made clear for me, unmistak[ab]le, plain and direct. It is right that I should teach school. It is my duty and this is what decided me. A visit from Mr [Charley] Sibley the sheriff to serve me with a writ or paper from Franklin and Brothers. The amount is ———— with interest. What a poor business woman I am. I have read it over half doz times and I only remember that it is $300 and something. Mr Thomas went in town this morning. I had just signed an order on Howard and Sons for $150.00 conscious while I did so that the river swamp was mortgaged and that we would probably lose it when we tried to settle up at the end of the year. Mr Thomas was annoyed, said I knew nothing of business and of this

---

10. All of the properties mentioned were heavily mortgaged.

11. Frederick Laurens Ingraham of Charleston, whom Mary Belle later married.

I am very conscious. I only know that we owed Jones & Norris Franklin and others at the end of the year when they advanced for us.

Mr Thomas left and as he drove off in the Buggy I thought "What's the use of my teaching. Everything will go anyway." . . . I remained seated, suspecting by this time that it was Mr Sibley, the sheriff. Very quietly I sat and looked at him as he entered the flower garden and approched the house. I suspected that he came in his official character but could not imagine what he came to levy upon. I was concious of a dim feeling of sympathy for his evident embarrassment, for Mr Sibley is a gentleman. He entered the piazzi. I rose shook hands with him and invited him to be seated. Declining to do so he handed me a paper. I knew at a glance that it was a legal paper. "What is this for Mr Sibley?" said I. "It is from Franklin and Brothers Mrs Thomas" he replied. "Oh yes! The people who have a mortgage on the land on the hill [Belmont], but what must I do with it Mr Sibley?" "Keep it Mrs Thomas" said he "and place it in the hands of your lawyers." "Mr Thomas expected to see you in Augusta today and pay you something for taxes." "Yes I know" he replied and then added, "I am so tired of my own and other people's troubles that I wish I was out of the office." To this I made no reply and bowing he left and I remained seated with the paper in my lap.

After a few moments I rose, entered the parlor and kneeling where yesterday I had reproachfully cried, "Oh Lord I don't know anything more now than I did before," I knelt again and cried, "Oh God I thank Thee that Thou hast made my way so clear," and great sobs which I strove not to render audible shook my whole being— sobs not of regret that that paper had been sent (for we owe the money) but of gratitude. Suppose I had decided to give up the school and Monday Mr Sibley had come—come when it was too late. How this law suit will end I do not know but the same Father who heard one prayer will hear again if I only pray for "daily bread."

My school room has been a lumber room during the summer. Rudolph made mattresses in there before camp meeting. The room has been made a receptacle for all kinds of things. I have only one servant and it has seemed a great task to put it in order. I believe that such things do me good—they rouse within me a spirit which is stronger than my human nature. I went into the school room and with Della (my cook) I swept, dusted, lifted and soon produced order out of the chaos which reigned before. . . .

. . .

Thursday, November 4, 1880 . . . Only a few days ago I was pasting in a new scrap book the letter which I wrote in June 1878 and published in the *Chronicle* and *Constitutionalist* appealing for the preservation of the Powder Mills chimney.[12] Last year Council granted a petition from the Confederate Survivors Association and placed the obelisk in the charge of that association— Day before yesterday the election for president of the United States took place but I was not as much interested as I am in the preservation of this chimney. Garfield[13] has been elected but I have never been able to arouse within myself the slightest enthusiasm for Gen Hancock. Enough for me to know that they were both Northern men who fought against us. Garfield promises nothing to the South and we will not be disappointed if we receive no marks of especial favor. Unlike Rose Ashleigh I cannot feel it an honour to have been introduced and to have shaken hands with Gen Hancock "the brave man who saved the Union" and Rose Ashleigh is the sobriquet over which Judge Aldrich's daughter writes.[14] She is Mrs Darling Duncan and seperated from her husband— She is from South Carolina!

. . .

November 26, 1880 . . . I do not know that I have mentioned that we have two boarders who are pupils of mine. One of them is Georgia Walton who has been with us one month and Ida Lou Thomas who has been with us one week. Julia Scales proposed to me to take them (as she could not) at 12 twelve dollars per month and I agreed and not for one moment have I regretted it. Georgia is a bright sweet child and very companionable for Kathleen. . . .

---

12. The powderworks chimney, 175 feet high, and Sibley Mills still stand as historic markers on the banks of the Augusta Canal.

13. James A. Garfield was elected president of the United States in 1880. His opponent was U.S. general Winfield Scott Hancock.

14. Rose Ashleigh, novelist, was the author of *His Other Wife* (1881).

I will only average 11 11/20 this month.[15] The Boggs children have not been during the month and Sallie Richards and Fannie Belle have had broken bone fever. I think Mr Neely wishes to get the school for his sister Mrs Sharpton. Ginnie Burch told me the other day that Jim Wiggins told them that Mrs Richards intended sending Sallie to Mrs Sharpton. I asked her to send Arthur to me but she said Mr Richards thought Ferdy ought to go to a man and he wished to send him to Mr Day and Arthur ought to go with him   I left the school room. I was very tired. Ginnie Burch's manner had annoyed me. I had been compelled to keep a great restraint upon myself during the morning.

All during the week I had been greatly tried with "the thorn in the flesh," that peculiar "messenger of Satan" which was intended to buffet me and had dealt me some heavy blows. I was not in a proper state of mind to rally from this additional trouble of having my school broken up. Had I given it up voluntarily that would have been different. The thorn in the flesh had irritated me, aroused the worst portion of my nature in a rebellious defiant spirit but now I was tired and oh I so much needed help. Going into the parlour I knelt and said not one word— After a while I arose came back in the school room and sat perfectly quiet until I had controlled myself to meet the children at dinner—but somehow—someway—I felt relieved. I believe I was almost glad I did not have to teach. I had done my best to keep it up. I could do no more. . . .

December 16, 1880 Today is the anniversary of my wedding day and I had forgotten it! Not until I dated the above line and tried to remember what day of the month it is was I reminded of it. Last week on Thursday the 9th of December I remembered it for that was Turner's birthday and he was 27— I have been married twenty eight years! Old enough to be supposed to have out grown sentiment. Yet I was sorry this morning when I found that Mr Thomas had left in his Buggy for Columbia County without bidding me good bye and giving me a kiss. Like myself I know he had forgotten that it was the anniversary of our wedding day. I was in the school room and busy. It was raining a little and I thought he would defer

---

15. Gertrude is referring to the number of pupils. She needed twenty to keep the school open.

going to the plantation. I can scarcely imagine a greater contrast than there is between my situation this afternoon and that of today one week ago. . . .

One week ago I was in Savannah. On Thursday of last week I was on the Atlantic Ocean! I scarcely know how to begin to tell how pleasant a week I spent. Surely more pleasure never was crowded into the same amount of time. I was so fortunate as to secure an invitation for Cora Lou and myself to join the party of excursionists who left Augusta last Tuesday Dec 7th for Savannah.[16] There were between two hundred and two hundred and fifty invitations accepted. I taught school Monday morning and that afternoon I left home for Augusta leaving my school in Mary Belle's care. . . .

I had that morning visited Mr [Joseph] Burch and explained to him that I wished to visit Savannah—that Mary Belle would take care of my school during my absence. He replied "Certainly Mrs Thomas. I have only one request to make of you." I bowed supposing that the request had some connection with the school and this is what he added, "I only hope that you will enjoy yourself to the utmost." My face flushed, the quick tears sprang to my eyes as I answered, "I shall certainly do that. I am much obliged to you Mr Burch" and left him, strengthened by his kindness—cheered by his sympathy. Dear old gentleman. He does not know how much good he did me when with the official permission he gave me he combined a chivalric politeness which many a younger man would do well to emulate.

An express train left Augusta between eleven and twelve oclock. The sun was shining gloriously. The wind blowing. The air cool and bracing and all things looking bright and lovely. As I looked out of the window at the rapidly shifting panorama, the bare fields the tall pines the most ordinary landscape assumed an additional beauty. Sufficient pleasure for me to rest and enjoy. I was resting both mind and body and wondering if among that gay group of girls either of them was to use one of their own expressions "having a better time than I?" We travelled through Waynesboro

---

16. The journal entry of October 3, 1880 (omitted here), speaks of "an excursion to see the new steamer *City of Augusta*. Mr. [Robert H.] May, the mayor of Augusta said he would furnish us with tickets so Cora Lou and I expect to go."

without stopping—six miles below we passed "Thomas Station." I looked out at our plantation now the property of Mr Dye and with the sigh of regret was mingled a pride in my husband's good taste which planned that quarter with its overseer's house and negro cabins. He selected the location—superintended the building of the substantial frame houses and constructed a quarter to which a Southerner might point with pride as a representative plantation in the antebellum days. Sherman's army camped on that plantation—burnt gin house and screw—several hundred bales of cotton and carried with him when he left valuable blooded stock—but I suppress the sigh and from there to Millen [Georgia] look out upon cotton fields white for the harvest. The incessant rains of November have prevented the farmers from gathering it. In large fields I observed two or three "hands" only picking—and this is December! . . .

Late in the afternoon we arrived in Savannah. Tom Scales had telegraphed to the Pulaski House and engaged two rooms. Col Snead had telegraphed to a friend to secure two rooms for him but we had received no answer. We drove to the Pulaski. When I was there before Mary Belle was a baby in long clothes—and I chaperoning a lively crowd of young people. Our rooms were given to us in the fourth story of the hotel. Opening the window I looked out upon the park—and Pulaski Monument[17]—my first view of Savannah in twenty years. Savannah by gas light! and as I looked, across my mind flashed the memory of the Christmas present Sherman gave to Lincoln fifteen years ago!

"The Mills of the gods grind slowly."[18] Lincoln is dead! Sherman has been branded a liar by Hampton—[19] Savannah smiles as she reclines with stately grace conscious that today her strength is greater than before. As for the future, young men and maidens will smooth away all the asperity of the past. I was impressed with this idea when the next day I saw a group of dark eyed Southern young

17. A monument erected to Count Casimir Pulaski, Polish patriot and hero of the American Revolution.

18. "Though the mills of God grind slowly, yet they grind exceeding small," from *Poetic Aphorisms: Retribution*, by Friedrich von Logau (1604–55).

19. Confederate general Wade Hampton III, who was elected governor of South Carolina in 1876.

gentleman and ladies exchange compliments and courtesy with a fair young Northern girl and her brother who had visited our genial clime in search of health—at all times the cultivated educated Northern people are welcome.

At night. . . . I turn the page and I find that I have only one more page to write before I finish this book. I will not have space to finish my account of my visit to Savannah— Is it ever thus, Will my life record be incomplete when called to join the innumerable caravan? Incomplete, unfinished, full of faults my life may have been but for the gift of life I render thanks—for my husband and my children I am grateful. Turner and Mary Belle are old enough to marry. Turner appears to have no intention of doing so and I think Mary Belle is yet in meditation fancy free. She has a friend who is quite devoted but this is a private affair. . . . I am on the last page of this journal. I have been two years writing it. During this time I have been busy striving to do my duty and in the performance of duty have met my reward. At times my duties have been extremely irksome—but only when worries outside of my school room unfitted me to cope with the trials within—

Some years ago I was in trouble. I met with a few verses from which I gathered much strength. . . . The morning I left Savannah I bought a Sea Side Library book called *Duty*— Seated in the cars I opened the leaves and my eye fell upon the same lines.

> "Put thou thy trust in God
>   In duty's path go on
> Fix on his word thy steadfast eye
>   So shalt thy work be done." [Martin] Luther

I read the verse with the name of the author attached, read that one verse and not one other line in the book that day. It fell idly upon my lap while memory recalled the past and I thought duty is not always pleasant. Sometimes it is very hard. . . .

15. Poverty and Trials

Money is very scarce.
—October 10, 1882

January 2, 1881   Yesterday was New Year's Day. All day long thick and fast the hail fell, freezing the snow which had fallen so silently and yet so constantly on Wednesday. Only in the middle of the road had it melted and all over the earth the feathery flakes had formed a carpet of beautiful snow. I returned from Augusta Friday in the buggy with Peter the coloured boy driving me. It was very fortunate that I did not postpone it until yesterday for it was as unpleasant a day as it was possible to be. Mr Thomas, Julian Kathleen and I are the only members of the family at home. We remained all day by a large fire and made an egg nogg to celebrate the day. . . . It is not late but I am sleepy and the children have gone up stairs to bed. Mr Thomas is asleep in this room and his loud breathing is not inspiring. . . .

January 5, 1881   I wish I had not begun a journal in this book for the paper is of an inferior quality and the pages being ruled is objectionable. Indeed I wonder sometimes why am I keeping a journal? I often wish that I was fond of sewing instead of writing—but a habit contracted early is apt to continue— For so long a time I have been accustomed with the end of an old year and the beginning of a New Year to write some record of the time that the necessity of continuing the custom forces itself upon me. I often feel that I would like to write but am so situated that I cannot, particularly in cold weather. We have but one fire burning constantly, besides the one in the school room, and all of us are together. I have but one woman, the cook (Della) and she is as annoying as it is possible for a servant to be. She teases Kathleen, is very disrespectful and noisy but she is the best I can command the services of. Indeed I feel that I am under some obligation to her for cooking for us during the past week for we have never known much worse weather. Christmas

417

Day was a very disagreeable day—raining all day but not very cold fortunately. . . .

Ah! me! in a few days I was so sorely tried, tempted to give up my school. Rain, constant rain fell—the clouds were heavy. It was cold and so dreary day after day. I went after a hurried toilette and still more hurried breakfast into the school room where a fire in a stove was burning. A few scholars came—just the number enough to keep me employed. Not the number to keep me interested in my work. I had driven around in the neighborhood and secured a promise from Mr Burch (Ginnie's father) and others that they would send their children.

My school room is bright and cheerful when the sun shines— but the sun did not shine. I have no shades to the room, the walls are not papered, no carpet on the floor—the stove smokes when the wind blows in a particular direction and during those short winter days I think the wind must have blown constantly in that particular direction. At last the last straw was heaped upon me in a visit from a young man known in the neighborhood as Jim Wiggins. He is the uncle of Charlie Wiggins, a bright little boy, eight years of age who is a pupil of mine. . . .

During my interview with Mr Wiggins I was very polite, altho he felt called upon to complain in several instances of my manner of instruction. "You cannot expect to give satisfaction to all of your patrons Mrs Thomas" said he, "people will prefer one teacher to another. I am a great friend of Mr Sharpton's and I think it is hard that he should be seperated from his wife when she goes off to teach school." I referred to Charlie's rapid improvement in writing (he has traced through two copy books). "Yes" he replied, "but he does not hold his pencil right—and I do not think he ought to write with a pencil." "Do I understand you sir," I enquired "to say that you prefer his using a pen and ink instead of learning to write with a pencil?" "Yes" was his reply. "In that case will you be so good as to see that he is supplied with them. The copy books and pencil which Charlie has used I have given to him." A few more words and he took leave, but after bidding him good bye I stood in the front door striving vainly to recover my composure.

It is enough for the parents to complain but when the "uncles, aunts and cousins" call me to account I am running the gauntlet. But I have little cause to complain of the interference of the parents or patrons as Jim Wiggins calls them. Instead I have to regret their indifference and neglect to furnish the necessary books. . . .

All the causes which I have enumerated led me to think that it was best to give up the school. To this was added a cogent reason which altho it had very great weight with me I shall not mention yet. I was very undecided. What was my duty? What ought I to do? At length not without making it again and again an especial subject of prayer I decided to resign the school—and in doing so thought it best to give it to Mrs Sharpton. I supposed her to be a good teacher, she told me that she was under a partial engagement in South Carolina but would break that engagement, that she had been requested by several of the patrons of my school to take charge of it (I have enquired since and cannot hear of one). That was Tuesday, Dec 21st.

Wednesday I taught school and that afternoon I drove in town to buy presents for the Christmas tree I was to give the children Thursday. I told Ma of the decision I had arrived at. Went up town, made the purchases and before breakfast the next morning Ida Lou and I drove out home. I was tired but happy. I felt that a great burden had been lifted from me. I wished people "Happy Christmas" whom I met. I felt ten years younger than a few days before. Now I was free—not to be idle but to read—write and who knows? perhaps publish.

Arriving at home the buggy filled with bundles I entered the sitting room. Mr Thomas was writing. "I have been thinking how we can get along if you give up this school Gertrude. Cannot you, Mary Belle and I keep it up?" I knew what that meant. . . . "What of Mrs Sharpton?" said I. "She has not had time to break her engagement in Carolina—and we are dependent upon the salary you earn." That morning I had met some of the patrons of the school. Mr Burch expressed great regret so did the children that I had decided to resign. Turner who is one of the trustees said "I need not feel discouraged &c." In a great hurry I wrote to Mrs Sharpton to prevent her breaking her engagement and told her "that I had reconsidered the subject and after seeing some of the patrons and trustees I had decided to retain the school." Her reply was "that it would make no difference in her plans whatever, that on the 1st of Jan she would open a school at the school house at Mr Carmichael's." . . .

I have been engaged most of the day writing. This has been a holiday week. Monday night Turner wrote me a note on the back of an envelope to let me know, "that all the schools have holiday." At that time the snow was all over the ground. The hail which fell all day long had frozen it hard. Sunday we had a sleigh ride. The children went with Mr Thomas first and then I went with him. We drove two horses. Went down by the church and afterwards drove up Belmont avenue. I remembered one other sleigh ride he and I took from Belmont in 1857 I expect.

. . .

Saturday, January 8, 1881 ... When I first took charge of this school I decided on Saturday, made my arrangements. On Monday morning I was ready to go in to see Mr [William H.] Fleming, the commissioner, when Mollie Richards called to see me and wished to know if I expected to teach. "In case I did not she wished to secure the school." I told her "Yes that I was going in to make arrangements for it, see the trustees and &c." I did so and was much astonished the next day to learn that Mollie had gone in and after assuring me, "that of course if I wished it she would not interfere," she had endeavoured to obtain the school. Mr Ben Neely would have liked to have secured it for her. She was a pupil of his and her securing the school would have reflected some credit upon him. I have been very polite to Mollie ever since but at the same time I did not like it.

During the week of Christmas and this week of holiday I have tried to think as little of the prospect of teaching again as I possibly could. I have not permitted myself to become very much interested in housekeeping for fear that it would make teaching less interesting. ... Thursday night Mrs Keener & Johnnie were over to see us. She told me that Mr Carmichael and Mr Richards had been to see Mr Burch to secure a school for Mrs Sharpton. Mr Thomas replied "Yes that Mr Burch told him so that day." After Mrs Keener left he told me that Mr C and R had proposed that Mrs Sharpton have a school she and I to be paid pro rata for the number of pupils. Mr Burch enquired "What objection they had to Mrs Thomas?" They replied that I "could not, or did not control the larger boys!" I think I can understand old Lear's outburst against ingratitude better than I did before—[1] That may be egotistical but I have striven so hard to do my duty by those children. I have one consolation, a clear con-

---

1. "Ingratitude, thou marble-hearted fiend," from Shakespeare, *King Lear*, act 1, scene 4.

science and the knowledge that hereafter those children will render me justice.

As to the charge that I did not control the boys, I have never had but one insubordinate boy in my school and he was Allen Neely, rendered so by home influence. . . . The real reason for Mr Richards' opposition is disappointment that Mollie did not secure the school. Mr Neely wishes to gain the salary for his sister (Mrs Sharpton) and Mr Carmichael wishes to rent his school house. Well! Well! I would not like to suffer as much humiliated pride as I did that night and yesterday.

At one time I thought I would go and see Mr Richards but I could not, I could not— I had requested them two or three times to send Arthur as well as Sallie but I really do not wish Ferdy. He is a dear good boy but he is too large to be in a school of girls. I might control their actions, I could not control their glances and I am considered responsible for their behavior on the road as well as in the school room. I could not nerve myself to go to see Mr Richards although I expected that those men would in order to obtain their point & file their complaint against me. Great tears of wounded pride would fill my eyes to be indignantly dashed aside. *Three* men against *one* woman! . . .

It is bad to be wounded by one's so called friends. Mr Thomas says I feel it too keenly. Perhaps so. Although it was raining this morning Mr Thomas went in. I am only afraid that in his anxiety to help me he may bring me into a publicity which I detest. I shall find out tonight what the result has been. In the afternoon yesterday Mr Thomas went to see Mr Richards who told him that it was Mr C's proposition to go to see Mr Burch and that he was sorry that he went. Today there has been a monthly meeting of the Board of Education which Mr Thomas will attend. . . . All of my neighbors wonder that I continue the school. They have an idea I am so well off that I can afford to do without it. I expect they think that I continue it as an amusement, hence neglect my duties. Ah, they do not know what real work it is.

Monday, January 10, 1881 I have written several letters tonight but I will take time to write that my school began this morning with six new scholars, John Boldosky and five of the Neely children. They looked so bright and happy that I kissed them everyone. I refer to the Neelys.

Yesterday morning Mr Neely called to see Mr Thomas. He was invited into the parlour and a few minutes after I went in to invite him into this room to the fire for it was very cold. I shook hands with him when Mr Thomas remarked to me "Mr Neely has called to see me Gertrude." Without a word I turned and left the room. I never respected my husband more than I did at that moment. I felt that it would be all as it should be. I came in here, took up a newspaper and commenced to read Dickens' *Christmas Carol* but I read over the lines two or three or four times without taking in the idea.

I could hear the hum of conversation and remembering how plainly Mr Thomas had spoken to Mr Richards with regard to Mr Carmichael and Mr Neely I thought it possible that a dispute might be the result. Mr Carmichael had informed Mr Neely that Mr Thomas had gone to the meeting the day before to prevent his reelection as Commissioner [of Education]. He came over here as he said to know if this was so? To this Mr Thomas replied that he did not know that Saturday had been the day for the election—that he had attended for a different purpose but that he did say that if I was interfered with that he would use his influence to make him lose his position.

I waited until I thought the gentleman had had sufficient time to converse and then I returned to the room. "Mr Neely" said I "what are your objections to me as a teacher?" He protested "that he entertained for me the highest respect, admired my talents, admitted that his children had never had a fair trial given them through lack of home cooperation, threw all the blame on Mr Carmichael and told me that he would send his children this morning. I invited him into this room to the fire and we had an earnest conversation. Mr Neely is one of the most nervous men I ever met in my life. If he was my husband he would worry me terribly. This morning he came over, told me that his children would come directly and stood talking, scratching one leg with the other foot. "Col" said he to Mr Thomas "have you any chewing tobacco?" Mr Thomas told him "no" but gave him several cigars. I am very glad that he has sent the children. Whatever the motive which prompted him it is a compliment to me which I appreciate.

Monday, January 17, 188[1] . . . As I said last week was very trying. I was so tired that I did not enjoy reading, writing or anything else. I have five classes in Geography in my little school. Ida Lou's class are in Europe. Annie Neely & Allen are in Africa, Fanny Bell's class are in the United States— John Neely who is in Cornell's Primary Geography has a lesson in South America and Sammy Burch who is in Cornell's First Steps has a lesson in North America. Those were the lessons I heard in Geography today. No wonder when I am through that my brain is somewhat confused. Class after class follow each other in rapid succession. I have no time to tell as I would like to do some incident connected with each place. I often think of what use is all my learning, the result of my college education and my twenty years of subsequent self culture, of what avail is it with the young pupils who are in my care? Why if I had a class of pupils all of the same grade in learning I could take a Geography and with every country, city and principal river I could blend some story—some association, some fact, some legend of poetry or romance which would make the hard dry names they study become bright and blooming as a rose. This week I will place two of [the] Geography classes together.

.   .   .

Monday, April 4, 1881 This is my birthday. Today I am forty seven and I realise that I am growing old. Oh for a calm serene middle age to be followed by an old age like that of Dr Lovick Pierce [Methodist minister]. Said he when he was ninety years old in one of his sermons, "Here I am an old man. My work done, or nearly so, waiting to go like a ripened fruit that still hangs in the sunshine to mellow." . . . Mr George I Seney has within the last few weeks given $50,000 to Oxford[2] and $50,000 to Wesleyan Female College in Macon. I write the figures $50,000 and it does me good to realise the idea. Dear old Alma Mater! I love Macon College and now and hereafter shall feel grateful to the generous man who aids our "Mother of Colleges" with so liberal a donation. . . . Mr Seney has spent thirty years in the Metropolitan National Bank of New York of which he is now president. . . .

I was pleased as a Methodist when I heard of the gift to Emory but when I heard of the additional donation to Macon College my heart gave one glad exultant throb and with it died the last faint *gleam of hostility* to the *North, conquered* by *kindness* after *near*

---

2. Emory College at Oxford, Ga.

sixteen years resistance. Mr Seney is only fifty three having been born in 1828. What a sensible man he proves himself, in that he bestows his money and attends personally to the distribution of it. . . . I know I but echo the sentiments of 800,000 Southern Methodists when I pray God that his richest blessing may rest upon our Northern friend and benefactor.

Dixie Farm, September 5, 1882 (nearly two years after) Turner is a candidate to represent Richmond Co in the Legislature subject to a primary election which takes place today. Cora Lou said this morning while she was sewing on a dress for Kathleen, "I wonder how the election is going on?" I think she thought because I had not said much I was not thinking of it. I have thought of little else, and often my heart has been lifted in prayer for Turner. Mr Thomas and Julian left for the poor house taking Frank a coloured man with them. Jeff went down to Pine Hill. Turner is in Augusta. *I* could do nothing. The places they went to are some of the places where the votes will be polled. I could not aid Turner in that way so I went into the parlour and I prayed for him. If it was best for him let him be elected. If not let me think it was for the best. . . . The polls close at 3 oclock. It will quiet my mother's heart to write. I take up my Journal which has not been written in for nearly two years. . . .

Just then Jeff came home from the Pine Hill precinct. He reported that only 19 persons were present and Mr Calvin as the country candidate was ahead of Turner. Soon after Mr Thomas and Julian returned from the Poor House and reported Turner ahead of Mr Calvin or Perrin the country candidates. Mr Thomas is very despondent because so few votes were polled. All of the "no fence" men remained away and few negroes voted. The largest number of votes for one man was given for Mr Brandt. He had friends working for him with a supply of whiskey and cigars. Mr Thomas thinks Mr Calvin will get so large a vote in Augusta. Well I will not worry about it. . . .

Wednesday, September 6, 1882 Turner did not return early this morning. I told Cora Lou I argued unfavourably from this. At length I heard him coming, riding rapidly to the house. "What news from the election?" cried Mary Belle. "Badly beaten" was his reply in as bright, joyous tones as if he had been announcing a victory. The papers which he brought us confirmed the news he gave me when he kissed me. Turner bears it bravely, tells good storys of the election and if he feels the defeat does not show it. He was badly beaten and Mr Thomas appears to feel it. I alluded to the brave front with which Turner faced it. "That does not alter it," Mr Thomas replies, "he was badly beaten." "Well what of it," I reply, "you would not have him cry, would you?" It is after twelve. Turner has gone to his room. I retire to my room, close the door and kneeling acknowledge I am disappointed, not so much at Turner's defeat as—how shall I express it—disappointment that my spiritual aid failed me. . . .

September 22, 1882   Julian has joined the Methodist church. God be praised. How glad! How rejoiced I am! Friday the 8th of September Richmond camp meeting began. During the meeting I privately said to Julian that I would like for him to go to the altar to be "prayed for" and "Julian," said I "my dear if you would like to unite with the church do not hesitate to do so. Your father nor I will object but will rejoice." This I said to him because I thought if the children do not unite with the church when young perhaps they never will. The meeting continued and several times Julian went to the altar. Tuesday night the last night of the meeting arrived and Mr Thomas of Asbury church preached. . . .

Then followed a proposition from the minister. He wished to know how many would come up and shake hands with him and thus testify their willingness to remain all night at the altar if necessary. I looked and saw Julian from inside the railing of the altar (with others) advance and shake the hand of the minister and returning kneel again. My heart gave one great throb and in a moment I was by his side. In a low tone I said to him, "Julian! Darling! Mama is here. I will remain all night if you wish to. I am going to my seat now but I will be near." Oh my God how a mother loves her child and how I love Julian. . . . The exercises continued. Mr Laprade came up to me. "Your son has united with us. He tells me he has not a clear conception," with some other words to that effect. "Julian is all right," was my reply.

I understood my honest, truthful boy. He did not understand some of the preacher's enquirys. He only knew that "God so loved the world that he gave his only begotten son, that whosoever believed on him should not perish but have eternal life." I do not know that he thought of that text. He only knew that he loved God and wished to do better than he had done before. Mrs Heard was shouting—men were singing and women were weeping, but Julian was calm. It is his nature so to be. I could have rejoiced aloud but ever when I feel most I wish to be alone. I was touched with Mr Thomas' solicitude with regard to Julian. An invitation had been extended to those who felt grateful to God to rise and testify. Many did so. I did not but that night when I returned to the tent I entered my room and *then* I told God how glad I was. . . .

Ah me, my poor human nature better understands the love of Mary, Christ's mother who followed him to the cross and my heart has always done homage to that touch of humanity which prompted Our Saviour to place his mother in John's care. My Saviour help another mother! A weak erring mother to so direct and guide her son that his may be a great and noble life.

Monday, September 25, 1882   I had expected Jeff would have been at home by this time but he has not come yet. Friday Flady Richards and Jeff went to Bath [Georgia] to attend a party given at Mrs Wood's. They expected to return last night after spending yesterday with the Byne girls. I am worried about Jeff because he was to have been in Augusta today to see Messrs Law and Deery with regard to a situation in a grocery store. . . . Joe [Thomas] has for several months been on the police force. It is a position which he would not have selected from choice as it is a step downward in social position but there was nothing else for him to do and he is of age and Pinck and Mamie have a large family of little people. Having become a policeman Joe has discharged the duty as well as he could. . . .

Monday afternoon.   Jeff was not to blame with regard to coming home. He went down with Flady Richards in his buggy and Flady drove down last night from Hepzibah to see Callie Allen a very pretty young girl with whom he is much pleased or as Jeff says "Flady has made a mash!" I only mention this as an instance of the present style of slang so prevalent among young people. . . . Jeff returned about dinner time and since then Mary Belle Cora Lou and himself have gone to the city. Jeff is to see "Messrs Deery and Law" and return tonight so that Mr Thomas can go in tomorrow. . . .

Last spring I was in Augusta. Coming down the street I saw Charlie Phinizy sitting before the door in the basement of his house. I called to him, "Mr Phinizy can I see you a few moments." He came to the gate and after shaking hands with me I proceeded to request of him that he would give Jeff a situation using his influence as president of the railroad. "I make this request of you" I said "not as the president of the railroad but as the friend I used to know so well." He smiled, assured me he would exert his influence that there were many positions and &c—shook hands cordially and we parted. Hearing nothing from him during the summer I was again in Augusta at Ma's. I knew Charlie was at home so I hastily penned a few lines to remind him of my request and seeing Mr Phinizy's carriage driver pass the house, I called him and gave him the note for Charlie.

This is September and since then I have received no answer to my note. I thought perhaps the boy neglected to give him the note but I am determined to know. In other words I will know the value of the old acquaintance upon which I made claim or the amount of courtesy possessed by the president of the railroad. Last week I was spending a few days in Augusta. Late on Tuesday afternoon I called to see Mrs Kolb (Charlie's sister Martha). She was one of my attendants when I was married and we have been friends (so called) ever since altho I know that were I to die tomorrow Martha would not grieve or shed a tear.

I was in the act of leaving and standing with Martha by the gate when Charlie Phinizy came in. Simply lifting his hat he passed on, but now was my opportunity. "Mr Phinizy" said I arresting his progress. He turned and I believe shook hands with me. "I wished to know" I proceeded to say "if you received a note I wrote you sometime ago?" "Yes'm" was his reply—only this and nothing more, no excuse no regret at apparent discourtesy—no promise of influence to be exerted. I waited for one instant, realising with a sigh, not a feeling of disappointment on Jeff's account for I expected nothing, but realising that I was of so little social importance. Had I been more influential Charlie Phinizy would not have had it in his power for one instant to have had me occupy the position of a suppliant for assistance. To my credit I will say that this feeling lasted only for the instant. Turning from him, after waiting for the explanation which did not come I resumed my conversation with Martha and Charlie went on in the house. . . .

Wednesday, September 27, 1882 . . . Turner has a new cutting machine with which he is much pleased. He has been cutting hay and Julian and Jeff, yesterday while Mr Thomas was in town, hauled up loads of it. This morning Jeff, Mr Thomas, Julian and others packed the large waggons with cotton and sent it up to Mr Ransom's to be ginned and packed. Jeff works very well altho he is unaccustomed to that kind of work. He went in Monday to see Mr Law but they gave him no satisfaction. They think that if Claude Shewmake leaves as he expects to that they can do with a young boy. Mr Law promised to let Jeff know and when he, Jeff, wished to know if he might call again replied "Yes," but I expect nothing from them. Yesterday I wrote a letter to Mr Grey of Waynesboro requesting him to give Jeff a place. We were boarding in the same house when we were in N Y last summer. . . .

For the last two years he [Jeff] has been with Loo Chong a Chinaman. He wishes to leave a situation which he thinks is degrading. Jeff is a man now and I agree with him. On my way to the prayer meeting I thought, I know this is a good beginning of the day. Leaving the church I was so confident of being "led by the spirit" I would not have been surprised if the first application had been successful.[3] I first spoke to Mr Rhodes. He was courteous, complimented Jeff but told me he had as many clerks as he wished in his store (a grocery store). I next enquired of Mr Calhoun if he wished a clerk in his store (a shoe store). He replied "no" and soon after I was joined on the street by Mary Vason (Mrs Foster). Of course while I was shopping with Mary I said nothing about Jeff. After leaving Mary I walked up to Richards' dry goods store, inquired of Allee Richards if they wished a clerk, and then all at once I thought "perhaps Col Dorsey may give Jeff a situation on the railroad." . . . One more application I made of Christopher Grey's dry goods house—conscious all the time that Jeff was not in the slightest degree familiar with the business. He does not know the difference between long cloth and cambric—Jaconet or swiss.

I expect persons ought to carry a little common sense into their religion as well as into everything. The next morning in prayer meeting Mr Richardson alluded to the distinction between "religious enthusiasm and fanaticism. In other words a man may be a fool in his religion." I shrank a little as I made the application and thought "which am I?" It must not be supposed that Jeff has been idle while I have been trying to assist him. He has made numerous efforts but there are so many wishing situations and for all heavy work in grocery stores coloured help can be obtained for a

---

3. Gertrude was spending several days in Augusta, attending meetings at St. James Church and making an effort "to procure a position for Jeff."

small price. Monday is the 1st of October. It is time he knew what he could do. Joe Thomas took the position of a policeman because there was nothing else for him to do and poor boy he has run the risk of his life in the discharge of his duty. . . .

. . .

Dixie Farm, October 3, 1882 . . . Tomorrow Cora Lou goes into the city. The next morning she leaves for *New York*. I think of Mary Bell's visit to NY and of Clanton (Little darling how few times I have written of you, but Mama does not forget) but I will remember *my* visit last summer and hope that we will keep well and happy. I was about to say— Ah me! Cora Lou is young. She can be happy but not I. While money cares weigh me down so heavily— but I will not permit a sad thought to trouble me now. I will the rather write of Ma's goodness in taking Cora Lou. My Mother! Oh my precious, darling mother. . . .

October 4, 1882 I began to write last night but I could not. I am worried and I will write because I can take pleasure in nothing else. Mr Dye is to the front again! Do you remember him my Journal? He is the man who owns our plantation in Burke. How long ago it seems since that awful time. I look out of the window and my eye falls upon the thick pine forest of Belmont and I try to realise that I am the same proud young creature who writhed in agony when first she learned that her husband's name had been protested—and later still—but "I'll drive such thoughts away."

How shall I write. Well two years ago Mr Thomas borrowed money from Mr Dye to pay taxes and failing to pay it last year gave additional security. The time arrives now for payment and Mr Dye says that if half is not paid he will levy upon the property and sell my lifetime interest. Monday Mr Thomas went in to see him. I had that thought to keep me company and my school opened with *four scholars. . . .*

Cora Lou left this morning in the spring waggon with Mr Thomas who has gone again to see Mr Dye. I was sad because I had so little money to give her. Mr Montgomery paid me through Mr Thomas fifteen dollars but it was required to pay the interest on a note due in bank. I feel too badly to write. I had wished to write thinking it would do me good but it does not.

Friday, October 6, 1882 I am always glad when Friday afternoon comes for I think I am that much nearer gaining the month's salary for which I am working. My duties have been very light this week for I have had so few scholars. I am glad to see Julian evince so much interest in his studies. After Christmas I hope to send him to the academy in Augusta. Ma, Cora Lou and Kate left yesterday morning. Mr Thomas gave Cora Lou six dollars. She bought her corset gloves and stockings. She will travel in her turban and brown plaid suit and looks very sweet. I do not know that I have ever written that I think Cora Lou quite pretty. She is tall and fine looking but she is better far than all this. She is a genuine comfort with her bright smile and willing hands. She is very fond of reading, principally novels, but she is very ingenious and quick with her needle. Going North will expand her mind, brighten her ideas and be of inestimable value to her. . . .

Tuesday, October 10, 1882 I am at home entirely alone with the exception of my cook (Mary Godbey). Since dinner we have had a busy time sending off a four mule team of cotton to Mr Ransom's to be ginned. Our screw is out of order and our mules so pulled down from hauling wood to fulfil a contract made with Mr W Mc-Coy that we thought it best to get Mr Ransom to gin our cotton at $2.50 pr bale. The cotton sent this afternoon will make eight bales we have sent from here. We pay by the hundred, 50 cts pr hundred and the tenants pick also. Our gin house has no lock on it so the cotton greatly to my annoyance has been kept in the back piazzi. I was so glad to get it out that Mary Belle, Julian, Kathleen, Marion Rood[4] and Mary my cook assisted the waggon driver Frank and his son Peter (about Julian's age) to fill the baskets. . . .

For two weeks I have been dreading that Mr Dye would press his suit and I thought that today my name would be published again. With this almost ever present thought I have taught, thankful that in the school room I was too busy to let it haunt me. I told Mr Thomas that I was willing to sell the swamp land which I received from Holt's estate and I think after I made up my mind to that purpose I felt better, but he does not think it is best, says we must keep it to mortgage to Mr Howard or we will not be able to purchase supplies. Meanwhile money is very scarce. The supplies

---

4. Marion Rood was the daughter of Kate Clanton Rood.

are to be bought cotton picking hands are to be paid and nothing is left over. Last night when Mr Thomas at a late hour returned I asked him if he saw Mr Dye. "No" was his reply "but I do not think he will do anything."

Not one word did I reply. I rose from the table and I went into the parlour and I knelt down by the sofa and in one great sigh of thankfulness I blessed God for the relief. No words came from my lips. My heart was too full and when my power of utterance came I could only say "I thank thee, I thank thee." Mr Thomas tells me that it is only temporary—only thirty days but I feel as a prisoner of the inquisition might have felt. For one blessed moment the pressure of the rack is relieved and I breathe freer. So far as I am concerned I have made up my mind that school teaching is to be my employment and if I were the only one to consult I would call my creditors together—make the best terms I could with them, try to secure some kind of support, give up everything and work the rest of my life. I would not have my existence so harrassed.

Dixie Farm, March 11, 1883   One week ago last night Gov [Alexander] Stephens died. That was March the 3d. Thursday Mch the 8th he was buried. It was a grand funeral, 75000 people were in Atlanta to do honor to the occasion— Statesmen, Senators, Congressman, eminent divines were present to pay their tribute of respect. . . .

My Journal Jeff is [in] Savannah. He has an excellent situation as an Express messenger between Savannah and Macon. One day is spent in the former—the next in the latter city. Some other time I will write about it. My pen is a very poor one.

My mind and thoughts are almost as dull as if my brain had been taken from my head to be weighed. The *Evening News* of Augusta thinks it a great pity Mr Stephens' brain had not been weighed "for the sake of science, as was Bonaparte's, and more recently Gambetta's."[5] What possible good could have been gained by it aside from the profanation. Would it have given the editors of the *Evening News* more brain. Did the weighing of Gambetta's brain increase the mental powers of anyone in France? . . .

If spirits know aught of mundane affairs as Mr Talmage preaches that they do I could imagine Gov Stephens and his brother

---

5. Leon Gambetta, a French statesman who died in 1882.

Linton smiling at the thought of Dr DeWitt Talmage[6] in the afternoon praying at the funeral of the late chief magistrate of Georgia and that night lecturing to the largest crowd that ever attended a lecture (the same crowd that attended the funeral) and keeping them "convulsed with laughter" by his lecture on "Big Blunders." Big man as he is Dr Talmage was unconscious that in selecting *that night* for his lecture he was the personification of the subject presented.

[The entry above was the only one for the year 1883. Gertrude Thomas wrote sporadically from 1882 through 1889. During those years, though she made no record of it in her journal, she became more active in organizations, including the Women's Christian Temperance Union. Her writing became more public than private. In December 1883, Mary Belle married Frederick Laurens Ingraham of Charleston, S.C., son of Commodore Duncan Nathaniel Ingraham, United States Navy hero (the Koszta Affair)[7] and Confederate States Navy captain. Frederick Ingraham was also the great-grandson of Henry Laurens of South Carolina, president of the Continental Congress, 1777–78.]

Wednesday, July 30, 1884 . . . Last night I told Ginnie Burch whose father died yesterday, "Ginnie I can bring you no comfort. It is one of those hard things we bear because we must bear them."

My mother died Sunday May 11th. It has been nearly three months and it feels like it happened years and years ago. How I felt then—how I have lived since I cannot tell. Just at first I was stunned. I moved, I lived because nature willed it so. I could not write. If I had my writing would have expressed the tumult of my thoughts. I had no christian resignation. I pretended to none. I bore

---

6. The Reverend Dr. DeWitt Talmage of the Brooklyn Tabernacle in New York was a popular preacher/lecturer who spoke frequently in the South. His sermons were published in the Augusta papers.

7. Martin Koszta, a Hungarian army officer in the uprising against Austria, 1848–49, fled to the United States in 1850 and filed for citizenship in 1852. In 1853 he traveled to Turkey, where he was illegally seized and imprisoned aboard the Austrian brig *Hussar* in Smyrna harbor. Duncan N. Ingraham, commanding the American sloop *St. Louis*, gained Koszta's release through an ultimatum that threatened the use of force. Ingraham became a national hero and received a Congressional gold medal for his daring exploit.

it stoically because I was obliged to. A few weeks after my mother's death I received a dear letter from Fred[8] and this is a portion of the letter I wrote him.

"I told you when you were with us that I could not find words to thank you but I will tell you this much. I have read your letter over and over again and it soothes and comforts me. . . . A few nights ago I looked upon a new moon and thought of my gifted young brother who died in Paris, and I said 'Holt, do you know that Ma is dead? Have you seen her? Are you in the same spiritual world?' Oh the memory of that hour when I stood alone and forgetting all things else, strove to penetrate the mystery which seperates us from those we love. Above me shone the young moon, which for fifteen years since Holt died[9] has told to me the same wondrous story of love and faith. Beside it were two stars shining brightly, the only ones visible in the boundless blue sky. I looked and looked in vain. I could read no new lesson of faith. I was searching for my mother. I missed her so." . . .

I wrote that letter of which the above is an extract and while writing knew I would not send it nor did I. I placed [it] in my writing desk and have until today made no attempt to roll the stone away from my mother's grave.

July 31, 1884 A few weeks ago I visited Mary Belle and remained ten days in Atlanta. It cheered my heart to see Mary Belle so happy in the love of her husband. She has been married seven months now. The visit did me a great deal of good. In the companionship of my gentle sympathetic daughter I began to regain my natural self. When I recall the awful time when my mother died and my state of mind after I can compare it to nothing. Would it be irreverent if I were to say to the condition of those angels who were hurled from heaven to hades? I was so happy in my mother's love, so blessed in her presence that when she had left us everything was a blank.

Sometime, not now I will try to tell how Ma was taken from us. For the first six weeks after her death, the material, the corruptible human nature portion of my being was so crushed, so agonized that I could not take in the idea of "mortality putting on immor-

---

8. Fred and Mary Belle Ingraham were living in Atlanta. They later moved back to Augusta.

9. Holt Clanton died in 1871, thirteen years earlier.

tality," "corruption becoming incorruption." I try, oh I try to lift my thoughts to a spiritual conception of my darling mother but Oh Mama darling I miss you so much.

Saturday, September 6, 1884 I am alone at home. Mr Thomas went down this morning to the swamp. Turner went to the plantation in Columbia Co prepared to rent the place to a man by the name of Squires. Cora Lou Julian and Kathleen have gone in the carriage for muscadines. They will call for Annie Neely. Just as they left the wife of one of our tenants brought some muscadines which she wished to exchange for soap. I engaged her to bring some more of them. I had intended driving with the children but the dining room has one side of the floor covered with watermelons. The figs and pomgranite and the Scupperno[n]gs in the yard are so much exposed when no one is in the house I concluded to remain at home. Mary Godby is cooking for me & Rudolph is in the yard but they are not to be depended on. The muscadines are for preserves and jelly. Camp meeting begins next Friday and I have made no preparations for it.

After the children left this morning I was on the front piazzi. In the flower garden were a number of beautiful white pigens picking up the stray bits of food scattered around. I came in and carried out some canary bird seed and threw to them. Startled they flew away, returning soon and ignoring what I had given them they began again their search, while within a few steps of them lay the bountiful feast which I with thoughtful hand and sympathetic heart had provided for them. As I looked I thought. If I from my superior standpoint of intelligence am interested in, and thoughtful of those little pigeons how much more is my Heavenly Father thought[ful] of and interested in me and then I tried to lift my thoughts higher and *oh it is so hard—* . . .

When my mother was dying, when the paralysis had attacked her body, when she was incapable of utterance, I thought her brain might be clear, that consciousness might yet linger with her and kneeling by her side I said "Mama darling, I will do everything I can for you" and in that promise I pledged myself for all time to act as I think Ma would like for me to— With that thought controlling every action, the division of my mother's furniture met my approval. My one idea was to preserve peace and family harmony— with the idea ever present with me, "Ma would have approved it."

I have resigned the school of which for five years I have had charge. I remembered how much my mother loved her home. She rarely referred to it but I knew how she disliked the thought that the house which my father built for her should pass into stranger hands. I remembered that during the last week of her illness two or three days before her death she walked to the window and looked out for the last time upon her flower garden. Remembering all this I have rented Ma's house—until it is sold— I will occupy Ma's room and God grant that the spirit of my mother may regulate and control my every movement. Mamie says she "does not understand how I can live there." Why I would like *to know* that Ma was around me at all times, and when I go to Augusta and enter the house I feel that I am reminded of Ma and I find myself saying "Ma, am I doing right in renting the house?" and I know that she would like it.

How I wish I could own my mother's house, not only because it is a fine large building but because *it was hers* and *Pa had it built*. I do not think that either member of the family has the love for it that I have unless it is Kate and she has rented one of Mr Hookey's houses on Centre St preferring to have a house of her own.

Today is the 6th of September—on the 11 of this month it will be four months since Ma was taken from us and to me it seems like ages have come and gone. Often I have thought that I would like to write about her death but I could not. I wrote only one letter telling of her death and that was to Althea Paul (Mrs Gregon) and that was two months after she died and this was a portion of what I wrote. "For nearly nine months Ma's health had been feeble. Dr Doughty[10] told us that she had heart disease but did not tell her and from that hour our effort was to prevent her knowing it. And our constant prayer was 'Good Lord! from sudden death deliver her.' She did not die suddenly. For more than a week she was confined to her bed. Relatives, children and grandchildren gathered by her bed side and affection soothed her last moments. A few days before she died Mr Adams the Presbyterian minister enquired of her, 'Mrs Clanton do you put your trust in Jesus?' 'Yes I do' was her simple childlike reply. My mother lived a life consecrated to the duties she was called upon to perform, that of a faithful wife and a devoted consci-

---

10. Probably William H. Doughty, Sr. William H. Doughty, Jr., also practiced in Augusta.

entious mother. Her children remembering her life of good deeds and earnest counsel, bless and revere her memory."

Dixie Farm Saturday, September 20, 1884   My little Kathleen has joined the Methodist church. Little darling in the coming years will you blame Mamma and say I acted wrong in permitting you to join so young? I will tell you my little girl why I thought it best. Hereafter you will hesitate to assume responsibility and perhaps like Turner and Jeff and Cora Lou refuse to unite with the church. . . . Again Kathleen said to me when the call was made for applicants for the church membership— "Mamma may I go?" "Yes" said I, "ask your Papa." Mr Thomas was a few seats in front of me across the aisle. I saw Kathleen go up to him as he stood on the side of the aisle and whisper to him. I suppose he objected for I heard her say in tones of entreaty "Let me, Let me" and in a moment more she came to me and said her papa said "Yes." Taking her by the hand I approached the altar and standing by my side my little Kathleen who will be ten years old the fourth of next January gave her hand to the church and promised "to try to be good." That is her idea of religion and I do not know that she can improve upon it. . . .

   Afternoon.   . . . After tea [yesterday] the good impression still lingered with me. I was reading to Mr Thomas in the parlour what I had written in the morning when Turner returned from Augusta bringing letters, among them one from Mr F Miller telling Mr Thomas that Mr Benson has placed in his hands a claim for 1800 dollars against us. I put the paper down that I was reading while Mr Thomas—well it does no good to write about such things but I haven't been on Mt Pisgah's top today. I knew the money was due and I had requested Mr Thomas to see Mr Benson and make arrangements with him—that I was willing to pay him from the first money given to me from Ma's estate. Had this been done probably Mr Benson would not have placed it in Mr Miller's hands and a lawyer's fee would have been saved.

16. Ill Health and Broken Spirits

What is to become of my journals?
—*August 28, 1889*

[Augusta] Two years later. September 10, 1886 This morning I looked for my long neglected journal. I thought I would write of last week's horror, the earthquake.[1] Julian returning from up town tells me that Cuba has been swept from the earth, that sailors report that the island is no longer to be seen. I have not read the morning paper but I cannot write of the earthquake now.

12 Oclock Friday. I have not heard what is the fate of Cuba but I will write and tell of the earthquake. Tuesday night Aug 31st I was at Dixie our home in the country. I had driven out in the Buggy with Mr Thomas the day before intending to remain several days. I was far from well, tired heart, soul and body. The night before I had prayed in importunate, reckless manner "Lift me higher, higher Lord to Thee." I was so tired of life's cares, so impatient so dragged down by sordid care. The next day Tuesday was an ideal day. I sat on the front piazzi at Dixie with a book in my hand which I did not read. A gentle wind whispered peace and brought loving thoughts of God's love. . . . All that day I was rested, soothed, comforted by the dear Mother Nature whom I so dearly love.

About twilight I stood by the window in the dining room looking towards Belmont. I never remember to have seen a greater number of stars. At the time I was impressed with the nearness of the constellations to the earth. The milky way seemed almost to touch

---

1. The earthquake of August 31, 1886, affected a large area of the southeastern coast. Charleston, S.C., suffered the greatest damage. In Augusta, there were thirteen shocks over the next week or ten days, and aftershocks continued for several months.

437

the earth. I stood and gazed and wondered as I had often done before at this mystery of God's creation. After tea Mr Thomas Turner and I sat by the table reading. I was reading *Daisy Chain*.[2] I stopped reading and undressed. A large rat was in the bed room and Turner and Mr Thomas chased it from the room shutting the door between my room and the bed room. A few moments after a musquito bit me on the shoulder and I asked Mr Thomas to rub it.

Just then a noise was heard right above my head as if a hundred rats might have been scampering. "Look out for the ceiling" said Mr Thomas, "run here," as he rushed into the bed room which is not plastered and exclaimed, "It is an earthquake." As that one horrible word, so potent with evil was uttered, as I glanced in his face, as I took in the meaning of the word some impulse prompted me to rush out into the front piazzi where I met Turner just escaping from the parlour. I do not think either of us uttered one word. Together we stood while the house shook and reeled like a drunken man, and still that awful, rushing, roaring sound is heard. I look, I see the piazzi sway to and fro (I seem to feel it now) and then as a man flees for his life I grasp Turner, and hand in hand we rush down the step and out into the front yard. I feel the earth sway to and fro. Oh God! the horror of that moment! Just then I expect the earth to heave and swallow us up. Has the day of judgement come? And as I sway with that awful, horrible motion, far away from the distant coloured church is heard the most pathetic, mournful wail I ever listened to.

I looked up for one instant. I expected the heavens to fall. Just where that day the lovely clouds floated, the stars now shone brightly. The sight steadied me thank God. Turner and I had seperated. He looked toward the house expecting it to fall. I had just time to glance towards the sky when another shock came. I heard Mr Thomas say "support your mother Turner." I felt my husband's arms around me. I was concious that I was falling. I was conscious of an intolerable pain in my back, and an awful nausea, and from that time through the successive shocks I was sick like unto death. A chair was first brought out into the yard. Later we went into the front piazzi where I lay covered with blankets, first resting in Mr Thomas' and then in Turner's arms. Every shock made me sick like

2. *The Daisy Chain or Aspirations, a Family Chronicle* (1856), by Charlotte Mary Yonge.

the throes of a woman in childbirth. I did not know that others had been sick. I could scarcely breathe. I was so sick while Mr Thomas and Turner were so free from sickness and after the first shock were calm. "What is the matter Gertrude?" said Mr Thomas in tones of surprise. "Are you so afraid to die?" While I, poor woman, awe stricken, gasping for breath, sick unto death in expectation of another shock could only shrink shiveringly with mortal terror from what I knew not.

During that time, after that one glance at the sky, I uttered not one word of prayer. I claim to be educated but I must be candid and admit that no untutored African was more thoroughly ignorant that night of earthquakes than I. I verily expected the earth would engulph us. And to my dying day I shall never forget the sensation of comfort, the very first gleam of comfort that awful night, which I derived when I heard the Savannah train of railroad cars go by. Verily I had not thought after that earthquake that there was solid foundation enough for the cars to travel upon.

Out on the piazzi we sat for half the night, we three. Oh that solemn night. May its terrible warning long linger with us. Later we retired to our room. I knelt and prayed God to let me sleep. I did not ask him to stop the earthquakes. I knew some wonderful machinery had been put in motion and I was not so presumptious as to think that I could influence its movements, but I did ask God to give me a cessation from my fright and sickness. I prayed for dear ones and all in trouble and God was good to me. I slept and was not conscious when two quakes came. Mr Thomas said I awoke, stirred, nestled closer up to him and then went to sleep again. The next morning Julian came down from Augusta and found us both in bed. Dear boy, he wished to see what had become of us and had ridden down to see. "No one," he said "had been to bed" and discribed everyone as being in an awful state of fright. Turner and Julian returned to the city. I remained with Mr Thomas.

Mr Thomas said he had no idea of leaving the house the night before. His one idea was to avoid the falling plastering. He brought the lamp out into the front piazzi to keep it from being overturned and setting the house on fire. He said that as he passed through the sitting room he could scarcely walk, the house was rocking and shaking in a terrible manner. He placed the lamp on the floor on the piazzi and then came to my assistance.

. . . With the morning had come calm, with the morning had come the knowledge that *others had been sick*. I have been told that those who received the shock on the ground suffered most. But neither Mr Thomas or Turner were sick but I remember now. Mr Thomas was in the house during the first shock and Turner during the second or third. . . .

After supper I sent to Mrs Keener to send me Lavender, Bromide of Potassium or some nervine, for tonight was to have suspense added to anxiety. She sent me a little brandy or whiskey. I do not know one from the other. I said my prayers, undressed, tied my clothes securely together to grasp at a moment's warning, drank one teaspoonful of brandy and went to sleep. Once during the night Mr Thomas called me to run but the quake passed off. I am a temperance woman but in a crisis like this it was better to drink the medicine than unnerve myself and others.[3] Not since the second night of the storm at Sullivan's Island[4] had I tasted brandy and then it was given me by good kind hearted Mr Ludekins who a few days ago lost his life bathing at the island. . . .

. . . .

January 5, 1887 Gertrude my little darling.[5] I would not have believed that you would be two years old and I made no mention of you in my Journal. Grandmamma has grown much older during the last two or three years. Business cares have pressed upon me and I have written nothing for two years in my Journal and very little for publication. My little dear. You are remarkably pretty and very bright. Someday I will write and tell some of your many pretty ways. While I am writing I hear the merry shouts of children and boys in the street playing at snow balling. Last night and this morning there was a heavy snow storm. I do not think I ever remember to have seen the snow fall so thick and fast. Yesterday was Kathleen's birthday. She was twelve years old. She began her journal yesterday and she recorded that yesterday morning at six oclock

---

3. This reference is the first indication that Gertrude had become involved with the temperance movement.

4. The hurricane that had struck Sullivan's Island, near Charleston, S.C., in August of the previous year was called the great storm of 1885. Gertrude was visiting the island with a group from Augusta and wrote an account of the storm that was published in the papers.

5. Gertrude is addressing Gertrude Clanton Ingraham, Mary Belle's daughter, born December 18, 1884.

there was an earthquake. We have not had one since Nov 7th. I think that was the last. . . .

About that time I was suffering very much from a boil on my neck. I was troubled about renting this house concious that we could not afford to give so much, and I think I was troubled with the size of it and the number of bricks contained in it, in case of an earthquake (And I am troubled about that now and wish I was in a wooden house). . . .

Meanwhile Mrs Allen had rented two rooms from me giving me an assured small income of eighteen dollars. Soon after I was well enough to sit up. Rebie Vason came down and took me to ride in her buggy (Mamie had taken me over in her buggy to Bessman's garden the afternoon before). I felt so much better when I came home with Rebie that I walked up to Sis Annie's. She insisted upon my dining with her. I went into the house and pulled myself up her long flight of stairs. Later I was lying on the sofa in her bed room talking to Rebie and Sis Annie about earthquakes. Sis Anne's chimneys had been mended. So had the plastering, her home having been condemned by the board. "Come up and stay with me while Mary and Rebie go to New York," said Sis Anne. "I would be afraid to sleep up stairs," I replied.

Just then Rebie looked up in a startled manner and rose from her chair. So did Sis Annie and then the house shook. The window panes rattled. "Let's go down," said Rebie. I rose and followed them. . . . I had gone up those steps with the feeble step of an invalid. I came down them with the activity of a young girl. Oh what a long flight it was. Just as I was half way down a second quake came and the house shook as if in the grasp of an angry monster. Panting out of breath, frightened all but to death, I sank into a seat. The shock was over but not the effect upon me. I could eat no dinner. Again I was nauseated. "I know you are a temperance woman Aunt Gertrude," said Mary, "but I believe you draw the line on earthquakes and cyclones. Take a glass of wine," offering me one. "No," said I "but I would like a strong cup of coffee." . . .

Today an election for sheriff and other county officers has been held at the city hall. The shouts of the negro men could be plainly heard as many of them had whiskey given them. Julian was expressing his opinion of a white man whose arm was thrown around a negro man whose vote he was trying to secure. "None of that in mine" said he. "I would not do it to be elected and I know I would not and run the risk of being beaten." Julian will be nineteen on the

23d of this month and in March he hopes to receive his diploma as a doctor.[6] He has attended the lectures last winter and this. He reads very closely and is much interested. My boy, my boy, you are almost a man now. Mother's little Julian, my little pet who cheered dark days at Belmont. I hope you will be a great and a good man.

April 5, 1887   Yesterday was April the 4th my birthday. Kathleen enquired of me "How old are you Mama?" And I was not jesting when I replied "I do not know." My journal has been lying on the table in my room for four [three] months since I wrote in January to record Kathleen's birthday party. Altho I made no mention of the birthday party I gave to her. Yesterday I thought of writing but did not. This morning I believe I will write but first I had to try and remember how old I was and a very womanly calculation I made. I really do not give the thought much attention during the year but my birthday is April the 4th and I never forget that I was married in 1852 on the 16th Dec. Nearly every year I have to count from those dates. I am fifty three years old.

Col U P Stovall died yesterday. He will be buried from St Paul's church this afternoon. He was seventy four years old and has lived in Augusta fifty years. I will have to live twenty one years more to attain to his age. Twenty one years does not appear a very long time but I am almost sure that I will not live that long. Do I really wish to live that long. What is that prayer "So teach me to number my days." How Col Stovall seemed to enjoy life and yet how marred his life was. I wonder if his wife is grieved or relieved by his death? She was not with him during his illness. How strange a thing is death and how strange a thing is life. I look out and the trees look as they did the spring Pa died. That was twenty three years ago and ever since I have hoped to meet my father again. My mother too I trust to see and am trying to realise the idea and accustom myself to the inevitable destiny which awaits me. What is natural is right. If a man die shall he live again. The trees which my father planted wave an assurance that all things follow their appointed destiny. . . .

.   .   .

---

6. Julian Pinckney Thomas graduated from the Augusta Medical College in 1887, the youngest in his class.

April 3, 1888. Augusta . . . I expect I shrink from what is before me. Tomorrow I will be fifty four years old and I could not obtain credit for fifty dollars. I own land, much of it, and it does not support my family.[7] For three years we have had complete failures on our river lands from high water. There is nothing to be obtained from my mother's estate.[8] Spring has come and I cannot buy a dress for Cora Lou or Kathleen. A pitiful confession to make to you my journal. I have written so little because I did not like to give expression to such trials *for they are trials.* Of late I have tried to be submissive. I am going (God willing) to do the duty which lies nearest to me. During the last month I have had only one servant. I give out the clothes to be laundried away from home. Cora Lou and I do the house work, that is the bed rooms. I cannot bear to owe a servant money which I cannot pay.

Dear Journal I have much to tell you much for which to be very grateful. Julian is north in Christ Hospital, Jersey City Heights [New Jersey]. He is House Surgeon I believe that is the position. Turner is in the Insurance business. Jeff is still with the Express Co. Mary Belle is happily married and is a great comfort to me. Cora Lou is all that a fond mother could desire while Kathleen my thirteen year old darling is a perfect treasure. Oh God I thank Thee for my children and my grandchildren.

Gertrude and Duncan[9] my dear little darlings I am sorry I can do so little for you but somehow, someway things are going to be different. I am going to pray to God to help me. Last year when my birthday came I was living in my mother's house. For three years we rented it for $500 dollars each year—the amount to be deducted from my interest in the house when it is sold. The second year I

---

7. All of Gertrude's property was mortgaged to the limit and beyond, and there were still the interest, taxes, and supplies to be paid.

8. Once again, the Thomases had expected a large legacy, but Mary Luke Clanton's properties were held by her only for her lifetime and then reverted to Turner Clanton's estate under the same terms as the other legatees. Her personal wealth, which was considerable before the war, had apparently dwindled away over the years. Also, Gertrude owed the estate $1,500 for three years' rent of the Clanton house in Augusta.

9. Duncan Nathaniel Ingraham was the first son of Mary Belle and Fred, born July 11, 1887. A second son, Henry (Harry) Laurens Ingraham, was born January 21, 1890.

rented the parlours to Dr and Mrs Patrick for sixteen dollars per month. I was sick that summer. I was unaccustomed to a summer in the city. The earthquakes came. I was undecided about renting the house. Mr Thomas thought it best.

Mrs Allen rented the parlours for the year at eighteen dollars pr month and in the spring for several months Mr Wynn with his wife and two children and sister in law Miss Mattie Nutting rented two rooms up stairs with the use of the parlour for $20 dollars pr month. I had forgotten to write that year before last Mr Robert Brown & his wife and two children rented two rooms for two or three months for eighteen dollars pr month. During . . . [several lines have been cut from the bottom of the page.] . . . [I rented] rooms to aid in supporting me and it gave me an income for buying dresses and bonnets but the privacy of my home was entirely destroyed. But I thought it was my duty. I think my long illness last summer was owing to the strain on my nervous system.

When Duncan was born down stairs in the wing room I was up stairs so weak from a long malarial sickness Dr Doughty would not let me know of it. My visit to Haywood White Sulphur and Waynesville in N C prolonged my life. Sis Anne gave me one month's board at the Springs thirty dollars, the regular price was forty dollars, but ours was a large party. I wrote home three letters, two for *Evening News* one for the *Chronicle*. I paid my board in Waynesville 15 dollars pr month and my travelling expense. Mr Foster and Mary invited me to be their guest at Battery Park hotel in Ashville from Saturday night until Monday morning and took Kate and I to drive Sunday afternoon to Richmond Hill and Col Connoly's. [More lines are missing here as a result of the page's being cut off at the bottom. Also, an entire page has been removed.]
. . . buy clothes for the children. On my birthday I wrote that I saw no way to provide for them and the very next day Kate gave Cora Lou twenty 20 dollars, as an Easter present she said. God bless Kate. She does not know altho she may guess how much Cora Lou appreciated it.

I was interrupted to receive a visit from Miss Weisiger. She is a cousin of Mr Sam Weisiger who has for two years past been very devoted to Kate. He is a widower with four children. I called to see her about eighteen months ago and this is the first time she has called. She is taking charge of Mr W's children. Not long ago she went with him to Richmond to visit her family while he went on to N York. I think she is in love with him. If Kate does not intend to marry him I wish she would not receive his attentions.[10] . . .

Well I have written until I have changed the current of my thought. After breakfast this morning I read in 1st Samuel and then kneeling I asked God's help and while I knelt the gong rang and a bill was presented for the second time for a pair of $1.50 cts shoes I bought from Murphey for Kathleen last week. I sent word "I would call and pay it" but how and when? A few minutes after came a bill for a vest for Kathleen from J B White for 35 cts. I thought it had been paid. Meanwhile I sent Malinda my cook to buy a 10 cts beef steak. (I never give more for one) and soon after Turner sent 50 cts lard and 50 cts meat. There was none in the store room and so I live, ~~literaly from hand~~ No I will not write that. I may be poor but I will not use slang. . . .

Dixie, August 28, 1889 I hesitated before I began to write. What is to become of my journals? "If you ever wish anyone to read them you will have to have them printed" said one of my sisters. I notice that my children are interested in references to their childhood. Kathleen is going to the depot for Cora Lou whom we expect home from White Oak[11] camp meeting. Cousin Polly (Mrs Walton) wrote inviting my family and Turner and Cora Lou went up Saturday morning on the Ga train. Fred Mary Belle and the two children went to Charleston two weeks ago. Mrs Hasell[12] was sick so they remained only a few days on Sullivan's Island. I was in town last Tuesday. Took dinner with Mary Belle who is housekeeping. We went up to Blythe's and I bought fruit jars and jelly glasses and I have been busy making pickle and jelly. Gertrude came out with me on the cars and Fred Mary Belle and Duncan came in the buggy Friday afternoon.

---

10. Kate Clanton Rood had been left a young widow with three small children when Henry Rood died of consumption in 1881 at age twenty-nine. Kate did later marry Sam Weisiger, a widower and Augusta businessman. There were no children from their marriage. Part of Kate's inherited property, the Clanton Rowell plantation, remained in her family until World War II, when it became part of Bush Field, Augusta's present-day airport.

11. White Oak was in Columbia County, Ga.

12. Mrs. P. Gadsden Hasell (Eleanor Ingraham) of Charleston was Fred Ingraham's sister.

Friday, August 30, 1889   Yesterday was a bright joyous day. Jeff was with us and I was happy. Returning from Augusta Wednesday afternoon Mr Thomas replied when I enquired Where is Cora Lou? "She and Jeff will be out in the morning." This he said as calmly as if Jeff had gone into Augusta the day before. "Jeff?" I exclaimed in glad surprise, "when did he come." "He has been at camp meeting" was the reply. Oh how glad I was. The next morning Jeff and Cora Lou drove out in Turner's dog cart.[13] Jeff is wearing a low straw hat with a white band. It is becoming to him, altho he wears a tall silk hat at times. I kissed him again and again and he loves me. Yesterday afternoon Cora Lou invited the Carmichaels Aphra Randolph and Julia to come over and play croquette. I gave the young people watermelon and apples. It was sweet to listen to Jeff sing last night.

This morning he returned to town. He does not know wether he will return. His doing so will depend upon a telegram. I stood in the piazzi and waved to him and I watched him until he drove as far as Mrs Keener's and all the way he would turn and wave in reply. I hope he will return. Jeff left Augusta in January and I have not seen him since except two hours one Sunday morning last spring when he spent the day in Augusta. His run in the express company is between Macon and Savannah. He boards with Mrs Hall in Macon and Gen [Lafayette] McLaws' family in Savannah. Mr Thomas went over to the camp ground yesterday to have the place and our tent arranged. This morning he sent over a load of articles. We will not regularly camp but we will try to be as comfortable as possible.

Last Friday night we had a club meeting, the first we have had since we moved back to Dixie. Last night I received a letter from Gertrude Clanton Flournoy.[14] I also received the subscription for *The Old Homestead* a magazine published in Savannah. In the August number was a paper I wrote on *Henry IV*. In September will be a paper on Ophelia from the play of *Hamlet*. I read both of them before the Hayne circle.[15] I have received many complimentary notices but little substantial encouragement to write.

---

13. A two-wheeled, horse-drawn cart with two seats back to back.

14. I have been unable to identify Gertrude Flournoy. She was perhaps a niece or cousin.

15. The Hayne Circle was a distinguished literary group of men and women whose members included newspaper editors, poets, essayists, and literary enthusiasts. It was named for Paul Hamilton Hayne (1831–86), a southern poet of national repute who was widely published. A native of Charleston, S.C., Hayne had adopted Augusta as his home and lived at nearby Copse Hill.

Epilogue

"If a higher field of usefulness is intended, a way will be made for me. Of this I am sure so I go on my way content."[1] These are idealistic words from a woman who had gone from wealth to poverty, given birth to ten children and buried four, borne the anxieties of war, suffered debilitating illnesses, survived years of unrelenting humiliation, and grown weary in mind and body. If her spirit of optimism had been less honest, she might be labeled a Pollyanna.

Eighteen months earlier, Gertrude Thomas had written, "I have had a disposition to shrink from making a record of my life."[2] Her journal was no longer a pleasure or a solace, and she wrote more and more infrequently until the remarkable account of forty-one years ended August 30, 1889. Disappointed in her efforts to write "for money"—though she did receive meager remuneration for a few articles—she changed her focus to activities outside the home and went on to fulfill her own prophecy of usefulness in a manner exceeding anything she could have imagined.

Thomas's diary reveals an intellectually astute woman devoted to family and keenly interested in community and political affairs, but that record is far from complete. It is evident that Thomas intended her scrapbooks to complement the journals and throw light on her public life. Fortunately, many of the later scrapbooks survive and it is through them that Thomas's story can be followed to the end of her life.[3] Her late-blooming career as a crusader and

---

1. Journal, May 15, 1880.
2. Journal, Dec. 31, 1878.
3. The scrapbooks of Ella Gertrude Clanton Thomas are unnumbered and are not arranged chronologically. Clippings are rarely dated, but information within the items and the events themselves usually establish the approximate date. The source of publication is seldom identified. The scrapbooks are in the

public figure is extensively preserved in print through newspaper clippings—articles written by her and about her. The scrapbooks disclose prodigious activity and make it easier to understand why Thomas no longer had the time or need for her journal. Her desire to write was achieved.

From her earliest organizational affiliations, she emerged as a leader—always holding office and in many cases serving as an official spokeswoman. The Methodist church and Wesleyan College were two of her lifelong interests. She delighted in attending meetings of the Wesleyan Alumnaen Association and served terms as a vice president of that group on at least two occasions, in 1866 and 1891. As secretary of the Ladies' Memorial Association of Augusta, she worked vigorously for a Confederate monument and Confederate Memorial Day. She was an officer of the Richmond County Grange, for which she wrote prizewinning essays, and she was rewarded by having some of them published in area magazines. One essay, on housekeeping, revealed more writing talent than expertise in the subject matter, while another discussed the problem of economy within the family and household—a subject near to her heart at the time. These and other articles on the theme of domestic relations reflected many of her personal problems and contained barely disguised allusions to her own resentment and disappointment.[4]

Home and family, nature, literature, and nostalgia for the Lost Cause were all acceptable subjects for a lady's pen, but even in the 1860s Thomas also used the press to voice her opinions on civic and political issues through regular letters to newspaper editors. Her busy pen became a weapon of considerable influence, and she was recognized as a talented and articulate speaker as well. An extrovert by nature, Gertrude Thomas was never timid in expressing her views, and over the years they took on added significance. Her letters to editors were sometimes picked up and published in other southern newspapers, thus widening her reputation. She wrote scathing denunciations of a plan to celebrate Sherman Day in Atlanta in 1881 and of suggestions that Benjamin F. Butler

---

possession of Gertrude Threlkeld Despeaux, who made them available for this book.

4. Gertrude Thomas, "The Housekeeper" and "Household Economy," 1876, scrapbook.

should run for president in 1884. She strongly supported Gen. John B. Gordon for the U.S. Senate in 1890 and in 1891 called on the Georgia legislature to establish a home for Confederate veterans.

Determined to establish her own identity, she began to sign many, though not all, of her letters and articles "Gertrude C. Thomas"—retaining "Mrs. J. Jefferson Thomas" in certain instances. During the late 1880s she began to speak out more confidently and in the 1890s her boldness reached its zenith. The budding feminist was coming into full flower.

Throughout her journal, Gertrude Thomas moralized on the importance of education. In 1887 she spoke candidly in support of the Blair bill for common education that would include blacks. "Education should be compulsory. Nor would I permit a man to vote who could not read and write. I know little of politics, but I do not undervalue the great privilege of the ballot box. . . . [L]et us remember we owe the colored race a debt of gratitude. I would rather be taxed to educate the colored families whose fathers labored faithfully for us, than to pay a pension to support the Union soldiers who fought against us. . . ."[5]

When Mattie Gordon, the evangelist, met with opposition in an Atlanta church, Thomas defended the right of women to preach and speak in public—a radical departure from the sentiment she had expressed in her journal on May 20, 1855: "But then again Paul has said 'Let not your women speak in public' and this aside from their natural diffidence would cause a female to remain silent upon such an occasion."

She wrote in favor of prison reform and called for police matrons in the jails: "Messrs. Editors, is there a police matron in Augusta? If not, the good women of the city should never be content until there is one. . . . Let every Georgia city follow Atlanta's example in this respect. Wherever there is a police station, insist upon the necessity for a female matron."[6] She also lashed out against wife abuse: "Wife beating is not confined to the lower classes. . . . By our laws we legalize the sale of whiskey and provide

---

5. Scrapbook. The source is not identified—most probably the *Augusta Chronicle* and the *Augusta Evening News*. There are often two clippings of the same article, differing slightly.

6. Scrapbook. The source is not identified—dateline Atlanta, Feb. 1893—probably from the *Augusta Chronicle*.

the cause for the crime of wife beating. . . . If the offence of wife beating is criminal make the punishment greater. . . . Think of the sacred obligation violated, the example and subsequent degradation of the children, but above all, think of the utter humiliation of the wife."[7]

In 1894 she joined Mary Latimer McLendon in campaigning for the Industrial School for Girls at Milledgeville, Georgia, which would prepare young women to earn a living. "What is to be done with them? How can they support themselves? It is one of the problems of the hour. . . . Give them help. There are ambitious girls in the state. Reach out a kindly hand, make those girls educated women, and the influence will be felt in the history of Georgia."[8]

Gertrude Thomas, a professed "temperance woman," never mentioned the Women's Christian Temperance Union (WCTU) in her journal, yet it was this organization, more than any other, that propelled her role as a public figure and ultimately led her into the suffrage movement. Her active participation, dating from the mid-1880s, was influenced, no doubt, by her cousin Jane Thomas Sibley, whom she mentioned often and in ways suggesting a close relationship. Cousin Jane, the wife of William Sibley,[9] was a prominent community leader in Augusta and state president of the WCTU. Together they were a strong team, and it was in the cause of temperance that Gertrude Thomas found her mission.

She served as secretary and vice president of the Augusta WCTU, as district president, and as a delegate to state and national conventions. She was an effective ambassador for the organization, using the full force of her writing skill in its behalf. She made emotional appeals for men to vote for prohibition, noting, "Men, you vote—I do not." Her primary concern was for the wives and children of men who drank. Reporting on a state convention in 1890, she commented that women of both races worked together in the common cause of temperance—a crisis in which white and black women alike were interested. "A colored woman's happiness," she wrote, "is as much involved in the temperance of her husband and sons as any white lady's."[10] In matters of race, she was

---

7. Ibid.

8. Scrapbook. The source is not identified—written in Atlanta, 1894.

9. William Sibley, son of pioneer Josiah Sibley, for whom the modern postwar Sibley Mill was named, was a wealthy Augusta businessman.

10. Thomas, "As to Temperance," 1889, scrapbook.

broad-minded and well ahead of her time in her thinking, as her journal proves.

There is little doubt that Gertrude Thomas's dedication to the temperance movement was influenced by personal experience—a speculation confirmed by family members. If Jefferson Thomas drank immoderately, she never explicitly said so in her journals, and yet innuendoes abound. Her veiled remarks about a "family skeleton," a "thorn in the flesh," a "subject to be avoided by mutual consent," and references to her husband's "inflamed eyes" all hint at a dark secret. She did mention the raving profanity, the convulsed lip and the "mask off," hardly the normal attributes of a man of Jeff Thomas's refinement and charm. There were other allusions. Writing of the intoxicated public behavior of another woman's husband, she said, "From this degradation I have been mercifully preserved,"[11] suggesting that Jefferson Thomas was discreet to some degree.

Perhaps the missing journal of 1871–78—that record of the most difficult and unhappy period of her life—would have shed light on the subject. It does seem probable that some character flaw was responsible for the missed opportunities and poor business acumen of an otherwise well-educated and charming man. Gertrude Thomas admitted to a keen sense of pride, particularly family pride, and that alone could have prevented her from writing about an alcohol problem in her home. Whatever her motive, the WCTU was her major public crusade for many years, in Augusta and later in Atlanta.

In 1893 Jeff and Gertrude, with their two unmarried daughters, Cora Lou and Kathleen, moved to Atlanta to live with their son Julian Thomas, who had established a successful medical practice and clinic there. The move was probably the only solution to their insurmountable problem of staggering debt.[12] There are no clues to tell exactly when and why the decision to move was made, but it is clear that Jefferson Thomas never recovered from the escalating debt, business and planting failures, and other problems brought on by emancipation and Reconstruction.

The Thomases' financial troubles were not resolved by the

---

11. Journal, May 20, 1855.

12. According to county records, Dixie Farm was, by that time, listed as the property of Turner C. Thomas. Mary Belle and her family lived there for several years.

move to Atlanta, nor would they be for several more years. In the end, there was nothing left of the Thomases' once sizable estate—nothing for them, nothing for the children. Nevertheless, relieved of everyday worries and harassments, Gertrude Thomas, with renewed energy, joined other women in the march toward the twentieth century. The scrapbooks are filled with clippings documenting her ongoing interest in church and literary groups, the WCTU, and the recently founded United Daughters of the Confederacy (UDC), in which she served as national treasurer and secretary. As an official representative of the WCTU and UDC, she traveled extensively to state and national meetings, routinely sending home reports for publication in the Augusta and Atlanta papers. She continued to stretch her own mind, and, after experiencing a Chautauqua in Atlanta, she wrote an inspired story commending that form of education and culture.

At every opportunity Thomas used her pen to further the causes of and promote equality for women. While still living in Augusta, she attended a meeting of the Southern Baptist Convention at which two women sought to be admitted as delegates. The effort was defeated, and, writing about it later, Thomas said she felt humiliated. She wrote: "It taught the women of the church that they were yet in a state of bondage. [I]t taught the children that mother was not the equal of father."[13] In another article, "Men and Women," dealing with changing opportunities in women's employment, she asked, "Does one wonder that women wish to be lawyers and gather in a few of the spoils of warfare?"[14] Given this background and Thomas's association with such women as Frances Willard, Rebecca Latimer Felton, and Mary Latimer McLendon,[15] all of whom she greatly admired, it was inevitable that her path led, finally, to active participation in the local and national suffrage movement.

The National American Woman Suffrage Association held its annual meeting in Atlanta in January 1895—an act of strategy because the Georgia groups were loosely organized at the time. Ger-

---

13. Scrapbook, from the *Augusta Evening News*, 1891.

14. Scrapbook, from the *Augusta Chronicle*, 1896.

15. Frances Willard was a leader of the Women's Christian Temperance Union and president of the national association. Rebecca Latimer Felton and her sister, Mary Latimer McLendon, both of Georgia, were leaders in the WCTU and were active in prison and education reform and the Georgia

trude Thomas attended as a fraternal delegate from the WCTU. Undoubtedly the events of that convention excited her to greater activity. It was on this occasion that she met Susan B. Anthony. Eight years later Anthony presented her with a book with the following inscription:

> Mrs. Gertrude C. Thomas
> *Atlanta—Georgia*
>   I present you this huge volume IV—because you are a *Life Member* of the *National Association*—and because I hope you will be able to place this book—together with its *three huge* companions in the *public libraries* of your city & business— your Colleges, your High Schools, your Normal Schools—&c— Where every student may find them and learn the *facts* about *women* during the 19th Century—*facts* that they can find *nowhere else*—
>
> Yours Sincerely
Susan B. Anthony
Rochester—N.Y.[16]

Feb. 15 1903.

Susan B. Anthony was eighty-three years old at the time of this presentation.

The first state convention of the Georgia Woman Suffrage Association was held in Atlanta in 1899. Gertrude Thomas was one of those who addressed the large assembly. With bold eloquence, she declared that "woman was not taken from the head of man—she is not his superior; she was not taken from his foot—she is not his inferior; but she was taken from his side and there she should stand, his equal in the work of the world."[17] At the same meeting, she was elected president of the association. She was sixty-five years old.

From the mid-1880s until shortly before her death, Gertrude Thomas lived her dream of a useful life. She received numerous honors and a wide recognition of her writing that must have given her deep satisfaction and joy. That she became a staunch feminist

---

Woman Suffrage Association. Mrs. Felton, of Bartow County, was the first woman ever to be seated in the U.S. Senate.

16. Susan B. Anthony and Ida Husted Harper, eds., *History of Woman Suffrage*, vol. 4 (Indianapolis, Ind.: Hollenbeck Press, 1902). This book is in the possession of Gertrude Threlkeld Despeaux.

17. *Atlanta Journal*, Nov. 28, 1899.

was probably as much the result of fate and personal experience as of conscious decision. Yet her independent thinking, concern for women, interest in politics, and intellectual ambition are clearly present throughout the journal of the girl and the woman, in good times and bad. Her zest for life was her strength.

The press was always complimentary of her, as these undated excerpts from scrapbook clippings attest: "Mrs. Thomas is a graduate of Wesleyan and that she does honor to the institution is proven by her letters and brilliant correspondence in the *Evening News*" (*Augusta Evening News*); "She is a woman of strong intellectual attainments and her facile pen frequently enlivens and adorns the columns of the daily press" (*Augusta Chronicle*); "She is broadminded and generous and in touch with everything that concerns her sex" (*Milledgeville Chronicle*); "This talented woman is known all over the state wherever the daily papers are read. She is a writer of considerable note" (*Atlanta Journal*). From Jackson, Mississippi, editor Kate Markham Power (*Kate Power's Review*) wrote an article on female writers of Georgia that named Gertrude Thomas as one who was well known in the South. The *Review* said: "Mrs. W. C. Sibley of Augusta . . . is a writer of great force as is Mrs. J. Jefferson Thomas, a lady of exalted character and wide influence."

Ella Gertrude Clanton Thomas died in Atlanta on May 11, 1907, and was buried in Magnolia Cemetery in her beloved Augusta. The lengthy newspaper notices of her death expressed genuine esteem for this courageous woman, and the *Augusta Chronicle* noted: "Mrs. Thomas was one of the most prominent women of Georgia and one of the most highly regarded. . . . She was almost an indisputable authority on Southern affairs . . . regarded as one of the most brilliant and brainy women of her time."[18] Gertrude Thomas "kept the vow,"[19] and she left the exciting legacy of her journal.

---

18. *Augusta Chronicle*, May 12, 13, 14, 1907.
19. "I vowed that I would dedicate my powers / To thee and thine; have I not kept the vow?" by Percy Bysshe Shelley, quoted in Journal, May 15, 1880.

Index

Names of family, friends, neighbors, servants, and the like are mentioned repeatedly by Gertrude Thomas. Not every one of them is indexed here, nor is every name randomly recorded in the journal listed. Many individuals or places briefly referenced in this abridged edition appear more frequently in the complete journal. The names of freedmen and hired servants are not included in the index. Within entries, Gertrude Thomas is abbreviated as EGCT, Jefferson Thomas as JJT.